Das *Institut für Theologie und Frieden* hat die Aufgabe, die ethischen Grundlagen menschlicher Friedensordnung zu erforschen und in den aktuellen friedenspolitischen Diskurs hineinzutragen. Mit den „Studien zur Friedensethik" wird eine friedensethische Vertiefung der außen- und sicherheitspolitischen Debatte angestrebt. Dabei geht es letztlich um die Frage: Durch welche Politik wird den heute von Gewalt, Armut und Unfreiheit bedrohten Menschen am besten geholfen und zugleich der Errichtung einer zukünftigen friedlichen internationalen Ordnung gedient, in der Sicherheit, Wahrung der Gerechtigkeit und Achtung der Menschenrechte für alle gewährleistet werden?

**Studien zur Friedensethik**
**Studies on Peace Ethics**

edited by
Prof. Dr. Heinz-Gerhard Justenhoven
Dr. Bernhard Koch

Volume 50

Heinz-Gerhard Justenhoven |
Mary Ellen O'Connell [eds.]

# Peace Through Law

## Reflections on *Pacem in Terris* from Philosophy, Law, Theology, and Political Science

Aschendorff Verlag

Nomos

BLOOMSBURY

Sponsored by: Herzog Erik von Arenberg Stiftung, Düsseldorf

**Die Deutsche Nationalbibliothek** lists this publication in the Deutsche Nationalbibliografie; detailed bibliographic data are available on the Internet at http://dnb.d-nb.de

ISBN HB (Nomos) 978-3-8487-1896-2
ePDF (Nomos) 978-3-8452-5961-1

ISBN HB (Aschendorff Verlag) 978-3-402-11694-4
ePDF (Aschendorff Verlag) 978-3-402-11703-3

**British Library Cataloguing-in-Publication Data**
A catalogue record for this book is available from the British Library.

| | | |
|---|---|---|
| ISBN: | HB (Bloomsbury): | 978-1-4742-2513-7 |
| | ePDF (Bloomsbury): | 978-1-4742-2512-0 |
| | ePub (Bloomsbury): | 978-1-4742-2511-3 |
| | xml (Bloomsbury): | 978-1-4742-2510-6 |

**Library of Congress Cataloging-in-Publication Data**
Justenhoven, Heinz-Gerhard / O'Connell, Mary Ellen
Peace Through Law
Reflections on *Pacem in Terris* from Philosophy, Law, Theology, and Political Science
Heinz-Gerhard Justenhoven / Mary Ellen O'Connell (eds.)
284 p.
Includes bibliographic references.

| | | |
|---|---|---|
| ISBN | 978-1-4742-2513-7 | (hardcover Bloomsbury) |
| ISBN | 978-1-4742-2512-0 | (ebook (pdf) Bloomsbury) |
| ISBN | 978-1-4742-2511-3 | (ebook (epub) Bloomsbury) |
| ISBN | 978-1-4742-2510-6 | (ebook (xml) Bloomsbury) |

Volumes 1 to 44 of the series 'Beiträge zur Friedensethik' and 'Theologie und Frieden' published by Verlag W. Kohlhammer, Stuttgart, Germany.

1. Edition 2016

# Table of Contents

Introduction 7

Pacem in Terris as Turning Point:
How the Catholic Church has Attempted to Overcome War
by its Ethics and Practice of Peace 11

*Johan Verstraeten*

The Quest for a "Global Public Authority"
in Contemporary Catholic Peace Ethics 31

*Heinz-Gerhard Justenhoven*

Belief in the Authority of International Law for Peace:
A Reflection on Pacem in Terris 45

*Mary Ellen O'Connell*

Does "ius cogens" exist in International Relations?
Philosophical remarks to the Encyclical "Pacem in terris" 65

*Matthias Lutz-Bachmann*

Global Constitutionalism: Fundamental Norms, Contestation
and the Emergence of Constitutional Quality 83

*Stefan Oeter*

A Global State, International Law and the Containment of
Persistent Conflict: An Anglican Response to Pacem in Terris 109

*Nigel Biggar*

Law and Security of Law 127

*Dietmar von der Pfordten*

Do We Need a World State? The Prospects of Multi-level Global Governance for the Organization of Peace in the 21st Century 143

*Andreas Hasenclever and Annette Schramm*

Global Governance vs. Global Government
Political Philosophy in Times of Globalisation 169

*Michael Reder*

Global Public Authority in Today's International Economic Legal Order: Towards Substantive and Institutional Convergence à la Pacem in Terris? 187

*Karsten Nowrot*

World Peace through International Adjudication? 215

*Christian J. Tams*

The International Criminal Court: A Global Public Authority? 255

*Samuel T. Tessema*

Authors 283

# Introduction

Two World Wars profoundly influenced the 20th Century. In the aftermath of those wars came renewed efforts to prevent further catastrophe. Charismatic figures led the way to founding the United Nations under a Charter in which the preamble declares: The "People of the United Nations are determined to save succeeding generations from the scourge of war." International law and international institutions have made progress toward this goal, but plainly the world is still a long way from effectively banning major organized violence between or within states.

Christians have engaged in a variety of efforts toward overcoming the problem of armed conflict by promoting peace through scholarship, through official Church teaching, prayer, and other action. In 1963, at the height of the Cold War and only a few months after the Cuban Missile Crisis, Pope John XXIII published his famous peace encyclical *Pacem in Terris*. It was an attempt to bridge the ideological gap between East and West and to offer a practical vision of how conflict could be resolved peacefully in a time of globalization. He offered something new, something beyond the accepted international policies of his time, such as normative ideas for reforming the UN. *Pacem in Terris* envisions a diverse world capable of living together without war. It calls for renewed commitment to the United Nations, to human rights, disarmament, development, and international law. John XXIII explained the role of public authorities within nation states in keeping the peace and working in general for the common good. He saw the need for similar authority for the international community. He implies that the UN could be that authority, given accomplishments such as the Universal Declaration on Human Rights adopted by the UN in 1948. The Pope called for the further development of the UN and international law in the direction of human rights, development, and disarmament.[1] The UN and international law have, in his view, the potential to play a pivotal and effective role in the maintenance of peace between nations. This conviction became a fundamental component of Catholic teaching. It is found in *Pacem in Terris*, the Pastoral Constitution *Gaudium et Spes*, one of the documents of the Second Vatican Council (1965), and in Pope Francis's encyclical *Laudato Sí* (2015).[2]

1 Pope John XXIII., Encyclical *Pacem in Terris*, No. 137: http://w2.vatican.va/content/john-xxiii/en/encyclicals/documents/hf_j-xxiii_enc_11041963_pacem.html

2 Cf. Pope Francis, Encyclical *Laudato Sí* (2015) No.175: "...there is urgent need of a true world political authority, as my predecessor Blessed John XXIII indicated some years ago". http://w2.vatican.va/content/francesco/en/encyclicals/documents/papa-francesco_20150524_enciclica-laudato-si.html

Fifty-years after John XXIII's inspiring message, this book looks again at his ideas for 'global political authority' and global law in the context of today. The discussants share their perspectives from theology, philosophy, international law, economics, and political science. *Johan Verstraeten* links contemporary Catholic peace teaching and practice to *Pacem in Terris*. The quest for a 'global public authority' is a cornerstorne in the normative design of Catholic peace teaching, *Heinz-Gerhard Justenhoven* argues. He notes that despite John XXIII and the Second Vatican Council's interest, few concrete ideas to substantiate 'global public authority' have emerged in the decades since 1965.

*Mary Ellen O'Connell* shares John XXIII's optimism about the capacity of both the United Nations and international law to serve as instruments of peace. International law developed over centuries, shaped by the world's religions and philosophies. Its core rule, a rule at the heart of the UN Charter, is the prohibition on military force. This rule owes much to Christianity. In O'Connell's view, what the world lacks today is not a global public authority but the John XXIII's insight as to the importance of international law and institutions.

In analyzing the encyclical, *Matthias Lutz-Bachmann* acknowledges that Pope John is transcending Kant's imperatives in "Perpetual Peace" of 1795 due to the globalized circumstances under which states are living and human rights being the normative basis of international community. The Pope's quest for a global public authority corresponds with the normative obligation of the international community to safeguard fundamental human rights. This is how the concept of 'ius cogens' in public international law is to be understood, *Lutz-Bachmann* argues.

For *Stefan Oeter* elements of successful law and authority are missing. He finds no "global people" or a global deliberative process. The international arena compares unfavorably to nation states equipped with government, law and constitutions. The world might, however, be able to develop a constitution.

Greater global organization and improved international law are unlikely and unwelcome in the eyes of Anglican theologian *Nigel Biggar*. He shares his doubts that international law will ever attract sufficient consensus to be effective law in our diverse world. He rejects global political authority in the form of a world state as "utopian and undesirable".

*Dietmar von der Pforten* offers a more positive perspective on international law. He takes up two prominent legal philosophical questions, pointing out that these questions pertain to international law as much as law within states. All law must deal with the problem of balancing legal stability with legal effectiveness. If the law changes too easily, it is policy, not law. If law never changes, it becomes anachronistic or worse. *Von der Pforten* also connects international law to the wider world of law in discussing the role of enforcement in legal theory. International law is widely (though mistakenly) believed to be unenforceable. Regardless, the focus on enforcement of law is overblown. Law depends more on acceptance and respect than coercive measures against law violators.

*Andreas Hasenclever* and *Annette Schramm* in analyzing world state concepts point to conceptual shortcomings, which inhibit their realization. They move away from the search for a world state to global governance concepts, and find evidence of such governance in the growing body of public institutions. They call these "islands of authority" where states delegate their own authority and pool their sovereignty. *Michael Reder*, too, describes global actors as "parts of complex and dynamic global networks" that deserve trust because of the cooperative problem-solving capacities of different actors in the global arena. Still, there is a negative aspect of these networks in that many global actors lack democratic legitimacy. Their political agendas are dominated by the focus of northern post-industrial state populations.

Nevertheless, within the international economic order that has supported the wealth of the north, *Karsten Nowrot* finds an ever-developing orientation towards the universal common good. What is lacking is institutional convergence. The world remains dominated by fragmented, inter-governmental organizations. While new international arrangements evolve, international courts are already playing a significant role. *Christian Tams* points to the value of courts in a subsidiary role within the UN system. For *Samuel Tessema*, the International Criminal Court fills, at least in part, the place of a global public authority. He outlines where the ICC is falling short and what needs to be done to reach the status of a true global court for holding accountable those who violate the most significant rules of the global system: human rights, law of armed conflict, and the UN Charter prohibition on the use of force.

The contributors do not ignore the widespread criticism and skepticism respecting "global public authority" and global law. Nevertheless, in the spirit of *Pacem in Terris*, the general view is more hopeful and constructive. More of the authors are optimistic than pessimistic about what can be accomplished toward a more peaceful and humane world.

Mary Ellen O'Connell Heinz-Gerhard Justenhoven

# Pacem in Terris as Turning Point: How the Catholic Church has Attempted to Overcome War by its Ethics and Practice of Peace

*Johan Verstraeten*

While *Rerum novarum* (1891) is regarded as the *Magna Charta* of Catholic social teaching in general, *Pacem in Terris* (1963) is unquestionably the "watershed document of the modern Catholic Peace movement"[1]. This "decisive breakthrough"[2] and "first ecclesial Charter of Human Rights"[3] is, together with the decrees of Vatican II, "the resolution of a crucial state of Roman Catholicism's long struggle with the modernizing and secularizing culture of the West"[4] and "the fullest general treatment of political morality to be found in modern Catholic social teaching "[5].

In this article I will first articulate why *Pacem in Terris* is a major shift in Catholic thinking about war and peace. Subsequently I will outline the evolution of the papal doctrine on war and peace after *Pacem in Terris*. Finally I will argue that the Catholic contribution to peace cannot be limited to official documents, but needs also to be interpreted in the light of the 'peace praxeology', or more concretely, peace advocacy and action by catholic movements such as *Pax Christi* and *Sant' Egidio*.

---

1 For example: Zahn, Gordon C. Afterword. In: Thomas A. Shannon (ed.). War or Peace. The Search for New Answers. Maryknoll ,NY, 1980, p. 233; Christiansen S.J., Drew. Commentary on Pacem in Terris. In: Lisa Sowle Cahill et al. (Eds.). Modern Catholic Social Teaching. Commentaries and Interpretations. Washington (D.C.), 2004, p. 233; Appleby, Scott. "In Truth, Justice, Charity and Liberty" Contesting Pacem in Terris in Our Time. In: *Journal of Catholic Social Thought*, 2004, 1, p. 39; Curran, Charles. The Teaching and Methodology of Pacem in Terris. In: *Journal of Catholic Social Thought*, 2004, 1, p. 17.

2 Eicher, Peter. Er ist Unser Friede. Von der Sicherheitsmoral zum Friedenszeugnis. In: Peter Eicher (ed.). Das Evangelium des Friedens. Christen und Aufrüstung. München, 1982, p. 77.

3 René Coste as quoted by Christiansen, Drew, Commentary, p. 239, footnote 29.

4 Langan, John, S.J. Human Rights in Roman Catholicism. In: Charles E. Curran, Richard A. McCorminck, S.J. (Eds.). Official Catholic Social Teaching (Readings in Moral Theology, 5). New York (NY), 1986, p. 110.

5 Christiansen, Drew, Commentary, p. 223.

*1. The turning point: Pacem in Terris.*

Written in the specific historical context of the cold war, nuclear deterrence and particularly the aftermath of the Cuba crisis *Pacem in Terris* has shifted the Catholic peace theology beyond classical just war thinking.

With regards to war as such and conscious of the destructive power of modern weapons, Pope John XXIII declares that "it no longer makes sense to maintain that war is a fit instrument with which to repair the violation of justice"[6]. More precisely the official Latin reads like this: "*Quare aetate hac nostra, quae vi atomica gloriatur, alienum est a ratione, bellum iam aptum esse ad violate iura sarcienda*"[7]. Despite the apparent clarity of the argument, there is no agreement among scholars about its precise meaning.

James Douglass interprets it as a pure pacifist assertion: "the conditions of modern war are such that no form of warfare can be justified"[8].

Paul Ramsey, followed by Charles Curran, interprets it as a reconfirmation of the teaching of Pius XII[9]. Curran refers to John Courtney Murray's interpretation of the war ethics of Pius XII according to which only defensive wars are justified and wars for avenging past offenses are rejected.[10]

According to René Coste the contention is about the "radical ethical irrationality of war". This irrationality is the reason why only in special circumstances, when armed violence is in perfect accordance ("coincides") with the justice of the cause, and the just way of waging war, war can eventually reach the level of moral rationality, but it can never do this on itself.[11]

Brian Hehir concludes that the dispute over the literal sense "remains unresolved and may not be open to definitive resolution". He proposes to

6 Pacem in Terris, nr. 127.

7 "Therefore, in an age such as ours, which prides itself on its atomic energy it is contrary to reason to hold that war is now a suitable way to restore rights which have been violated" (PT 127). According to Charles Curran the dispute is mainly caused by the original authorized but erroneous English translation from Latin.

8 Hehir, J. Brian. The Just-War Ethic and Catholic Theology: Dynamics of Change and Continuity. In: Thomas A. Shannon (ed.). War or Peace? The Search for New Answers. Maryknoll (NY), 1980, p. 20; Douglass, James. The Nonviolent Cross: A Theology of Revolution and Peace. New York (NY), 1966, p. 84.

9 Hehir, The Just War Ethic, p. 20.

10 Ramsey, Paul. The Just War. Force and Political Responsibility. New York (NY), 1966, pp. 78, 208-210; Curran, The Teaching and Methodology of Pacem in Terris, p. 30.

11 Coste, René. Théologie de la Paix (Cogitato Fidei, 203). Paris, 1997, pp. 186-187. This interpretation is quite different from his earlier interpretation in Morale Internationale, pp. 354-355, where he writes that it is not a direct and absolute condemnation of nuclear war. Pope John makes an appeal to the 'common sense'; one cannot understand any more that a nuclear war with its risk of escalation could still be a just war.

read the encyclical in the light of later documents as "not proscribing the defensive use of force under very restricted conditions". But according to him this is nothing more than "toleration of the use of force, not a moral endorsement"[12].

I personally think that *Pacem in terris* nr. 127 must be interpreted in the perspective of the whole of the encyclical. Its focus is not on war but on the conditions for a sustainable peace: "relations between states, as between individuals, must be regulated not by armed force, but in accordance with the principles of right reason: the principles that is, of truth, justice and vigorous and sincere co-operation"[13].

This can be read as a shift in focus "from casuistry to vision and a program for peace"[14], a program that Czempiel had suggested in the title of his significant article: "The Christians and Foreign Politics. Just War Doctrine or *Praxeology of Peace*?"[15]

*Pacem in Terris* is clearly an example of the latter: it describes the necessary conditions for a sustainable international peace based on human rights and the universal common good. According to Drew Christiansen Pope John's reference to the order of love as basis for peacemaking is the crucial hermeneutic key. The encyclical proposes in nr. 164 an "*hermeneutic of political life and contemporary history in which love and the unity of the human family are the heuristic tools. That is, Christian love enables one to see in ambiguous historical developments opportunities and positive accomplishments, ignored by realists, which contribute to the growing unity of the human family*"[16].

There is, however, more than merely an ethic of love because Pope John's endorsement and particular interpretation of the human rights discourse is at least as important. In order to understand this adequately three perspectives must be taken into account: Pope John's reinterpretation of natural law in terms of the nature of the human person, his new attitude towards the world underpinned by a theology of the 'signs of the times' and, his qualified endorsement of the Universal Declaration of Human Rights in the perspective of the 'universal common good'.

---

12 Hehir, The Just War Ethic, p. 20.

13 Pacem in Terris, nr. 114.

14 Curran, The Teaching and Methodology of Pacem in Terris, p. 22.

15 Czempiel, Ernst Otto. Die Christen und die Auswärtige Politik. Lehre vom Gerechten Krieg oder Praxeologie des Friedens. In: Civitas. Jahrbuch für Christliche Gesellschaftsordnung, 6. 1967, pp. 20-45.

16 Christiansen, Commentary, p. 226.

### *1.1 Natural law, the dignity of the human person and human rights*

*Pacem in Terris* begins with an assertion of "the necessity of human rights for the good order of society"[17]. These rights are, according to Thomas Merton, the whole basis of the encyclical. While Machiavelli and many political leaders consider authority as resting "on force and ruse, ruthlessness and cruelty, to the ability to seize power and hold on to it against all contenders", *Pacem in Terris* rests on "the objective reality of man, on the natural law, that is on the inner orientation of man to freedom, and on the obligation which this entails"[18]. With this summary Merton grasps the essence of the encyclical. Human rights are not presented as merely self-evident or as simply the consequence of a solemn proclamation by the United Nations, but as grounded in natural law.[19]

That does not mean that *Pacem in Terris* is simply reiterating the philosophical understanding of natural law as articulated in the Catholic tradition.

According to Charles Curran the encyclical puts "more stress on the human person and not on human nature as such"[20] because the inviolability of the human person is interpreted as "the direct consequence of his dignity"[21]. In other words: the focus is on the "nature of the human person" and on the capacity that human beings "can use their God-given reason to discover the order that the Creator put into the world"[22]. "While the framework appears to be one of natural law, natural law has been turned inside out. Human nature, not nature is the touchstone. Conscience, rather than cosmic law is the foundation of the moral order" [23]

Drew Christiansen rightly observes that with this shift in emphasis *Pacem in Terris* reconnects official Catholic social thought with the late medieval/early Catholic rights theory "[…] and its belief "that rights rest on the *ius naturale* as the human power of reason"[24].

Indeed, the basic moral principle is the human person as described in *Pacem in terris* nr. 9: "*Any well-regulated and productive association of men in society demands the acceptance of one fundamental principle: that*

---

17 Langan, Human Rights, p. 110.
18 Merton, Thomas. Seeds of Destruction. New York (NY), 1964, pp. 164-165.
19 Cardinal Renato R. Martino. Pacem in Terris on the International Common Good and World Authority. In: *Grace & Truth. A Journal of Catholic Reflection for Southern Africa*, 2004, 1, p. 23.
20 Curran, The Teaching and Methodology of Pacem in Terris, p. 19
21 Coste, René. Morale Internationale. L'humanité à la recherché de son âme (Bibliothèque de théologie. Serie 2 : Théologie Morale). Paris, Desclée, p. 238.
22 Curran, The Teaching and Methodology of Pacem in Terris, p. 18.
23 Christiansen, Commentary, p. 224.
24 Christiansen, Commentary, p. 240, footnote 43 and his excursus pp. 333-335.

*each individual man is truly a person. His is a nature, that is, endowed with intelligence and free will. As such he has right and duties, which together flow as a direct consequence from his nature*".

This criterion reflects the 'personalist' turn in natural law thinking as endorsed by *Mater et Magistra* (1961), in which Pope John XXIII had grounded Catholic social teaching "*on one basic principle: individual human beings are the foundation, the cause and the end of every social institution [...] for men are by nature social beings*"[25].

Today most Catholic theologians agree that that the personalist emphasis on human freedom and human rights is a significant development in the Catholic understanding of natural law. Thomas Merton expresses this succinctly: as follows: "Pope John teaches that when authority ignores natural law, human dignity, human rights and the moral order established by God, it undermines its own foundations and loses its claim to be obeyed, because it no longer speaks seriously to the *conscience of free men*" [26].

### *1.2 A more positive attitude and the theology of the signs of the times.*

Pope John's reinterpretation of the natural law in terms of protecting human freedom and free conscience had such far reaching consequences for the future of Catholic peace thinking, that it is not surprising that, in the beginning, it was not received by all theologians without reservation. Drew Christiansen notes that immediately after the publication of *Pacem in Terris* some scholars have expressed their fear that the emphasis on human freedom (as inspired by the thinking of Pietro Pavan) would particularly run the risk to create misunderstandings about the commitment of Catholics in the realm of politics: "At issue was the independence of the Catholic faithful from hierarchical supervision when they engaged in politics"[27]. The Dominican papal theologian Luigi Chiappi "suspected the document of inclining towards liberalism and indifferentism" and Georges Jarlot s.j., editor of *Etudes*, warned against a potential ideological contamination by Marxism[28].

But, was a more positive attitude towards Marxism and representative of the communist world so negative? The critical voices have insufficiently taken into account that Pope John XXIII had made two fundamental dis-

25 John XXIII, Mater et Magistra, 219.
26 Merton, Seeds of Destruction, p. 170.
27 Christiansen, Commentary, p. 222.
28 Christiansen, Commentary, p. 222.

tinctions in order to hold out his hand to 'people of good will', also to the 'enemies' on the other side of the iron curtain.

First he distinguished between the human person "who retains in every case his dignity as a person" and "the philosophies to which he sometimes adheres"[29]. A person who adheres to an unacceptable worldview is still to be respected as a person with dignity.

Secondly, he made a distinction between "false philosophical teachings", which he still rejected, and "movements even if these movements owe their origin and inspiration to these false tenets," since such movements "contain elements that are positive and deserving of approval"[30]. In quite diplomatic terms, Pope John suggests that such movements can change history. At times it can occur that "meetings for the attainment of some practical results which previously seemed completely useless now are either actually useful or may be looked upon as printable for the future"[31]. Curran thinks that the logic of these contentions is "tactful but crystal clear"[32]. Without forgoing the necessity of great prudence, they are "a call for a thaw in the cold war" and "an opening to the left" which involves "a movement away from intractable opposition to dialogue"[33]. *Pacem in Terris* paved the way towards the *Ostpolitik* of Pope Paul VI and his secretary of State Casaroli.

On the individual level Pope John acknowledged the 'prudential' freedom of the laity to be engaged in alliances across ideologies (on the condition that they remained loyal to the principles of the official social teaching)[34]. His recognition of prudential freedom was according to Donal Dorr "a significant change of attitude by the Vatican in the political field"[35]. Indeed, the recognition of the prudential freedom of the laity was in fact combined with a shift in the official Catholic policy with regards to left wing movements and the opponents of the 'free west' during the Cold War.

This open attitude towards historical movements, which contribute to peace, is underpinned by a fundamental new theological interpretation: secular movements cannot only do good but their historical action can be theologically qualified as 'signs of the times'. With this expression Pope John anticipated the theology of the pastoral constitution *Gaudium et spes*.

29 Pacem in Terris, nr. 158.
30 Pacem in Terris, nr. 159.
31 Pacem in Terris, nr. 160.
32 Curran, The Teaching and Methodology of Pacem in Terris, p. 29.
33 Curran, The Teaching and Methodology of Pacem in Terris, p. 29. See also Dorr, Donal. Option for the Poor. A Hundred Years of Catholic Social Teaching. New York (NY), 2003, p. 144.
34 Pacem in Terris, nr. 160.
35 Dorr, Option for the Poor, p. 144.

Indeed, *Pacem in Terris* proposes fundamentally not a deductive approach, despite the impression it gives in so far as every level of analysis (personal, intra-state, international) is judged on the basis of its conformity with the natural order "as the order established by God"[36].

The peace encyclical reconfirms *Mater et Magistra* in which John XXIII endorsed the method of Joseph Cardijn and the Christian workers movement ("see, judge, act", MM 236), but he did this with an important addition: what appears in the analysis as a positive contribution to peace and the common good, gets now theological significance as 'signs of the times'. As such the word is not used, but the intention of Pope John is crystal clear: what he describes in *Pacem in Terris* nr. 39-45 as 'nota' are in fact '*signa temporum*'[37]. The text enumerates three signs of the times: (1) The progressive improvement in the economic and social condition of working men (which began by claiming their economic and *social* rights, but now also includes their '*political* rights'); (2) The part that women are now playing in political life (which is a sign of "the increasing awareness of their natural dignity"), and (3) the political independence of former colonies (with an additional remark about the elimination of racial discrimination). These are three concerns from the emancipatory agenda, to which he adds others signs as well, such as the increasing interdependence.

For Pope John the concept of "signs of the times" is so fundamental that even respect for human rights and duties is implicitly interpreted as such a sign: they are a way to God. According to Pope John, respecting human rights and duties not only leads to a better understanding of truth, justice, charity and freedom [in this order![38]], but also to "a better knowledge of God"[39]. Such way of thinking anticipates what a year after Pacem in Terris will be articulated in the Pastoral Constitution *Gaudium et spes* 11 as "deciphering authentic signs of God's presence and purpose in the happenings, needs and desires" in which the people of God "has a part along with other men of our age".

With the introduction of the expression "signs of the times" *Pacem in Terris* began "a new style of experience based religious reflection to social questions"[40]. But there is more. In a most insightful article Mary Elsbernd

36 Pacem in Terris, nr. 1.

37 In fact, *Pacem in Terris* mentions more than 3 signs of the times. Archbishop Denis Hurley mentions 12 different signs of the times in the encyclical in his article Reading the Signs of the Times 1963-2003. In: *Grace &Truth. A Journal of Catholic Reflection for Southern Africa*, 2004, 1, pp 9-11.

38 In the Compendium of the Social Doctrine of the Catholic Church the order is different: truth, freedom, justice and love.

39 Pacem in Terris, nr. 45.

40 Christiansen, Commentary, p. 233.

and Reimund Bieringer observe that before *Pacem in Terris* pope John had used the expression '*signa temporum*' at least twice. In his apostolic constitution *Humanae salutis* (25 Dec. 1961) he writes: "*Christ exhorts us to discern the signs... of the times*". In his "act of faith" of 24 March 1963 Pope John acknowledges that he learned from his acquaintance with a diversity of cultures that "*the moment has come to acknowledge the signs of the times, to understand the possibilities that they offer and to look much forward into the future*"[41].

This sentence is of the utmost importance since it anticipates to what pope Paul VI will later on articulate as a 'forward looking imagination'. For Paul VI a "forward looking imagination" is a *conditio sine qua non* for the creation of a more peaceful and just world.[42]

Reflecting upon the implications of pope John's vision on the signs of the times, pope Paul VI rightly pointed out that an indispensable aspect of the theology of the signs of the times requires not only an analysis of facts or of "what is", but also of what can be. According to him a 'forward looking imagination' makes it possible to

> (1) "to perceive in the present the *disregarded* possibility hidden within it" and
>
> (2) It enables people to direct the present "towards a fresh future".

Instead of continuing to discuss issues in terms of mere 'facts' or old frameworks of meaning, pope Paul VI proposes a profound scrutiny of political and social realities as a complex social field that contains hidden, and even *disregarded* possibilities for new developments. In other words: Beaten paths must be left. We need a method to discover the perspectives which the dominant discourse(s) do not allow us to perceive. According to Pope Paul VI, this scrutiny, moreover, "sustains social *dynamism* by the *confidence* that it gives to the *inventive powers* of the human mind and heart". For Paul VI – confirming here the positive attitude of his predecessor – such an imaginative dynamism requires breaking down the mental walls

---

41 Quoted in Elsbernd, Mary/ Bieringer, Reimund. Interpreting the Signs of the Times in the Light of the Gospel: Vision and Normativity of the Future. In: Johan Verstraeten (ed.). Scrutinizing the Signs of the Times in the Light of the Gospel (B.E.T.L. 208). Leuven, 2007, p. 44.

42 The idea of a 'forward looking imagination' reappeared in a document from the pontifical council for justice and peace on the financial crisis: Towards Reforming the International Financial and Monetary Systems in the Context of Global Public Authority (published October 24, 2011).

that narrow the mind. According to him the fresh future can be defined theologically as (1) the fruit of the spirit of Christ which also "*breaks down the horizons" within which our understanding "likes to find security"* and (2) as transgressing the limits to which our activity "would willingly restrict itself". Hence his conclusion that the crucial task is "to go beyond every system and every ideology" because they constitute the hermeneutical horizon that limit our understanding of the reality of the contemporary crisis.

I think that this open, imaginative and future oriented way of thinking, which in an embryonic form is already present in *Pacem in Terris*, is perhaps the most important contribution the Church can make to a world without war, since it fully matches with what John Paul Lederach proposes as a way toward sustainable conflict transformation. According to Lederach, it is necessary "*To imagine responses and initiatives that, while rooted in the challenges of the real world, are by their nature capable of rising above destructive patterns and giving birth to that which does not yet exist. In reference to peace-building, this is the capacity to imagine and generate constructive responses and initiatives that, while rooted in the day-to-day challenges of violent setting, transcend and ultimately break the grips of those destructive patterns and cycles*"[43].

### *1.3 The Universal Declaration of Human rights and the Universal Common Good.*

Inspired by David Hollenbach, John Langan characterizes *Pacem in Terris* as containing "the most complete and systematic list of ... human rights in the modern Catholic Tradition"[44]. While both the hierarchy of the Catholic Church and theologians have "been for a long time suspicious about the doctrine of human rights, because of the context of a laicist and anticlerical historical context in which they have emerged"[45], *Pacem in Terris* embraced the human rights discourse positively.

For René Coste the enumeration of human rights is in a way comparable with the Universal Declaration and this is "one of the most original parts of the document, which has most impressed the world opinion". Notwithstanding the fact that pope John's endorsement of the Universal Declaration is not 'unqualified[46]', it leaves no doubt that he interpreted it as "a step in

43 Lederach, John Paul. The Moral Imagination. The Art and Soul of Building Peace. Oxford, 2005, p. 182.
44 Langan, Human Rights, p. 113.
45 Coste, Morale Internationale, p. 240.
46 Pacem in Terris, nr. 144.

the right direction, an approach toward the establishment of a juridical and political ordering of the world community," and as "a solemn recognition of the personal dignity of every human being; an assertion of everyone's right to be free to seek out the truth, to follow moral principles, discharge the duties imposed by justice, and lead a fully human life"[47]. This positive attitude is clearly different from the opinion of contemporary thinkers according to whom Catholicism is incompatible with the human rights tradition because of the presumed incompatibility of Catholicism with modernity[48]. This is a thesis which is convincingly refuted by Charles Taylor nuanced analysis of modernity, and by David Hollenbach's argument for the capability of the catholic tradition to enrich the human rights tradition from within by way of giving freedom rights a communitarian interpretation (as preconditions for life in community with others)[49]. In any case it is undeniable that for pope John respect for rights and duties is a necessary condition for peace.

A significant aspect of his endorsement of the human rights discourse is the fact that he inserts it in the perspective of a global ethic. The text does not use the word globalization as such, but it already points to the implications of a global interdependence. As ethical counterpart of this the encyclical proposes a more inclusive vision of the common good. While Pope John's predecessors had applied it mainly to the sphere of the national state, he now refers to the "universal common good", which is a truly "innovative concept"[50].

For Pope John the idea of a universal common good is connected with the conviction that an international order based on the anarchy of states is no longer capable of resolving problems[51] "*Under the present circumstances of human society, both the structure and form of governments, as much as the power that public authority wields in all the nations of the world, must be considered inadequate to promote the universal common good*"[52]. Hence his argument for a world-wide public authority, not conceived as a monolithic world state, but a complex authority structure guided by the principle of subsidiarity[53]. An 'international authority' is needed which must recog-

---

47 Pacem in Terris, nr. 144.

48 See for example Rowland, Tracey. Culture and the Thomist Tradition: After Vatican II. New York (NY), 2007.

49 Hollenbach, David, A.J. A Communitarian Reconstruction of Human Rights: Contributions from Catholic Tradition. In: R. Bruce Douglass, David Hollenbach (Eds.). Catholicism and Liberalism. Contributions to American Public Philosophy. Cambridge (MA), 1994, pp. 127-150; Taylor, Charles. A Secular Age, Cambridge (MA), 2007.

50 Christiansen,Commentary, p. 231.

51 Appleby, In truth, p. 38.

52 Pacem in Terris, nr. 135.

53 See for this: Martino, Pacem in Terris on the Universal Common Good and World Authority, pp. 22-23.

nize the dignity and rights of all individuals and which, respecting the principle of subsidiarity, will not replace individual states, while being "better able to address the many worldwide issues that individual states cannot adequately address"[54].

## 2. Developments after Pacem in Terris

### 2.1 Gaudium et spes

The next decisive step in the development of the Catholic ethics of peace and war was the Pastoral Constitution *Gaudium et Spes* (1965), which confirmed and even reinforced the positive peace approach of *Pacem in Terris* with the words: "peace is not merely absence of war; nor can it be reduced solely to the maintenance of a balance of power between enemies; nor is it brought about by dictatorship. Instead, it is rightly and appropriately called an enterprise of justice"[55].

Simultaneously the council fathers did not hesitate to praise "those who renounce the use of violence in the vindication of their rights"[56]. They also acknowledged explicitly the choice of Christians to become conscientious objectors and they called for laws that would guarantee them a humane treatment. "At the time, Catholic pacifists regarded this rather limited official acknowledgement as a notable achievement" [57].

Moreover, without using the term genocide as such, the text radically condemns "the methodological extermination of an entire people, nation or ethnic minority" as an horrendous crime, a condemnation followed by a rejection of blind obedience to commands[58].

On the other hand the right to armed defense continues to be acknowledged "as long as the danger of war remains and there is no competent and sufficiently powerful authority at the international level" and military service is described as "a genuine contribution to the establishment of peace" provided that troops fulfill their role properly[59]. But, as mentioned, this is balanced with the endorsement of conscientious objection.

---

54 Curran, The Teaching and Methodology of Pacem in Terris, p. 27.
55 Gaudium et spes, nr. 78.
56 Gaudium et spes, nr. 78.
57 Finn, James. Pacifism and Justifiable War. In: Thomas A. Shannon (ed.). War or Peace? The Search for New Answers. Maryknoll (NY), 1980, p. 8.
58 Gaudium et spes, nr. 79.
59 Gaudium et spes, nr. 79.

The most famous proposition is, however, the condemnation of "total war". More precisely, the condemnation of war acts directly intended to kill civilians: "any act of war *aimed* indiscriminately at the destruction of entire cities or extensive areas along with their population is a crime against God and men itself"[60].

Unfortunately the Latin and official version of this text remains somewhat ambivalent because, under the pressure of a powerful US lobby, the original "*pertinet ad*" or "*secumfert*" (both referring to real bombardments) was replaced by "*tendit in*". The USA lobby feared that a clear condemnation of the nuclear attacks on Hiroshima and Nagasaki would harm the national interest of the USA. Via the insertion of "*tendit in*" the US lobby tried to solve the problem by distinguishing between the condemnation of the *intention* to destroy entire cities and, a massive destruction of population centers as unintended effect of a presumed well intended act such as ending the war earlier or reducing the ultimate number of its victims. According to Norbert Glatzel the condemnation of total war can be read as an act with double effect reasoning, but I think that this is an erroneous interpretation. Following the convincing argument by John Ford with regards to obliteration bombing[61], even with a "*tendit in*" terminology, there is no justification possible of a "counter city" bombardment, because the massive killing of civilians is in this case the *direct intention* and not the unintended indirect effect of the act. Consequently it is not possible to 'escape' the condemnation of the nuclear attacks on Hiroshima and Nagasaki via a reference to an act with double effect reasoning. According to Dubarle, secretary of the sub-commission which drafted the text on peace in *Gaudium et spes*, it was *not* the intention of the council fathers to weaken the condemnation or to avoid references to Hiroshima. This is confirmed by Eduard Herr's detailed analysis of the genesis of the text: an attempt to let the '*tendit in*' be preceded by a '*per se*' was rejected with a '*non placet*'[62].

About the deterrence system the text of GS is altogether quite diplomatic, although the arms race is finally judged to be not a safe way to preserve a steady peace and it is, moreover, criticized as a system the costs of which do harm to the poor. [63]

---

60 Gaudium et spes, nr. 80.

61 Glatzel, Norbert. Neueste Kirchliche Lehrverkündigung. In: Norbert Glatzel, Ernst Joseph Nagel (Eds.). Frieden in Sicherheit. Zur Weiterentwicklung der katholischen Friedensethik. Freiburg, 1981, pp. 133-136.

62 Herr, Eduard. Sauver la paix. Qu'en dit l'Eglise? Bruxelles, 1991, pp. 33-65.

63 Gaudium et spes, nr. 81.

### *2.2 Later developments*

After Vatican II, the popes have not ceased to criticize the arms race and the deterrence system.

According to Pope Paul VI "the question of war and peace presents itself today in new terms". "It is not that the principles have changed... But today war has at its disposal means which have 'immeasurably magnified its horrors and wickedness'" (message to the special session of the UN General Assembly, 1978).

In fact the 'new terms' were articulated in many ways.

In *Populorum progressio* (1987) Pope Paul VI introduced 'development' as the new name of peace. As such he confirmed the positive peace vision of *Gaudium et spes* according to which peace is not only an absence of war but a process which requires the creation of just institutions and respect for the rights of poor. Later on, in liberation theology which radicalized the development approach, institutional injustice, theologically interpreted as structural sin, will be seen as one of the main causes of violent conflicts.

One of the most striking initiatives by Pope Paul VI was, moreover, the idea to deliver yearly peace messages on the occasion of the world day of Prayer for Peace, held on the 1st of January every year. An analysis of these messages reveals that gradually, particularly since the pontificate of John Paul II, the ecological agenda was inserted into the peace agenda.

In *Sollicitudo rei socialis* (1987) Pope John Paul II reformulated the device of Pius XII, "*opus justitiae pax*" as "*opus solidaritatis pax*". It is by way of radical solidarity as a response to the global interdependence and structural sin, that a more just and peaceful world will be created.

In many other regards Pope John Paul II contributed to developing the Church' vision of peace. He enriched the teaching on human rights and human dignity with a "Christocentric" theology (Encyclical Redemptor Hominis). He also radically rejected violence as a legitimate means to realize justice and he opted for nonviolent strategies. Inspired by the Sant' Egidio community he took initiatives for the reconciliation between religions (such as the interreligious meetings in Assisi).[64]

The most important evolution after Vatican II was the increasing role of bishops' conferences in developing a Catholic peace ethic. Particularly in

64 For a detailed articulation of the Peace ethics of JP II see Justenhoven, Heinz-Gerhard. The Peace Ethics of Pope John Paul II. In: Heinz-Gerhard Justenhoven/ William Barbieri (Eds.). From Just War to Modern Peace Ethics (Arbeiten zur Kirchengeschichte , 120). Berlin, 2012, pp. 313-344.

the 1980s several bishops' conferences in the USA and Europe issued inspiring documents concerning peace in general and new developments in the deterrence system such as the installation of SS20, Pershing II and cruise missiles in Europe. The most influential of these letters was the '*Challenge of Peace*' published in 1983 by the bishops of the USA. This document not only presented an excellent ethical reflection on deterrence and inspiring peace theology, but also and above all a new method of open conversation about the various drafts of the text by scholars and activists, diplomats and policy makers. This open consultation method did not receive much sympathy from cardinal Ratzinger, head of the Congregation for the Doctrine of the Faith.

A most important document is the '*Compendium of the Social Doctrine of the Catholic Church*' published in 2004. The chapter on the promotion of peace, the last version of which is clearly influenced by Cardinal Martino's expertise as former president of *Pax Christi*, reaffirms the earlier developments in papal teaching and above all the positive definition of peace in terms of being the fruit of justice and love.

Modern war is criticized in sharp terms, as well as deterrence and several sorts of weapons, but the right to legitimate defense remains conditionally accepted. The Compendium also endorses an important recent evolution in international law which limits the 'sovereignty of state' thinking with regards to humanitarian intervention. Priority must be given to "the duty to protect". The text refers to the proposition by Pope John Paul II (1993) that "the principle of national sovereignty cannot be claimed as a motive for preventing an intervention in defense of innocent victims"[65]. The Compendium also reconfirms the magisterium's support for the International Criminal Court.

The Holocaust/Shoah (in these words[66]) and terrorism[67] are radically condemned, but simultaneously the compendium pleads for a "courageous and lucid analysis of the reasons behind terrorism", which is in diplomatic terms a clear rejection of the simplistic idea of 'war on terror'.

65 Compendium nr. 506.
66 Compendium nr. 506.
67 Compendium nr. 514.

### *3. Broadening the scope: the role of peace movements in the praxis of the Church*

The Catholic Church's attempts to avoid war cannot be reduced to the production of texts. More important are concrete actions for conflict transformation and war prevention. The Holy See and its diplomacy have played a crucial role in this regard[68]. But the Catholic Church is more than its official diplomacy, since the whole people of God is responsible for the mission of the Church to promote peace. Movements such as *Pax Christi* and *Sant'Egidio* are representative bearers of this general responsibility.

The most prominent movement is *Pax Christi*, which acknowledges *Pacem in Terris* as its "*magna Charta*"[69]. Founded in France in 1945 to promote reconciliation between the French and the Germans following World War II, Pax Christi was endorsed by Pope Pius XII a few years later as an official Catholic peace movement in which members of the hierarchy, clergy and laypeople work together on an equal and democratic basis. Its presidency is shared by a bishop and a lay woman, both of whom are elected. As an international organization *Pax Christi* began to play an important role since the Dutch cardinal Alfrink became its president in 1965. Since the 1970ies *Pax Christi* advocates against the arms trade and under the impulse of bishop Dom Helder Camara it started advocating more strongly for non-violence. In 1979 it was given special consultative status at the UN, and it is working at UN centers in Geneva, New York, Vienna and Paris. It is also officially represented at the African Union and the Council of Europe and has regular access to the European Parliament, the European Commission and NATO. In 1983 *Pax Christi* received the UNESCO peace education prize and in 1987 the UN peace messenger award. In all the years since its foundation *Pax Christi* played an important role in the transformation of conflicts. During the war in Bosnia it offered practical help in refugee camps and organized interreligious meetings in Serbia, Albania, and Kosovo. It organized reconciliation meetings in Northern Ireland. It participated in successful coalitions such as those working to ban landmines and cluster

68 See for example Araujo, Robert, S.J. The Holy See as International Person and Sovereign and Participation in International Law. In: Heinz-Gerhard Justenhoven/ William A. Barbieri ( Eds.). From Just War to Modern Peace Ethics (Arbeiten zur Kirchengeschichte, 120). Berlin, 2012, pp. 249-273; Buonomo, Vincenzo. La pace e l'attività internazionale della Santa Sede. In: Vitorio Alberti (ed.). Il Concetto di Pace. Attualità della Pacem in Terris nel 50° Anniversario (1963-2013). Pontificio Consiglio della Giustizia e della Pace. Citta del Vaticano, 2013, pp. 407-440.

69 What follows is based on an internal document from Marie Dennis and additional information received from Paul Lansu.

munitions and in actions to stop the use of child soldiers. *Pax Christi* was co-founder of the International Action Network against Small Arms and Light Weapons. It promoted the establishment of the International Criminal Court and did a lot of work in the Middle East, where it co-sponsored the *Ecumenical Accompaniment Program* in Israel and Palestine. Other contributions were a successful mediation between the Lord's Resistance Army and the government of Uganda to initiate peace talks in 2006; a multi-year strategy to address deep-seated racism in U.S. communities; a closed door dialogue between civil society actors from the greater Middle East, including Israel and Palestine; establishing "sports for peace" programs in South Sudan and Haiti; action for community-based reintegration of former combatants in the Democratic Republic of Congo; dialogue between youth from Kosovo and youth from Northern Ireland; courses in preventive reconciliation using the principles of Aikido in the Philippines; work at a national and international level for the abolition of nuclear, chemical and biological weapons; a high level solidarity delegation to post-coup Honduras; "peace week" initiatives, many of them annual, in the Netherlands, Belgium, Germany, France, UK, the African Great Lakes region, Kosovo, Russia, Croatia, the Philippines and Colombia.

In short, *Pax Christi* "initiated a new way of thinking and praxis into the church" since it " has incorporated a wide range of conflict transformation and peace building practices into its collective program (…)".

A very effective part of *Pax Christi* is its international office, which describes itself as follows. "Guided by the faith and by the social teachings, we attempt to raise a voice in the face of grave human rights' violations and threats to peace".[70] As a faith-based Catholic movement, *Pax Christi International* pays special attention to the impact of religion in relation to violent conflicts, recognizing that intolerance and extremisms toward or associated with any religious group can cause or exacerbate violence. Simultaneously, "*Pax Christi* believes that the resources of faith traditions, including the Christian tradition, can make a significant contribution to peace". It member proclaim that "The starting point of our advocacy is God, our desire to love and serve God. Our goal is to build a just society, based on gospel values".

---

70 See Lansu, Paul. Spirituality of Advocacy in Pax Christi International. Brussels, Updated version 2010. See also an advisory package prepared by the international *Pax Christi* secretariat, entitled: Avenues for Advocacy in the U.N. Human Rights Council; A *Pax Christi International* Advisory Package (Internal ref. 2009-0379-en-gl-HR).

Focusing on the human person its advocacy serves mainly "those who suffer and are victims of selfishness and unjust structures", and at the same time *Pax Christi International* wants "to be present where decisions are made in order to wield a transformative influence on the complex issues of those injustices".

For *Pax Christi International* advocacy means "a planned piece of work that seeks to bring about change in a given context". It encompasses:

a. Policy analysis, evidence-based research and strategizing;
b. Campaigning, awareness raising and mobilizing; and
c. Lobbying and influencing decision- and/or policy-making.

One of the most important features of the *Pax Christi* advocacy is that it is based on spirituality from below. In this regard it differs from classical diplomacy. "Traditionally, in times of peace at least, only diplomats conducted international politics. Economic growth, democratization in the west, the increasing importance of issues such as human rights, disarmament, and development have all helped broaden the actors of international relations from just the professional diplomat to a wider range of actors: non-diplomatic civil servants, non-state lobby groups, development aid groups, and other NGOs. This 'new diplomacy,' modeled on values rather than state sovereignty, works through coalitions – or networks – of state and non-state actors", hence for *Pax Christi*. "Advocacy is more than critically engaging decision-makers on behalf of the poor, oppressed, and other victims of violence. It is political *action with, and by the marginalized* executed in order to amplify their voices within the democratic framework of nation states and international governmental bodies. This necessarily involves mass mobilization on certain issues, strengthening collective bargaining, and democratic and non-violent struggles and campaigns. The thrust is towards policies that enact a special concern for those impoverished and oppressed." One of the focal points in the strategy of *Pax Christi International* is a "globalization from below" and establishing a "network from below for justice and peace", which starts from "listening to the victims of violence". Starting bottom up from the level of the people means first of all: "to listen to their stories and to learn from them. We can only realize what they have to teach us if we humbly accept that they have the knowledge of the issues affecting them, while we arrive as marginally informed outsiders. It is this act of humility that allows us to advocate from the perspective of victims and the poor, the only perspective that makes our work credible in the eyes of those we want to influence".

*Sant'Egidio* is another Catholic movement which excels in building up 'networks for peace', based on "personal and organizational contacts across religious boundaries"[71]. Its mediation in Mozambique is one of the best examples of an effective contribution to a sustainable peace agreement in a context where classical diplomacy had failed. Scott Appleby labels *Sant'Egidio* as the "most successful conflict mediators of the 1990ies"[72]. According to him there are two 'secrets' behind its success: first, "the community builds an unimpeachable record for integrity and good offices in the societies it comes to serve. Through various initiatives, from orchestrating international humanitarian relief to providing direct services to the needy, *Sant'Egidio* practices nonpartisan social action that underscores its equanimity and commitment to the common good". "Second, the community does not seek political or economic power for itself, but neither is it averse to drawing on its powerful friends for the cause of peace."[73]

## *Conclusion*

The two examples of Catholic peace movements demonstrate that the Catholic Church' contribution to overcome war and to build peace is more than a matter of papal messages. However since *Pacem in terris* official texts remain indispensable as expressions of the fundamental shift from just war thinking to peace ethics, but they are not sufficient since, as John Paul II has acknowledged, the teaching of the Church "will gain credibility more immediately from the witness of actions than as a result of its internal logic and consistency"[74].

But even when we acknowledge the necessity of effective action for peace by movements like *Pax Christi* or *Sant'Egidio*, one thing remains a *conditio sine qua non*: war will never be overcome without a profound inner conversion and for this inner combat the church offers rich spiritual resources.

Indeed, as *Pacem in Terris* suggests, "the world will never be a dwelling place of peace, till peace has found a home in the heart of every man"[75]. As such *Pacem in Terris* resonates what great spiritual masters have always understood. Etty Hillesum articulates this as follows. We must fight war and

71 Appleby, R. Scott. The Ambivalence of the Sacred. Lanham (MD), 2000, p. 157.
72 Appleby, The Ambivalence, p. 157.
73 Appleby, The Ambivalence, pp. 162-163.
74 Pope John Paul II, Centesimus annus nr. 57.
75 Pacem in Terris, p. 165.

all its excrescences "by releasing, each day the love that is shackled inside us and giving it a change to live"[76] and each of us "must turn inward and destroy in himself all that he thinks he ought to destroy in others (…) every atom of hate we add to this world makes it still more inhospitable"[77]. Or, as Christian de Chergé, the assassinated abbot of the abbey of Tibhirine wrote: we can't wish somebody peace without going to the extreme in struggling against the hatred in ourselves, "a*nd nobody can say he has sufficiently done it…*"[78]

76 Smelik, Klaas A. (ed.). Etty. The Letters and Diaries of Etty Hillesum 1941-1943. Grand Rapids (MI), 2002, p. 307 (28 March 1942).
77 Smelik, Etty, p. 529 (23 September 1942).
78 Quotation from my own memory.

# The Quest for a "Global Public Authority" in Contemporary Catholic Peace Ethics

*Heinz-Gerhard Justenhoven*

Since the end of the 19th Century, the Catholic Church has developed peace ethics in which the primary objective is to overcome war through an international legal system. Political peace between people and states should arise from the realization of an actively efficient international legal system including the required international institutions. In this case, the Catholic Church can tie in with the deliberations of theological tradition from Augustin, Thomas Aquinas, Francisco de Vitoria to Francsico Suarez[1] and their relation of peace and law. Simultaneously, the Church also takes up the debates of pacifistic inspired humanitarian law (Walter Schücking, Hans Wehberg), which in the 19th and 20th centuries were driven by the thoughts of overcoming war through international law.[2]

## *1. The Quest for Commitment, Effectiveness and Institutionalization of Public International Law*

Supporting the initiative of President Woodrow Wilson, Pope Benedict XV. suggested establishing the "States united under the Christian law".[3] In his appeal for peace on the 1st of August 1917[4], as the end of the First World War is in sight, his answer to that disaster was "that all States, putting aside mutual suspicion, should unite in one league"[5], through which the nations could protect themselves from future wars. "So would each nation be assured not only of its independence but also of the integrity of

1 Cf. Heinz-Gerhard Justenhoven/William Barbieri, Eds., From Just War to Modern Peace Ethics, (Berlin-Boston: de Gruyter), 2012.

2 Cf. e.g. the publications of Walter Schücking and Hans Wehberg.

3 Benedikt XV., *Pacem Dei* 18, in: http://w2.vatican.va/content/benedict-xv/en/encyclicals/documents/hf_ben-xv_enc_23051920_pacem-dei-munus-pulcherrimum.html [12.1.2015].

4 For Benedicts peace initiatives see John F. Pollard, The Unknown Pope. Benedíct XV. (1914-1922) and the Pursuit of Peace, (London 1999), 177-123.

5 Benedikt XV., *Pacem Dei* 17.

its territory within its just frontiers."[6] Following the theological tradition, Benedict uses an argument from creation theology whereas international or national borders do not constitute a counter-argument. The foundation of Benedict's recommended *nations foederatis,* "must be that the moral force of right shall be substituted for the material force of arms that substitutes the material power of weapons"[7]. According to the Pope's suggestion for the institutionalization organization, the international community could orient itself to the Church as "the most perfect type of universal society" (*societas universalis*) [8], both in regard to the organizing principle as well as the institutions.

Pope Benedict was aware of the weaknesses of the *Permanent Court of Arbitration* in The Hague, which was based on the complete voluntariness of the parties in conflict.[9] Therefore he requested "as a substitue for armies the institution of arbitration with its peace-making function, subject to regulations to be agreed on and sanctions to be determined against the State which should refuse either to submit international questions or to accept its decision"[10]. With this call for mandatory arbitral jurisdiction, the sovereignty of the states would be limited in two crucial areas: Firstly, Benedict demanded the abdication of the legality of warfare as an accepted means of the sovereign state to persue its political goals. In the future, the states would be obligated to carry out their matters of dispute in the international court. The states would be refused recourse to military deployment of political objectives. Secondly, the states must accept an authority capable of making compulsory decisions in reference to international conflicts, and if necessary, to implement their judgments accordingly. In my opinion, this is the reason for Pope Benedict's demand to establish security measures against those states refusing to accept the decisions made by the Court of Arbitration. The propinquity between the suggestions made by Woodrow Wilson on the 22nd of January 1917, and those of Pope Benedict in August of the same year, leads to the conclusion that the Pope was aware of the Wilson's League of Nations concept.[11] Benedict focused on laying open the

---

6 Benedikt XV., *Pacem Dei* 17.

7 Benedict XV., Exhortation *Dès le Début* to the Belligerent Peoples and to their Leaders, in: Principles for Peace. Selections From Papal Documents, (Washington DC 1943), 229-232, 230.

8 Benedict XV., Pacem Dei 18.

9 John Merrills, International Dispute Settlement, (Cambridge: Grotius 2nd Ed. 1991), 87.

10 Benedict XV., Dès le Début 230.

11 Cf. Gerhard Beestermöller, Die Völkerbundsidee, (Stuttgart: Kohlhammer 1995), 143ff.

basic ethical principles of international law. He viewed himself as an "interpreter and preserver of eternal laws" (*interpres et vindex legis aeternae*)[12]. He calls for the "Law of the Love of the Gospel" (*evangelica lex caritatis*), that equally applies to the individuals as well as to the states and the people[13]. From that perspective, Benedict views it as "one of the Pope's most important tasks", "to explain that justice may not be infringed upon by any one person or for any reason."[14] Due to the state of affairs during the First World War, Benedict was only capable of urging for peace and point out the ethical principles of a peace order.[15]

It was Pope Pius XII. who then rendered new impulses to the Catholic Church's peace teaching, which were systemized in the famous Papal encyclical *Pacem et terris* issued by his successor Johannes XXIII. Spread amongst his numerous statements and communiqués, Pius systematically laid the foundation of the teachings of peace, which to this day, still continue to have effect. To solve the war problem, the human race must develop a universal, world-embracing political order. This order is not limited to a state, nation or another particular dimension. Pius perceives the legal order and subdivision of the international community in analogy to the order of the states, which focuses on the people.

Andreas Niederberger argues against this analogy with respect to the disanalogy of individuals and republics: "*Republiken sind selbst politische Entitäten, die zu einem bestimmten Zweck entstanden sind, nämlich dazu, den öffentlichen Rechtszustand zwischen den Individuen zu sichern. Als solche können sie nicht selbst als ‚ursprüngliche' Entitäten begriffen werden, die der Schaffung eines öffentlichen Rechtszustandes bedürfen, um ihre Ansprüche geltend zu machen. Ihre Existenz hängt normativ an dem Zweck, den sie für die Individuen erfüllen, so dass sie nur in dem Maß eigenen ‚Verpflichtungen' unterliegen können, in dem diese durch die Zweckbestimmung abgedeckt sind.*"[16] But this is exactly the argument the popes are using: In time of globalisation the wellbeing of the indivdual cannot be aspired through the state alone but has to be strived for in the global community.

---

12 Benedict XV., Allocuzione *Convocare Vos* (22.1.1915) in: http://w2.vatican.va/content/benedict-xv/it/speeches/documents/hf_ben-xv_spe_19150122_convocare-vos.html (Original text in Italian).

13 Benedict XV., Pacem Dei 14.

14 Benedict XV., Allocuzione *Convocare Vos*.

15 Cf. Heinz-Gerhard Justenhoven, Der Friedensplan Papst Benedikts XV. im Ersten Weltkrieg, in: Ökumenische Rundschau 3, (Leipzig 2014), 360-369.

16 Andreas Niederberger, Demokratie unter den Bedingungen der Weltgesellschaft? (Berlin – New York: de Gruyter), 2009, 274.

## 2. Effective Enforcement of Public International Law through a Global Public Authority

Although welcoming the plans of Dumbarton Oaks concerning the establishment of the United Nations' organization in 1944, Pius XII. concurrently warned of the fact that the new League of Nations must avoid "structural errors and the failures of previous solutions"[17]. The emerging United Nations, as one can interpret this, required a League of Nations under international law, in which not only fairness and freedom are recognized as indispensable fundamental values, but its application must also be effectively enforced.

The United Nations to be established must „do everything possible to, once and for all declare that war of aggression, as a permitted solution of international tension and as a tool of national endeavor, is morally outlawed"[18]. According to Pius XII. there is an anlogy between the international community and a state: Just as the law in a state is not only based on the consensus and acceptance of law, but also on legal security, i.e. the enforcement of law and the monopoly of power, the international legal system needs continuous developement in this very direction.[19] Therefore Pius demanded as early as 1944 an effective international political authority with statutory power as the "recognition of its immorality" does not suffice for ostracizing war. According to the Pope, it requires "the threat of a legal intervention of the nations and a punishment superimposed upon the aggressors by the international community"[20] so that ostracism can be effectively enforced. As he would like "to see the authority of the UN increased“[21].

> "Clearly, the UN Charter did not meet all the Pope's requirements on these issues."[22]

17 Pius XII., Nuntius Radiophonicus (Radio message on Christmas 1944), in: Acta Apostolicae Sedis 37 (Typis Polyglottis Vaticanis 1945), 10-23, 18 (in Italian),or:: http://w2.vatican.va/content/pius-xii/it/speeches/1944/documents/hf_p-xii_spe_19441224_natale.html [13.1.2015].

18 Pius XII., Radio message on Christmas 1944, 18.

19 Cf. Guido Gonella, The Papcy and World Peace. A Study of the Christmas Messages of Pope Pius XII, (London: Hollis & Carter 1945), 165f.

20 Pius XII., Radio message on Christmas 1944, 19.

21 Pius XII., Nuntius Radiophonicus (Radio message on Christmas 1956), in: Acta Apostolicae Sedis 49 (Typis Polyglottis Vaticanis 1957), 5-22, 21 (in Italian), or: http://w2.vatican.va/content/pius-xii/it/speeches/1944/documents/hf_p-xii_spe_19441224_natale.html [13.1.2015].

22 Robert J. Araujo, John A. Lucal, Papal Diplomacy and the Quest for Peace. The United Nations from Pius XII. to Paul VI. (Philadelphia/PA: Saint Joseph's University Press 2010), 15.

Pius goes far beyond the political reality of his time and repeats the demand that the UN "(must) have the right and power to pre-empt every case, in which a state contemplates military attacks in another states regardless of any excuse used"[23]. That said, Pius demanded the abolishment of the veto right of the five powers in the Security Council. While abstaining from any suggestions regarding the United Nations' institutionalized organization, Pius XII. did purport normative principles: the United Nations Organization must be carried by a consensus of the states and should be democratically and federally structured. The international authority should be effective, however subsidiary.[24]

The peace encyclical *Pacem in terris* by Pope John XXIII. from 1963[25] became globally renowned and praised. Regardless of its new, consensus-accentuated style, its agenda of political order remains within the systematic framework set by Pope Pius XII.[26] When John XXIII. speaks about the international community in his encyclical, two models are imaginable. On the one hand, he could view the international community primarily as a community of states; the states were to be regarded as juridic persons of international law. In traditional international law until the early 20$^{th}$ century it is conceived as such. However, Catholic peace ethics view the individual human being and not the individual state as a constitutional member of the international community. Only because of this presupposition, John XXIII. can conceive the abstract concept of the international community as a global state. Let's look at his arguments in more detail:

Through globalization, the efficiency of a traditional state has been pushed to its limits. On their own, "no State can fittingly pursue its own interests in isolation from the rest"[27]. They are dependent upon one another. "Hence, there will always be an imperative need", Pope John concludes, "to promote in sufficient measure the universal common good; the good, that is, of the whole human family"[28]. The description of growing dependency within the human race, according to Pope John, endorses the conclusion of universal public welfare as a requirement that is based in human nature.

---

23 Pius XII., Radio message on Christmas 1956, 20.

24 Cf. Pius XII., Radio message on Christmas 1944, 18 and 19.

25 John XXIII., Pacem in Terris, in: http://w2.vatican.va/content/john-xxiii/en/encyclicals/documents/hf_j-xxiii_enc_11041963_pacem.html [13.1.2015]

26 Cf. Yves Congar, The Four Pillars of Peace, in: Herbert Schambeck, Ed., Pro Fide et Iustitia. Festschrift für Agostino Kardinal Casaroli, (Berlin: Duncker & Humblot 1984), 369-380, 369.

27 John XXIII. Pacem in terris Nr. 131.

28 John XXIII. Pacem in terris Nr. 132.

As an individual state alone, for example in issues concerning security and peace, is not capable of guaranteeing the dignity and development of a human being, the universal common good must also be promoted beyond the states' public welfare. The rights of the individual are also the focal point of universal common good as well. This, as John further infers, can only be ensured through a respective global authority. "Today, the universal common good presents us with problems which are world-wide in their dimensions; problems, therefore, that cannot be solved except by a public authority with power, organization and means co-extensive with these problems, and with a world-wide sphere of activity. Consequently the moral order itself demands the establishment of some such general form of public authority."[29] As his predecessor Pius, Pope John also assumes that analog to the state authority, the global issues to be regulated can only be solved through a universal authority. As far as I can see, no other model of order is being discussed.

However, those asking what this global model of order could look like will find no further answers; this is open to further deliberations. Hence Pope John lets it rest upon two important criteria setting limits to global authority: it must be set up "with the consent of all nations"[30], thus, working according to the principle of the unanimous vote. And "it is no part the duty of universal authority to limit the sphere of action of the pubic authority of individual States"[31]; hence, only becoming subsidiarily active.

In his peace encyclical and based on his thoughts of universal public welfare, John XXIII. inferred the necessity of an international, political authority. According to the Second Vatican Council, to overcome war is the most important political and moral challenge. Therefore, a fundamental reform of the international order must be realized.

To reach this end, it „undoubtedly requires the establishment of some universal public authority acknowledged as such by all and endowed with the power to safeguard on the behalf of all, security, regard for justice, and respect for rights."[32] Just days after adoption of the council's text, and in the first speech of a Pope to the United Nations General Assembly, Pope Paul VI. repeated this statement almost verbatim: "Who can fail to see the need and importance of thus gradually coming to the establishment of a

29 John XXIII. Pacem in terris Nr. 137.

30 John XXIII. Pacem in terris Nr. 138.

31 John XXIII. Pacem in terris Nr. 141.

32 Second Vatican Council, Pastoral Constitution *Gaudium et Spes* Nr. 81 (1965), http://www.vatican.va/archive/hist_councils/ii_vatican_council/documents/vat-ii_const_19651207_gaudium-et-spes_en.html [13.1.2015].

world authority capable of taking effective action on the juridical and political planes?"[33]

As far as I can see, the debate covering the order model within the Catholic peace ethics has not been continued since then. The Popes that followed absorbed this stand of the Council's debate, without driving them further. In his Social Enzyclical *Caritas in Veriate* Benedict XVI. states: "there is urgent need of a true world political authority" as a political instrument to "manage the global economy; to revive economies hit by the crisis; to avoid any deterioration of the present crisis and the greater imbalances that would result; to bring about integral and timely disarmament, food security and peace; to guarantee the protection of the environment and to regulate migration"[34]. This public global authority is explicitly qualified by Benedict: "Such an authority would need to be regulated by law, to observe consistently the principles of subsidiarity and solidarity, to seek to establish the common good, and to make a commitment to securing authentic integral human development inspired by the values of charity in truth."[35] Benedict XVI. concisely summarized his predecessors' peace ethics.

Whereas his predecessors also did, John Paul II. stood for the outlined ethical ideal and saw the United Nations as an important step of development to a global public authority.[36] In lieu of frequent defiance, he asked how development in the required direction could be brought into place, respectively how it could be held in motion. The Pope demanded that the existing law as well as the respective institutions be respected by the states as relevant players, due to the fact that there were yet no effective international authority capable of enforcing legal compliancy vis-à-vis the states. While the idea of promoting the United Nations to become a "global public authority" is looked at with suspicion or even harsh critique.[37]

In his address to the members of The Permanent Court of Arbitration and the International Court of Justice in the Peace Palace in The Hague in 1985,

---

33 Paul VI.: Address to the United Nations Organization (4.10.1965): http://www.vatican.va/holy_father/paul_vi/speeches/1965/documents/hf_p-vi_spe_19651004_united-nations_en.html [13.1.2015].

34 Benedict XVI., Caritas in Veritate Nr. 67: http://www.vatican.va/holy_father/benedict_xvi/encyclicals/documents/hf_ben-xvi_enc_20090629_caritas-in-veritate_en.html [13.1.2015].

35 Benedict XVI., Caritas in Veritate Nr. 67.

36 Introductions to the Peace Ethic of Pope John Paul II.: Heinz-Gerhard Justenhoven, The Peace Ethics of Pope John Paul II., in: From Just War to Modern Peace Ethics, ed. Heinz-Gerhard Justenhoven/William Barbieri, (Berlin-Boston: de Gruyter), 2012, 313-344. Ugo Colombo Sacco, John Paul II and World Politics. Twenty Years of Search for a New Approach (1978-1998), (Leuven: Peeters 1999).

37 Cf. Nigel Biggar's position in this book, pp. 109-126.

Pope John Paul II. emphasized the interest of the Holy See in reference to the international system of justice that reached back to the commencement of The Hague institutions. Whilst referring to the engagement of Leo XIII., he emphasized that the "Church has consistently supported the development of an international administration of justice and arbitration as a way of peaceful resolving conflicts and as part of the evolution of a world legal system."[38] Although the states, starting with the Peace Conference 1899 in The Hague, endeavored substantial progress in the development of public international law, yet as always, a consensus to bow to the law was lacking within the community of states. "Will the constitutional states ever reach a consensus and build a community that waives every legal exemption?"[39] is how the Pope worded the core problem of the necessary abdication of sovereignty. As the states reserve the right to decide whether they want to resolve conflicts within the framework of public international law or seek a final decision through the deployment of political power, and should the situation arise, through military instruments of power, Johannes Paul II. announced his conclusion by stating that "the present Court is no more – but it is also no less – than an initial step toward what we hope one day will be a totally effective judicial authority in a peaceful word."[40] If conflicts are ever to be resolved based on law, the states must decide to come to a consensus and surrender further sovereignty. Johannes Paul II sees the specific contribution of Catholic peace ethics for the further development of international jurisdiction in pointing out "the criteria which the development of an international system of law must satisfy"[41].

As a justice-oriented regulating system, the law should secure "peace by means of fair regulation of the relationships between people and between the people and their institutions"[42]. Such as the principle of equality applies as a legal principle between individuals, so must it also apply as a principle under international law amongst the subjects of international law. The

38 John Paul II., Address to the International Court of Justice in The Hague (13.5.1985), http://www.vatican.va/holy_father/john_paul_ii/speeches/1985/may/documents/hf_jp-ii_spe_19850513_corte-internazionale_en.html [13.1.2015].

39 John Paul II., Appel aux Membres du Corps Diplomatique, http://www.vatican.va/holy_father/john_paul_ii/speeches/1990/february/documents/hf_jp-ii_spe_19900201_corpo-dipl-ciad_fr.html [13.1.2015].

40 John Paul II., Address to the International Court of Justice.

41 John Paul II., Address to the International Court of Justice.

42 John Paul II., Discours aux Représentants des Institutions et Organismes de la Communauté Européene, http://www.vatican.va/holy_father/john_paul_ii/speeches/1985/may/documents/hf_jp-ii_spe_19850515_european-community_fr.html [13.1.2015].

article of Claus Kreß in this volume shows in more detail how much the international judical system is becoming part of a global public authority just as the papacy from Leo XIII. to John Paul II. envisioned it.

*Summary*

The question should be pursued, in which manner a global peace order should be further developed within the peace ethics of the Catholic Church by implementing international law and through legal instantiating institutions. Since their establishment, international law and existing international institutions up to the International Court of Justice have been supported and suggestions enunciated in reference to their further development which would fully validate them as legal institutions. Ultimately, the requirements are justified in the fact that the dignity and fundamental rights of a human being should be the point of reference for every political community. The protection of a person's dignity through respect and safeguarding of human rights requires legal institutions. The Catholic peace ethic reasons this with the term of public welfare: Although the realization of public welfare is primarily the responsibility of the respective state; however, where the individual states reach their limits, a global political authority becomes necessary. A global political power, that in the second degree, takes over the essential responsibilities and such, which protects the international public welfare.

The necessity of a global politic authority arises from the international public welfare's need; as an analogy between the individual state's public welfare and that of the international community. Both communities can only aspire to build their public welfare on the foundation of a functioning legal system and respective institutions. In this case, the ecclesiastic peace ethics presume that legal security is not achievable without the institutions being equipped with the respective authorizations, and only on a voluntary basis. For this reason, a global public authority should have effective competencies towards the states and based on the states' previous voluntary consent, this global public authority should be capable of intervening in the states' sovereignty.

From this perspective, the existing international peace institutes are deemed a correct and important step towards an international order. The existing international law should be further developed into an international legal order that is oriented to human rights and is capable of ensuring legal security between the peoples and states. International conflicts should be carried out in the international jurisdiction in an obligatory manner.

### 3. Wars in Syria and Ukraine revealing the deficits of the international community

While the *Charta of Paris* from November 21, 1990 was optimistic about the international community's ability of conflict resolution,[43] the last years have given reason for disillusionment: Looking at the wars in Syria and eastern Ukraine the international community's deficit in avoiding and solving conflicts is obvious. Currently we witness a series of violent conflicts from the Sahel region through the Middle East with Syria and Iraq as nucleus to Central Asia with Afghanistan and Pakistan as hot spots and Eastern Europe with a focus on Ukraine. In each case the root cause is a local conflict over the distribution of power and wealth. A people or part of the population has risen and fought for its share of the cake: for political and economic participation. The early stage of the wars in Syria and Ukraine are examples of this pattern. Those in power showed unwillingness to share and used violence to maintain their privileges. This phase of instability of the state is used by foreign powers, regional and international, trying to extend their sphere of influence – calling opposing powers into the arena, who are fearful of losing traditional influence in the region. A weak state is obviously an invitation to powers in search of extension of their influence, as conflicting parties in the civil war try to improve their cards in the game by asking outside forces for support.

A weak or fragile state is unable to exert the monopoly of power within its borders and thus leaves the door open for outside powers to interfere in the local conflict; the state is no longer able to protect its population and to provide security. As we have seen in Syria, those in power can be the root cause for escalating a political conflict into a violent one and thus become the security threat for at least part of the population instead of protecting it. When there is little hope that the government being a party in a violent conflict can serve as a broker for a peaceful solution, help has to come from the outside players. But so far in Syria regional and international powers have been more part of the problem then a help for a solution: The Shiite regime of Iran with the Hisbollah as its dependent militia is supporting the Assad regime against Sunni Saudi Arabia with its allies, the Gulf emirates who were in support of different islamistic militias. With the US supporting the opposition against Assad, Russia sided with the government for not losing its last stronghold in the Middle East after Qaddafi's overthrow by Nato-forces.

43 Cf. Charta of Paris, http://www.osce.org/mc/39516?download=true [17.12.2014].

From a Machiavellian perspective regional and international powers have no choice than behaving exactly this way: Should they decide to quit the mutual power play, they would not only lose influence but endanger their own security; the opposing power will make use of the power vacuum a rewithdrawing power leaves behind, will accumulate more influence and try to eliminate the old counterpart. As Hans Morgenthau, Machiavellis most learned scholar, has shown with convincing evidence, the power play is insuperable within the current international order.[44] Morgenthau himself has criticized US-President Franklin D. Roosevelt for ignoring this reality while laying the foundation of the United Nations. According to Morgenthau states have to lobby for their interests to be able to protect their people, i.e. to provide wealth and security; doing so they have to use power to enforce their interests. The use of power is essential for a state aiming at its core goals. As states do have conflicting interests, it is evident according to Morgenthau – and history has proven this – that states need to make use of their power to enforce their interests against the will of opposing states. These political conflicts tend to turn into military conflicts, as powerful states want to enforce their will wherever they can and as long as possible. Political, economic and – as last resort – the use of military means is in view of Morgenthau and his political realism a logical consequence of the existing international order. Ignoring these facts by creating a United Nations that is unable to eliminate the structure of international politics while at the same time put hope of being able to overcome this structure has led to sharp critic from political realists and still does nowadays. Political realism seems to be condemned to live with a violent world with no hope of change.

## *4. Impartiality as normative challenge of the international system*

The UN is engaged in trying to broker peaceful solutions in Syria and many other conflicts, yet the UN's ability to engage in conflicts is limited by the interests of its member states: by powerful members and the Permanent Five Members of the Security Council especially. With their veto they can bloc the UN: in obstructing a Security Council resolution deciding whether or not a conflict is interpreted as a threat to world peace and measures to be taken. Intentionally the security council was meant to decide impartially in

44 Cf. Hans J. Morgenthau, Politics among Nations: The Struggle for Power and Peace, (New York: Knopf 5th Ed. 1978).

the name of all the member states; in reality impartiality is lacking in many cases. From a normative point of view the inability of the UN to act in similar cases without differentiation, i.e. to act impartial, is its greatest challenge.

Following the Kantian philosophical approach of Otfried Höffe, I argue that the states are obliged to overcome the status of anarchy in which they still remain until the reign of law in international affairs despite a number of improvements in the 20th century.[45] The impartiality of the international system can only and needs to be overcome by a justice oriented, mandatory and effective international law. Regarding international security and the issue of war and peace the existing international law can be described as an intermediate stage between a law that serves primarily the interest of the dominant powers and an international law that is really impartial. From a normative point of view the states are obliged to overcome the remaining impartialities in international law. According to Otfried Höffe it is in the interest of states to agree to a justice oriented international law with respective institutions to enforce it: the inherent impartiality of the international system in combination with the growing globalisation is a severe threat to sovereignity. They endanger the security and political freedom of individual states, as no state can be sure not to be overtoppled by other states – as long as international relations are not ruled by a mandatory, effective and justice oriented law. The practical relevance of legal rules is only given, when law is accepted by the consensus of the members of the legal community, mechanisms and institutions for conflicts resolution are existing and in the end there is legal security by law enforcement as last resort. Therefore Otfried Höffe can show that from an ethical point of view impartial global public authorities to enforce the international law are required.[46] As a legal philosopher Höffe comes to very similar conclusions as the Catholic peace ethics as shown above. While the popes and the II. Vatican Council do not elaborate their quest for a universal public authority, Höffe develops a full scheme of a 'subsidiar and federal world republic'[47]. I understand Höffe's approach as one attempt to solve the normative problem of a lacking impartiality in the international system. The question that Catholic peace ethics rises, i.e. what an 'impartial global public authority' can look like or how it can be constructed, is obviously open. But the pure fact that we have no clear institutional idea yet is no argument against the normative quest.

45 Cf Otfried Höffe, Democracy in an Age of Globalization, (Dordrecht: Springer 2007), 157.
46 Cf Höffe, Democracy in an Age of Globalisation, 305.
47 Cf Höffe, Democracy in an Age of Globalisation, 157-237.

While Samuel Tessema, Karsten Nowrot and Christian Tams describe approaches of existing international institutions as steps toward more impartiality in their articles in this volume, Global Governance theories challenge the quest for a global public authority.

## *5. Global governance and the quest for impartiality*

Global Governance theories value the expanding numbers of global actors as relevant players on the international scene. NGOs like Amnesty International and Greenpeace should be understood as advocators of the "international public interest" as Jost Delbrück puts it and this way have a necessary and constructive function in polity.[48] Together with civil societies, religions and many others Michael Reder describes them as "parts of complex and dynamic global networks" in this volume. Global Governance theories according to Reder therefore take the different potentials of self-governance and governing others as starting point trusting in the cooperative problem-solving skills of global actors in order to manage complex global interactions.[49] For normative Global Governance theories this seems to be the best available solution and getting as close as possible towards peace and justice in the world as there are no other existing forms of adequately solving global conflicts.

Global Governance theories manage to grasp the complex network of international relations and shed light on the problems solving capacities of different actors in the global arena. This is obviously their indispensable contribution and needs to be integrated into the systematics of Catholic peace ethics. But what about the problem of impartiality? Reder points to the deficits of the reliance of the global civil society as described: NGOs, while contributing to the *bonum commune internationalis* lack democratic legitimacy and depend on the focus of those financing them: the public of the wealthy societies of the northern industrial states and their take of global problems. It seems an open question to me of how to introduce more impartiality into the system of global NGOs; will it happen by itself without any regulations?

48 Jost Delbrück, Von der Staatenordnung über internationale institutionelle Kooperation zur ‚supraterritorial or global governance': Wandel des zwischenstaatlichen Völkerrechts zur rechtsordnung des Menschen und der Völker? In: Weltinnenpolitik, ed. by Ulrich Bartosch und Jochen Wagner, 55-65, (Münster: Lit 1998) 63.

49 Cf. Michael Reder, Global Governance vs. Global Government. Philosophy in Times of Globalisation, in this volume pp. 169-186.

While Global Governance theories help understanding the dynamics and cooperative character of the international system as it is existing, the key issue that papal peace teaching raised seems undealt: How can a higher degree of impartiality in the international system be secured. While it needs to be acknowledged that a multitude of global actors contribute to the orientation towards a *bonum commune internationalis*, there are those left behind, damnified or ignored: indigenes, ethnic minorities, religious groups and others with no or little political influence. The quest for a 'global public authority' is the normative quest to overcome impartiality in a globalized world – even if we don't know yet how.

# Belief in the Authority of International Law for Peace: A Reflection on Pacem in Terris

*Mary Ellen O'Connell*

> ...[L]aws clearly indicate how a man must behave toward his fellows in society, and how the mutual relationships between the members of a State and its officials are to be conducted. They show too what principles must govern the relations between States; and finally, what should be the relations between individuals or States on the one hand, and the world-wide community of nations on the other.
>
> --*Pacem in Terris, 11 April 1963*[1]

The religious leaders who gathered in Rome for the Second Vatican Council recognized the value of law in all human relations. Law's most essential purpose is the prevention and settlement of disputes. Certainly that is its most essential purpose at the international level.[2] In other words, the purpose of law is peace. As the quotation above indicates, Pope John XXIII, now St. John, well understood the linkage between law and peace. In his encyclical, *Pacem in Terris*, he called on humanity to take steps toward greater peace, including through recognition of and respect for the potential of law in ordering human affairs without violence. This chapter is an investigation of how international law supports the quest for peace, with the aim of renewing respect for law drawing inspiration from Pope John's extraordinary encyclical.

International law is the law that governs relations at the level of the "worldwide community of nations." It is law relevant not only to states and international organizations, but to individuals and groups when their activities or experiences have international impact. Despite the evident importance of international law, too many in the world today doubt that international law is truly law and, therefore, doubt that international law can play the role in fostering peace aimed at in *Pacem in Terris*.[3] The widespread

1 Pope John XXII. Pacem in Terris: Encyclical of Pope John XXIII on Establishing Universal Peace in Truth, Justice, Charity, and Liberty, 1963, http://www.vatican.va/holy_father/john_xxiii/encyclicals/documents/hf_j-xxiii_enc_11041963_pacem_en.html [15.9.2015].

2 See Brownlie, Ian. The Peaceful Settlement of International Disputes in Practice. In: *Pace International Law Review*, 1995 (7), p. 257.

3 For example, the United States representative at the United Nations, John Bolton, who served in that position from August 2005 to December 2006, argues that international law is a form of morality, not law, in Bolton, John. Is there Really 'Law' in

violence in our world is evidence that supports these doubts about the efficacy of international law. This chapter presents the alternative case, arguing that with greater understanding and compliance, international law can play a far more constructive and successful role in fostering an end to violent conflict. In particular, the international law rules restricting the use of force need acceptance and respect. As will be emphasized in the discussion to follow, the rules on the use of force are based on the same moral conviction that inspired *Pacem in Terris*: the necessity of peace for the flourishing of humanity and the natural world. Legal scholars can find new inspiration in good Pope John's words of decades ago to work for peace by creative scholarship supporting the world's law against war.

## *1. International Law as Law: Authority and Enforcement*

Turning first to the problem of even discussing "law" for peace, many people in the world today, including influential political scientists and even government officials, doubt that international law is really law. Two particular misunderstandings drive much of the doubt: One misunderstanding concerns the source of international law's authority. The other misunderstanding concerns how international law is enforced. Doubts surrounding the source of international law's authority arise from the fact that law within states is explained on a different basis than law between states. People are familiar with explanations for the authority of national law – law within states – but these explanations do not apply to international law. Law within states centers on constitutions and government institutions. The legitimacy of both is often explained by the story of a "social contract". Over time, the social contract can become part of a state's shared historical and cultural experience. In other words, doubts about international law have been built in some cases on a hypothetical about national law. A better theory of national law authority turns out to be one equally true of international law.

The other misunderstanding concerns international law's means of enforcement. The lack of a police force, judicial system with compulsory jurisdiction, and an executive branch charged with implementing the law suggest that international law cannot really be law. In fact, the way interna-

International Affairs? In: *Transnational Law and Contemporary Problems*, 2000, 10, p. 1. See also the discussion below of Goldsmith and Posner's The Limits of International Law.

tional law operates is in reality not so different from national legal systems, despite the different institutional structure.

Turning first to the question of authority, individuals who openly doubt that international law has authority may have difficulty explaining the authority of national law. They may point to a state's constitution, institutions of government, and the practice of voting to support their assumption. Yet, it should be asked, what imparts authority to a constitution or government? In many cultures and for many centuries, the answer has been that God institutes governments and designates leaders. Hugo Grotius, the renowned 17th century jurist, theologian, diplomat, and reputed father of international law, said of all law, not just international law: "What God has shown to be his Will, that is law."[4]

Today, few outside a theocracy like that in Iran believe that one looks to God for the source of legal or governmental authority. The Age of Enlightenment moved humanity to seeing science and the scientific method as the sole basis for supporting arguments. For almost two centuries, concepts required material proof to be considered worthy of recognition. Consent, which could be depicted as some physical or material act of saying "yes", became the hypothetical basis of post-Enlightenment legal and political theory. Indeed, the term "social contract" (a society-wide act of consent) remains the most widely used explanation for the basis of law and government in the West. The social contract is a heuristic device most associated with the English philosopher John Locke. It holds that citizens within nations have consented to be governed. Of course, no one actually consents in this sense of making a statement or signing a document.[5] The reality is that the governed everywhere accept government and law passively.

People are born into these arrangements and accept them as essential to social life. Acceptance is demonstrated in ways ranging from law compliance to refraining from revolution. Some populations may reject the type of government they have or the identity of government officials; the rejection may even result in violent rebellion, an all too common feature of contemporary life. Some rebellion is motivated by a desire of people to create states with closer cultural affinity. This is true respecting late 20th and early 21st century separatist movements in Congo, Nigeria, the Philippines, Iraq, Syria, Ukraine, the former Yugoslavia, Indonesia, Sri Lanka and Western China to name a few. The ethnic clashes in these states are not about the dif-

4 Grotius, H. De Jure Praedae Commentarius: Commentary on the Law of Prize and Booty. The Hague, 1868, ch. 2.

5 For a discussion of the fictional "social contract," see O'Connell, Mary Ellen. The Power and Purpose of International Law. Oxford, 2008.

ficulty of successful law in culturally diverse communities, as much as the sense that a particular government is not treating all citizens fairly. People want law and government. They also want law and government to be fair, honest, and competent.

People everywhere value law. It is accepted, even where governments that produce it within states are rejected. No social contract hypothetical is needed to try to explain the acceptance of law in distinction to the need to defend particular forms of government or constitutions.[6] The basis of authority in international law is also acceptance. Since the rise of the modern state with the end of the Thirty Years War in Europe, individuals, states, and organizations have accepted the need for formal and neutral law to regulate relations that reach beyond international borders. Because international law defines statehood, identifies borders, establishes treaties, and affects myriad other features of daily life in an increasingly connected world, only a global cataclysm could result in its displacement. Indeed, no government today openly questions the status of international law as a binding system of authority. The real focus of doubters and deniers is on particular bodies of rules, especially the rules restricting the use of force.

As for institutions and culture to support international law, the international community has both – and both have existed far longer than those of any but a few modern states. Global institutions and culture have different characteristics from the analogs of nation states. Institutions for implementing and enforcing international law include the United Nations Security Council, the International Court of Justice, the International Criminal Court, as well as national and regional courts, police, and administrators applying international law.

Some decry the lack of popular participation in the making of international law and the selection of officials to lead international organizations. However, government representatives, who are elected popularly, participate. Moreover, new technology is creating participation in all aspects of international life.[7] Consider the drafting of the 1998 Rome Statute for the International Criminal Court and the review conference in Kampala in 2010. Further, the international community has its own identity, which can support international law as national law is supported by a state's common culture. Philip Allott

6 See Hart, H.L.A. The Concept of Law. Oxford, 1961.

7 A great deal has been written about popular participation in international law-making and governance. One excellent account is by Reisman, Michael. The Democratization of Contemporary International Law-Making Processes and the Differentiation of their Application. In: Rüdiger Wolfrum, Volker Röben (Eds.). Developments of International Law in Treaty Making. Heidelberg, 2005.

has referred to the international community as the "society of all societies."[8] Addis Adeno speaks of the international community as a community of diversity. He describes a central purpose of international law being to preserve diversity through prohibiting crimes of genocide, slavery, and aggression.[9] International law is not in conflict with the diverse cultures of national communities. It supports them and in so doing creates a meta-culture.

In addition to the basis of authority, another widespread myth about international law is that it has no means of enforcement. Scholars, especially of political science, have used this erroneous conclusion to help make the argument that international law is not real law and that militarily powerful states need not comply with it – at least when it comes to the regulations on resort to force.[10]

In fact, international law has means of enforcement and those means play much the same role in supporting the authority of international law as the police play in supporting the authority of law within states.[11] Within states, police do not enforce each rule – far from it. Police are active almost exclusively in enforcing the criminal law. Contract law, tort, administrative law, procedural law, and other categories of law are self-enforcing, or, where disputes occur, are resolved through a variety of dispute resolution mechanisms. Most law compliance occurs with no thought for the potential of coercive enforcement. Moreover, as everyone knows, a great deal of law within states is never enforced. This is true of rules such as traffic laws, but it is also true of far more important rules such as the criminal laws against murder, domestic violence, theft, and rape. Enough rules are enforced to indicate that the community supports the law. The fact that each rule has the potential for coercive enforcement is what makes it a legal rule. That potential for enforcement plays a role in why the rule is accepted as law.

It is the same in international law – international law has armed measures and countermeasures, commonly known as sanctions, as well as international organization penalties and measures ordered by courts.[12] These forms of coercion are available to enforce any conduct rule. As with national law, coercive measures are not taken with respect to every violation and are not the only means of dispute resolution. The wealthy and powerful get away with

8 Allott, Philip. The True Function of International Law. In: *Indiana Journal of Global Legal Studies*. 1998, vol. 5 (2), p. 391 ff.

9 Addis, Addeno. Imaging the International Community. In: *Human Rights Quarterly*, 2009, vol. 31, pp. 145-50.

10 The German-American political scientist Hans Morgenthau made this conception of international law enforcement a common belief among students of political science in his widely used textbook, Politics Among Nations, first published in 1948.

11 This topic is taken up in detail in my book, O'Connell, Power and Purpose.

12 O'Connell, Power and Purpose, ch. 4-9.

more law violation than the weak and poor. In this respect, international law is remarkably similar to domestic law. Observing the practice of states and other relevant actors supports the view that sufficient enforcement occurs to explain the wide recognition of international law as binding law.

Ignorance about these aspects of international law has been particularly prevalent in recent years in the United States. American legal scholars are justifiably proud of the U.S. constitutional system and the nation's immense economic and military power. These scholars sometimes give in to the temptation of comparing international law with U.S. law and find international law deficient. Often the scholar reaching such a conclusion knows relatively little about international law. The result has been a wave of publications perpetuating misunderstandings and myths, particularly with respect to the basis for authority, the means of enforcement, and the reality of international legal rules restraining the use of force.

For example, a Bush administration lawyer co-authored THE LIMITS OF INTERNATIONAL LAW, and two other Bush administration lawyers involved with the torture memos, John Yoo and Robert Delahunty, published an article in the prestigious MICHIGAN LAW REVIEW, with the title: *Peace Through Law? The Failure of a Noble Experiment*.[13] Both the book and the article contain significant errors.[14] The fact that highly rated journals and presses have produced such publications supports one thesis of this chapter: failure to comply with international law is due in part to lack of knowledge of international law. Ignorance is undermining respect for international law principles.

Properly understood, international law can play a more robust role in the pursuit of peace, and the associated goals of protecting human rights, supporting prosperity, and conserving the environment. If international law had been taken seriously by American, British, and Australian leaders, they would not have invaded Iraq in 2003; torture would not have been carried out in secret detention sites; and so-called "targeted killing" would never have become the preferred counter-terrorism tool of the United States.

---

13 Goldsmith, Jack/ Posner, Eric. The Limits of International Law. Oxford, 2006. In addition, Eric Posner published The Perils of the Global Legalism with the University of Chicago Press in 2009. Delahunty, Robert J./Yoo, John C. Peace Through Law, The Failure of a Noble Experiment. In: *Michigan Law Review*. 2007, (106) p. 923 ff. Yoo and Delahunty propose a rule that is already the law.

14 Delahunty/ Yoo, Peace Through Law, p. 939. See also O'Connell, Power and Purpose, ch. 3 for a lengthy analysis of errors in Posner/ Goldsmith. See also numerous book reviews critiquing Posner/ Goldsmith, e.g. van Aaken, Anne. To Do Away with International Law? Some Limits to the Limits of International Law. In: *European Journal of International Law*, 2006, p. 289 ff. and a symposium issue, Symposium: The Limits of International Law. *Georgia Journal of International and Comparative Law* 2006, vol. 34 (2).

These dramatic examples from the first two decades of the 21st century are the result of years of declining respect for international law, beginning in the 1960s.[15] Pope John XXIII was prescient to call for respect for law and international institutions. The post-World War II consensus against war and in favor of international organization and law was already showing signs of weakening by the early 1960s. Indeed, outside the area of arms control, no international legal development to advance the law of peace has occurred since the drafting of the Charter in 1945. By contrast, much has been done to weaken the law against war.

Legal scholars have persistently argued for greater rights to use force, for a variety of reasons that have changed with political trends. During the existence of the Soviet Union, within the Soviet bloc it was argued that force could be used for the good of spreading communism.[16] In the West, similar arguments were used to justify force to spread democracy.[17] During the Cold War, no wholesale attacks on international law or the law against force tended to be made. Each Superpower realized the benefit of being able to cite the law against its opponent and took care not to provide an excuse to the other for law violations. Still, political scientists were beginning to make theoretical arguments aimed at undermining the basis of international legal authority, and misinformation began to spread.

U.S. foreign policy-makers were listening to these erroneous theories about international law from scholars espousing political science realism. International law scholars provided few responses because so many of the best and brightest minds, certainly in the U.S., had turned from international law toward a focus on constitutional law. It was a turn away from the law of the world community. Only in such an internally oriented context could the U.S. Attorney General promise, as he did in 2013, not to use drone attacks to kill Americans on U.S. territory unless the individual was involved in combat.[18] The senator who demanded the promise saw no need to get the same guarantee for such citizens of all nations.[19]

---

15 This is when the views of Hans Morgenthau began to influence U.S. foreign policy. See O'Connell, Power and Purpose, ch. 2.

16 See Kovalev, Sergei. Sovereignty and the International Obligations of Socialist Countries. In: Pravda, 26.09.1968.

17 For a debate on the Reagan Doctrine and international law, see Louis Henkin et al. (Eds.). Right v. Might: International Law and the Use of Force. Washington (D.C.), 1991.

18 The promise was a response to a query from Sen. Rand Paul (R-KY), in a letter available on the *Washington Post* website: https://www.washingtonpost.com/blogs/post-politics/files/2013/03/Senator-Rand-Paul-Letter.pdf [15.9.2015].

19 Archbishop Desmond Tutu of South Africa has protested the lack of concern for the rights of non-U.S. citizens in a letter to the New York Times, 12.02.2013, available

In point of fact, international law protects the entire world community from drone attacks outside combat zones. Fifty years after *Pacem in Terris*, the time is ripe to renew the call of Pope John for a commitment to the law that governs human relations at all levels. As this chapter seeks to show, if international law was important in 1963, it is even more important fifty years later in our more globalized world. To reduce violence and shift efforts toward health, the environment, human rights, and prosperity, international law needs to be understood and respected. With greater understanding should come action, action for peace on earth.

## *2. The Evolution of International Law Restrictions on War*

The international law restricting the use of force of today has its origins in the thinking of St. Augustine, Bishop of Hippo in North Africa in the 5th century.[20] Augustine was faced with the challenge of a heretical sect known as the Donatists who preyed upon Augustine's pacifist flock. The Donatists took literally the words of scripture that reported Christ's admonition to his followers to put away their swords. The Donatists never touched swords – they substituted clubs, beating and robbing pacifist Christians. In response to this and other provocations, Augustine moved away from strict pacifism. He considered force in self-defense to be morally acceptable for Christians. Augustine was a student of St. Ambrose who taught wars of defense could be ethical for Christians, a teaching that built on classical Greek and Roman notions that war fought to re-establish peace respected the priority of peace over war. Augustine adopted these views as his own, adding that the way a war is fought will determine the likelihood of long-term peace. If people are so brutalized, if everything is taken from them so that all that is left is to fight on, the cause of peace is doomed. In this observation lies an early rationale for rules governing the conduct of war.

at: http://www.nytimes.com/2013/02/13/opinion/drones-kill-lists-and-machiavelli.html?_r=0 [15.9.2015]. See also his foreword to Cohn, Marjorie (ed.). Drones and targeted killing, legal, moral and geopolitical issues. Northampton (MA), 2014.

20 For an excellent general history of international law on the use of force, see Neff, Stephen. War and the Law of Nations. A general history. Cambridge, 2005. For specialized studies of the Just War Doctrine and international law, see Barbieri, William/ Justenhoven, Heinz-Gerhard (Eds.). From Just War to Modern Peace Ethics. Berlin-Boston, 2012; Conforti, Benedetto. The Doctrine of Just War and Contemporary International Law. Italian Yearbook of International Law, vol. 12 (2002). Leiden, 2003; and von Elbe, Joachim. The Evolution of the Concept of the Just War in International Law. In: *American Journal of International Law* 1939, vol. 33 (4) pp. 665-688.

The 13th century Dominican priest St. Thomas Aquinas developed these ideas into something closer to a legal code. His ideas persist to this day almost unchanged under the label of the Christian Just War Doctrine. Despite the advances for society found in Aquinas's thinking about war, his views began to be challenged by those who rejected his explanation of the basis for legal authority. Aquinas taught that legal authority flows from the Divine; the implementation of law depends on the Church and lay leaders loyal to the Church. With the Reformation, these foundations were questioned and subsequently weakened. What the pope or the Holy Roman emperor said with respect to law was no longer accepted as a matter of faith.

Scholars increasingly looked to the law itself to fill the void left by the Church's diminished role in law. St. Thomas's followers, the Spanish scholastics, including Las Casas, Vitoria, Suarez, and others, contributed to the idea of the law, rather than human authority, as the ultimate governor of human action. They, too, promoted the Just War Doctrine to constrain the use of force between societies, but they had no ready solution for those who rejected papal authority.

It was Hugo Grotius, the renowned Dutch Protestant scholar, theologian, and diplomat, who provided a persuasive argument for law as the substitute for the pope and the emperor. Grotius rejected the thinking of those who wanted to leave each prince supreme in his own realm, relying on his own conscience as to the just cause of war or the need to comply with a treaty.[21] Grotius disliked the results of leaving matters to the consciences of European leaders of his day. The devastating Thirty Years' War (1618-1648) was, at least on the surface, about clashing consciences – Catholic versus Protestant and Protestant versus Protestant. In this context, Grotius disagreed with another Protestant international law scholar, Alberico Gentili. Gentili argued that each prince could form his own views on the morality of resort to war. No one of equal status could judge him. For Grotius, resort to war could be judged against objective standards. Grotius made his arguments in the seminal work, *On the Law and War and Peace* (1625). He wrote hoping to help end the Thirty Years' War and mitigate its barbarism. He wanted to inspire greater humanity in the conduct of the war and encourage the establishment of a legal order superior to the warring factions after the war. A group of legally co-equal sovereign states did in fact emerge in Western Europe after the war to organize the terms of the peace agreements, known as the Peace

21 See O'Connell, Power and Purpose, ch. 1. For more on Gentili, Kingsbury, Benedict/ Straumann, Benjamin (Eds.). The Roman Foundation of the Law of Nations. Alberico Gentili and the Justice of Empire. Oxford, 2010.

of Westphalia (1648). Grotius's comprehensive treatise provided the legal blueprint for the new world order.

To have an impact, Grotius had to respond to those who shared Gentili's view but also to those who shared Machiavelli's.[22] Machiavelli (1469-1527) saw no law above sovereigns, but he went further, rejecting the idea that a prince had to listen to his conscience. For Machiavelli no action was unjust if a ruler found it expedient. Grotius, by contrast, according to Hersch Lauterpacht, saw "an intimate connexion between the rejection of the ideas of 'reason of State' and the affirmation of the legal and moral unity of mankind. [Grotius] insist[ed] that if no association of men can be maintained without law, 'surely also that association which binds together the human race, or binds many nations together, has need of law.'"[23] Grotius saw law as possible in every type of human community because he understood human beings as "being intrinsically moved by a desire for social life, endowed with an ample measure of goodness, altruism, and morality, and capable of acting on general principle and of learning from experience."[24]

By contrast, law above nations was impossible for Machiavelli and the prominent 17th century political theorist, Thomas Hobbes, because of their view that, again in the words of Lauterpacht, "man is essentially selfish, anti-social, and unable to learn from experience."[25] For them, "the basis of political obligation is interest pure and simple; the idea of a sense of moral duty rising supreme over desire and passion is a figment of imagination.... This is the typical realistic approach of contempt towards the 'little breed' of man."[26] Grotius felt no such contempt. He believed in the Christian law of love and held the optimistic view of people's capacity contained in Christianity. He built his conception of international law on the Spanish Scholastics, moving farther in the direction of a secular understanding of natural law than they had, in order to avoid the religious controversies swirling as he wrote. He emphasized the use of human reason to understand the law ordained by nature and the universal principles of morality. He explained that while much of international law is positive law, natural law is the more important part because it provides the basis of positive law authority and is the measure of the aspirations of law.

---

22 Lauterpacht, Hersch. The Grotian Tradition in International Law. 23 British Year Book of International Law. Oxford, 1946, p. 31.

23 Lauterpacht, Grotian Tradition, p. 31; citing Grotius, de Jure belli ac Pacis, Proleg, p. 23.

24 Lauterpacht, Grotian Tradition, p. 24.

25 Lauterpacht, Grotian Tradition, p. 24.

26 Lauterpacht, Grotian Tradition, pp. 24-25.

The next important figure in the history of international law was Emmerich de Vattel. Vattel, though a self-identified believer in natural law and follower of Grotius, helped pave the way for positivism to replace natural law as the reigning theory of the sources of international law.[27] His principle work was a widely read book: *The Law of Nations* (1758). Indeed, it was read by America's founding fathers. Vattel was a professional diplomat and wrote the book out of very different motivations to those of Grotius. While Grotius wrote in reaction to the horrors of the Thirty Years' War, Vattel wrote in service to sovereigns. He shared with Grotius an understanding that a higher law governed human affairs, but he left it to each individual sovereign to judge his or her own compliance. No sovereign could sit in judgment of another. Vattel preceded and inspired Bodin and others usually given credit for the rise of the idea of absolute sovereign authority within states. Vattel's vaunted view of states and their leaders was also aligned with the rise of science and the importance of objective evidence. The combination undermined natural law theories that supported the authority of international law as law over states, leaving positivism as the dominant theory – but it is incorrect to say that natural law explanations disappeared completely.[28]

In many accounts of the 19th century, it is thought that the rise of positivism and the concept of absolute state sovereignty meant the end of legal restraint on force. However, for many scholars and government officials the Just War Doctrine continued to govern. This fact is often overlooked in accounts on the use of force. Few European governments failed to justify the use of force in terms of some lawful end. Natural law – the idea of law superior to the sovereign – continued to be an important part of legal theory. Positive sources of law in the form of treaties and customary international law existed, but general principles of international law and international law's authority to bind continued to be described as based in natural law, much as Grotius had taught. While several prominent international law scholars in Britain and the United States began crusading for the elimination of natural law from the "science" of international law, natural law never disappeared.[29] Indeed, in recent years, new interest has emerged in understanding the place of natural law in the international legal system.[30]

---

27 See O'Connell, Power and Purpose, ch. 1.

28 On the persistence of natural law theory as part of the jurisprudence of international law through the 19th century, see Neff, Stephen C. Justice Among Nations. A History of International Law. Cambridge (MA), 2014, p. 261.

29 See Oppenheim, Lassa. International Law. London, 1905.

30 See, e.g., opinions of Judge Antonio Cançado Trindade, especially his dissenting opinion in Jurisdictional Immunities of the State (Ger. v. Italy) 2012 ICJ 179 (Judgment of Feb. 10).

While theoretical contests were being waged among international law scholars on the nature of law against war, in the wider world, popular peace groups made the advancement of peace through law a major goal of their activism.[31] By the time of the First World War, these groups had grown to impressive size. They began with Christian pacifists, but over the centuries evolved toward large, secular organizations, some of which continue today, such as the Women's International League for Peace and Freedom. The groups advocated alternatives to war such as the use of arbitration under international law. Largely through pressure from the peace movement, alternatives to war were added to the agenda of the first Hague Peace Conferences of 1899. The conference had been called by the Russian Tsar initially to reach certain arms control agreements since Russia was losing the European arms race of the later 19th century. Little was done about reducing or outlawing weapons, but the states present did agree to attempt to use arbitration and other third-party dispute resolution methods before resorting to war.

Many in the mass peace movements of Europe and North America wanted more. They wanted robust legal obligations prohibiting resort to war, and they wanted an international court. Leaders of the movement reasoned that if the United States Supreme Court could keep the peace among semi-sovereign states, a world court could do the same for the international community. In 1905 and 1906, techniques of mediation and fact-finding had been used to good effect to end the Russo-Japanese War and to prevent a war between Russia and the United Kingdom. All of these factors and others led to the convening of another Hague Peace Conference in 1907. Some strides were made at the conference. The most important accomplishment was the drafting of a treaty detailing rules for the conduct of armed conflict, as well as belligerent occupation. These rules, especially regarding occupation, continue to bind as current law.

The new commitment to peaceful settlement of disputes was, of course, quickly forgotten in 1914 as militaries from around the world clashed in Europe. During the peace negotiations that followed, the decision was taken to finally develop a world court. Eighteen leading international law specialists gathered in Geneva and developed the Statute of the Permanent Court of International Justice (PCIJ). The members of the League of Nations adopted the statute and the court began operations in 1920. The United States, having not joined the League or the PCIJ, worked to promote peace in another form. Together with France in 1928, it initiated the Kellogg-Briand Pact, or

31 Cortright, David. Peace: A History of Movements and Ideas. Cambridge, 2008.

Pact of Paris, a treaty prohibiting resort to war as an instrument of national foreign policy.

In addition to the League of Nations, the PCIJ, and various substantive legal obligations to delay or forgo resort to force, the post World War I peace regime was also built on disarmament. This part of the consensus, however, failed dramatically. Germans came to see the outlawing of war as favoring the United Kingdom with its vast empire built on wars already fought, a view underscored when the disarmament effort failed. The British and Americans would not be obliged to massively reduce their ships and weaponry. If Germany did not re-arm too, it would remain in a seriously weakened military, economic and political condition compared to other powers.

The prominent German international and constitutional law scholar, the Catholic Carl Schmitt, argued that Germany should not allow itself to be dominated by other countries through accepting their interpretations of what international law meant and required of Germany.[32] Schmitt and others successfully advocated German resurgence despite the requirements of treaties and the League. By the 1930s, the League was failing and German leaders saw little reason to heed its mandates.[33]

Through all of these momentous events, international law scholars continued to search for better ways to explain international law and its authority in international affairs, as well as to improve its function in the international community.[34] By the end of the First World War, some legal scholars concluded that declining respect for international law could be explained by the theory of sovereignty. In the 1930s, scholars pointed to the cult of sovereignty that placed the state and its leaders above the law. Positivism, which is based on state practice, had no winning argument to use against the dictators emerging in Europe with aggressive designs on other states. Those designs were, after all, an exercise of state will. Nor could positivists explain why persons who were opposed to the absolute power of the state should not be treated as enemies of the state.

Hans Kelsen, an Austrian legal scholar of great renown in the first half of the 20th century, conceived of turning away from a focus internal to the state and to international law. For Kelsen law is a logically constructed idea. In its purest form, law must emanate from a source with authority to command obedience backed by a sanction. He argued that the community responds to law violations with coercive measures, which are not permitted for social

---

32 O'Connell, Power and Purpose, ch. 2.

33 O'Connell, Power and Purpose, ch. 2.

34 See e.g., Lauterpacht, Hersch. The Function of Law in the International Community. Oxford, 1933.

or moral violations. International law has, and has always had, sanctions for law violation. Sanctions provide the evidence of what the international community understands to be law.[35]

Kelsen responded to those who believed all war to be unlawful by saying that the only way to respond to unlawful war was with war. The sanction for Kelsen is the ultimate motivation for law compliance. Where Kelsen parted company dramatically with Schmitt was in the source of law's authority. For Kelsen, because the sovereign itself has to be empowered, the ultimate source of legal validity must be found elsewhere – in the community's belief in and acceptance of the law: a natural law explanation.

Kelsen is associated with positivism, but his views of authority and the place of war in the international legal system present a broader picture. Kelsen credited Augustine, Aquinas and Grotius with having developed the idea of war being forbidden except in a good cause. The breakdown of the Just War Doctrine in international law in the 19th century came in connection with theories of absolute state sovereignty. Those theories challenged all international law, not just the limitation on war. For Kelsen, the problem in permitting war and reprisals to enforce the law inevitably came back to the issue of who decides the law has been broken. The theory of absolute sovereignty had developed in the absence of a decision-maker superior to each state. This conundrum led Kelsen to become a strong advocate of international courts.[36]

When the League gave way to the United Nations at the end of World War II, the PCIJ continued under a new name, the International Court of Justice, but now associated with the UN. The document establishing the United Nations, the UN Charter of 1945, included in Chapter I, Article 2(4) a general prohibition on the use of force. To support the prohibition, Chapter VI of the Charter lists alternatives to war that states should use to settle disputes, and Chapter VII provides authority for the UN Security Council to react to threats to the peace, breaches of the peace and acts of aggression. Chapter VII also includes the only two express exceptions to the prohibition in Article 2(4). These exceptions are narrowly drafted in the interest of fulfilling the opening words of the Charter: "To save succeeding generations from the scourge of war…"

Despite Kelsen's influence, the UN regime for preventing and ending conflict is center on the Security Council, not the World Court. The Council's job was to enforce the peace, not the law. The UN Charter regime

35 O'Connell, Power and Purpose, ch. 2.
36 O'Connell, Power and Purpose, ch. 2.

against the use of force is robust but arguably too limited in scope. The use of armed force was finally prohibited for all states in UN Charter Article 2(4), except when the UN Security Council authorizes force or in limited cases of self-defense to an armed attack until such time as the Security Council acts.[37] The Security Council has authority to take measures in response to threats to the peace, breaches of the peace, and acts of aggression.[38] The drafters of the Charter gave the victorious powers of World War II the right to veto any resolution mandating action. The understanding and respect for the international law restricting resort to force was well established among post-war leaders. For just one example, in 1956, when the United Kingdom, France, and Israel colluded to use military force to re-take the Suez Canal from Egyptian control, both the United States and the Soviet Union condemned the unlawful use of force in violation of the Charter.[39] The Charter does not, however, require states to resort to the International Court of Justice or other means of resolving disputes peacefully. In hindsight, the prohibition on force would have been strengthened with a world court possessing compulsory jurisdiction.

---

37 Article 2(4) All Members shall refrain in their international relations from the threat or use of force against the territorial integrity or political independence of any state, or in any other manner inconsistent with the Purposes of the United Nations.
Article 51 Nothing in the present Charter shall impair the inherent right of individual or collective self-defense if an armed attack occurs against a Member of the United Nations, until the Security Council has taken measures necessary to maintain international peace and security. Measures taken by Members in the exercise of this right of self-defense shall be immediately reported to the Security Council and shall not in any way affect the authority and responsibility of the Security Council under the present Charter to take at any time such action as it deems necessary in order to maintain or restore international peace and security.

38 Article 39 The Security Council shall determine the existence of any threat to the peace, breach of the peace, or act of aggression and shall make recommendations, or decide what measures shall be taken in accordance with Articles 41 and 42, to maintain or restore international peace and security.
Article 40 In order to prevent an aggravation of the situation, the Security Council may, before making the recommendations or deciding upon the measures provided for in Article 39, call upon the parties concerned to comply with such provisional measures as it deems necessary or desirable. ...
Article 41 The Security Council may decide what measures not involving the use of armed force are to be employed to give effect to its decisions... .
Article 42 Should the Security Council consider that measures provided for in Article 41 would be inadequate or have proved to be inadequate, it may take such action by air, sea, or land forces as may be necessary to maintain or restore international peace and security. Such action may include demonstrations, blockade, and other operations by air, sea, or land forces of Members of the United Nations.

39 For details, see Bowie, Robert. Suez 1956. International Crisis and the Role of Law. Oxford, 1975.

By the 1960s, however, Carl Schmitt was again attracting followers, and he continues to do so today. Among his early adherents was Hans Morgenthau. Morgenthau had engaged the work of both Kelsen and Schmitt while a student and young scholar of international law in Germany and Switzerland. He preferred Schmitt. Even after becoming a victim of Nazism like Kelsen, Morgenthau turned decisively away from international law and toward promotion of the United States, where he found asylum, as the world's dominant power. He thought that security lay only in having greater power than others, and became one of the creators of the dominant theory of political science today, realism. For Morgenthau, international law, with its ineffective sanctions and inadequate theory, was too weak to command respect in the ultimate questions of power. He, like Schmitt, believed the state needed a strong man to advance its interests and those interests centered on amassing power – not living peacefully in the community of states. Morgenthau's thinking has had a profound impact in the United States. He launched the realist school of international relations scholarship that continues to hold a highly dismissive view of international law.

At the same time that Morgenthau was transforming the American view of international law, the Second Vatican Council was working to renew the Roman Catholic Church. Part of this effort included support by the Church for the UN, human rights, and international order. The Church presented these ideas just as the critics of international law were in the ascendant. The Church was not alone in countering criticism of law and institutions. International law has never lost its defenders in the academy and among government officials. Chief among the defenders was a devout Jewish legal scholar, Louis Henkin. Henkin responded to Morgenthau, explaining that law, whether national or international, is not dependent on the sanction to qualify as law.

Following the British legal philosopher H.L.A. Hart, Henkin explained that law depends on acceptance and voluntary compliance far more than the sanction. International law attracts this acceptance and compliance because, in Henkin's view, it offers substantial practical advantages to policymakers who really could not manage without some system of rules. Henkin offered a more realistic picture of international life than the realists. Henkin, however, devoted the rest of his scholarship to human rights and the United States Constitution. Knowledge of international law in general, its source of authority, and its enforcement declined.

In the era of civil rights and women's liberation, constitutional law became the prestige subject. Interest in international law narrowed to interest in human rights. Increasingly, legal scholars working in the area of human rights had little or no background or training in general international law. At certain points in the 1980s and 1990s, such prominent U.S. law schools as Stanford, Pennsylvania, Chicago, and Texas had *no* scholars focused principally on public international law. At Yale, international law scholars were experimenting with their own creation, dubbed the New Haven School, which probably created more confusion than clarity about the nature of international law. So as political science realists were critiquing international law, international law theorists were largely absent from the debate. Compounding all of this, in the 1980s a new form of realism emerged with the post-modern movement. The proponents of the new realism, critical legal theorists or "crits", joined the traditional realist attack on international law. They, too, pointed to the theoretical weaknesses of international law. However, instead of holding states back, as Morgenthau had seen it, the critical legal theorists tended to see the opposite: international law supporting state power, patrimony, hierarchy, hegemony, and imperialism.

By the end of the 20th century, all of these critics were joined by a small group of American political theorists, known as neoconservatives. They advised using American military power to advance the U.S. position in the world. They advocated the spread of democracy as the preferred internal political order for states – a form of governance that would allow greater U.S. influence within states. Plainly, these policies conflicted with core principles of international law on state equality and the non-use of force. The neo-conservatives shared a pro-military intervention philosophy with large numbers of human rights advocates. Both groups championed a form of military force known as "humanitarian intervention." In 1991, the United States led NATO forces in using force against Serbia and Montenegro to induce President Slobodan Milosevic to pull national forces out of the province of Kosovo. For 78 days, NATO bombed in the first major use of force involving the United States for which the U.S. State Department provided no legal justification in terms of the United Nations Charter.

The Kosovo Crisis apparently weakened regard for the prohibition on the use of force among NATO member states. In the wake of the 9/11 tragedy, the U.S. also sought a military solution to the problem of terrorism. In 2003, the United States, the United Kingdom, and Australia invaded Iraq, officially to destroy weapons of mass destruction. When the UN Secretary General stated that the invasion violated the UN Charter, U.S. foreign policy leaders seriously discussed leaving the UN. The Secretary General placated concern by launching a thorough review of the UN rules, institutions, and practices devoted to peace and security. The review was completed and the member states – including the U.S. – took up the results at a world summit in New York in September 2005. The World Summit Outcome Document recommitted the world to the rules of the Charter as written.

> 78. We reiterate the importance of promoting and strengthening the multilateral process and of addressing international challenges and problems by strictly abiding by the Charter and the principles of international law, and further stress our commitment to multilateralism.
>
> 79. We reaffirm that the relevant provisions of the Charter are sufficient to address the full range of threats to international peace and security. We further reaffirm the authority of the Security Council to mandate coercive action to maintain and restore international peace and security. We stress the importance of acting in accordance with the purposes and principles of the Charter.[40]

### *3. The Future of International Law for Peace*

We can conclude with some hope and optimism that the international law prohibition on the resort to force "forged in two world wars" remains in place. Nevertheless, two inter-related issues should be of great concern to anyone committed to peace as a religious, ethical, or even practical matter. Firstly, despite the fact that the prohibition on force remains in effect, little is done through international law or other social institutions to improve compliance with it. This may be in part due to the second issue: many leading scholars support expanding the right to use force for a variety of purposes. Rather than research, write and teach about law compliance, they devote their work to finding loopholes in the prohibition, advocating for flexible interpretations, or overriding the rules through various proposals. Those in the academy who might wish to work on compliance seem to spend their time replying to this advocacy rather than thinking creatively about how to win respect for the law of peace.

A good deal of the advocacy for flexibility comes from those who sincerely believe major military force is an effective response to the problems of terrorism, human rights violations, and weapons proliferation. Neverthe-

40 2005 World Summit Outcome, UN GAOR, 60th Sess., at 22-23, U.N. Doc. A/60/L.1 (Sept. 15, 2005).

less, the legal advocates for opening international law to permit the use of major force very likely include scholars who know national political leaders have reached a point where they lack creative and courageous policies to respond to complex social issues. At the end of the Cold War, astonishing levels of resources continued to be poured into militaries. Failing to think of anything else, leaders have turned to the military option. The United States has been involved in major combat almost every year since 1990, yet terrorism continues, as do human rights atrocities and weapons proliferation. Little is done in the meantime about the causes of civil war, climate change, poverty, or global health crises.

## *Conclusion*

During a commemoration of World War I, at a cemetery where 100,000 Italian troops killed during that war are buried, Pope Francis said, "War is madness."[41] International law needs this message from our moral leaders in the world. *Pacem in Terris* is a blueprint for leading us away from war through international law and institutions. Bringing the world's attention back to alternatives to war may help to create a new demand for peace through law. It may inspire a renewal within the field of international law toward solving the challenges of theory and practice that continue to beset the rules for peace. Understanding that international law scholars can answer a higher calling than pleasing those with momentary political power may be exactly what is needed to end the undermining of the UN Charter and renew the search for peace through law. Reminding scholars of this is another lesson we can learn from John XXIII and Francis, who took the name of the saint of peace.

41 Garay, Gavino. War is Madness. In: New York Times, 13.09.2014, http://www.nytimes.com/video/multimedia/100000003112598/pope-francis-war-is-madness.html [15.9.2015].

# Does “ius cogens” exist in International Relations? Philosophical remarks to the Encyclical “Pacem in terris”

*Matthias Lutz-Bachmann*

“Peace on earth”: In April 1963 Pope John XXIII. published his famous encyclical in addressing the imminent dangers for peace of his time. His statement gained great attention in a complicated situation of world politics which was determined by the enormous tensions among the political powers USA and USSR and the persistent danger of war between the West and the East. Deeply anchored in the tradition of modern papal teaching on social and political affairs since Leo XIII., the encyclical is focused on the problems of international politics in the second half of the 20th century. While pointing out the risks for the whole world stemming from nuclear weapons, the ongoing nuclear arms race and the proliferation of weapons of mass destruction as the expression of a wrong political and social world order Pope John is arguing for the constitution of a new universal political authority constituted by strong normative reasons. This universal political authority may allow to overcome the conflicts in the international order of nation-states. In spite of the urgent problems the encyclical finally is pointing at the new chances and expressing even optimistic prospects for the future in global politics. The Pope’s final optimistic views are justified by important developments within the sphere of public international law after World War II., especially with respect to the Charter of the United Nations Organizations (1945) and the Universal Declaration of Human Rights (1948) which have been recognized as very important steps in the right direction. The existence of these legal documents seems to confirm the Pope’s optimism towards the normative necessity and the political possibilities to build a global political order in which the biblical and philosophical imperative “Peace on earth!” may become real in politics.[1]

In my paper I will refer to the text of the encyclical in order to identify the arguments in favor of the perspectives of the proposed new global political order based on both states and societal movements. This order is thought to be constructed according to the normative impact of moral and political

1 Cf. Luke 2,14 as well as Kant, Immanuel. The Metaphysics of Morals. Akademie-Ausgabe VI, p. 354.

principles like the human rights. An effective human rights protection in a political order is presupposing the legal constitution of robust juridical structures which may allow the expectation to obtain coercion. The recommendation of Pope John to develop a new political order across the globe containing these reliable juridical structures for the preservation of peace and human rights has not been realized until today. It seems that we are farer away from the implementation of Pope John's ideas today than we might have been some years ago in the time shortly after the end of the cold war. The question therefore arises how the postulates of peace and human rights can be preserved in the political arena of the world without the accomplishment of strong political institutions which might observe the legal commitments of the states concerning the demand for peace and human rights.

As a substitute for the proposed new political order on earth modern international law is claiming the status of 'ius cogens' for the legal validity of at least some fundamental human rights like the prohibition of aggression, genocide, enslavement, race discrimination and torture. Its claim for cogency is based on the consent of the signatory states of the 'Vienna Convention on the Law of Treaties'. But we have to confess that this claim of cogency for these legal postulates is missing a reliable political and juridical structure which is able to effectively protect peace and human rights globally and impartially. This is true even if the statement of 'ius cogens' is obviously an important step to overcome the constitutional weakness of classical international law. But the claim of 'ius cogens' in international law today is not yet satisfactory if compared with the farer reaching recommendations of Pope John and his proposal of a new political global order, based on the principles of human rights and able to preserve peace effectively. "Peace on earth" is therefore a document which is still of high systematic moral and political importance until today. It is addressing us, that means the audiences of states and churches, public and private actors including individual human beings in a situation of the world where warfare and military conflicts are more and more omnipresent and increasingly dangerous in different ways. Our world is still waiting for a better political order which is built upon principles able to protect peace and human rights efficiently. That implies global political structures which are able to defend human beings by legal procedures and civic coercion instead of using military force and warfare against both the aggression of official states and of private organizations like groups of terrorists.

In the first section of my article (1.) I will refer to the basic normative arguments of the encyclical, which may claim a general and in part even philosophical character, in the second section (2.) I will refer to the analysis of the international and global relations and in the third section (3.) I will discuss the contribution of the encyclical concerning a future global political body which I will connect with the topic of 'ius cogens' today.

*1.*

Pope John is starting his papal letter[2] "to the bishops, clergy and faithful" in the Catholic world as well as to all human beings of "good will"[3] with the programmatic statement that 'peace on earth' has been and still is the highest aim of striving throughout human history and as such 'peace on earth' is declared to be the most important goal of all political acting.[4] In the language of the Aristotelian tradition of political philosophy the avoidance of war and the state of peace on earth can be called 'the highest good' and the final goal for collective human acting at all. In the tradition of Kant the state of peace is the necessary and unconditioned postulate of practical reason which should become realized by the constitution of a legal order following the principles of republicanism. Both philosophical perspectives are systematically present in the text as we will see. But nevertheless Pope John is convinced that this final goal of human practical endeavor is not to be reached at "except by the diligent observance of the order" which is constituted by God.[5] How can we understand this statement of the Pope? Is the practical goal of peace something which can be reached only by religious people believing in God or is it open to everybody in a secular public?

First of all we have to recognize that the order to which the encyclical is pointing here is of course not the 'outer order' of the physical world. This kind of outer 'nature' is the subject of the sciences and technologies. According to the Pope's statement they are able to explain more and even better in modern times its mechanisms through their methods of observation and explanation. And it is the positive expectation of the Pope that the results of the scientific explanation of the world will finally allow in a comprehensive reflection to identify the magnitude of God's creation which becomes more

2 I'm referring to the official version of the encyclical "Pacem in terris" in the Latin and English version which sometimes contain slight divergences from each other. For the citation I follow the numbering of paragraphs in the English translation of the text.

3 Cf. para. 1: „universis bonae voluntatis hominibus".

4 Cf. ibid.: „Pacem in terris, quam homines universi cupidissime quovis tempore appetiverunt".

5 Cf. ibid.: „condi confirmarique non posse constat, nisi ordine, quem Deus constituit, sancte servato".

and more obvious according to Pope John's statement through modern scientific research. But the encyclical reference to 'nature' is not addressing the question of a final theoretical or 'metaphysical' goal of human cognition but dealing with the most inclusive practical aim of human desires and activities. The topic of 'peace on earth' is nothing else than the final goal of yearning in the history of human beings and in so far peace is defined to be the 'summum bonum' in the order of political acting. This statement makes us aware that Pope John's text is a contribution to the reflections of practical philosophy as well as to the tradition of moral doctrines.

The insight in the 'nature' of the 'highest good' is referring to what is called the 'inner order' whose recognition is to be reached by reasonable reflections. These considerations have to take into account that in the case of a reflection on human acting we are reflecting upon ourselves not only as 'mere objects' in a 'third persons perspective', but also as the 'first' and 'second persons' who are already involved in a certain intersubjective practice[6]. It is interesting to see that this epistemological distinction of the theoretical and practical order of human insight as well as the reference to the language of an 'outer' and the 'inner' order of 'nature' is following both above-mentioned traditions, namely the Aristotelian[7] and Kantian[8] epistemologies which include the conviction that the epistemic logic of practical reflection in search for normative principles has to start with the explanation of the practical experiences of human beings and their reflections upon what 'we' practically 'owe each other'.

These epistemological premises are present in the moral theory of Thomas Aquinas[9] as well and are necessary for a proper understanding of the term "nature of humans" by the encyclical. In the theory of Aquinas the moral insight of the "lex naturalis" or the "natural law" is "the good" which "falls under the apprehension of practical reason, which is directed to action"[10].

6 For these epistemological questions see my introduction into "Ethics": Matthias Lutz-Bachmann, Grundkurs Philosophie Band 7: Ethik, Stuttgart 2013, p.13-26.

7 Cf. Aristotle, The Nicomachean Ethics, Book I.

8 Cf. Kant, Critique of Practical Reason, Introduction.

9 Cf. Thomas Aquinas, S.th. I-II, q. 90 ff. and Thomas Aquinas, Commentary on Aristotle's Nicomachean Ethics Book I; cf. e.g. the recent Latin-German edition: Thomas von Aquin, Kommentar zur Nikomachischen Ethik, herausgegeben, übersetzt und eingeleitet von Matthias Perkams, Herders Bibliothek der Philosophie des Mittelalters, HBPhMA Band 33, Herder Verlag, Freiburg i.Br. 2014. See additionally: Die Epistemologie der praktischen Wissenschaften im 13. und 14. Jahrhundert, hrsg. von Matthias Lutz-Bachmann/Alexander Fidora, Akademie Verlag, Berlin 2008; Erkenntnis und Wissenschaft. Probleme der Epistemologie in der Philosophie des Mittelalters, Akademie Verlag, Berlin 2004.

10 Cf. Thomas Aquinas, S.th. I-II, q. 94, a. 2.

This argument of Aquinas is important since it realizes the state of practical reasoning of us as the source of normativity. On this background the encyclical of Pope John is pointing therefore to the specific character of the 'natural law' which constitute the basic character of normativity. The command of 'natural law' can be recognized only through the insight of practical reason. As a result of such reasoning the encyclical offers the self-description of humans as free 'persons' endowed with certain unalienable basic rights. Accordingly the correct insight in these natural laws of human practical reasoning 'teaches' us how we should not only interact morally correct in modern society with all the other human persons[11] but also in the field of politics. From here the encyclical is drawing the basic arguments concerning the normative questions how we should interact politically with each other as political citizens in modern states and as political citizens of the world. According to the encyclical the insight in these 'laws' will give us the right recognition of the principles of the correct relations among the states as well as among individuals and states and at least for the society of all nations on earth. This global community of all human beings is according to Pope John a necessary replenishment to the given order of single nation-states and should finally become established since the constitution of a global political community of all humans irrespective of their culture or race, their belief and their national identity is in the common interest and advantage of all[12]. This community is not only reasonable and insofar just a possible option for practical reasoning. It is a necessary condition for the achievement of the goal of 'peace on earth' which was defined as the highest moral good and the final political goal of all human acting.

Chapter I. of the encyclical is dealing with the basic and general definition of the social order which is necessary from a normative point of view.[13] It starts with an assertion that any well-regulated and suitable association of humans is to be built upon one fundamental principle: The insight, that each

---

11 Cf. Lex and Ius. Essais on the Foundation of Law in Medieval and Early Modern Philosophy, ed. by Alexander Fidora/Matthias Lutz-Bachmann/Andreas Wagner, Frommann-Holzboog Verlag, Political Philosophy and Theory of Law in the Middle Ages and Modernity Vol. II,1, Stuttgart-Bad Cannstatt 2010.

12 Cf. para. 7: „His enim legibus praeclare erudiuntur homines quibus primum modis mutua sua commercia in humano convictu moderentur; quibus deinde modis rationes componendae sint, quae civibus cum publicis suae cuiusque civitatis magistratibus intercedunt; quibus tum modis mutuo contingantur respublicae; quibus postremo modis inter se contineantur hinc singuli homines et civitates, illinc universarum gentium societas; quae, ut tandem condatur, communis omnium utilitas vehementer requirit."

13 Cf. para. 8: „De ordine …, quem inter homines vigere necesse est.

human being is a person. That means according to the text that each human being is endowed by his/her proper nature with intelligence, the capacity of practical reasoning and a free will. As such each human being has rights and duties which proceed from this 'nature' of all humans, immediately and simultaneously. "These rights and duties are universal and inviolable, and therefore altogether inalienable".[14]

According to the logic of the text this statement is the result of a philosophical argumentation that means an insight which is to achieve at least by a philosophical reflection which is not in opposition to the biblical view of the human. The theological doctrine of the 'nature' of the human as a person and the implications of this sentence is somehow founded on both the philosophical insight and the biblical tradition. This becomes clear when Pope John adds to the already mentioned considerations on the 'nature' of humans an additional statement, an assertion for which he is claiming the standpoint of the theological perspective. For a Christian theology the human being is possessing not only the 'natural' property of personhood and the original or natural rights and duties, inherent to all persons by their proper 'nature', but additionally the theological attributes: "being redeemed" by Jesus Christ, "being made a friend of God" and becoming a "heir/heiress" to eternal glory. These qualifications of the human being are obviously deduced from theological premises according to the texts of the New Testament, while the assertion of the personhood of each human being as well as the original human rights and duties are considered to be drawn from an insight in 'human nature'. From a practical point of reflection the Pope is claiming an insight which is universal, in principle open to everybody and is claiming for its position an epistemic independency from religious traditions or special cultural sources. The encyclical is therefore drawing very general conclusions from the insight in the necessity of peace and the original state of human rights towards the structure of the political order of the world and its postulates are addressing "all human beings of good will".

A first evidence for the here required universal validity may be concluded from the developments of public international law in 20th century, especially from the 'Universal Declaration of Human Rights' within the United Nations Organization. In the emergence of these legal norms and principles by international politics after the experienced enormous destructions and crimes against humanity in international politics of the first decades of 20th century we can identify the political agreement of the existing community of states to the fundamental normative norms. These norms include the in-

14 Cf. para. 9: „Quae propterea, ut generalia et inviolabilia sunt, ita mancipari nullo modo possunt".

sight that all human beings are 'as such' or 'by their proper nature' subjects of an original freedom and holders of basic rights. From a philosophical point of view we can conclude that all humans are endowed with reason and conscience by which the prerequisites of the legal norms are legitimate and necessary postulates in the political arena. This document of the Declaration of Human Rights may demonstrate that there is indeed already something like a general agreement of states given in the international arena as a matter of fact. The encyclical is on the one hand pointing affirmatively to these historic facts and is on the other hand arguing beyond that situation. It is claiming the universal and unconditioned validity of human rights as the basis for a new global political order which overcomes the real world of powers and states after World War II. For a correct understanding of the encyclical it is therefore important to realize that the reference to what Pope John called "human nature" and its philosophical meaning is indeed containing an appropriate and reasonable justification for the universal validity of the "human rights" which are just asserted or stated but not justified or further deepened by the document of the United Nations.

In his text Pope John is stating something like a list of basic rights upon which a human acting either in society or in politics should be built. The "right to live" is according to him the most basic right followed by the "right to bodily integrity" as well as the right "to the means necessary for the proper development of life, particularly food, clothing, shelter, medical care, rest and, finally, the necessary social services."[15] The list of human rights is continued with the "right to be looked after" in the events of illness, disability, widowhood, old ager and enforced unemployment or the human person is deprived of the means of livelihood without being responsible for. These rights show a much higher degree on societal and economic appropriation than the articles of the 'Universal Declaration of Human Rights' of the UN. Here we might identify a special outcome of the general papal tradition in social teaching. The same is true for the rights the Pope is claiming in the next paragraphs concerning the cultural, moral and religious practice of humans. With regard to the important questions of the special 'political rights' the encyclical is stating not only a right for each human being to actively participate in public life but also in the political affairs of her/his country. This right is accompanied by the right to emigrate as well as to immigrate. Here we can identify not only the consequences drawn from the insight into the universality of the human rights and the statement that each individual human is the holder of these rights, but also the impact the papal doctrine

15 Cf. the English translation, p. 11.

of human rights contains with reference to international law. The Pope declares that the fact that the human being is (usually) a citizen of a particular state "does not deprive her/him of membership in the human family, nor the citizenship in that universal society, the common world-wide fellowship of human."[16] Here the Pope is obviously pointing at his vision of a global political community of all human beings which is going beyond the limits of the real order of powers which is still presupposed by the Charter of the UN and the principles of the old international law. The idea of a 'global political order' that means a political body which is including all humans on earth in a strict sense, based on the constitution of human rights as a cogent legal order has not been realized in the given international order of states and powers in the year of 1963 when the encyclical was published. But according to Pope John's arguments the constitution of such a new legal order is necessary in order to protect the 'peace on earth', based on the human right, in the structure of politics and international relations, and conflicts and challenges which stem from the danger of nuclear weapons and the proliferation of weapons of mass destruction and other dangerous developments in international relations until today. In section 3.) I will refer to theses aspects.

It is the purpose of this paper to search for specific arguments which may lead the discussion to the legitimation of a 'ius cogens' in international relations today. It is therefore important to see that the encyclical is stating that each human being is "entitled to the legal protection" of her/his basic rights. According to the text it is normatively necessary that "such protection must be effective, unbiased, and strictly just."[17] Here we can identify the first but nevertheless important indication that the above-mentioned list of rights is more than a collection just of moral postulates but includes a stronger political program to enforce these rights effectively, that means by institutions in the realm of societal-political acting. Pope John therefore postulates the normative necessity to constitute effective legal and juridical systems in which and by which the basic human rights are imposed in a fair, unbiased and over all just manner. This at least worldwide constitution of an order of legitimate law is according to the encyclical the only possible way to protect not only these rights but to defend the state of peace in which

16 Cf. the English translation, para. 25. In the Latin original we can read that each human is not only a citizen of her/his political state („res publica“) but also a member of the human family („membrum humanae familiae“), as well as a „universal citizen“ („civis universalis“) of this global society and general union of all humans („illius societatis et coniunctionis omnium hominum communis“).

17 Cf. the English translation, para. 27. In the Latin original we read: "Ad humanam personam quoque pertinet legitima suorum iurium tuitio: eademque ad effectum valens, aequalis, ad versas iustitiae normas conformater."

every individual human being is recognized as an original subject of rights in the national as well as in the international arena.

As a consequence of these arguments of Pope John we can conclude that this doctrine is leading to the postulate that the individual humans must become subjects and holders of cogent rights even within the international law whose 'classical construction' in modern times since the Peace Treaty of Westphalia had merely been focused on 'nation-states' and their predecessors. Additionally we can derive the postulate that a national, state-centered as well as an international or even better global order of legal coercion is necessary and legitimate if the normative claim for human rights shouldn't fail. We will see how these considerations are prepared in Chapters III and IV of the encyclical where Pope John is referring to the problem how an order of peace, based on human rights, can be preserved in the international arena.

*2.*

In Chapter III. Pope John argues that all states – like all human beings – are "subjects of reciprocal rights and duties". According to him "the same law of nature that governs the life and conduct of individuals must regulate the relations of political communities with one another."[18] As we have seen above the Pope's reference to a 'law of nature' or to the 'lex naturalis' which is claiming validity for human beings is nothing else than the "inner order" of normativity whose insight and recognition are given to us by 'practical reason'. That means by reasonable reflections considering the implications of the cognition that each individual being is a human person and as such a subject of inalienable rights and duties. With his position the Pope is in agreement not only with the Aristotelian-Thomistic line of arguments in the Catholic tradition but also with modern philosophers like Kant. Nevertheless the encyclical is presenting its own set of arguments. In the text we can identify an interesting argumentation since Pope John in his next steps is referring not directly to the rights and duties of the states as such but indirectly in pointing to the persons who act in the name of the states in the arena of international polities. The "political leaders" are, even when they act as representatives of their states, "still bound" by the insight in the normative force of the "law of nature" that means the non-coercive power of human reasoning and conscience regarding the unconditioned claim of validity which are inherent in the basic human rights. "The political leaders"

18 Cf. the English translation, para. 80.

are therefore, even if acting strategically and persecuting the mere interests of their prevailing countries, obliged to practically acknowledge the basic normative principles like the human rights and "they have no authority to depart" from their precepts.[19] According to these arguments the logic of political acting of the states is never allowed to leave the ground of the moral self-reflection of us being humans.

In the following paragraphs the text of the encyclical is reflecting the normative principles for the interaction of states like the avoidance of racial discrimination on which first the colonial and later all imperialist ideologies of the so-called 'enlightened' western countries from the 16th until the 20th centuries have been based[20]. Accordingly no state and no nation is allowed to dominate other nations. The imperative of justice among states leads the Pope to the postulate that all states have "the right to existence, to self-development, and to the means necessary to achieve this."[21] Conflicts among states may be the consequence of diverging interests but "states are not allowed to settle these differences, by armed force nor by deceit or trickery."[22] Here Pope John is talking about the limitation of the civil authority of each state and its necessary orientation towards not only the "common good" of the state but also the "common good of the entire human family."[23] "In pursuing their own interests, civil societies, far from causing injury to others, must join plans and forces whenever the efforts of particular states cannot achieve the desired goal."[24] This leads the encyclical to the insight in the necessity of something like a commonwealth of nations beyond the limited space of the single nation-states and organized by states and civic organizations: "The universal common good requires the encouragement in all nations of every kind of reciprocation between citizens and their intermediate societies."[25] States and international organizations, civilians and individuals can and have to cooperate in order to support single nation-states in the case when they are failing to reach their prevailing legitimate goals and to help the community of all states as well as of the individual human beings to practically achieve what the Pope called "the universal common good of all". As we have seen above in the center of this reference to the claimed "universal common good" we can identify the postulate of peace

19 Cf. the English translation, para. 81.
20 See e.g. Max Horkheimer/Theodor W.Adorno, Dialectic of Enlightenment, transl. and ed.by J.Cumming, Continuum Publishing Company, New York 1994
21 Cf. para. 92.
22 Cf. para. 93.
23 Cf. para. 98.
24 Cf. para. 99.
25 Cf. para. 100.

based on human rights alone - and not on oppression, on the power of arms, on unjust orders or on the enslavement of humans.

There can be no doubt that the constitution and preservation of peace belongs to the most important goals of all humans and insofar the idea of a universal political order of peace is the inherent element of his reference to the concept of a universal common good. Here we can easily identify the enormous political and juridical significance of the papal letter. Pope John is rejecting the strategic principle of the modern security policy of almost all states of his time based solely on the power of arms even if the ideologies of the so-called realists in international relations claimed and still claim evidence for the principle that "peace cannot be assured except on the basis of an equal balance of armaments."[26] This policy is leading to a situation in which "one country is equipped with atomic weapons, others consider themselves justified in producing such weapons themselves, equal in destructive force."[27] The strategic logic of this kind of security politics is according to the Pope's observation not only morally wrong, it is in its own logic nothing else than self-contradictory, contra-intuitive and that means not only irrational but additionally dangerous since it undermines the fundaments for peace and security in real politics. "Consequently people are living in the grip of constant fear. They are afraid that at any moment the impending storm may break upon them with horrific violence. And they have good reasons for their fear."[28]

Against this logic of an "equal balance of armaments" and an international politics based on deterrent the Pope postulates first the "need of disarmament" and second a general banishment for nuclear weapons worldwide. Both political requirements are – analog to the categorical imperative of pure practical reason in Kant's moral and political philosophy[29] –, like Pope John puts it, "dictated first of all by reason".[30] From this insight the encyclical draws the normative conclusion that "there is a general agreement – or at least there should be – that relations between states, as between individuals, must be regulated not by armed force but in accordance with the principles of right reason: the principles, that is, of truth, justice and vigorous and sincere cooperation."[31]

---

26 Cf. para. 110.
27 Cf. para. 110.
28 Cf. para. 111.
29 Cf. Immanuel Kant, To Perpetual Peace, transl. by T.Humphrey, Hackett Publishing Company, Indiapolis/Cambridge 1983, p. 107-139.
30 Cf. para. 114.
31 Cf. para. 114.

The goal of this argumentation of the Pope is a binding legal order of states, constituted by "treaties which are sincere, lasting and beneficial in their effects"[32] on the basis of the free consent of the partners. In his text Pope John is pointing to the fact that this vision which is based on a normative reflection is not just a contra-factual ideal but somehow already effective – even in preliminary ways – in the real political developments and in the evolution of international law since the end of World War II. Subjects of these occurrences are the humans. They are more and more convinced "in our time that any disputes or conflicts which may arise between nations must be resolved by negotiation and agreement, and not by recourse to arms."[33] He names these developments in the public sphere of the world "signs of the time", a metaphor which has already been used in the New Testament. In the biblical context the term "signs of the time" is addressing the messianic symbols pointing to the fact that the future of the divine salvation of human beings is already present with the appearance of Jesus Christ. With this reference to the very strong messianic language in mind Pope John finally states that in the time of nuclear weapons the traditional theory of the possibility of a just war has become obsolete, once and for all.[34] It is obvious that this statement is marking an explicit break with earlier doctrines on warfare in the Catholic tradition in the light of the modern challenges to peace.

## *3.*

As we know, the classical doctrines of the just war started with the premise that in a given situation of conflict there was structurally no solution left for a peaceful agreement among the conflicting partners on the basis of a just decision addressing a responsible and mutually accepted law court.[35] What are the systematic answers to this problem the encyclical is able to develop after its clear rejection of the just war-theory for the time after the production of the nuclear weapons of mass destruction? In Chapter IV. of the encyclical we can identify at least some elements of an answer to this question. These arguments take us to the instrument in international law which is

32 Cf. para. 118.
33 Cf. para. 126.
34 Cf. the Latin text, para. 127: "Quare aetate hac nostra, quae vi atomica gloriatur, alienum est a ratione, bellum iam aptum esse ad violata iura sarcienda."
35 Cf. e.g. Lutz-Bachmann, Matthias. „Peace" and „justice" in the tradition of „just war-theories". In: Gunther Hellmann (ed.). Justice and Peace. Interdisciplinary Perspectives on a Contested Relationship. Campus Verlag, Frankfurt/New York 2013, p. 90-99.

called nowadays 'ius cogens' and which was introduced to the doctrine and legal practice of public international law at least by the Vienna Convention on the Law of Treaties[36] in 1969, six years after Pope John published his encyclical. This is by the way the reason why the text of the encyclical does not refer to the concept of 'ius cogens' explicitly.

The arguments of Chapter IV. are well structured and lead the reader in a first reflection to a normatively grounded affirmation of the United Nations Organization and the Universal Declaration of Human Rights (1948) by the Pope. In a second reflection we can realize that the arguments of the encyclical are pointing clearly to a new order of the political powers and states which is laying beyond the legal order of the Charter of the United Nations of 1945. With his reflections Pope John is transcending even the imperatives we can deduce from Kant's philosophy. In his famous article 'To Perpetual Peace' of the year 1795[37] Kant is arguing for a commonwealth of peace-keeping states which is not constituting a sphere of cogent law including global institutions which are able to preserve peace and human rights by civic and pure juridical coercion[38]. But this is exactly the goal of the encyclical 'Pacem in terries' which is following the general idea of "peace through law" and not by military enforcement.

Pope John is starting his argumentation with reference to the fact that due to the enormous progress in sciences and technology human beings all over the world are extending their societal collaboration and are intensifying their association with one another. We can summarize this description of the societies and human interactions by the Pope in applying the modern concept of 'globalization' which is not used in the text. As economies are growing they become more and more interdependent. One of the evident consequences of these developments is according to Pope John's observation the politically important fact that states, in former times perhaps isolated from each other, are today the longer the more not able to achieve their own goals or to realize their special interests independent from the other states. Here we can diagnose a still increasing interdependency of the politi-

---

36 Cf. Articles 53 and 64 in the "Vienna Convention on the Law of Treaties" (VCLT) from 23rd of May 1969 which came into effect in 1980.

37 Cf. Frieden durch Recht. Kants Friedensidee und das Problem einer neuen Weltordnung, hrsg. von Matthias Lutz-Bachmann/James Bohman, Suhrkamp Verlag, Frankfurt 1996; Recht auf Menschenrechte. Menschenrechte, Demokratie und internationale Politik, hrsg. von Hauke Brunkhorst/Wolfgang Köhler/Matthias Lutz-Bachmann, Suhrkamp Verlag, Frankfurt 1999; Weltstaat oder Staatenwelt? Für und wider die Idee einer Weltrepublik, hrsg. von Matthias Lutz-Bachmann/James Bohman, Suhrkamp Verlag, Frankfurt 2002.

38 See Kant, To Perpetual Peace, Akademie-Ausgabe 354-357.

cal bodies of the states and their actors. These factual occurrences underline the normative importance of the question concerning the universal common good for humanity. As we have already seen the questions addressed by the concept of the universal common good are above all related to the topics of war and peace everywhere on earth.

In former times states realized their particular goals under highly different circumstances. The traditional system of states, following the Peace-Treaty of Westphalia (1648) seemed to be functionally appropriate to the dominant interests of the modern states. Their representatives or rulers cooperated "through the normal diplomatic channels, or by top-level meetings and discussions, treaties and agreements, in using the ways and means suggested by the national law, the law of nations or international law."[39] This more or less functional reconstruction of the appropriateness of international law in the history of the states in the Westphalian order leads the encyclical to the argument that due to the deep changes within the process of modern globalization the international order of the states has to be reconsidered and transformed. The reason for this statement is focusing at the change of the mutual relationships between the states in consequence of the ongoing process of globalization. Here we can identify the demand for new legal instruments, juridical structures and political institutions if the preservation of peace and of human rights in international and even in inner-state affairs shouldn't fail. Pope John therefore resumes: "We are thus driven to the conclusion that the shape and structure of political life in the modern world, and the influence exercised by public authority in all nations of the world are unequal to the task of promoting the common good of all peoples,"[40] which consists – as we have seen above – in the power of politics to guarantee peace and justice based on the normative principles of the human rights. This proposal includes much more institutional requirements than e.g. Kant's ideas concerning a treaty of the peaceful republics which is considered to be limited on the question of peace based on the agreement of all actors without a stronger institutional order[41].

39 Cf. para. 133; see the Latin text: " … sive per suae nationis legatos, sive per convenus et colloquia hominum in civitate praestantissimorum, sive per pacta et conventa: viis nempe instrumentisque adhibits, quae vel iure naturali, vel iure gentium, vel iure omnibus nationibus communi describebantur".

40 Cf. para. 135; see the Latin text: "In hodiernis igitur humanae societatis adiunctis, tum rerum publicarum constitution ac forma, tum vis, qua in universis terrarium orbis nationisbus pollet publica auctoritas, bono onmium populorum communi provehendo sunt impares habendae".

41 Cf. Matthias Lutz-Bachmann, Kants Friedensidee und das rechtspolitische Konzept einer Weltrepublik, in: Frieden durch Recht, ibid., p.25-44.

Pope John is calling for a new institution of global political authority which is responsible for the global common good,[42] especially for the topic of peace, which was politically urgent concerning the above-mentioned arms race as well as the proliferation of nuclear weapons and other weapons of mass destruction. Today, we have to admit that these problems are not yet solved and seem to become more and more difficult since new forms of warfare, of threatening and of world-wide terrorism are generating new challenges for the 'order of peace'. The new institution of global political authority with responsibility for security and global peace which the Pope is arguing for should be founded on the human rights principles and "must likewise have as its special aim the recognition, respect, safeguarding and promotion of the rights of the human person."[43] These considerations draw the normative consequences from the reflections on the basic principles of politics. Here it becomes clear that the public global authority Pope John is arguing for contains necessarily an effective juridical character claiming cogency – much more than further executive structures according to the well-known structures of governments in single states. In other words, Pope John is not arguing in favor of a 'world republic' but for an institutional authority with effective protection of peace and human rights. From here we can conclude that the power of this institution of global authority is thought to be a limited one, functionally defined by the principle of subsidiarity: "Its essential purpose is to create world conditions in which the public authorities of each nation, its citizens and intermediate groups, can carry out their tasks, fulfill their duties and claim their rights with greater security."[44]

On the background of these arguments Pope John deeply affirms the Charter of the United Nations Organization and the Universal Declaration of Human Rights as legitimate and important legal steps in the right direction. But he is aware that there are structural elements in the order of the UN which are not yet sufficient or are even obstacles on the way to an appropriate public authority. Pope John therefore calls both the UN as a legal body of public international law and the Declaration of Human Rights "a step in the right direction, an approach toward the establishment of a juridical and political ordering of the world community."[45] And he adds the final thought:

---

42 Cf. para. 137: "Today the universal common good presents us with problems which are world-wide in their dimensions; problems, therefore, which cannot be solved except by a public authority with power, organization and means co-extensive with these problems, and with a world-wide sphere of activity."

43 Cf. para. 139.

44 Cf. para. 144.

45 Cf. para. 144.

"It is therefore our earnest wish that the United Nations Organization may be able progressively to adapt its structure and methods of operation to the magnitude and nobility of its tasks. May the day be not long delayed when every human being can find in this organization an effective safeguard of his personal rights."[46]

As we know this institutional development the Pope is arguing for has not yet been realized after so many years and the legal constitution of the United Nations is still based on those principles of international law stated by the former founding member of the UN in the year of 1945. Here we can identify some of the reasons why the UN is failing too often in its effort to protect peace and human rights. But nevertheless we can identify some progress in public international law since then. International law theories today apply the concept of 'ius cogens' to some of the most important regulations in international affairs. The statement of cogency is considered to help to overcome a specific 'weakness' of the traditional public international law which is still affirmed in Kant's theory[47] and is present in the Charter of the UN. Its weakness consists in its enervation or better lack of institutional power to impose the prevailing legal norms by civic means if the states as the legal subjects of international law are unwilling to obey. This 'weakness' is of course the consequence of the fact that in contrast to the legal realm within the single states there is no ordinary legislator and executor of law in the international arena endowed with the institutional power to impose the prevailing norms. In his encyclical Pope John is exactly pointing at this 'incompleteness' in international law. This incompleteness becomes evident with regard to the new challenges which arise for the global community of human beings and of states in the ongoing process of globalization and the still increasing dependency of each single state not only on the collaboration with other states but also on the cooperation even with sphere of civic societies, and that means with the humans beings themselves and their immediate communication and interaction around the globe in which the human actors are not any longer mediated by the representatives of the former nation-states. The new global political order Pope John is arguing for has to serve primarily in order to help to preserve the state of peace in this new situation of mankind. That implies not only the avoidance of warfare between and within the single states against the classical state actors like governments but also against private actors and new formations of military coercion, of economic power, of cultural impact or of religious

46 Cf. para. 145.
47 Cf. Kant, To Perpetual Peace, Akademie-Ausgabe 357.

groups, movements and interests. And additionally it means to protect the universal claim of the validity of human rights for every human being on earth on the background of these developments.

These are precisely the original intentions of proclaiming the concept of 'ius cogens' when it was introduced into public international law. The above-mentioned 'Vienna Convention on the Law of Treaties', signed in 1969, has been prevailing law since 1980 for the signatory states and has been claiming a cogent force within the given international relations. The treaty of Vienna makes explicit what has already been accepted by the members of the United Nations Organization in the declaration of the human rights: the statutory prohibition of aggression, genocide, enslavement, race discrimination and torture. The constitution of the International Criminal Court is another important step in order to overcome the structural "weakness" [48] of international law towards a more effective institutional power for the basic legal norms of the world community of humans and states. But even if we can agree that these efforts will be further important steps towards the direction of Pope John's suggestions we have to concede that these elements have not yet been the constitution of a new legal order which is proposed by the text of the encyclical in 1963.

The serious question remains whether or not the development of international law towards a more compelling and powerful force for the basic legal norms is satisfactory since appropriate for the protection of peace and human rights on the global. Especially with regard to the statement of 'ius cogens' in public international law we have to admit that this enforcement of at least some basic principles of human rights is not only insufficient with regard to its effective implementation but sometimes leading to new conflicts among states and public agencies. Without a new constitutional order among states and globalizing societies, like the one Pope John is calling for, the claim of a concept of a 'ius cogens' is sometimes fictional and pure rhetoric, sometimes effective and real. Until now its legal power is still depending on 'sovereignty' of states which is claimed to be more or less 'unconditioned' by protagonists of international politics and accordingly on the acceptance by these actors, but not on the 'authority' of a new political body or on the 'effectiveness' of a juridical structure 'above' the single ac-

48 Cf. e.g. Matthias Lutz-Bachmann, The threat of violence and of new military force as a challenge to international public law, in: Legitimacy, Justice and International Law, ed. by Lukas H.Meyer, Cambridge University Press, Cambridge 2009, p.252-269 and recenty: Human Rights, Human Dignity, and Cosmopolitan Ideals. Essays on Critical Theory and Human Rights, ed. by Matthias Lutz-Bachmann/Amos Nascimento, Ashgate Publishing Limited, Farnham/Burlington 2014.

tors in the global arena which was the goal of Pope John's arguments. What we need today are more efforts to constitute political global institutions independent from the particular interests of the states and equipped with legal and juridical power to secure effectively peace and to protect human rights. It is obvious that the UN of today is not able to realize these tasks due to its constitutional dependence on the particular state-interests, especially the power-interests of the privileged veto powers in the Security Council, and on the affirmation of the principle of sovereignty of the states. If the world community of all 'human beings of good will' would hear the appeal and could recognize the arguments of the encyclical 'Peace on earth', one could imagine the possibility of a reform of the UN. This could help to secure peace and justice with the outcome that "every human being can find in this organization an effective safeguard of his/her personal rights."[49]

49 Ibid.

# Global Constitutionalism: Fundamental Norms, Contestation and the Emergence of Constitutional Quality[1]

*Stefan Oeter*

## *1. Introduction*

There is an old dream of human beings, a dream which has been in the minds and hearts of human beings since time immemorial – the dream of "Peace through Law". Theologians have cultivated this dream all over the history of Christianity, starting with St. Augustine, and the 'bellum iustum' doctrine constituted a decided attempt to operationalise such dream in moral theology, moral philosophy and law.[2] Some people thought this dream to be nonsensical – like many German authors in late 19th and early 20th century.[3] But even in late 19th century, many responsible statesmen thought it worth to try at least steps in the direction of "Peace through Law", as the history of the two Hague Peace Conferences of 1899 and 1907 demonstrates clearly.[4] An organized peace movement developed already at this time,[5] and more and more international lawyers thought it worth to struggle for a transformation of international law, from a world order characterized by a 'liberum ius ad bellum' to a new world order with a strict prohibition of use of force in international relations. Mankind has gone a long way throughout the 20th century, surviving a number of

1 This text partly draws on the proposal for a Collaborative Research Centre (SFB) on "Constitutionalism Unbound" prepared by Antje Wiener and Stefan Oeter.

2 See Justenhoven, Heinz-Gerhard/ Barbieri, William A. (Eds.). From Just War to Modern Peace Ethics. Berlin, 2012; Köhler, Michael/ Hössl, David (Eds.). Si vis pacem, para pacem? Friede durch internationale Organisation als Option für das 21. Jahrhundert. Frankfurt/M., 2008.

3 See as an exemplary study Degenhardt, Frank. Zwischen Machtstaat und Völkerbund: Erich Kaufmann (1880-1972). Baden-Baden, 2008, pp. 16-37.

4 See Kalshoven, Frits (Ed.). The Centennial of the First International Peace Conference: Reports & Conclusions. The Hague, 2000, pp. 44, 166, 261; Eyffinger, Arthur. The 1899 Hague Peace Conference: The Parliament of Man, the Federation of the World. The Hague, 1999, pp. 42, 102, 204 (Eyffinger, 1899 Hague Peace Conference); Dülffer, Jost. Regeln gegen den Krieg? Die Haager Friedenskonferenzen von 1899 und 1907 in der internationalen Politik. Berlin, 1981, pp. 54, 80, 101, 273.

5 See Eyffinger, 1899 Hague Peace Conference,1981, pp. 42-79.

horrible catastrophes where 'civilization' slided back into hatred, aggression and ruthless violence. At least in normative terms, the UN Charter of 1945 constituted a decisive step forwards[6] – but the use of military force as a tool in political power struggles still continues to be a scourge of mankind.

The expansion of international law seems not to have done the full job. International law seems still to be too much a creature of some dominant powers, the powerful and ruthless, ready to oppress people by the exercise of military force – and not the defence of the oppressed and the powerless.[7] Politics still seems to be the dominant force, and law its maiden, not the other way round. But "Peace through Law" requires politics to be disciplined – at least in some respect – by legal rules. And where has this operation of binding politics to legal bounds been successful? Our most convincing example is the modern nation-state, with its monopoly of force and a constitution that disciplines politics and binds it to the core values of democracy, rule of law and human rights – although this model seems much less successful outside Europe and North America than originally hoped.

Why not trying to create a 'Constitution' for the international community? Should it not be possible to go the way from the "anarchical society of states" to a "global community" based on "Peace through Law"? The resulting quest for "constitutionalising" the global legal order seems logical – and keeps writers of international law and political theory busy since some two decades. There exists a growing body of literature dealing with phenomena of 'constitutionalisation' – and such 'constitutionalisation' usually is seen as a progress towards a more just world order, towards "Peace through Law".[8] The UN Charter has been called the 'Constitution'

6 Concerning the historical background of the UN Charter see Mazower, Mark. No Enchanted Palace. The End of Empire and the Ideological Origins of the United Nations. Princeton (NJ), 2009, in particular pp. 149-189.

7 See Oeter, Stefan. Chancen und Defizite internationaler Verrechtlichung: Was das Recht jenseits des Nationalstaates leisten kann. In: Bernhard Zangl, Michael Zürn (Eds.). Verrechtlichung – Baustein für Global Governance? Bonn, 2004, pp. 46-73.

8 Compare the literature reviews by Wiener, Antje et al. Why a New Journal on Global Constitutionalism? Editorial. In: *Global Constitutionalism*, 1, 2012, 1, pp. 1-15; Cohen, Jean L. Globalization and Sovereignty. Rethinking Legality, Legitimacy, and Constitutionalism. Cambridge, 2012, p. 45ff.; Schwöbel, Christine E.J. Global Constitutionalism in International Legal Perspective. Leiden, 2011, p. 11 ff.; Peters, Anne. The Merits of Global Constitutionalism. In: *Indiana Journal of Global Legal Studies*, 16, 2009, 2, p. 397-411; Peters, Anne. Compensatory Constitutionalism. In: *Leiden Journal of International Law*, 19, 2006, 3, pp. 579-610; Brown, Garrett Wallace. The constitutionalization of what? In: *Global Constitutionalism,* 1, 2004, 2, pp. 201-228.

of the international community,[9] we have become used of talking of a 'Constitution of Europe',[10] and phenomena of 'constitutionalisation' are even detected in seemingly technical regimes such as the WTO.[11] But we should be careful in order to avoid the epistemological traps of finding what we want to see. Utmost care is needed for two reasons: firstly, we do not exactly know what characteristics really make up 'constitutionalisation', ending up in a rather fuzzy use of the concept, and, secondly, we do not always know for sure that every kind of 'constitutionalisation' really carries moral progress with it – 'constitutionalisation' may also be seen in the hardening of legal regimes that consolidate at its outset an unjust order, characterized by asymmetries of power, oppression of the powerless, ruthless exploitation and unacceptable distributional inequalities. With other words: the descriptive category of 'constitutionalisation' does not tell us anything about 'constitutional quality' in a normative sense, about the legitimacy of a normative order and its 'justness' in terms of moral philosophy. An academic study of 'global constitutionalism' thus requires more than just an empirical analysis of phenomena of 'constitutionalisation', linked to specific kinds of progress in institutionalisation of international regimes; it requires a closer look to 'legitimacy' and 'justness'[12]. The following reflections will outline the challenges that result from such initial observation, will try to sketch out a research program for future research on 'global constitutionalism'. These reflections have not fallen from a blue sky; they are rooted in a growing body of academic literature and take up themes, assumptions and first insights of an ongoing collective research project at Hamburg under the title "Constitutionalism Unbound", coordinated by my political science colleague Antje Wiener and myself.[13]

---

9 See Fassbender, Bardo. We the Peoples of the United Nations: Constituent Power and Constituent Form in International Law. In: Neil Walker/ Martin Loughlin (Eds.). The Paradox of Constitutionalism: Constituent Power and Constitutional Form. Oxford, 2007, pp. 269-290.

10 See e.g. Weiler, Joseph H.H./ Wind, Marlene (Eds.). European Constitutionalism Beyond the State. Cambridge, 2003.

11 See Petersmann, Ernst-Ulrich. From State-centered towards Constitutional 'Public Reason' in Modern International Economic Law. In: Giorgio Bongiovanni (Ed.). Reasonableness and Law. Dordrecht/ Heidelberg, 2009, pp. 421-458; Petersmann, Ernst-Ulrich. Human Rights, Constitutionalism, and the World Trade Organization. In: *Leiden Journal of International Law* 19, 2006, 3, pp. 633-667.

12 See in this regard the seminal work by Franck, Thomas M. The Power of Legitimacy among Nations. Oxford, 1990.

13 See the project website at: http://www.wiso.uni-hamburg.de/professuren/global-governance/forschung/fertiggestellte-projekte/constitutionalism-unbound.

## *2. Phenomena of 'Constitutionalisation'*

As already mentioned, an abounding strand of literature is looking for phenomena of 'constitutionalisation' throughout the entire range of international law.[14] There is neither a clear definition nor a robust consensus of what constitutes in detail 'constitutionalisation'. The use of the term varies a lot, and its meanings are far from evident. The starting-point, however, seems beyond dispute: International law has not only gone through a process of rapid expansion, with more or less no area of social practice regulated by law that has not its own set of international legal rules, but has entered into a process of strong institutionalisation.[15] The phenomenon of 'international organizations' is not really new, but the decades since 1945 have seen an enormous growth of such international organizations.[16] There is practically no body of international legal rules that is not linked to some kind of a sectorial organisation. International organisations (IOs) are again creatures of states, but they cannot be modelled in a simple principal-agent relationship. Even very traditional strands of (state-centred) rational choice theorists admit that IOs are actors on its own terms, actors that shape international law, bypass states, pursue their own agendas and

14 See O'Donoghue, Aoife. Constitutionalism in Global Constitutionalisation. Cambridge, 2014; Peters, Anne. Are We Moving Towards Constitutionalization of the World Community? In: Antonio Cassese (Ed.). Realizing Utopia: The Future of International Law. Oxford, 2012, pp. 118-135; Fassbender, Bardo/ Siehr, Angelika (Eds.). Suprastaatliche Konstitutionalisierung: Perspektiven auf die Legitimität, Kohärenz und Effektivität des Völkerrechts. Baden-Baden, 2012; Pernice, Ingolf (Ed.). Konstitutionalisierung jenseits des Staates: Zur Verfassung der Weltgemeinschaft und den Gründungsverträgen internationaler Organisationen. Baden-Baden, 2012; Kleinlein, Thomas. Konstitutionalisierung im Völkerrecht: Konstruktion und Elemente einer idealistischen Völkerrechtslehre. Heidelberg, 2012; Habermas, Jürgen. Die Krise der Europäischen Union im Lichte einer Konstitutionalisierung des Völkerrechts. In: Jürgen Habermas. Zur Verfassung Europas. Berlin, 2011, pp. 39-96; Pfeil, Florian. Globale Verrechtlichung: Global Governance und die Konstitutionalisierung des internationalen Rechts. Baden-Baden, 2011; Frowein, Jochen Abr. Konstitutionalisierung des Völkerrechts. In: Klaus Dicke et al. (Eds.). Völkerrecht und Internationales Privatrecht in einem sich wandelnden internationalen System: Berichte der Deutschen Gesellschaft für Völkerrecht Bd. 39. Heidelberg, 2000, pp. 427-447.

15 See Zürn, Michael. Regieren jenseits des Nationalstaates. Globalisierung und Denationalisierung als Chance. Frankfurt/M., 1998, p. 166 ff.; König-Archibugi, Matthias. Introduction: Institutional Diversity in Global Governance. In: Mathias Koenig-Archibugi/ Michael Zürn (Eds.). New Modes of Governance in the Global System. Basingstoke, 2006, pp. 1-29.

16 See Klabbers, Jan. An Introduction to International Institutional Law. 2nd ed. Cambridge, 2009, pp. 14-37.

coalesce with a variety of actors in order to overcome blockades in the diplomatic set-up.[17]

It seems clear that 'constitutionalisation' is more than mere 'legalisation'. Legal regimes still can serve as strategic tools for state actors, manipulated and exploited for the selfish interests of powerful actors.[18] 'Constitutionalisation' mostly is used where a claim might legitimately be made that law is liberated from the dominance of politics, gains a systemic autonomy that allows it to put limits to political practice. In national legal orders, such 'liberation' of law from total subjection to the logic of politics is task of the constitution, defining the structural coupling of law and politics, with no clear dominance of one over the other.[19] The systemic 'hardening' of legal regimes means that certain types of political action must be justified in terms of legal discourse – and political actors cannot evade such 'justification discourse' in legal terms, but are forced into it, like political actors inside the nation-state cannot avoid of justifying their actions in constitutional terms.[20] A decisive step towards such a systemic 'hardening', in the sense of emerging systemic autonomy, is the creation of mechanisms of obligatory judicial dispute settlement, or of other authoritative dispute resolution by third organs.[21] The success story of its dispute settlement has made the WTO a candidate for 'constitutionalisation' discourses,[22] and the sweeping powers of authoritative decision-making at the hands of the UN

17 See Collins, Richard/ White, Nigel D. (Eds.). International Organizations and the Idea of Autonomy. Institutional Independence in the International Legal Order. Abingdon, 2011.

18 See Oeter, Chancen und Defizite internationaler Verrechtlichung, p. 46 ff.

19 See Neves, Marcelo. Symbolische Konstitutionalisierung. Berlin, 1998, p. 60; Oeter, Stefan. Verkoppelung von Recht und Politik im europäischen Verfassungsdenken. In: Claudio Franzius/ Franz C. Meyer/ Jürgen Neyer (Eds.). Strukturfragen der Europäischen Union. Baden-Baden, 2010, pp. 67-83.

20 See Ladeur, Karl-Heinz. Der Staat gegen die Gesellschaft: Zur Verteidigung der Rationalität der „Privatrechtsgesellschaft“. Tübingen, 2006.

21 See Justenhoven, Heinz-Gerhard. Internationale Schiedsgerichtsbarkeit: Ethische Norm und Rechtswirklichkeit. Stuttgart, 2006.

22 See Stoll, Peter-Tobias. Constitutional Perspectives on International Economic Law. In: Marise Cremona/ Peter Hilpold/ Nikolaos Lavranos (Eds.). Reflections on the Constitutionalisation of International Economic Law. Liber amicorum for Ernst-Ulrich Petersmann. Leiden, 2014, pp. 201-213; Petersmann, Ernst-Ulrich. Multilevel Judicial Governance as Guardian of the Constitutional Unity of International Economic Law. In: *Loyola of Los Angeles International and Comparative Law Review*, 30, 2008, 3, pp. 367-418; Hilf, Meinhard. Die Konstitutionalisierung der Welthandelsordnung: Struktur, Institutionen und Verfahren. In: Wolff Heintschel von Heinegg et al. (Eds.). Entschädigung nach bewaffneten Konflikten. Die Konstitutionalisierung der Welthandelsordnung. Berichte der Deutschen Gesellschaft für Völkerrecht Bd. 40. Heidelberg, 2003, pp. 257-282.

Security Council have induced many authors to perceive the United Nations in a constitutionalist perspective.[23]

The UN Security Council with its broad powers and its byzantine decision-making, however, illustrates at the same time the dangers inherent in such a model of 'constitutionalisation'. It is far from clear that the Security Council, as the supreme organ for the maintenance of peace, is himself bound by the same values and fundamental norms that it seeks to impose on states.[24] Gross and consistent patterns of human rights violations are now generally perceived as a "threat to international peace" in the sense of Article 39, justifying a military intervention mandated by the Security Council.[25] But at the same time, the Security Council does not accept to be bound in its own operations by human rights standards. The notorious Kadi case with the European Court of Justice as well as the appalling lack of judicial remedies for victims of human rights violations in cases of UN-directed interim administrations (like in Kosovo) illustrate these imbalances.[26] As a consequence, we are confronted with some challenging questions. Does 'constitutionalisation' empower the *addressees* of global governance norms? For example, is the protection of fundamental rights of individuals improved as a result of changing the rules of procedure of the World Trade Organisation (WTO) or the United Nations (UN)? Given the reference to 'constitutionalisation', we would expect that the "publics", asking for such changes by contesting existing fundamental or constitutional norms, potentially perceive these processes of 'hardening' of legal regimes as positive steps towards 'peace through law' and global justice – but there are quite a number of examples where the contrary seems true.

23 See Fassbender, Bardo. The United Nations Charter as the Constitution of the International Community. Leiden, 2009.

24 See on the resulting problems of legitimacy Frowein, Jochen Abr. Issues of Legitimacy Around the United Nations Security Council, In: Jochen Abr. Frowein (Ed.). Verhandeln für den Frieden. Liber amicorum Tono Eitel. Berlin/ Heidelberg, 2012, pp.121-139; see also De Wet, Erika. The Chapter VII Powers of the United Nations Security Council. Oxford, 2004, p. 133 ff. (De Wet, Chapter VII Powers).

25 See De Wet, Chapter VII Powers, pp. 149-172, as well as Oeter, Stefan. Menschenrechte, Demokratie und Kampf gegen Tyrannen als Probleme der Friedenssicherung? Voraussetzungen und Grenzen der Autorisierung militärischer Gewalt durch den Sicherheitsrat der Vereinten Nationen. In: Thomas Bruha/ Sebastian Heselhaus/ Thilo Marauhn (Eds.). Legalität, Legitimität und Moral. Können Gerechtigkeitspostulate Kriege rechtfertigen? Tübingen, 2008, pp. 183-209.

26 See Avbelj, Matej (Ed.). Kadi on Trial. London, 2014; De Wet, Erika. From Kadi to Nada. In: *Chinese Journal of International Law*, 12, 2013, 4, pp. 787-807.

### 3. *Global Constitutionalism and its Three Schools*

In an ideal world, the growing interdependencies of societies and states resulting from globalisation would lead to a global polity with a global constitution. Peoples of the world would unite in a genuine 'international community' which then would operate as a constituent power ('pouvoir constituant') organising a process of drafting and adopting a formal constitutional document. But the world is not ideal, and the path towards a formal 'world constitution' is completely utopian. Although some philosophers argue that there is a necessity for such a 'world state',[27] nobody knows how such a polity could be organised. Nobody wants a global Leviathan that takes over control and suppresses the freedoms of the diverse societies populating the world.[28] But there is also no concept how a 'global democracy' could be organised – the problems of representation and democratic decision-making on a global scale seem insoluble, at least at the current stage of development of world society.[29] Formal constitutionalism, according to the model we know from the nation-state, is not a viable option for world society. But the pressing needs of the 'global village' require more and more common solutions. States have concluded myriads of treaties in order to deal with these pressing needs, and have founded hundreds of international organisations to cope with the challenges haunting inter-state cooperation.[30]

What about the legitimacy of such an array of fragmented, technocratic treaty regimes? Input-legitimacy is scarce;[31] the regimes largely have no alternative than to rely on output-legitimacy.[32] But is that sufficient to convince citizens that their needs are catered for in an adequate way? And does that really solve the most basic problems of political organisation at global level, such as preservation of peace and the promotion of rule of law in international relations? Most people are not convinced that this is the case, and such a perception is not really false. The international community has a

27 See Höffe, Otfried. Demokratie im Zeitalter der Globalisierung. München, 1999.

28 See Oeter, Stefan. Internationale Organisation oder Weltföderation? Die organisierte Staatengemeinschaft und das Verlangen nach einer „Verfassung der Freiheit". In: Hauke Brunkhorst/ Matthias Kettner (Eds.). Globalisierung und Demokratie. Frankfurt/M., 2000, pp. 208-239.

29 See Held, David. Democracy and the Global Order: From the Modern State to Cosmopolitan Governance. Stanford (CA), 1995.

30 See Peters, Anne. The Growth of International Law between Globalisation and the Great Power. In: *Austrian Review of International and European Law*, 8, 2003, pp. 109-139.

31 See Krisch, Nico. Beyond Constitutionalism: The Pluralist Structure of Postnational Law. Oxford, 2013, p. 264 (Krisch, Beyond Constitutionalism).

32 See Krisch, Nico. The Decay of Consent in International Law in an Age of Global Public Goods. In: *American Journal of International Law*, 108, 2014, 1, p. 1 ff.

constitutional problem, but the traditional way of dealing with that – formal constitution-making – is not available.[33] As a result, international lawyers and international relations specialists are looking around to find alternatives. 'Constitutionalisation' seems to be such an alternative.[34] If we cannot agree on a formal constitution, there is at least hope that the reason of history leads to a gradual accumulation of bits and pieces of constitutional arrangements in international law and institutions. Constitutionalism shifts to a paradigm of 'organic' emergence of constitutional arrangements, with a growing body of customary institutions that fulfil constitutional functions – thus the inherent optimism of studies on global constitutionalism.[35] The paradigm is not entirely new, but has been developed already more than twenty years ago and has kept lawyers and political scientists busy throughout the last two decades. The focus of the relevant studies differs – some authors are mapping phenomena which – they think – can adequately be described as 'constitutionalisation', whereas others start more from a normative angle and call for some kind of 'constitutionalisation' as a normative 'must'. But the underlying idea of a cumulative emergence is common to all.

As mentioned already, a significant number of authors have been dealing with these challenging issues since quite some time. Usually these authors are categorized as writers belonging to the new academic current of 'global constitutionalism'. But, again, this term is rather fuzzy, used for a variety of authors that have different academic interests and work with different paradigms and methodologies. Thus, before going into detail of 'constitutional quality', we need to revisit briefly the different schools of 'global constitutionalism' that we can find in academic writing.[36]

In a rough generalization, which unavoidably contains some degree of simplification glossing over the more subtle differences between authors and schools of thought, we can distinguish three schools according to their respective approaches – functionalist, normative and pluralist approaches. While all schools share the observation of a qualitative shift from global-

33 See Krisch, Beyond Constitutionalism, p. 38 ff.

34 See the references in footnote 14.

35 See – as some of the most influential works – the collective volumes of Dobner, Petra/ Loughlin, Martin (Eds.). The Twilight of Constitutionalism? Oxford, 2010; Klabbers, Jan/ Peters, Anne/ Ulfstein, Geir (Eds.). The Constitutionalization of International Law. Oxford, 2009; Loughlin, Martin/ Walker, Neil (Eds.). The Paradox of Constitutionalism: Constituent Power and Constitutional Form. Oxford, 2007.

36 The following mapping takes over the categorization developed by Antje Wiener – see Wiener, Antje. Global Constitutionalism. Oxford, 2012. Oxford Bibliographies Online, Available at http://www.oxfordbibliographies.com/ view/ document/obo-9780199743292/obo-9780199743292-0092.xml?rskey=CnfQ7M&result=1&q=antje%20wiener #firstMatch.

ised towards constitutionalised legal relations, the concept of global constitutionalism as applied by the contributors to each school reflects different assumptions, hypotheses and expectations. Nevertheless, there are some characteristics that are common to all these schools of thought – in particular the understanding that global constitutionalism (as a new field in the Social Sciences and Law) is not predominantly informed by single disciplinary approaches but combines methodological approaches and orientations of various disciplines. The distinction according to three schools is practice-based, informed by the different ways in which the underlying concepts are approached and applied.

Their respective main distinctive features have developed according to a choice of either mapping or shaping the global realm according to constitutional standards. Leading questions address the purpose and possibilities of constitutionalism with regard to developing the most feasible approach to justice and legitimacy in the global realm. While all three schools generally share the observation of enhanced constitutional quality beyond the nation-state as a result of processes which can be summarised as a major shift from globalised towards constitutionalised international relations, the consequences derived from this observation are rather divergent and lead to quite different orientations.

The normative school would consider global constitutionalism a strategic move towards establishing or accommodating a global constitution or, at least, compensate for constitutional loss at the national or subnational level by purposeful constitutionalisation in the global realm. While agreeing on the preference of shaping the world order according to modern principles of constitutional law and justice, the normative school differs sharply between supporters and contenders of a global constitution. In sum, this school engages in the project of shaping the global order according to specific normative principles. The key conceptual approach of this group thus rests on the extension of principles, norms and rules of modern constitutionalism beyond the modern state with the goal of constructing an institutionalised and legitimate global order. Jürgen Habermas has become famous as proponent of such an approach with his 2011 essay which puts forward his long-time argument that while a global constitution is neither necessary nor desirable, a neo-Kantian politically constituted world society is.[37] Another example for that school of thought is the special issue of Peters and Armingeon 2009 that stands out as an interdisciplinary collection of articles edited

37 Habermas, Jürgen. Die Krise der Europäischen Union im Lichte einer Konstitutionalisierung des Völkerrechts. In: Jürgen Habermas. Zur Verfassung Europas. Berlin, 2011, pp. 39-96.

by a political scientist and a lawyer.[38] A third example may be given with Fassbender's 2009 book that represents what might be called a stand-alone perspective in the debate by maintaining the argument that the UN Charter should be considered a global constitution.[39]

The functionalist school typically studies processes of constitutionalisation which are revealed through bargaining and negotiations in the environment of international organisations. This school focuses on the impact of constitutionalism by mapping the global terrain according to new standardised procedures and regulatory agreements. The key concept for this school is therefore that of constitutionalisation. A good example for this school is offered by the 2009 book of Dunoff and Trachtman.[40]

The pluralist school takes a critical approach to universalist assumptions and theorises constitutional change as contextualised, contingent and constitutive. Its authors would typically question the uncritical reference to the regulative ideal of liberal community ideals as stable regulative frames for constitutional change in the global realm. This school takes account of the social practices of constitutionalism as they extend beyond modern state boundaries, with the intention to identify the variety of possible and desired principles, norms and rules of constitutionalism that are considered appropriate by a plurality of global actors. Good examples of the school are Nico Krisch[41] as well as Daniel Halberstam[42] and Peer Zumbansen[43]. James Tully, to mention another important author, develops a critical approach to democratic constitutionalism in his 1995 book and demonstrates its value added for studying real world politics.[44] This approach is further substantiated by his new book on 'Public Philosophy in a New Key'.[45]

38 Peters, Anne/ Armingeon, Klaus. Introduction: Global Constitutionalism from an Interdisciplinary Perspective. In: *Indiana Journal of Global Legal Studies*, 16, 2009, 2, pp. 385-395.

39 Fassbender, Bardo. The United Nations Charter as the Constitution of the International Community. Leiden, 2009.

40 Dunoff, Jeffrey L./ Trachtman, Joel P. (Eds.). Ruling the World? Constitutionalism, International Law, and Global Governance. Cambridge, 2009.

41 Krisch, Nico. Beyond Constitutionalism: The Pluralist Structure of Postnational Law. Oxford, 2012.

42 Halberstam, Daniel. Constitutional Heterarchy: The Centrality of Conflict in the European Union and the United States. In: Jeffrey L. Dunoff/ Joel P. Trachtman (Eds.). Ruling the World? Cambridge, 2009, pp. 326-355.

43 Zumbansen, Peer. Comparative, Global and Transnational Constitutionalism: The Emergence of a Transnational Legal-Pluralist Order. In: *Global Constitutionalism*, 1, 2012, 1, pp. 16-52.

44 Tully, James. Strange Multiplicity: Constitutionalism in an Age of Diversity. Cambridge, 1995.

45 Tully, James. Public Philosophy in a New Key. 2 vol. Cambridge, 2008 and 2009.

Despite the distinct standpoints on how to use global constitutionalism, it is important to acknowledge that the boundaries between the schools are fuzzy. Often a scholarly perspective is developed from a two-tiered perspective which comfortably combines different approaches. Examples for this eclecticism are Anne Peters' call for purposeful constitutionalisation to compensate for normative deficits following globalisation,[46] Mattias Kumm's functionalist distinction between small and large constitutionalism on the one hand, and his cosmopolitan claim for constitutionalism "as a jurisprudential account claiming to describe the deep structure of public law".[47] Other paradigmatic examples are Jo Shaw's postnational approach to European constitutionalism which advances a normative argument for responsibility while discarding the modern constitutional architecture favoured by the normative school's main protagonists,[48] or Nico Krisch's combination of the functionalist and pluralist schools when writing with Kingsbury and Stewart on Global Administrative Law,[49] on the one hand, and when developing the concept of postnational constitutionalism,[50] on the other. Another way in which two schools combine is the shared focus of some members of both the normative and pluralist schools on the way that non-state actors are able to exercise agency – to shape the development of constitutional norms.[51]

## *4. The Role of Contestation in 'Global Constitutionalism'*

The emerging global legal order is of an essentially contested nature.[52] There are few fundamental norms of global law that are so settled that no contestation on their normative validity and content takes place. Admittedly, there exist some normative principles (and also some rules) that are universally

46 Peters, Anne. The Merits of Global Constitutionalism. In: *Indiana Journal of Global Legal Studies* 16, 2009, 2, pp. 397-411.

47 Kumm, Matthias. How Does European Union Law Fit into the World of Public Law? Costa, Kadi and Three Conceptions of Public Law. In: Jürgen Neyer/ Antje Wiener (Eds.). Political Theory of the European Union. Oxford, 2011, pp. 111-138.

48 Shaw, Jo. Process and Constitutional Discourse in the European Union. In: *Journal of Law and Society* 27, 2000, 1, pp. 4-37.

49 Kingsbury, Benedict/ Krisch, Nico/ Stewart, Richard B. The Emergence of Global Administrative Law. In: *Law & Contemporary Problems* 68, 2005, 3, pp. 15-61.

50 Krisch, Beyond Constitutionalism.

51 Forst, Rainer. Kritik der Rechtfertigungsverhältnisse. Perspektiven einer kritischen Theorie der Politik. Frankfurt a.M., 2011; Wiener, Antje. The Invisible Constitution of Politics: Contested Norms and International Encounters. Cambridge, 2008.

52 See Wiener, Antje. A Theory of Contestation. Heidelberg et al., 2014, pp. 39-42.

accepted as fundamental norms, at least in a principled perspective.[53] The prohibition of the use of force could be mentioned here, the principle of self-determination, the protection of territorial integrity of states, the prohibition of genocide, to name some of the few.[54] Most norms claimed to be fundamental norms are contested already at the level of validity. But even the (in principle) uncontested norms have no clear meaning as soon as operational questions are concerned.[55] As a result, the concrete 'meaning-in-use' usually tends to remain contested.[56] 'The degree of contestation might differ quite a lot, but the fact that the meanings of fundamental norms are contested is a part of normalcy – even in constitutional orders at national level.[57] Agreeing on a basic constitutional principle or rule does not necessarily mean that anybody agrees what such an agreed norm means in detail. The phenomenon of contestation is ambivalent in that regard. A strong degree of contestation may be perceived as an indicator of problems of legitimacy – but it could also be just the other way round. If contestation of operational legal arrangements is voiced under reference to 'sacred', generally shared fundamental norms, contestation even strengthens the normative power of the fundamental norm.[58] Contestation here demonstrates the shared belief in the relevance of the norm.

However, dramatic challenges are lying beneath the surface. States produce – via the myriads of treaty regimes they have created – huge masses of normative output in order to improve coordination and to solve problems of global governance. But do citizens believe in the ethical validity, as well as efficacy, of such norms? State-centred international law seems to be less and less capable of securing legitimacy of its normative output any more.[59] Individuals and civil society actors do not feel to be represented adequately by states and their organs and demand for their own voice in norm-setting.

53 See Wiener, Theory of Contestation, p. 35 ff.

54 These more or less uncontested norms (at least at the level of principles) are largely identical with the core non-dispositive norms of international law usually qualified as 'ius cogens'- see e.g. Frowein, Jochen Abr. Jus cogens. In: Max Planck Encyclopedia of Public International Law. Oxford, Online ed., 2013.

55 See Wiener, Theory of Contestation, pp. 35-39.

56 As to the category of 'meaning-in-use' see Milliken, Jennifer. The Study of Discourse in International Relations: A Critique of Research and Methods. In: *European Journal of International Relations*, 5, 1999, 2, pp. 225-254.

57 Tully, James. Strange Multiplicity: Constitutionalism in an Age of Diversity. Cambridge 1995.

58 See Wiener, Theory of Contestation, pp. 8, 10; Tully, James. Struggles over Recognition and Distribution. In: *Constellations* 7, 2000, 4, pp. 469-482.

59 See e.g. Koskenniemi, Martti. The Fate of Public International Law: Between Technique and Politics. In: *Modern Law Review* 70, 2007, 1, pp. 1-30.

In a general perspective, studies of contested compliance suggest that the legitimacy problem of global governance becomes ever stronger;[60] yet, a parallel increase of contestation and constitutionalisation would seem to be paradoxical, unless one takes contestation as a symptom of shared belief in the guiding force of the fundamental norms to which contestation usually refers as yardstick. In this sense, the drastic rise of incidences of contestation could be conceptualised as indicative of the existence of a constitutionally warranted right to access to contestation.[61] As Daniel Halberstam notes, the "process of constitutional contestation reveals that the conflict in each system surrounds three primary values of constitutionalism: voice, expertise, and rights. Constitutional heterarchy means that none of these values is predictably associated with any particular level, unit, or institution of governance."[62]

Accordingly, there are two understandings of contestation: *First*, considering moments, in which constitutional or fundamental norms are contested as empirical indicators; and *second*, examining ways in which legitimacy may be established through constitutionally warranted access to contestation outside modern state generated settings of justice.[63] If seen from the angle of the discursive processes by which a society develops 'shared meanings-in-use' of its normative foundations, the quantity and quality of instances of contestation must not be misunderstood as an indicator of normative challenges to the existing order – it could be taken also as just the opposite, as indicator of a lively and dynamic normative discourse that over time is capable to achieve ever deeper forms of 'shared meanings-in-use'. Under such a perspective, legitimacy deeply depends on contestation, and the first and foremost condition for building legitimacy is access to contestation.[64] Only when every segment of society has the feeling that its voice is heard, its values and interests are respected and taken on board in political decision-making, and that it can make its voice heard by contestation, will

60 De Búrca, Grаínne. The European Courts and the Security Council: Between Dedoublement Functional and Balancing of Values. In: *European Journal of International Law* 20, 2009, 3, pp. 853-887; Kingsbury et al., Global Administrative Law; Slaughter, Anne-Marie. A New World Order. Princeton (NJ), 2004; Zürn, Michael/ Hasenclever, Andreas/ Wolf, Klaus-Dieter (Eds.). Macht und Ohnmacht internationaler Institutionen. Frankfurt a.M./New York (NY), 2007.

61 For the latter, see e.g.Tully, Strange Multiplicity.

62 Halberstam, Daniel. Constitutional Heterarchy: The Centrality of Conflict in the European Union and the United States. In: Jeffrey L. Dunoff/ Joel P. Trachtman (Eds.). Ruling the World? Cambridge, 2009, pp. 326, 354.

63 See e.g. Pettit, Philip. Legitimacy and Justice in Republican Perspective. In: *Current Legal Problems* 65, 2012, pp. 59-82.

64 See Wiener, Theory of Contestation, p. 10.

the normative order gradually emerging over time be perceived as legitimate. In a complex twist, contestation thus has a close linkage not only to legitimacy but points also to issues of 'constitutional quality'.

Constitutional arrangements, and the fundamental norms laid down in such arrangements, need societal validation.[65] Their content cannot be invented from a blue sky, but must correspond to a large degree with the values and cultural orientations of a given society – thus the problematic character of constitutional transplants.[66] It may be possible to impose a formal constitution on society that has not that much to do with the values and cultural orientations of society – but the price paid for such imposition will always be a lack of legitimacy of the constitutional order, and a strong component of brute force needed to secure the respect of citizens towards such order. The 'constituted power' of a state ('pouvoir constitué')[67] may write a constitution that fits to its needs and preferences[68] – think of imposed constitutions after a military 'coup d'état' that enshrine the dominance of the military over society. There should be no doubt, however, that such an imposed constitution giving precedence to the needs of the 'pouvoir constitué' over the needs of the people (as the 'pouvoir constituant') will rarely manage to gain a degree of legitimacy that would guarantee its stability over time even if the regime imposing it will fall one day.[69] The normative force of a constitution ultimately does not rest on the force of guns and prisons, the policemen and soldiers enforcing it, but on the shared normative consensus that underpins its validity as rules of the political game.[70] We are touching here the paradoxical nature of the relation between the constituent power and the constituted power, a relation that has always remained a conundrum for political theory to a certain degree. Most authors have tended to rely here on the paradoxical assumption of a constitutional moment.[71] Here a normative consensus of a given society

65 See Wiener, Invisible Constitution of Politics, pp. 4-5, 26-30.

66 See e.g. Forsyth, Miranda/ Haggart, Blayne. The False Friends Problem for Foreign Norm Transplantation in Developing Countries. In: *Hague Journal on the Rule of Law*, 6, 2014, 2, pp. 202-229.

67 As to the temptations of the 'pouvoir constitué' see Thornhill, Christopher J. A Sociology of Constitutions: Constitutions and State Legitimacy in a Historical-Sociological Perspective. Cambridge , 2011, p. 219 ff.

68 See also Mazmanyan, Armen. Failing Constitutionalism: From Political Legalism to Defective Empowerment. In: *Global Constitutionalism*, 1, 2012, 2, pp. 313-333.

69 See also O'Donoghue, Aoife. Constitutionalism in Global Constitutionalisation. Cambridge, 2014, pp. 56-59.

70 See Wiener, Invisible Constitution of Politics, pp. 4-5.

71 See e.g. Loughlin, Martin/ Walker, Neil. Introduction. In: Martin Loughlin/ Neil Walker (Eds.). The Paradox of Constitutionalism: Constituent Power and Consti-

crystallises in a constitutional document and thus founds an institutional order with an arrangement of 'constituted powers'.[72] These 'constituted powers', however, show a strong tendency to manipulate the constitutional results and to create – if needed – artificially their (claimed) 'constitutional moments' when they think a change of constitutional order is pertinent. As a result, the relation between the two – constituted and constituent powers – tends to be much more complex than traditional constitutional theory was willing to admit.[73]

Accordingly, we cannot expect research immediately to shed new light on the paradox of 'constitutional moments', and linked to that on the relationship of constituted and constituent power.[74] What we need instead is a more hands-on claim about legitimacy. By focusing on the diversity of groups that raise constitutional claims, and on the diverse form and substance of different instances of contestation, we can expect to learn more about the presence or absence of shared validation of constitutional norms in the global realm. The legitimacy of global governance claims to exercise legitimate authority depends on such shared validation. Only with shared validation of fundamental norms will the international community develop a common understanding of the underlying rules of the game – and such a common understanding, an operative consensus of the underlying fundamental norms, is the essence of 'constitutional quality' in the global realm.[75] Accordingly, what is needed is an attempt to identify the degree of shared validation indicated by the external "source of authority" of a constitutional script, be it a written or an unwritten one. Global regimes develop such 'constitutional scripts', but the legitimacy of such 'scripts' remains open to dispute.

---

tutional Form. Oxford, 2007, pp. 1-8.

72 See Lindahl, Hans. Constituent Power and Reflexive Identity: Towards an Ontology of Collective Selfhood. In: Martin Loughlin/ Neil Walker (Eds.). The Paradox of Constitutionalism: Constituent Power and Constitutional Form. Oxford, 2007, pp. 9-24.

73 See in particular Thornhill, Chris. Contemporary Constitutionalism and the Dialectic of Constituent Power. In: *Global Constitutionalism*, 1, 2012, 3, pp. 369-404; compare also Dyzenhaus, David. Constitutionalism in an Old Key: Legality and Constituent Power. In: *Global Constitutionalism*, 1, 2012, 2, pp. 229-260.

74 As to the paradigm of 'constitutional moments' applied to constitutionalism beyond the nation-state see Kotzur, Markus. Constitutional Moments in globaler Perspektive – eine völkerrechtliche Spurensuche. In: Jahrbuch des Öffentlichen Rechts, 62, 2014, p. 445 ff.

75 See Wiener, Invisible Constitution of Politics, pp. 21-30.

## 5. *The Question of 'Constitutional Quality'*

If we want to get a more clear answer to questions of legitimacy of the 'constitutional scripts' in the global realm, we thus need to raise the question of 'constitutional quality'.[76] In analyzing the normative substance of the observed phenomenon of constitutionalisation in the global realm, the first key challenge is presented by the criterion of the constituent power (or its proxy). The category of 'constituent power', at least as soon as we apply the category to normative orders beyond the nation-state, seems to be an oxymoron.[77] Global constitutionalism undoubtedly cannot relate to a predetermined community, as a 'pouvoir constituant' in a traditional sense. Constitutionalisation in the global realm, however, refers to a notion of 'global community' or 'humankind', as a potential legitimating subject.[78] In the best-case scenario, through the process of constitutionalisation as a recursive process of transferring constitutional elements into the global realm, the global community gradually constitutes itself as a 'pouvoir constituant', in the same process in which it accumulates shared normative understandings as the underpinnings of constitutionalisation. In that case, constitutional quality should accrue to such a degree that world society organizes itself as a polity with a normative ordering of substantial constitutional quality. However, whether this best-case scenario is a possibility remains to be shown.

In principle, according to constitutional theory, a constitution serves to check societal actors in their interrelation, warrant access to the protection, and entitles the governing institutions (the pouvoir constitué) to act on behalf of the community of citizens.[79] A constitution keeps law and politics 'in check'. A constitution thus organises the relationship between law and politics, by putting both in a framework where politics decides to a certain degree on the content of law (in given procedures) while politics at the same time is put in the straightjacket of legal rules and procedures that discipline the political process.[80] The relations between the constitution and

76 See Wiener, Invisible Constitution of Politics, pp. 13-16.

77 See e.g. Thornhill, Contemporary Constitutionalism, pp. 369-375.

78 See Paulus, Andreas. The International Legal System as a Constitution. In: Jeffrey L. Dunoff/ Joel P. Trachtman (Eds.). Ruling the World? Cambridge, 2009, p. 69 ff.

79 See Möllers, Christoph. 'We are (afraid of) the people': Constituent Power in German Constitutionalism. In: Martin Loughlin/ Neil Walker (Eds.). The Paradox of Constitutionalism: Constituent Power and Constitutional Form. Oxford, 2007, pp. 87-106.

80 See Schmidt, Rainer. Verfassungskultur und Verfassungssoziologie: Politischer und rechtlicher Konstitutionalismus in Deutschland im 19. Jahrhundert. Wiesbaden, 2012, pp. 11-24.

the community are guided by constitutional principles and norms. Given that a constitution's substance is stable, and that its principles, norms and procedures remain valid over time notwithstanding the changing group of citizens as members of this community, the reference to the citizenry as the constituent power is a necessary condition for a text to be 'of constitutional quality'.[81] Such reference might be fictitious to a large degree, but it must be made – and the citizenry must in principle believe that the text was made on behalf of it and serves its needs.

However, it is important to note that – whether written or unwritten – a constitution derives its authority from sources that are external to the constitutional text (or routine as e.g. in the UK context). That means, a constitution's legitimation stems from normative foundations that are found outside the constitution itself, that are socially constructed in a discursive process where society accepts the constitutional arrangement as being made on its behalf.[82] This external source of authority is contingent on the larger historical context in which a political community is constituted.

With the establishment of the international community through international conferences, conventions and treaties, and in parallel the strengthened and growing political authority of modern nation-states,[83] constitutionalised communities emerged as 'state-bound' – and continue to exist in the bounded context of statehood.[84] That is, throughout the period of modern state-building constitutions are expected to refer to a specific population, a territory, and a government.[85] Given that in the UN only states are admitted as members, this process of 'state-bound' constitutionalisation was largely considered as completed with the 20$^{th}$ century, which again served as the basis for the strengthening of international organisations such as the UN – organisations that rest upon states and rely heavily on the organisational resources and the capacities of states to implement international legal rules. This starting-point has manifold consequences. On the one hand, there is a growing debate on global constitutionalism with the 'sovereigntist' strand of international law[86] where 'sovereigntists' claim that international law

81 See e.g. Thornhill, Contemporary Constitutionalism, pp. 378-391.

82 See Reus-Smit, Christian. The Constitutional Structure of International Society and the Nature of Fundamental Institutions. In: *International Organization*, 51, 1997, 4, p. 555-589.

83 See Tilly, Charles. The Formation of National States in Western Europe. Princeton( NJ), 1975.

84 As to the emergence of state-bound constitutionalism see Brunkhorst, Hauke. Legitimationskrisen. Verfassungsprobleme der Weltgesellschaft. Baden-Baden, 2012.

85 See Grawert, Rolf. Staat und Staatsangehoerigkeit. Berlin, 1973.

86 See Posner, Eric A. The Perils of Global Legalism. Chicago, 2009. Also the critical review of Posner by Cohen, Heather. Book Review – Eric A. Posner's The Perils of

must necessarily remain state-centred and cannot transform into some kind of 'global law' where states, international organisations and non-state actors cooperate and negotiate on new legal arrangements on equal footing. On the other hand, post-colonial strands and law and development studies question the role of the state in the real functioning of international law.[87] The outreach and control of states is fragile in large parts of the world; states are used to coalesce with societal power-holders and to delegate large parts of their functions to non-state actors, which diminishes the power (and the capacity) of states to monopolise force inside their polities and to implement effectively rules set under international law.[88]

It is becoming more and more obvious that the paradigm of state-bound constitutionalisation includes two serious shortcomings: The process of creating modern statehood throughout the world, mostly in the framework of the colonial state, involved drawing new political boundaries that did not overlap with social borders (especially in Africa, but also in Asia and Latin America).[89] The post-colonial states inheriting the structures of statehood from the former colonial powers knew precisely that they were sitting on a minefield and had to guard the pandora's box of revision of boundaries – thus the (nearly obsessive) insistence of regional state communities in Latin America and Africa on territorial integrity and uti possidetis.[90] In addition, state-bound constitutionalism put constitutional arrangements that were not linked to the central institutions of the state to one side, as can be seen with the First Nations in Canada and the United States, the Maori in New Zealand, and a lot of other indigenous peoples throughout the world.[91] The ensuing problem of how (post-colonial) statehood and (autochtonous) indigenous communities with its inherited structures of social organisation, of

Global Legalism (2009). In: *German Law Journal*, 13, 2012, 1, pp. 67-75.

87 See Anghie, Antony. Imperialism, Sovereignty and the Making of International Law. Cambridge, 2004, pp. 196-244; Ordord, Anne. A Jurisprudence of the Limit. In: Anne Orford (Ed.). International Law and its Others. Cambridge, 2005, pp. 1-32; Esclava, Luis/ Pahuja, Sundhya. Beyond the (Post)Colonial: TWAIL and the Everyday Life of International Law. In: *Verfassung und Recht in Übersee*, 45, 2012, 2, p. 195.

88 See Oeter, Stefan. (Fragile) Staatlichkeit und Entwicklung. In: Philipp Dann/ Stefan Kadelbach/ Markus Kaltenborn (Eds.). Entwicklung und Recht. Baden-Baden, 2014, pp. 471- 497.

89 See Makau wa Mutua. Why Redraw the Map of Africa: A Moral and Legal Inquiry. In: *Michigan Journal of International Law*, 16 (1995) 4, p. 1113 ff.; Okafor, Obiora Chinedu. Redefining Legitimate Statehood: International Law and State Fragmentation in Africa, The Hague, 2000.

90 See e.g. Giuseppe Nesi, Uti possidetis Doctrine. In: Max Planck Encyclopedia of Public International Law. Oxford, Online ed. 2011.

91 See Tully, Strange Multiplicity.

collective decision-making and dispute-settlement fit together – or should be related to – has remained mostly unresolved and remains a challenge for the future. It is a rather recent phenomenon that states of Latin America and Africa start bridging the gap between these competing structures of organisation, with the objective of creating a new (inclusive) social and political order.[92] At the same time, non-state actors are radically gaining in importance also in the established states of the North[93] – think of multinational firms that often have a cash-flow and social power that oversteps that of middle-sized states. The nation-state loses in significance and is forced to negotiate (and coalesce) with new actors on an equal footing.[94]

The resulting conceptual argument therefore is that the process of (previously state-bound) constitutionalisation has become 'unbound', with the rise of a plethora of new actors, but also with the transfer of constitutional norms and principles from the domestic realm into the global realm. The literature has dubbed this process "global constitutionalisation" or "constitutionalisation beyond the state".[95] While the literature addressing this phenomenon is relatively recent, an emerging interdisciplinary field of global constitutionalism is noticeable nonetheless. It distinguishes the three mentioned schools, functionalist, normative and pluralist.[96] According to the first school, constitutionalisation in the global realm is based on a functionalist rationale. It has been developed with reference to "taxonomic" rather than "normative" criteria[97] to enhance the legitimacy of global governance institutions.[98] The second takes the opposite view, arguing that global con-

92 See e.g. Bernot, Sabine. Die verfassungsrechtliche Anerkennung indigenen Rechts, Rechtspluralismus und Menschenrechte – untersucht an den Beispielen Südafrika und Bolivien. PhD thesis, Hamburg, 2014.

93 See Jönsson, Christer/ Tallberg, Jonas (Eds.). Transnational Actors in Global Governance. Basingstoke, 2014.

94 See the contributions in Peters, Anne et al. (Eds.). Non-State Actors as Standard-Setters. Cambridge, 2009.

95 See e.g. Weiler, Joseph H.H./ Wind, Marlene (Eds.). European Constitutionalism Beyond the State. Cambridge, 2003; Dunoff/Trachtman, Ruling the World? Constitutionalism, International Law, and Global Governance. Cambridge, 2009 (Dunoff/Trachtman, Ruling the World?); Peters, Anne. The Merits of Global Constitutionalism. In: *Indiana Journal of Global Legal Studies*, 16, 2009, 2, pp. 397-411; Klabbers, Jan/ Peters, Anne/ Ulfstein, Geir (Eds.). The Constitutionalization of International Law. Oxford, 2009.

96 See Wiener, Antje. Global Constitutionalism. Oxford, 2012. Oxford Bibliographies Online, Available at http://www.oxfordbibliographies.com/ view/document/obo-9780199743292/ obo-9780199743292-0092.xml?rskey= CnfQ7M&result=1&q=antje%20wiener#firstMatch.

97 See e.g. Dunoff/ Trachtman, Ruling the World? p. 4.

98 See Buchanan, Allen/ Keohane, Robert O. The Legitimacy of Global Governance Institutions. In: *Ethics and International Affairs* 20 (2006) 4, p. 405-437, as well

stitutionalisation is a necessary normative corrective, given that through the transfer of constitutional norms and principles, state-bound constitutionalisation has lost normative quality.[99] The third school takes a pluralist view that expects, and endorses, the parallel existence of different types and degrees of constitutionalisation.[100] It conceptualises constitutional quality as socially constituted rather than meta-theoretically given.

Against this background of 'unbound' constitutionalisation defined as a process that effectively unbinds previously state-bound principles and norms, future research must raise a question about constitutional quality: Does the transfer of constitutional norms beyond state borders change constitutional quality? To answer this question, one must probably embrace a global approach to pluralism, which includes a potential global plurality of constituent powers and external sources of authority rather than working with the assumption of a bounded plurality of constitutional authority including internal and external constitutional pluralism pending on given "sites of power".[101]

Some clarifications are necessary at this stage. We define the term constitutionalism as a theoretical framework (rather than a phenomenon). As such, constitutionalism guides research on constitutionalisation. Accordingly global constitutionalism is defined as a framework approach to study constitutionalisation in the global realm. Following the law-in-context approach[102] we define constitutionalisation is a practice category and therefore a phenomenon, which remains to be assessed through empirical observation. In turn, constitutionalism is understood as a theoretical framework including different cultural and temporal contexts, an academic "artefact" that comprises the stipulation of constitutional norms, principles and proce-

---

as Slaughter, Anne-Marie. A New World Order. Princeton( NJ), 2004; comp. also critically Cohen, Jean L. Globalization and Sovereignty. Rethinking Legality, Legitimacy, and Constitutionalism. Cambridge, 2012.

99 See e.g. Peters, Anne. The Merits of Global Constitutionalism. In*: Indiana Journal of Global Legal Studies*, 16, 2009, 2, pp. 397-411; Habermas, Jürgen. Zur Verfassung Europas. Berlin, 2011.

100 See e.g. Walker, Neil. Flexibility within a Metaconstitutional Frame: Reflections on the Future of Legal Authority in Europe. In: Grainne De Burca, Joanne Scott (Eds.). Constitutional Change in the EU. From Uniformity to Flexibility? Oxford, 2000, pp. 9-30; Maduro Poiares, Miguel. Courts and Pluralism: Essay on a Theory of Judicial Adjudication in the Context of Legal and Constitutional Pluralism, In: Dunoff/ Trachtman, Ruling the World? pp. 356-380.

101 Compare Maduro, Courts and Pluralism, pp. 357-358.

102 See Kratochwil, Friedrich. Leaving Sovereignty Behind? An Inquiry into the Politics of Post-modernity. In: Richard Falk, Mark Juergensmeyer and Vesselin Popovski (Eds.). Legality and Legitimacy in Global Affairs. Oxford, 1989, pp. 127-148; Onuf, Nicholas. The Constitution of International Society. In: *European Journal of International Law*, 5, 1994, 1, pp. 1-19.

dures in other than state-bound environments. This practice-based approach examines unbound constitutionalisation from a comparative perspective that takes into account cultural diversity as a formative and distinctive dimension of constitutionalism.[103] Rather than applying what specialists of international law and international relations disciplines often dub a "Westphalian discourse" of state-bound constitutional communities, Global Constitutionalism should encourage alternative visions of community. Unbound constitutionalisation involves 'state-plus' actorship, yet it is increasingly distinct from the group of citizens as the constituent power of nation-state communities. A *plurality of actors* (state-plus) therefore is a distinctive characteristic of unbound constitutionalisation. [104]

With the reference to either a notion of 'global community' or 'humankind'[105] and to a 'community interest'[106] as the overriding orientation of international law, constitutionalisation in the global realm does point to a potential legitimating subject (compare, for example, the references in the United Nations Convention of the Law of the Sea of 1982). In sum, unbound constitutional quality[107] is indicated by two criteria: First, it requires a reference to 'humankind' as the potential constitutional community; second, it must facilitate access to contestation to its constituents, thus alliterating to the process of self-constituting community in a recursive process.[108] Even though each serves as an indicator of constitutional quality, both are necessary criteria. For example, in the global context, the reference to 'mankind' as the external source of authority in the UNCLOS serves as an indicator for constitutional quality, while the existence of the constituent power is less clearly identifiable, given that UNCLOS is not signed by all member states of the UN as a possible community of reference, and, arguably even more importantly, the reference group is a group of states rather than citizens.[109] An innovative move thus is needed – a move shifting the focus on *unbound* constitutionalisation that includes transferring erstwhile 'state bound' constitutional elements such as norms, principles and procedures into the glob-

103 See Wiener, Invisible Constitution of Politics, pp. 39-41.

104 See also O'Donoghue, Aoife. Constitutionalism in Global Constitutionalisation. Cambridge, 2014, pp. 200-241.

105 See e.g. Paulus, Andreas. International Community. In: Max Planck Encyclopedia of Public International Law. Oxford, Online ed., 2013.

106 See Feichtner, Isabel. Community Interest. In: Max Planck Encyclopedia of Public International Law. Oxford, Online ed., 2007.

107 As to the concept of 'constitutional quality' see Wiener, Invisible Constitution of Politics, pp. 21-36.

108 See Wiener, Invisible Constitution of Politics, pp. 197-212.

109 See Kratochwil, Friedrich. The Status of Law in World Society. Meditations on the Role and Rule of Law. Cambridge, 2014, pp. 75-100.

al realm. By introducing the concept of unbound constitutionalisation, we might break with the routine of linking constitutionalism intuitively with state-bound concepts of constitution.[110] According to this approach, however, one cannot expect constitutionalisation any more to generate constitutional quality in any case – by all means and on all accounts.

Instead, I would argue that whether or not unbound constitutionalisation is actually constitutive for constitutional quality needs to be proven empirically, given the change of context from the familiar national or domestic political realm towards the global realm. As such, it includes the practices of, for example, solemnly declaring a collective reference to shared principles, setting norms following public deliberation or legal contestation, or stipulating constitutional procedures in an official document.[111] Notably, constitutional quality is therefore considered as the more encompassing normative concept while constitutionalisation is defined as a process, which consists of a set of empirically observable social practices. These practices are distinguishable according to their respective context(s) of emergence as legal, political or societal practices as well as from the top-down towards the bottom-up perspective on constitutional quality.

## *6. Concluding Remarks*

The reflections set out above should demonstrate that a lot more needs be researched than simply looking – in a more or less descriptive fashion – to phenomena of 'constitutionalisation'. Traditional research on 'constitutionalisation' already suffers from a theoretical indeterminacy – we do not really know what characterises 'constitutionalisation', what makes up the 'constitutional quality' that might justify using the attribute 'constitutional'. But at the same time, behind the writings on 'constitutionalisation' there is an important analytical and theoretical challenge that must be taken seriously. Human beings quest (quite rightly) for order and stability not only at national level, but also at the level of the international community, and thus demand for "peace through law" – and this clearly implies an ideal of 'rule of law' in global politics.[112] But binding politics to law in the global realm, i.e. beyond

110 See also O.Donoghue, Constitutionalism, pp. 44-50.

111 See Craig, Paul. Constitutions, Constitutionalism, and the European Union. In: *European Law Journal*, 7, 2001, 2, pp. 125-150; Bermann, George A./ Pistor, Katharina (Eds.). Law and Governance in an Enlarged European Union. Oxford, 2004.

112 See e.g. Marshall, David/ Modirzadeh, Naz (Eds.). The International Rule of Law Movement. A Crisis of Legitimacy and the Way Forward. Cambridge( MA), 2014.

the nation-state, requires the emergence of a normative set-up that fulfils functions that we ascribe in national legal orders to constitutions – and at the same time globalisation and the shift of government functions from the national realm into the global realm weakens and erodes the constitutional framework of legally bounded politics at national level.[113] This might explain the longing for the emergence of a 'global constitution', or at least the drive towards 'global constitutionalism'. We must pay attention, however, that our search for constitutional elements in the global realm does not become an exercise in wishful thinking, where we take our wishes for reality, with the constitutional arrangements we believe to see being mere chimera.

Such danger is pertinent. This does not say that the whole debate on constitutionalisation is completely illusionary, that the constitutional elements claimed to be found in global governance are simply the emperors' new clothes. Looking for constitutional elements in the global legal order is more than a mere exercise in legal utopia[114] – obviously there are processes that might be perceived in constitutional terms and bits and pieces in global governance that fulfil constitutional functions. The crux of the matter, however, is that we do not really know whether the processes of 'constitutionalisation' change things to the better, whether there is any 'constitutional quality' behind the described phenomena, a normative substance that could contribute to the legitimacy of global governance.[115] Law (and constitution) are first and foremost formal tools of social organisation.[116] The debate on 'legalisation' tells us that we can find more and more legal frames in global governance, and the debate on 'constitutionalisation' tells us that global governance contains more and more elements from the toolbox of constitutional forms that serve constitutional functions. What these debates do not tell us, however, are the contents of such formal tools. Law is no good or bad in itself – it can be filled with completely different contents. It can serve for the improvement of human condition, can free human beings from terror and serfdom – but it can also serve as a tool of repression and terror,

113 Compare also Kratochwil, The Status of Law in World Society, pp. 261-290.

114 But there is also a legitimate place for legal utopia in international law; see Allott, Philip. Eunomia – New Order for a New World. Oxford, 2001; see also Cassese, Antonio (Ed.). Realizing Utopia – The Future of International Law. Oxford, 2012; Koskenniemi, Martti. From Apology to Utopia. The Structure of International Legal Argument, 2nd ed. Oxford, 2005.

115 As to the concept of legitimacy in global governance see e.g. Wheatley, Steven. The Democratic Legitimacy of International Law. Oxford, 2010; Buchanan, Allen E./ Keohane, Robert O. The Legitimacy of Global Governance Institutions. In: *Ethics & International Affairs*, 2, 2006, 4, pp. 405-437.

116 See Kratochwil, The Status of Law in World Society, pp. 50-74.

as an instrument of serfdom and injustice. The same is true for constitutions. The fully-fledged framework of constitutionalism at nation-state level takes certain care that the latter does not happen.[117] By requiring an inclusive procedure of drafting and adopting a constitutional document, at best with a final referendum requiring the consent of at least a strong majority of citizens to the constitutional text, traditional constitutionalism at national level contains certain safeguards which ensure that the constitutional text to a large degree reflects the preferences, values and cultural orientations of the citizenry.[118] These safeguards are not always respected – the temptations of constituted powers to manipulate the constitutional process are always present, and quite often constituted powers fall victim to these temptations, brushing aside the participation of citizenry in constitutional process and more or less imposing constitutional documents. The costs of such a sin-fall are usually dramatic – the constitutional text then will have no chance of gaining legitimacy, of societal validation as a widely shared set of fundamental rules.

The mentioned safeguards of national constitutionalism do not work in the global realm, however. There is no agreed formal framework of setting constitutional rules; 'constitutionalisation' as an 'organic' process of emerging bits and pieces of constitutional function has no implicit frame of how these principles and rules come about.[119] They 'emerge', but we do not know that much about the formal framework, the inclusiveness and fairness of the processes leading to such emergence.[120] Often these principles and rules will emerge from the international legal process, thus will be set by states as the core actors of the international community. The community of states, however, is plagued by dramatic asymmetries of power; the international legal process is not necessarily inclusive and fair, but knows a huge array of selective and asymmetric processes where quite biased and parochial outcomes may be the results.[121]

We are here at the core of the problem. "Peace through law" does not simply require the replacement of force by law, whatever content such law

117 See Thornhill, Contemporary Constitutionalism, pp. 392-396.

118 See e.g. Arato, Andrew. Conventions, Constituent Assemblies, and Round Tables: Models, Principles and Elements of Democratic Constitution-Making. In: *Global Constitutionalism*, 1, 2012, 1, pp. 173-200.

119 See also Brown, Garrett Wallace. The Constitutionalization of What? In: *Global Constitutionalism*, 1, 2012, 2, pp. 201-228.

120 On these preconditions of a legitimate global legal order see Franck, Thomas M. The Power of Legitimacy Among Nations. Oxford, 1990.

121 See Allott, Philip. The Health of Nations. Society and Law beyond the State. Cambridge, 2002, pp. 342-398.

may have. Law may also be brute force disguised in legal forms. "Peace through law" requires specific types of law with certain characteristics that secure its dignity. Law must fulfil certain conditions – in terms of process as well as content – in order to achieve such dignity. In terms of process, law must be the result of decision-making processes that guarantee certain inclusiveness – thus access to contestation is so important. Only such inclusivity enables legal rules to develop 'shared meanings-in-use' when it comes to operational application. In terms of content, a certain degree of fairness and respect of minimal requirements of distributive justice is needed in order to enable legitimacy of the principles and rules resulting from the legal process. International law does not contain any guarantees that these requirements are fulfilled. Accordingly, 'constitutionalisation' must be viewed with a strong dose of scepticism – the constitutional elements may be legitimate, but may also be very problematic. And we do not have clear analytical tools and/or normative yardsticks to distinguish the different outcomes.

In order to find answers to these pertinent questions, we must reflect much more thoroughly on the issue of normative validation and legitimacy – a research agenda that we are trying to take up with our Hamburg project on 'Constitutionalism Unbound'. While working on this project during the last two years, I have made the basic experience of any researcher entering uncharted waters of research – the old insight that, the more I manage to learn, the more I am becoming aware of how limited my knowledge is. But we definitely must know more on 'global constitutionalism' if our eternal project of "peace through law" shall succeed.

# A Global State, International Law and the Containment of Persistent Conflict: An Anglican Response to Pacem in Terris

*Nigel Biggar*

## *1. Pacem in Terris: admirable, but naive*

*Pacem in Terris* says much that is admirable. What Christian or person of good will could cavil at the rhetorical question, "Is there anyone who does not ardently yearn to see war banished, to see peace preserved and daily more firmly established?" (115).[1] Who could quarrel with Pope John XXIII's urging that we should spare no labour to ensure that world events follow "a reasonable and humane course" (117), or that we should give "serious thought" to the problem of a peaceful adjustment of relations between political communities on a world level (118)? And even though we might want to quibble with it, we can nevertheless endorse the general thrust of the statement that "it is hardly possible to imagine that in the atomic era war could be used as an instrument of justice" (315). All this exhortation to peacemaking can only be applauded.

But there are times when *Pacem in Terris* is not unobjectionably pacific, but dubiously pacifist. Thus we are told that "disagreements [between nations] must be settled, not by arms ... but rather in the only manner which is worthy of the dignity of man, i.e., by a mutual assessment of the reasons on both sides of the dispute, by a mature and objective investigation of the situation, and by an equitable reconciliation of differences of opinion" (93). We are also told, by appeal to Pius XII, that "Nothing is lost by peace; everything may be lost by war" (116). Here the encyclical becomes less admirable, because more evasive and doubtful. Of course, it is far preferable that international disputes be settled by diplomacy rather than war, and we should strive to see that they are. Nevertheless, "[t]he Whiggish view that there [is] a rational solution to all problems and all that [is] needed [is] to find a modus vivendi comfortable to all parties" and that these parties "[are] rational ... [and] sincerely [want] to reach

1 John XXIII. Pacem in Terris.In: William J. Gibbons, S.J (ed.). Seven Great Encyclicals. New York (NY), 1963.

solutions"[2] – a view that Andrew Roberts attributes to Lord Halifax in the 1930s and which certain passages in *Pacem in Terris* appear to echo – is naïve and hardly (Augustinian) Christian. Sometimes a party to a conflict is so wedded to a gravely unjust policy by fear or greed or a lust for domination or racist contempt that he will not be dissuaded from it by sympathetic patience and sweet reason.

To make the point more concretely, I offer this example. At one point, the encyclical affirms that, if civil authorities allow anything contrary to the moral order, neither the laws made or authorisations granted can bind the conscience (51); and shortly afterwards it tells us that, if any government violates the rights of man, its orders completely lack juridical force (60). Suppose, then, that a state or an ethnic majority is gravely abusing human rights – say, committing murder on a massive scale – and suppose that diplomatic appeals to peace and justice fall on deaf ears. What is to be done? Or rather, since there is no end to the pious wringing of hands, what is to be done that would be *effective* in stopping the violation? If Pius XII's dictum were true, then peace is always to be preferred to war – even when peace involves mass atrocity. But the dictum, taken at face value, is not true. Peace is not simple, and much (for some) can be lost by it. Peace for the member-states of the United Nations Security Council (UNSC) in 1994 was not peace for the 800,000 Tutsis being hacked to death in Rwanda; and peace for the European Union (EU) and NATO in 1995 was not peace for the 7,000 Muslim men and boys slaughtered at Srebrenica.

As peace is more morally ambiguous than *Pacem in Terris* allows, so the prospect of global government is more utopian. Pope John tells us that international agreement is no longer able to meet the requirements of the universal common good (135), and that what is needed is a public authority with "world-wide power" (137, 145). This should come about by consent, not force, since "there would be reason to fear that a supranational or work-wide public authority, imposed by force by the more powerful political communities, might be or might become an instrument of one-sided interests; and even if this should not happen, it would be difficult for it to avoid all suspicion of partiality in its actions" (138). In this paper I intend to show why global government is both utopian and undesirable, why the development of international law is preferable, why this will continue to be hindered by conflicting national interests and interpretations, but why it is nevertheless possible.

2 Roberts, Andrew. The Holy Fox. A Life of Lord Halifax. London, 1992, p. 115.

## *2. Global government: both utopian and undesirable*

International order can be based either on global government or international law. In the latter case, nation-states recognise certain norms and consent to be ruled by them. They might also consent to the enforcement of such norms against law-breakers – currently, through the UNSC – or they might not. If they do so consent, then they will have to provide the military means, since the United Nations (UN) itself possesses no standing military forces. In the case of global government, however, the enforcement of international law would be out of the hands of individual nation-states and at the command of a trans-national body with its own (military) law enforcement agency. In other words, there would be a global state analogous to a nation-state. I think that such a global state is at once utopian and undesirable.

It is utopian for two related reasons, one historical and one cultural. In Europe, national judicial and policing systems came into being because they were imposed, usually coercively, by strong royal central government. For sure, the history of the formation of the federal United States (US) and of the confederal European Union suggests that policing coherence can be negotiated, and need not always be coerced. However, in the case of the US such negotiation was made possible by a very high degree of cultural homogeneity, by the short histories of the individual constituent colonies, and by the recent experience of common endeavour in fighting the British. The much longer histories of the member states of the EU, their much more limited cultural similarity, and the lack (so far) of the unifying experience of a *common* struggle for survival has meant that the very nature of the desired unity remains contested, and the process of unification has been much more prolonged and might never be as complete. In the absence of a single state that is able and willing to use force to create and sustain a comprehensively global empire, therefore, we can expect that the deep cultural differences between the West and the likes of China, India, and even Russia – differences that have been entrenched by centuries and even millennia of largely separate historical development – will continue to hinder agreement on the creation of a standing trans-national police force, and on the cession to a global government of the authority to deploy it.

However, even if the prospect of a global state were not utopian, its realisation would still be undesirable. Popular confidence in government requires that rulers are not too distant from the ruled, that the former are sensitive to the particular circumstances and needs of the latter. The recurrent phenomenon of political disturbance when groups feel that their interests are not sufficiently considered by government, the growth of the movement for democratic representation, the disintegration of formal global empires, and the current popular disillusionment with the European Union all bear witness to that. Confidence in government also requires that the different groups of the ruled trust each other – and the fairness of the political system that arbitrates their rival interests – sufficiently to tolerate moments of political frustration and defeat. In a global state, however, the geographical and cultural remoteness of rulers from the ruled, and of the different groups of the ruled from each other, would make such confidence and trust impossible to elicit and sustain. What is more, a global state would have a monopoly of armed force, which would make it vulnerable to tyranny; and this tyranny, being global, would be without rival and therefore without significant challenge.

### *3. Why international law is preferable*

The advantage of an international order based on international law and international institutions lies in its contingency upon the consent of nation-states. This has the obvious benefit of preventing the overwhelming concentration of global power and, provided that the states themselves are democratically accountable, of enabling the international order to elicit and maintain sufficient popular support, or at least consent. Given that Protestant Christianity was born in reaction against what was perceived to be the overweening power of the Pope and of the Holy Roman Empire, it is probably not a coincidence that there is at least one Protestant tradition that has consistently championed an *inter*-national order over a *trans*-national one since the mid-19th century.

I speak of my own (British) Anglican tradition. Thus, notwithstanding his membership of a world-wide British empire, in 1869 F. D. Maurice affirmed "the sanctity of national life";[3] distinguished a nation's reverence for its own language, laws, and government from a contempt for foreigners;[4] envisaged Christ's kingdom as "a kingdom for all nations" and not a "world-empire";[5] and argued that war is lawful only as "a struggle for Law against Force; for the life of a people as expressed in their laws, their language, their government, against any effort to impose on them a law, a language, a government which is not theirs".[6] Such views survived the First

3 Maurice, F.D. Social Morality. London, 1893, p. 183. These lectures were first published in 1869.
4 Maurice, Social Morality, p. 191.
5 Maurice, Social Morality, p. 180.
6 Maurice, Social Morality, p. 179.

World War. In his 1928 Henry Scott Holland Memorial Lectures, William Temple affirmed the variety of nations against a non-national cosmopolitanism; and argued that a state has not only the right, but a duty, to defend itself against annihilation, because "each national community is a trustee for the world-wide community, to which it should bring treasures of its own; and to submit to political annihilation may be to defraud mankind of what it alone could have contributed to the general wealth of human experience."[7] A little later in his 1935-36 Gifford Lectures, Hensley Henson drew a sharp distinction between genuine patriotism, which is an extension of neighbourly love, and "self-centred, vainglorious nationalism": "Patriotism pictures humanity as a composite of many distinctive national types, enriched with the various achievements of history. Nationalism dreams of a subject world, an empire of its own wherein all men serve its interests and minister to its magnificence".[8] Most recently, this Protestant, Anglican affirmation of distinctive national life against global imperialism or cosmopolitanism has found expression in the thought of Oliver O'Donovan. In his *The Desire of the Nations: Rediscovering the Roots of Political Theology* (1986), O'Donovan invokes biblical authority in favour of an international order that is unified by universal law rather than by universal, imperial government, and which is constituted by a plurality of nations, each with their own cultural integrity.[9] Unlike empire, "[l]aw holds equal and independent subjects together without allowing one to master the other".[10]

### *4. Why the development of international law will continue to be hindered by conflicting moral views, national interests, and legal interpretations*[11]

I believe that the gradual, piecemeal development of international law and institutions is preferable to the creation of a global state and government as a means of managing conflict. Nevertheless, here too we should avoid unrealistic optimism of the sort that I detect in Mary Ellen O'Connell's thought.

---

7 Temple, William. Christianity and the State, Henry Scott Holland Memorial Lectures 1928. London, 1928, pp. 172, 156.

8 Henson, Hensley. Christian Morality: Natural, Developing, Final, Gifford Lectures 1935-36. Oxford, 1936, p. 269.

9 O'Donovan, Oliver. The Desire of the Nations: Rediscovering the Roots of Political Theology. Cambridge, 1986, pp. 70-73.

10 O'Donovan, Desire of Nations, p. 236.

11 Much of this section and the following ones has been drawn and slightly adapted from Chapter 6 of my In Defence of War. Oxford, 2013, pp. 219-28, 231-5, 237-9, 240-3.

She describes international law as "the closest thing we have to a neutral vehicle for taking on the world's most complex issues and pressing problems".[12] She writes enthusiastically of increasing worldwide participation in the formation of the law, and in the discovery of international values. She endorses Abdullahi An-Na'im and Christopher Weeramantry's Habermasian quest for universal consensus through dialogue, commenting that they understand that international laws should be those "to which all possibly affected persons could agree as participants in rational discourses".[13] She acknowledges that international law enforcement still functions considerably through self-judging and self-help, but reckons that "with the growth of courts and tribunals this problematic aspect of the law is diminishing".[14] And while, in the search for higher norms and general principles, different courts and tribunals may yield conflicting results, she believes that these can be ordered in terms of the hierarchy of courts.[15] In the closing paragraph of her book she writes that the world's problems "will not be solved by armed conflict… People everywhere believe in law, believe in this alternative to force… International law reflects that the international community's shared goals today are peace, respect for human rights, prosperity, and the protection of the natural environment".[16]

I fully respect the aspiration; but I cannot quite share the faith. My Protestant appreciation of the value of nation-states will not allow it.[17] Nor will my Augustinian-cum-Niebuhrian 'realism' about the inevitable role in international relations of national interests and differential power. Nor will my scepticism about Habermas's sunny views of the possibility of homog-

12 O'Connell, Mary Ellen. The Power and Purpose of International Law: Insights from the Theory and Practice of Enforcement. New York (NY), 2008, p. 14.

13 Habermas, Jürgen. Between Facts and Norms. Cambridge (MA), 1997, p. 107; quoted by O'Connell, Power and Purpose, p. 141.

14 O'Connell, Power and Purpose, pp. 7-8.

15 O'Connell, Power and Purpose, p. 144.

16 O'Connell, Power and Purpose, p. 370.

17 I suspect that my disagreement with Mary Ellen O'Connell has something to do with our divergent ecclesial allegiances – she teaches at the University of Notre Dame, one of the United States' leading Roman Catholic institutions of higher learning; I am an Anglican clergyman. This possibility first occurred to me when reading her statement, quoting Alfred Rubin, that the international authority of the Pope and the Holy Roman Emperor declined because of "the Reformation's perception of the Church as a human institution with fallible officers" (O'Connell, Power and Purpose, p. 23), and that just war doctrine "broke down when the authority of the Church was lost to determine the justness of any cause" (O'Connell, Power and Purpose, p. 148n.192). It strikes me that that O'Connell looks to the UN to recover what was lost to international order at the Reformation, whereas my Inner Protestant regards the Church and the UN with equal scepticism.

enously rational consensus.[18] I do not think that we can expect international society – even as it manifests itself in international courts – to be free of intractable moral disagreement and political conflict.[19] I do not deny that the more the international community can agree on legal norms to govern international behaviour, the better. But what those abstract norms are taken to mean, and what they are taken to require practically in concrete circumstances, will often differ according to the moral views and political interests of nation-states. Consensus commonly covers a multitude of rival rational construals.

### *5. The case of legal controversy over Kosovo*

The best way to show this is by way of a particular example. Take, then, the case of the controversy over the 1999 military intervention in Kosovo by the North Atlantic Treaty Organisation (NATO). The most basic objection levelled by critics of NATO's intervention was that, lacking authorisation by the Security Council, it presumed to run rough-shod over international law, thereby weakening the law's authority and setting a precedent for any sufficiently powerful state to invade another's sovereign territory on moral grounds of its own choosing. As a result, it was argued, the security of states everywhere had been weakened and relations between them made more distrustful. NATO's high-handed action had made the world a considerably more dangerous place.

That, however, was only one view, for the legal status of NATO's action was – and is – a point of controversy, on which eminent experts in international law have taken opposing sides.[20] There is no doubt that the UN Charter forbids the unilateral use of force, except in self-defence; and that it

18 For an explanation of why I regard Habermas' aspiration to universal consensus as naïve, see "Not Translation, but Conversation: Theology in Public Debate about Euthanasia" and "Conclusion" in Nigel Biggar and Linda Hogan (eds.) Religious Voices in Public Places. Oxford 2009, esp. pp. 162-73, 191-3, 312-24.

19 According to O'Connell's account, it seems that I am more or less aligned here with the New Haven School of International Law in its "skepticism about the possibility of cabining law from policy or politics, as well as scepticism about the possibility of objectivity in the law" (O'Connell, Power and Purpose, p. 70).

20 For example, on 10 May 1999 at the International Court of Justice in The Hague Ian Brownlie argued on behalf of the Government of the Federal Republic of Yugoslavia that NATO's action was illegal, while his counterpart at the London School of Economics, Christopher Greenwood, argued the opposite on behalf of the Government of the United Kingdom.

restricts all other use of force to what is specifically mandated by the UNSC for the maintenance of international security and peace. Controversy arises, however, over whether or not this is the last word on the matter of armed intervention for humanitarian purposes. On the one hand, Ian Brownlie, former Professor of Public International Law at Oxford University, thought that it is. He argued that the Charter's position is clear and that it remains unqualified. In support of his argument he made the following points: that the preparatory work of the Charter indicates unequivocally that intervention for special motives was ruled out; that the Charter's position was confirmed in 1970 by the Declaration on Principles of International Law concerning Friendly Relations and Cooperation in its restatement of "the principle concerning the duty not to intervene in matters within the domestic jurisdiction of any State"; and that there is no evidence of the development of a doctrine of humanitarian intervention in customary international law. To demonstrate this last point, Brownlie cited statements made between 1971 and 1999 by seven legal authorities of various nationalities, including (most powerfully) a British Foreign Office document that contains this passage:

> In fact, the best case that can be made in support of humanitarian intervention is that it cannot be said to be unambiguously illegal.... But the overwhelming majority of contemporary legal opinion comes down against the existence of a right of humanitarian intervention, for three main reasons: first, the UN Charter and the corpus of modern international law do not seem specifically to incorporate such a right; secondly, state practice in the past two centuries, and especially since 1945, at best provides only a handful of genuine cases of humanitarian intervention, and, on most assessments, none at all; and finally, on prudential grounds, that the scope for abusing such a right argues strongly against its creation.... In essence, therefore, the case against making humanitarian intervention an exception to the principle of non-intervention is that its doubtful benefits would be heavily outweighed by its worth in terms of international law.[21]

On the other hand, against this position it can be argued that the UN Universal Declaration of Human Rights (1948), and subsequent treaties on the maintenance of human rights, have subjected the internal conduct of sovereign states to international norms: "From their inception these texts were regarded as a significant attack in the shell of state sovereignty".[22] It is doubtful, however, that they establish a right of unilateral intervention

21 Foreign Policy Document No. 148, The British Year Book of International Law, 57 (1986), p. 619. Brownlie's argument as a whole may be found in the Record of the public session of the International Court of Justice, 10 May 1999, to hear the case of Yugoslavia v. Belgium et al. concerning the legality of the use of force.

22 Hehir, J. Bryan. Just War Theory in a Post-Cold War World. In: *Journal of Religious Ethics*, 20/1, Fall 1992, p. 244.

in defence of the rights they affirm.[23] Such a right might be inferred from Article 1 of the Genocide Convention (1948), where the signatories "undertake to prevent and punish" genocide. However, arguably, this is then qualified by Article 8, according to which contracting parties "may call upon" the UN to take action under its Charter. Certainly, it is generally taken for granted that all subsequent treaties are to be read as subordinate to the Charter.

Nevertheless, there remains good reason to doubt whether the Charter's rule of non-intervention should be understood as absolute, applying always and everywhere. Like any other human document, the Charter's inception had an historical context – one in which particular concern about certain kinds of intervention was predominant. Like any others, its rules draw their specific meaning from certain typical cases. In 1945 the typical cases of intervention were expansionist and (neo)-colonialist. This is borne out in the aforementioned 1970 Declaration on Principles of International Law, whose commentary on the principle of non-intervention specifies its meaning in these terms:

> No State may … coerce another State in order to obtain from it the subordination of the exercise of its sovereign rights and to secure advantage of any kind.… Every State has an inalienable right to choose its political, economic, social and cultural systems, without interference in any form by another State.[24]

So far, as Brownlie claimed, this confirms the UN Charter's position. But it also develops it by making specific mention of a case that is unlikely to have been in the minds of the Charter's authors in 1945:

> … no State shall organise, assist, foment, finance, incite or tolerate subversive, terrorist or armed activities directed toward the violent overthrow of the regime of another State.[25]

If the meaning of the Charter can be developed in the light of a new case, surely it can also be revised by one. Is it not highly improbable that the Charter's signatories, acting in the immediate aftermath of the Holocaust, envisaged a case where a state is perpetrating genocide against a minority

23 *Pace* Hehir, who seems to assert such a unilateral right: "…the UN texts affirm an obligation on the part of states to defend human rights in states found guilty of persistent and gross violations of rights" (Hehir, Just War Theory).

24 Quoted by Brownlie before the International Court of Justice, 10 May 1999. See Section III of his speech.

25 Quoted by Brownlie before the International Court of Justice, 10 May 1999. See Section III of his speech.

within its own borders, and is thereby posing a threat to international peace and security, but where the UN is powerless either to act itself or to authorise another body to act instead, because a single member of the Security Council vetoes action for reasons of regional politics? And is it not highly probable that they agreed to outlaw unilateral intervention on the (idealistic) assumption that the UN would be able both to recognise genocide when it saw it, and to decide to act against it – by force of arms, if need be?[26] If this is not so, then the signatories to the Charter must be deemed to have agreed that in a case where the next Hitler decides upon a Final Solution for a minority group within the borders of his own state, cannot be dissuaded from this policy by diplomatic or economic pressure, and restrains himself from invading a neighbour; and where the politics of the Security Council preclude sufficient unanimity to enable armed intervention by an authorised body; then international law would forbid any state to intervene instead. Those who do not find this supposition plausible (and I am among them) have good reason, therefore, to regard the case of NATO's military action in Kosovo as an exception to the UN Charter's rule prohibiting unilateral intervention, rather than a transgression of it.

Whatever the intentions of the original signatories to the UN Charter, it is clear that many of their successors recognise that, under present circumstances (where the power of the UN to enforce international law is so weak and trammelled), an unconditional prohibition of unauthorised humanitarian intervention is intolerable. This is evidenced in part by the tendency of international lawyers and diverse states to undertake "creative exegesis"[27] of international law. So, for example, while it is true that India did eventually justify its intervention in East Pakistan in 1971 in terms of a strained claim

---

26 Richard Lillich made this historical-contextual point in an exchange with Ian Brownlie as far back as 1974, when he wrote that "[d]octrinal analysis of Article 2(4), much of it written shortly after the Charter's adoption or based upon attitudes and expectations formed during the immediate post-war period, frequently fails to mention that, to the extent that states consciously relinquished the right to use forcible self-help, they took action under the assumption that the collective implementation measures envisaged by Chapter VII soon would be available. Yet even staunch supporters of the collective approach, such as Judge Jessup, admitted that unilateral humanitarian interventions might be permissible if the United Nations lacked the capacity to act speedily" ("Humanitarian Intervention: A Reply to Ian Brownlie and a Plea for Constructive Alternatives". In: J.N. Moore (ed.). Law and Civil War in the Modern World [1974]; reprinted in Mary Ellen O'Connell (ed.). International Law and the Use of Force: Cases and Materials. New York (NY), 2005, p. 309.

27 The phrase is Tom J. Farer's in A Paradigm of Legitimate Intervention. In: Lori Fisler Damrosch (ed.). Enforcing Restraint: Collective Intervention in Internal Conflicts. New York (NY)1993, pp. 330, 340.

to self-defence,[28] she did so only for the political reason of winning support from the Security Council. Her preferred, original justification was humanitarian,[29] and the international community's reluctance to countenance it moved the Indian ambassador to berate other members of the Security Council. "What ... has happened to our conventions on human rights, self-determination, and so on?", he challenged on one occasion; and on another, "What has happened to the justice part [of the UN Charter]?".[30] Further evidence of dissatisfaction with reading international law simply in terms of the express statements of treaty law is furnished by the wide acceptance in the 1990s of humanitarian interventions that were not explicitly authorised by the Security Council – this 'wide acceptance' being expressed in the form either of a supportive Security Council resolution in prospect, or of a refusal by a majority of the Security Council to issue a condemnatory resolution in retrospect. Two examples of the former are the Anglo-American intervention in northern Iraq in 1991 to save the Kurds, and the imposition of a no-fly zone in southern Iraq to aid the Shi'ite Muslims.[31] An example of the latter is the Council's refusal, by twelve votes to three, of Russia's proposed resolution condemning NATO's intervention in Kosovo in 1999.[32]

---

28 Proponents of a legal basis for unauthorised humanitarian intervention commonly claim India's 1971 intervention as a supporting case of state practice, and so of customary law. Opponents commonly point out that India's primary ground of justification was self-defence, not humanitarian intervention (e.g., Chesterman, Simon. Hard Cases Make Bad Law: Law, Ethics, and Politics in Humanitarian Intervention.In: Anthony F. Lang (ed.). Just Intervention. Washington (D.C.), 2003, p. 49), and that this ground was weak (e.g., White, Nigel D. Democracy Goes to War: British Military Deployments under International Law. Oxford, 2009, p. 209). What opponents fail to point out is that self-defence was only offered *faute de mieux*, politically speaking.

29 Fisher, David. Morality and War: Can War be Just in the Twenty-first Century? Oxford, 2011, p. 225.

30 UN Security Council Resolutions, 1606th Meeting, 4 December 1971, and 1608th Meeting, 6 December 1971; quoted in Fisher, Morality and War, p. 225.

31 Stanley Hoffman wonders whether the protection of the Kurds might have been "a simple extension of the classical security operation against Iraq, that would have never have occurred if Iraq had not invaded Kuwait", rather than the application of a new principle of humanitarian intervention on behalf of oppressed minorities (The Ethics and Politics of Humanitarian Intervention. Notre Dame (IN), 1996, p. 28). While it was, no doubt, diplomatically convenient to have the intervention ride on the coat-tails of the Security Council's authorisation of the Allies' defence of Kuwait against Iraq, it is hard to see how it could plausibly be described as an 'extension' of that defence.

32 In their highly tendentious article, "Has US power destroyed the UN?", Simon Chesterman and Michael Byers say that Russia's proposal was defeated "in large part" by the votes of the five NATO countries then on the Council (*London Review of Books*, 29 April 1999, p. 29). They discreetly omit to mention the role of the

There is, therefore, a widespread view that international treaty law, strictly read, prohibits what it should not. Implied in this is an appeal to a moral authority that transcends treaty-texts – proximately customary law, ultimately natural law. Since dissatisfaction with a strict reading of treaty law is not universal, and since evidence of the recognition of customary law in the history of state practice is controversial, the appeal to customary law carries limited social authority. Nevertheless, according to Christian just war thinking, as expressed by that patriarch of international law, Hugo Grotius, the appeal is entirely rational. In cases of *iudicium cessans*, where public authority fails to enforce the law against grave and massive injustice, the natural unilateral right to oppose it by force revives – other, prudential, things being equal.[33] In addition, sceptical readings of the history of state practice are vitiated by the simplistic assumption that where national interests are at play, humanitarian motives must be either absent or spurious. The appeal to customary law is rationally stronger and more authoritative than many recognise.

The crucial question then arises as to whether this unwritten law should be allowed to interpret and qualify that which is inscribed in treaties such as the UN Charter.[34] I believe that it should, because otherwise international law would become so rigid as to be incapable of learning from situations that its original authors never envisaged, and of revising itself accordingly – and that would certainly detract from its authority. If customary law is permitted to play this qualifying role, then NATO's intervention in Kosovo has a reasonable claim to legality.

---

other *seven* votes cast against Russia by non-NATO states. Quite how a minority of five votes can inflict a defeat 'in large part' is a puzzle.

33 Grotius, Hugo. Rights of War and Peace, 3 vols.Richard Tuck (ed.). Indianapolis (IN) 2005, II.XX.VIII.5, p. 970: "[T]he antient [sic] liberty, which the law of nature at first gave us, remains still in force where there are no courts of justice", or when they malfunction – for example, "when complaint having been made to the judge, he does not render justice in a certain time"; ibid., II.XX.IX.5, p. 975: "even in this punishment [for the satisfaction of the offended party] … there remain some footsteps of the antient [sic] right in those places, and among those persons, who are not subject to any established courts of judicature; and even among those too who are so subject, in some particular cases". The phrase '*iudicium cessans*' derives from Grotius: "… in a private war, the right of defence is as it were, only momentary, and ceases as soon as one can apply to a judge. Whereas a public war, arising only between those that acknowledge no common judge, or when the exercise of justice is interrupted [*ubi cessant iudicia*]; the right of defence has here some continuance, and is perpetually maintained, by fresh injuries and damages received" (Grotius, II.I.XVI, p. 416 and note).

34 This is the basic point of disagreement between Brownlie (who denied it) and Greenwood (who affirmed it). For Brownlie's position, see his speech before the International Court of Justice. For Greenwood's, see his article Yes, but is the war legal? In: The Observer, 28 March 1999, p. 22 and the report on Law and Right in *The Economist*, 3 April 1999, pp. 19-20.

### 6. *Intractable legal controversy and its empirical, political, and moral roots*

Now let us move from the particulars of the controversy over Kosovo to make some general observations about the nature of controversy over the interpretation of international law. On the one hand, Ian Brownlie argued that international law's prohibition of unauthorised military intervention for 'humanitarian' purposes is unequivocal. In support, as we have seen, he cited the text of the UN Charter, the Declaration on Principles of International Law, and the statements of a variety of national legal authorities over a period of almost thirty years. He also denied that the history of state practice evidences an informal international consensus about a unilateral right to intervene, which could be held to constitute customary international law.[35] On the other hand, Richard Lillich argued that the doctrine of humanitarian intervention can claim the authority of jurists such as Grotius and Vattel; that pre-Charter history furnishes ample evidence of relevant state practice; that the Charter does not "specifically abolish the traditional doctrine"; that the Charter attributes *two* main purposes to the post-war international legal regime, the maintenance of peace *and* the protection of human rights; that humanitarian intervention serves the latter purpose; and that it only offends against Article 2(4), if it threatens the 'territorial integrity' or 'political independence' of the state subject to intervention.[36] Brownlie implied that such a "flexible and teleological interpretation of treaty texts" is weak;[37] while Lillich approvingly cited another commentator's view of Brownlie's interpretation as "an arid textualist approach".[38]

35 In his 1974 exchange with Richard Lillich, Brownlie argued that before 1945 history can be found to yield only "one possible genuinely altruistic action", namely, the intervention of 1860 in Syria to prevent further massacres of Maronite Christians. The collective intervention in Greece in 1827, he said, did not use a legal justification; and the American intervention in Cuba in 1898 was justified by the Joint Resolution of Congress in terms of American interests. In the period between the UN Charter and 1974 Brownlie found state practice of humanitarian intervention "totally lacking" (Brownlie, Ian. Humanitarian Intervention. In Mary Ellen O'Connell (ed.), International Law and the Use of Force: Cases and Materials. New York (NY), 2005, p. 301).

36 Lillich, Richard. Humanitarian Intervention: A Reply to Ian Brownlie. In: Mary Ellen O'Connell (ed.) International Law and the Use of Force: Case and Materials. New York (NY), pp. 307-8. As evidence of pre-Charter state practice of humanitarian intervention, Lillich cited collective action against Ottoman suppression of the Greeks in 1827; against Ottoman persecution of Christian Cretans in 1866-68; against Turkish oppression in the Balkans 1877-78; and against Turkish oppression in Macedonia 1903-8.

37 Brownlie, Humanitarian Intervention, p. 300.

38 Lillich, Humanitarian Intervention: A Reply to Ian Brownlie, p. 308.

The struggle between textualist and contextualist lawyers for the true meaning of international law resembles nothing so much as the struggle between conservative and liberal theologians for the true meaning of the Bible. In both cases, while the text itself does constrain what can plausibly be attributed to it, the variety of plausible interpretations is considerably determined by extra-textual factors. In the case of the interpretation of international law, prominent among these factors are the empirical, political, and moral assumptions that legal interpreters bring to the texts of treaties and to the 'text' of the history of state practice. So we observe that Brownlie assumed a generally cynical view of the motives of governments, when he wrote of "the near impossibility of discovering an aptitude of governments in general or carefully moderated, altruistic, and genuine interventions to protect human rights"[39] and that "[t]he whole field [of humanitarian intervention] is driven by political expediency and capriciousness".[40] Along the same lines, Simon Chesterman judges that "[t]he capriciousness of state interest is a theme that runs throughout the troubled history of humanitarian intervention",[41] and the fact that "[m]ilitary action under … [the Security Council's] auspices has taken place only when it was in the national interests of a state that was prepared to act" he deems "a troubling trend through the 1990s".[42] That genuinely moral action is altruistic and entirely lacking in self-interest is a particular, quasi-Kantian moral view, which, as I have argued elsewhere, is a false one.[43] Similarly, it is not necessary to attribute the selectivity of humanitarian intervention to grubby expediency and capriciousness. Sometimes the decision to intervene in one place rather than another can be an expression of the moral virtue of prudence.[44]

Brownlie also expressed scepticism about the efficacy of military action, arguing that civil conflicts "cannot be 'solved' by a use of force", and that those advocating military intervention "need to produce more evidence" that such action achieves benefits greater than the costs it imposes.[45] It is clear enough that he doubted that such evidence can be produced, because he did not believe that intervention is worthwhile. Whatever its truth, this is not a textual claim but an empirical one – and an empirical claim that involves an inarticulate and controversial moral ranking of the values that comprise

39 Brownlie, Humanitarian Intervention, p. 303.
40 Brownlie, Humanitarian Intervention, p. 304.
41 Chesterman, Hard Cases Make Bad Law, p. 47.
42 Chestermann, Hard Cases Make Bad Law, p. 55.
43 See Biggar, In Defence of War, pp. 231-3.
44 See Biggar, In Defence of War, pp. 233-5.
45 Brownlie, Humanitarian Intervention, p. 304.

costs and benefits (for example, bare lives, a just political environment, and the maintenance of international order), together with an opaque and spurious 'calculation' of them. Such scepticism about military action also fuels O'Connell's opposition to unilateral humanitarian intervention, which stiffens her interpretation of international law. She reckons that one of the two main objections to military intervention for humanitarian purposes is "the severe pragmatic difficulty of protecting human rights through war".[46] She suggests that the desire to see more military force used to enforce human rights "may result from an unrealistic understanding of the good that can actually be accomplished by major armed force".[47] "[O]ne can question", she writes, "whether the US attack [on Libya in 1986] was proportional".[48] She refers to "[t]he deaths and devastation caused by the bombing [of Yugoslavia by NATO in 1999] and the terrible aftermath, during which Serbs and UN Peacekeepers were killed".[49] And she suggests that the continued use of massive aerial bombardment after the fall of the Taliban regime in 2001 "was arguably disproportionate".[50] The issue that Brownlie and O'Connell raise is both appropriate and important, but it is a moral-empirical issue, not a legal-textual one. Moreover, as is inevitable, their judgements of proportionality are necessarily less-than-scientific, highly controversial, and difficult to substantiate.[51] O'Connell herself signals this by the consistently tentative manner of her assertions: "may result", "one can question", "arguably".

The interpretation of international law offered by Richard Lillich is, of course, no less influenced by extra-textual considerations. However, unlike the textualists, Lillich thought that international law *should* be interpreted with reference to such factors. Thus he quoted with approval Michael Reisman's comment that Brownlie lives "within the paper world of the Charter",[52] and he complained that "there is little evidence that Brownlie has contemplated the costs in terms of life and dignity his construction of the Charter demands"[53] and that he makes no mention of the problem of "the

46 O'Connell, Power and Purpose, p. 181. The other main objection is that intervention weakens the legal regime for peace.

47 O'Connell, Power and Purpose, p. 148. See also O'Connell, Mary Ellen. Responsibility to Peace. 27 Dec. 2007, http://www.sef-bonn.org/de/veranstaltungen/index.php.

48 O'Connell, Power and Purpose, p. 183.

49 O'Connell, Power and Purpose, p. 180.

50 O'Connell, Power and Purpose, p. 188.

51 For a fuller discussion of the meaning and permissiveness of the criterion of proportionality, see Biggar, In Defence of War, Chapter 4.

52 Lillich, Humanitarian Intervention, p. 313.

53 Lillich, Humanitarian Intervention, p. 311. Martti Koskenniemi agrees: a formalistic, strictly textual reading of international law "seems arrogantly insensitive to the

obvious procedural defects" of the UN and is "wholly devoid" of constructive alternatives.[54]

While the extension of consensus about international norms – which constitutes the development of international law – is to be warmly welcomed, we should not delude ourselves into supposing that this consensus will ever be absolute to the point of permanently transcending intractable conflicts of interpretation. The diversity of moral views and political interests is certainly a persistent feature of human life *in hoc saeculo*, and probably a permanent one. That is why, as Adam Roberts and Dominik Zaum have observed, "the era since 1945 has witnessed – alongside the new institutions of the United Nations and the multilateral diplomacy that it embodies – the continuation of all the classical institutions of the international system: great powers, alliances, spheres of interest, balances of power and bilateral diplomacy".[55] They judge the 2004 report of the UN High Level Panel on Threats, Challenges, and Change to be "hopelessly optimistic" in aspiring to set up a comprehensive security system through the UN,[56] which they regard as an "impossible ideal".[57] This is because the fault lies, not simply with the unruly behaviour of particular states or even with the right to veto in the Security Council,[58] but with "deep and enduring problems of world politics".[59] "The Security Council", they write, "is not an impartial judicial body, but a deeply political organisation",[60] whose members have "very different perspectives on the world and the threats it faces".[61]

---

humanitarian dilemmas involved" ("'The Lady Doth Protest Too Much': Kosovo and the Turn to Ethics in International Law". In: *The Modern Law Review*, 65/2, March 2002, p. 163.

54 Lillich, Humanitarian Intervention, p. 313.

55 Roberts, Adam and Zaum, Dominik. Selective Security: War and the United Nations Security Council since 1945. Adelphi Paper 395. London, 2008 p. 24.

56 Roberts and Zaum, Selective Security, p. 18.

57 Roberts and Zaum, Selective Security, p. 76.

58 They point out that no veto prevented the Security Council from addressing the Khmer Rouge's auto-genocide in Cambodia from 1975-9, and that Council members have sometimes acted in spite of a veto, e.g., over the Suez crisis in 1956 (Roberts and Zaum, Selective Security, p. 37).

59 Roberts and Zaum, Selective Security, p. 19.

60 Roberts and Zaum, Selective Security, p. 20.

61 Roberts and Zaum, Selective Security, p. 28. Edward Luck concurs: "As an innately political body composed of member states with individual interests ..., the [Security] Council's determinations about ... whether a government's ... suppression of some of its population ... threaten[s] its neighbors or more distant states ... may often be controversial" (UN Security Council: Practice and Promise, Global Institutions series. London, 2006, pp. 82-3).

Accordingly, on the one hand, many regimes (such as those in Russia and China) continue to insist that *only* the Security Council may authorise military intervention, and that only directly authorised intervention is legal. They insist on this because their overriding concern is to limit the power of the West, especially the US; because they are not much moved by humanitarian concerns; and because they do not trust the grounds on which others might want to intervene, fear that they themselves might become subject to such intervention, and therefore want to control it as much as possible. On the other hand, there are other states that are not content with an international system that allows the politics of the Security Council, and especially the casting of a veto, to stymie effective action, sometimes military, against a regime's grossly atrocious behaviour. The recent fate of *The Responsibility to Protect* report in international debate gives no ground for hope that this crucial point of disagreement is going to be resolved any time soon.[62]

### *7. Stepping back from scepticism, looking forward with chastened hope*

There are, I think, good reasons to be sceptical of idealistic claims for the development of international law and institutions – as well as idealistic hopes for the creation of a global state. Nevertheless, there are also grounds to be hopeful about the prospect of the extension of international consensus, if not of its absolute completion. One of these grounds is the recent history of attempts to persuade the international community to formally endorse the doctrine of the Responsibility to Protect.

Upon his appointment as Secretary General of the UN in 1997, Kofi Annan began to press the international community to achieve a greater measure of collective clarity over humanitarian intervention by explicitly affirming what he asserted to be "this developing international norm in favour of intervention to protect civilians from wholesale slaughter", and by agreeing rules for its effective application under international law. "The choice", he told the UN's General Assembly in September 1999, "... must not be between [Security] Council unity and inaction in the face of genocide – as in the case of Rwanda, on the one hand; and Council division, and regional action, as in the case of Kosovo, on the other".[63] Two years later Annan's ef-

62 See Bellamy, Alex J. Responsibility to Protect: The Global Effort to End Mass Atrocities. Cambridge, 2009.

63 Quoted by Luck, Edward C. In: UN Security Council: Practice and Promise. Global Institutions series. London, 2006, p. 85.

forts received major backing, when the report of the Canadian government's International Commission on Intervention and State Sovereignty (ICISS) articulated a doctrine of a 'responsibility to protect' ('R2P').[64]

Unfortunately, progress in winning international endorsement was hindered by the highly controversial invasion of Iraq in 2003, which stiffened opposition to any loosening of the reins on unilateral action. As a consequence, the report of the Secretary General's High Level Panel on United Nations Reform in 2004, the Secretary General's own report of September 2005, and the Outcome Document of the 2005 UN World Summit all reaffirmed the prohibition on the use of force without prior Security Council authorisation, except in the case of armed attack;[65] and the Panel expressly rejected the claim that force can sometimes be legitimate, even if unlawful.[66]

On the other hand, progress, while hindered, was nevertheless made. The World Summit did declare that "[e]ach individual state has the responsibility to protect its population from genocide, war crimes, ethnic cleansing and crimes against humanity", and the gathered heads of state and government did pledge that "we accept that responsibility and will act in accordance with it", promising to take collective action in a timely and decisive manner through the Security Council, should a national authority "manifestly fail" in its responsibility to protect.[67]

The question of what may or should happen, when the UNSC next fails to authorise collective action, has been left hanging. International consensus about the norms of international relations therefore remains a long way short of completion. Nevertheless, it *has* advanced. So, if the creation of a global state is both utopian and undesirable, further progress in the development of international law is not only desirable, but also possible. Such gradual development will not abolish conflict, but it will help to contain it. It will not establish peace on earth once and for all, but it will extend it.

64 Report of the International Commission on Intervention and State Sovereignty, The Responsibility to Protect. Ottawa: International Development Research Centre, 2001.

65 O'Connell, Power and Purpose, p. 227. Thus they rejected the ICISS's recommendation that, where the Security Council rejects a proposal or fails to deal with it in a reasonable time, unilateral action by a regional or sub-regional organisation under Chapter VII of the UN Charter would be permissible, subject to its seeking subsequent authorisation from the Security Council (Responsibility to Protect, XIII).

66 O'Connell, Power and Purpose, p. 147. This claim had been made by the Swedish government's Independent International Commission on Kosovo in its report in 2000 (O'Connell, Power and Purpose, p. 225).

67 Luck, UN Security Council, p. 85.

# Law and Security of Law

*Dietmar von der Pfordten*

## *1. Introduction*

How can we reach peace through law?

Peace is the main *aim* which human beings try to attain in their lives and thus in their actions. Law is one important *mean* to reach this central aim of peace. But how can law do this? One decisive way by which law can foster peace is via the *security of law*, especially the *security of international law*. So in order to reach peace through law one has – among other things – to augment the security of law, especially the security of international law. But what is this, the security of law, and how can we understand it?

*Human actions* are necessarily directed towards *aims*. Therefore, they are fundamentally *intentional*. In order to attain these aims they use *means*. So, human actions are comprised of at least two necessary elements:[1] an *aim* and some *means* (broadly conceived) to realize this aim. *Peace* is one central aim of human actions. And we know a lot of very different means to attain this aim: trade, confidence building, disarmament, friendly relationships among nations, the abolishment of hunger and poverty, just terms of economic relations, the balance of powers, deterrence, democratic structures within states, international political institutions like the UN or the WTO etc., and last but not least: *law*. *"Law"* is understood here in the sense of *human law* only. So *natural law* or *ius cogens* in international law or with a more modern expression: *normative ethics* will not be meant by "law" in this text.

Peace can be generally improved by human law, e.g. by the codification of human rights standards in constitutions and treaties. Human law can be used as a means to keep or reach peace, e.g. via peace treaties. However, only one aspect of peace through law will be investigated in this article: the security of law, especially the security of international law.

One main part of the security of law is *effectiveness* (for other parts see point 6.). The effectiveness of all the above mentioned means to keep or

---

1 Concerning the necessity of an aim in every action see e.g. Aristotle. Nicomachean Ethics. Rackham, Harris (transl.). Cambridge (MA), 1968, 1094a1; Searle, John. Intentionality. An Essay in the Philosophy of Mind. Cambridge, 1983, p. 107.

reach peace is questionable and debated. And the same problems hold for law as a means to keep or reach the aim of peace. Especially concerning international law the security in the sense of effectiveness is often unsettled and open to question. We know of peace treaties which were able to keep peace effectively, like the peace treaties of Munster and Osnabruck in 1648, which ended the Thirty Years' War in Europe and led to the so called Peace of Westphalia. However, we also know of peace treaties which were not able to keep peace effectively e.g. the Munich agreement in 1938 between Hitler, Mussolini, Daladier and Chamberlain.

So the effectiveness of law as a means of the security of law to keep or reach peace seems to be quite empirical and contingent. Not completely, but to a large extent, it depends on the empirical and contingent connection with other means and facts – for example those mentioned above and others like the parties' compliance with legal obligations, the existence of hegemonic political aims, the economic situation which makes military armament possible or impossible etc. Because of its empirical and contingent character the question concerning the security of law and especially the effectiveness of law in connection with these other means is an empirical question which has to be answered by legal sociology and political science.

But isn't there also a philosophical i.e. necessary and conceptual dimension of the question concerning the security of law? Does not the *concept of law* essentially include some sort of security or at least effectiveness? To answer this question we have to look into the necessary properties of the phenomenon law i.e. the necessary conditions of the concept of law.

## *2. The Question regarding the Necessary Properties of Law*[2]

Law is necessarily a kind of *human action in the widest sense* (including its consequences, whether these are in fact intended or can at least be expected).[3] If law, by conceptual necessity, is a form of human action, then it can only be understood if one takes into consideration the necessary qualities of human actions mentioned above: aims and means.[4] So law is not only a mean in respect to the external aim of peace. It is in itself an action which contains *aims* and *means*. But which are those?

2 See for the following: von der Pfordten, Dietmar. What is Law? Aims and Means. In: *ARSP* 97, 2011, pp. 151-168; von der Pfordten, Dietmar. Rechtsphilosophie. Eine Einführung. München, 2013, pp. 53.

3 Radbruch, Gustav. Rechtsphilosophie. Dreier, Ralf/ Paulson, Stanley (Eds.). 2nd ed., Heidelberg, 2003, p. 11.

4 Grice, Paul. Meaning, in Studies in the Ways of Words. Cambridge, 1989, p. 219.

### 3. Aims and Means in Understanding the Law

In the history of legal philosophy, the views of the significance of law's aims and means have changed dramatically.

From the beginning of philosophy in ancient times up to the late Middle Ages, great emphasis was laid on quite specific and demanding aims in order to distinguish law from other phenomena. For Plato and Aristotle, the aim of law and politics was the *good*, explained as *justice,* and, especially for Aristotle, *eudaimonia* and the *common good.*[5] The means did not play a great role. Cicero stressed justice as the aim of the law, too.[6] Thomas Aquinas then defined law as: an ordinance of reason for the *common good*, made by him who has care of the community, and promulgated.[7] The aim, therefore, is the *common good.* However, Aquinas still mentions *justice*, especially in respect of the positive law.[8]

In the seventeenth century this emphasis on the specific aim of law vanished. The good, justice, eudaimonia and common welfare were no longer considered to be the main aims of law and politics. The means became more and more important. Thomas Hobbes proposed a reduced but still quite specific aim of law and politics: *self-preservation.*[9] Furthermore, he stated that law in general consists of commands.[10] John Locke assumed the *preservation of property* – understood in a wide sense to include life, liberty and ownership of material goods – as the main aim of law and politics.[11] Montesquieu saw *freedom* as the main aim of law.[12] And Kant defined law similarly with respect to a liberal and very limited aim: Law comprehends *the whole of the conditions under which the voluntary actions of any one person can be harmonized with the voluntary action of every other person, according to a universal law of freedom.*[13]

5 Plato. The Republic. Emlyn-Jones, Chris/ Preddy, William (Eds. and transl.). Cambridge (MA), 2013, 327a1, 433a; Aristotle. Nicomachean Ethics I 1, 1094a; V 1, 1129a; Politics. Rackham, Harris (transl.). Cambridge (MA), 1967, 1328a36.

6 Cicero. On the commonwealth and On the laws. Zetzel, James E.G. (ed.). Cambridge, 1999, I, 29.

7 Aquinas, Thomas. Summa Theologiae. Questions on God. Davies, Brian (ed.). Cambridge, 2006, II-I, qu. 90. Questioning the course of the Queastio, these four elements are developed. The final definition is at the end in the answer to article 4.

8 Aquinas, Thomas. Summa Theologiae, II-II, qu. 57 ff.

9 Hobbes, Thomas. Leviathan. Tuck, Richard (ed.). Cambridge, 1991, chap. 17, 1.

10 Hobbes, Thomas. Leviathan, chap 26, 1.

11 John Locke. Second Treatise on Government. Cambridge, 1991, §§ 3, 6, 7, 123, 124.

12 de Montesquieu, Charles-Louis. De l'Esprit des Lois. Paris, 1973, Book XI, XII.

13 Kant, Immanuel. Metaphysik der Sitten, Metaphysische Anfangsgründe der Rechtslehre. Akademie-Ausgabe. Berlin, 1969, § B.

For Hegel, too, the aim of law is *freedom*.[14] And the utilitarians still assumed a specific aim, but in a reduced form: *maximising happiness*, understood as a collective effort to promote the individual and contingent state of pleasure.[15] But in the following decades of the nineteenth and twentieth century scepticism concerning necessary aims, value relativism, and a general positivism in the philosophy of science led to a nearly complete dismissal of specific aims of the law and an almost exclusive reference to the means as the fundamental aspect of law. In England, John Austin characterised law as "sanctioned commands".[16] In Germany, Rudolf v. Jhering defined law in a purely formal way, namely as the valid coercive norms of the state.[17] For him, norms and coercion are the crucial means of law. However, Jhering also proposes an aim of law, if only a relative and rather unspecific one: securing the fundamental conditions for the existence of a society.[18]

Hans Kelsen did not identify any specific aim of the law. In his theory, law is distinguished from other social facts only by its specific means: by forming a hierarchical and dynamic system of coercive norms which confer validity on other, inferior norms with a basic norm as the necessary assumption and unifying ground of validity.[19] The same applies to the differentiation of law from other social orders like morals. Here, the specific means of law are the necessary use of coercion to guarantee obedience, and its quality of being a dynamic system, that is, the fact that the hierarchy of validity is not based upon correspondence in content but upon formal authorization.[20]

H. L. A. Hart, too, finds the distinguishing feature of modern, developed law, "the heart of a legal system", only in means, namely in a system of

14 Hegel, Georg Wilhelm Friedrich. Grundlinien der Philosophie des Rechts oder Naturrecht und Staatswissenschaft im Grundrisse. Frankfurt a. M., 1970, Works 7, § 40, 98: ‚Das Recht ist zuerst das unmittelbare Dasein, welches sich die Freiheit auf unmittelbare Weise gibt.', § 4, 46: ‚Der Boden des Rechts ist überhaupt das Geistige und seine nähere Stelle und Ausgangspunkt der Wille, welcher frei ist, so daß die Freiheit seine Substanz und Bestimmung ausmacht und das Rechtssystem das Reich der verwirklichten Freiheit, die Welt des Geistes aus ihm selbst hervorgebracht, als eine zweite Natur, ist.'

15 Bentham, Jeremy. The Principles of Morals and Legislation. Buffalo (NY), 1988, chap. 1, I, 1.

16 Austin, John. The Province of Jurisprudence Determined. Rumble, Wilfrid E. (ed.). Cambridge, 1995, pp. 12, 21-37.

17 v. Jhering, Rudolf. Der Zweck im Recht (1877). 3rd ed., Leipzig, 1893, vol. 1, p. 320.: ‚Recht ist der Inbegriff der in einem Staate geltenden Zwangsnormen.'

18 v. Jhering, Zweck im Recht (1877), p. 443. On p. 446, Jhering stresses the relativity of aims. On p. 511, both conditions are put together.

19 Kelsen, Hans. Reine Rechtslehre. 2nd ed., Wien, 1960, pp. 3, 196.

20 Kelsen, Reine Rechtslehre. p. 34.

primary and secondary rules.[21] He identifies three forms of secondary rules: rules of change, rules of adjudication and a rule of recognition. The rule of recognition is in particular the necessary means to identify the other rules of law.[22] An aim of law is mentioned by him only *en passant,* and it is only a very unspecific aim, which holds for many other social facts. Hart says: 'I think it quite vain to seek any more specific purpose which law as such serves beyond providing guides to human conduct and standards of criticisms of such conduct.'[23]

Joseph Raz, in his definition of law, omits the two-level requirement and adds "authority" as the decisive feature.[24] But "authority" is still another means – like norms, sanctions, and second-order rules. No one accepts authority as a final aim of law. Ronald Dworkin famously distinguished between rules and principles, which is, basically, a distinction in terms of means: ultimately, it is only a distinction between two types of rules: "all-or-nothing" rules on the one hand, and rules that are susceptible to deliberation on the other hand.[25]. But in his main work *Law's Empire*, he introduced, beside justice and fairness, a specific virtue or conviction of law makers: *integrity*.[26] He does not, however, propose that this virtue or conviction of law-makers is a necessary aim of law and hence a necessary condition of the concept of law. Integrity is only an "ideal" which ought to be accepted by political communities and law-makers like judges and legislators.[27]

One of the few philosophers of law in the twentieth century who identified a specific and decisive aim of law was Gustav Radbruch.[28] In a return to pre-modern roots, Radbruch proposed *justice* as the necessary aim or "idea" of law.[29] For him, justice (in a wide sense) encompasses three sub-

21 Hart, H.L.A. The Concept of Law. 2nd ed., Oxford, 1994, p. 98.
22 Hart, Concept of Law, p. 79.
23 Hart, Concept of Law, p. 249.
24 Raz, Joseph. Legal Positivism and the Sources of Law. In: Joseph Raz. The Authority of Law. Essays on Law and Morality. Oxford, 1979, p. 43: 'Put in a nutshell, it [law] is a system of guidance and adjudication claiming supreme authority within a certain society and therefore, where efficacious, also enjoying such effective authority.'
25 Dworkin, Ronald. Taking Rights Seriously. London, 1977.
26 Dworkin, Ronald. Law's Empire. Cambridge, 1986, pp. 166-167, 176.
27 Dworkin, Law's Empire, pp. 189, 214-215, 218.
28 His disciple Arthur Kaufmann follows him in the assumption of this aim. See Kaufmann, Arthur. Rechtsphilosophie. 2nd ed., München, 1997, chap. 9, p. 135. Hermann Kantorowicz, a friend of Radbruch, first gave a definition with an aim and then a definition lacking any aim: Kantorowicz, Hermann. The definition of law. Cambridge, 1958, p. 12: „Law is a body of rules aiming at the prevention or the orderly settlement of conflicts.“, p. 21: „A body of rules prescribing external conduct and considered justiciable.“
29 Radbruch, Rechtsphilosophie, p. 34.

aims:[30] justice as formal equality that is justice in a narrow sense, expediency (*Zweckmäßigkeit*), and the security/certainty of law (*Rechtssicherheit*). In the early pre-war version of his theory Radbruch holds that for judges security of law is sufficient to attain the aim of justice.[31] But then also justice in a narrow sense can be sufficient. So it seems to follow that security is not a necessary element of law in Radbruch's opinion.

The problem with Radbruch's explication of justice, in my view, is that legal security is quite concrete (being only a sub-aim or a means), while expediency is very abstract and unspecific. In fact, the latter merely refers to the necessary condition that we have found not only in law but also in every human action: attaining an aim. Also justice in the sense of formal equality – the first sub-aim of justice in a comprehensive sense – and maybe even justice in the general sense could be one such aim. So what we need is to identify a more specific aim. Radbruch's attempt to characterize justice in the general sense in terms of those three qualifications remains, in my view, quite unsatisfying. The reason for this is that his account combines quite different elements of the means-end-correlation without clarifying how they relate to that correlation. But what account could do better?

### *4. The Necessary Aim of Law: Mediation between Possibly Contrary Concerns*

My proposal is this: The conceptually necessary aim of law (and, thus, necessary feature of its concept) is

> the mediation between possibly contrary, conflicting concerns.[32]

For instance, statutes mediate between various general concerns of people, judges' holdings mediate between interests in particular conflicts, administrative acts mediate between the specific wishes of individual citizens and/or the interests of the general public, international treaties and international organizations mediate between the different interests of nations.

So we have four elements of the necessary aim of law: (1) at least two concerns or interests, (2) which are contrary/disparate, (3) the possibility that these concerns may conflict, and (4) a form of mediation. These elements need careful explanation:

---

30 Radbruch, Rechtsphilosophie, pp. 54, 73.

31 Radbruch, Rechtsphilosophie, p. 85

32 See von der Pfordten, What is Law? Aims and Means, pp. 151-168; von der Pfordten, Rechtsphilosophie, p. 53ff.

(1) Concerns or interests (for the present purposes, these concepts are used synonymously) are not reducible to an economic or egoistic will. An important concern or interest, for example, is that one's children be able to attend a good school. The concept "concern" is derived from more concrete properties: *strivings*, *needs*, *wishes* and the *aims* of individuals who can be thought to be bearers of interests. In order for the mediation of concerns to be legally relevant, the concerns in question must be sufficiently weighty.

(2) The concerns must in some way be contrary/disparate. If they are perfectly parallel there is no need for law to solve a conflict between them, as a conflict cannot arise between them. Nonetheless, the contrariness /disparity does not need to be actual, only its possibility suffices.

(3) Even if two concerns are contrary/disparate to each other, a conflict between them – or, more precisely: about them – may be impossible for other reasons. In that case, there is neither a possibility nor a reason for mediation. Consider the following example: A farmer wants rain, the tourist sunshine. For as long as local weather cannot be influenced, there cannot be a conflict between their contrary/disparate concerns. Mediation by law is neither possible nor necessary.

(4) There must be a weighing or considered decision between these possibly contrary/disparate concerns. That does not mean that law must be good or just in a perfectionist sense. The necessary condition is only that the entities which are of concern have to be taken into consideration in some way. If persons are murdered or their assassination is ordered – that is, if they are killed without a criminal inquiry or fair trial –, this cannot be law, because it does not mediate between conflicting concerns or at least ones that are contrary in nature.

In this sense, killings in war are not law, though, of course, they may be allowed from the point of view of international law or ethics, for instance, as a means of self-defence. Similarly, for conceptual reasons the total disfranchisement of certain social groups cannot be law. The qualification, for example, of an ancient slavery law depends upon whether the concerns of the slaves are taken into account, even if only to a minimal degree.

The conditions of law proposed here are relatively abstract and weak. Law does not have the fulfilment of all or even the main demands of morality or ethics as its necessary aim. But it does have a conceptually necessary aim, without which it is impossible to identify a social fact as law. We may call this aim "justice" in some weak sense. This is to be taken, however, not as a normative, ethical standard, but as a conceptually necessary constituent of the concept of law.

### *5. Other aims: Peace, Security?*

How about peace then? Peace is one main realisation of the more abstract aim of law that is the *mediation between possibly contrary/disparate, conflicting concerns*. Peace is a special form of the mediation between possibly contrary/conflicting concerns, a form, where *no violent means are used*. But as such a realisation and special form of the necessary aim of law, peace is contingent and therefore not a necessary element of the concept of law. So some law will realize peace, while another law will not, like the *jus ad bellum*, e.g. Art. 39-51 UN-Charta, and the *jus in bello*. The only thing we can add is that law in itself as a certain type of human speech act is not a violent mean. But it can be used to justify and foster the use of violent means.

Is security a necessary aim of law? I doubt this, at least in respect to security in the all-encompassing abstractness of the concept. We create and use some quite insecure laws in order to try to attain the aim of the mediation between possibly contrary conflicts. International treaties are the best example of such insecure means.

But perhaps some aspects of the all-encompassing concept of security are at least necessary means of the law. Therefore, we have to ask for some more concrete aspects of the security of law. One could distinguish at least six of these more concrete aspects: *categorical character*, *externality*, *formality*, *immanence*, *coercion/force/sanctions* and *effectiveness/effectivity*.

In order to reflect on these means we first have to answer more generally: Is not the state a necessary source of the law? This answer is important, because if the state is a necessary source of the law, then the security of law is somewhat automatically and therefore necessarily sustained by the power and the might of the state.

### *6. The State as Necessary Source of All Law?*

There was and is a tradition, starting with Hobbes and Spinoza and continued by Austin, v. Jhering, G. Jellinek and others,[33] which assumes that the state is the necessary source of all positive law. One outcome of this

33 Hobbes, Leviathan, chap. 26; de Spinoza, Baruch. Tractatus politicus, Oeuvres Bd. V, Paris 2005, III, § 1, 2; Austin, The Province of Jurisprudence Determined, p. 26; v. Jhering, Zweck im Recht (1877), p. 320; Jellinek, Georg. Allgemeine Staatslehre. 3rd ed., Kronberg/Ts, 1976.

doctrine is that the law of nations is not considered as law but as some sort of morals.[34]

Against this doctrine – which was criticized by many scholars, e.g. Eugen Ehrlich[35] – many non-state law creators can be named: churches and other religious communities, clubs, local communities, international organizations like sport or internet organizations which do not have state quality, the source of the lex mercatoria. It is empirically true that in modern times most of the law is created by states. But this empirical fact must not be taken as a conceptual necessity which could restrict law to the norms which are issued by states. The aim of law, that is the aim of mediation between possibly contrary conflicting interests, can be and is in reality an aim of non-state communities and organisations like churches, religious communities, clubs, associations, organizations, groups etc. as well.

## *7. The Necessary Means of Law: Categorical Character, Externality, Formality, Immanence*

What are the necessary means of law, which also foster the security of law? By reference to the aim of mediation between possibly contrary/disparate concerns, we can distinguish law from many social facts. But some social facts have the same aim, or at least a similar one, e.g. morals, politics, religion, and non-moral conventions. Law can be distinguished from these social facts only by reference to its necessary means:

### *7.1 Conventions*

Law does not only comprise voluntary norms, but also at least some categorical obligations, that is, obligations which do not have as a necessary condition the concrete agreement of those obligated (which does not mean that all legal norms are categorical). So law is – like morals – distinguished from pure *conventions* by its partially *categorical character*.[36] Its categorical character is one aspect of the security of law. This categorical character does also hold for international law. It is clear that international treaties, in-

34 See Delbrück, Jost/ Wolfrum, Rüdiger. Völkerrecht, Band I/1 Die Grundlagen. Die Völkerrechtssubjekte. 2nd ed., Berlin, 1989, p. 34.

35 Ehrlich, Eugen. Grundlegung der Soziologie des Rechts. 4th ed., Berlin, 1989, p. 32.

36 Note that categorical character has to be carefully distinguished from coercion.

ternational custom law and the fundamental principles of the law of nations bind categorically.

### 7.2 Morals

Law has, in all its various manifestations, only external sources and means (judging, agreeing, issuing, ordering, voting) but no purely internal source, such as the human conscience, which is one necessary source of morals.[37] So the distinctive feature of law, in comparison to *morals*, is its *externality* in all singular instantiations. Its external character is another aspect of the security of law. The norms of international law are also external.

### 7.3 Politics

Law, in all its manifestations, is marked by a certain formality in its making, promulgation, or application, which simple political acts, for example a decision in foreign politics, do not have, not even in the form of a rule like the Monroe Doctrine or the Brezhnev Doctrine.[38] By contrast, resolutions of the UN for example have this formality. So the distinctive feature of law in comparison to *politics* is its *formality* in all its singular instantiations. This formality of law lends support to *legal security*, e.g. when peace treaties are signed in a solemn procedure and documents are exchanged.

### 7.4 Religion

Human law refers to immanent states of affairs within human life and agency. By contrast, religion, as the practice of a faith, also refers to a transcendental goal – the goal, say, of beatitude, reincarnation, or eternal peace of the soul. Accordingly, the distinctive feature of law in comparison to *religion* is its *immanence* in all its singular instantiations. This holds at least under the condition that law and religion are separated in reality and are not more or less interwoven, as in Jewish or Islamic law. Also its immanence

37 This was already stated by Kant, Immanuel. Metaphysics of Morals, Metaphysical Foundations of the Theory of Law, Introduction.

38 See for a comprehensive study of the formality of law: Summers, Robert. Form and Function in a Legal System. Cambridge, 2006.

contributes to the security of law. The starting point of the immanence of international law can be estimated quite clearly: It was in 1625 when Hugo Grotius published “De Jure Belli ac Pacis”.

To sum up: We have identified four elements of the concept of security as necessary means of law, which hold also in international law: its *categorical character*, its *externality*, its *formality* and its *immanence*. What about the two others, *coercion/force/sanctions* and *effectiveness/effectivity* which can be seen as two elements of “enforcement”,[39] an element that is often proposed from a positivistic perspective?

### *7.5 Coercion/Force/Sanctions*

In Kant’s “Metaphysics of Morals“ one can find the famous phrase “Das Recht ist mit der Befugnis zu zwingen verbunden.” (“Law is connected with the authority to coerce.”).[40] But firstly coercion is here not understood in a physical sense or in the sense of another sort of sanction e.g. a monetary fine. It can also be a mere verbal obligation. So it coincides with the categorical character of every law, above mentioned. And secondly one has to note the expression “Befugnis” (“authority”). Kant does not state anything about coercion, force or sanction as a necessary factual property of law. He holds instead that somebody who has a subjective right is ethically *entitled* to use coercion in this wide sense of verbal obligation. So Kant cannot be taken as a witness that law is necessarily connected with force, coercion or sanctions.

Every lawyer knows that there are legal norms which are not enforceable. We distinguish between *ius cogens* and *ius dispositivum*.[41] Ius dispositivum is per definition not enforced by the authorities. There are *leges imperfectae* (e.g. contracts according to §§ 656, 762 German Bürgerliches Gesetzbuch/BGB). And § 1 of the German Richtgeschwindigkeitsverordnung states 130 km/h as suggested speed, without any sanctions. Even the sociologist Max Weber acknowledged that not all law is guaranteed by force or coercion.[42]

39 See O’Connell, Mary Allen. The Power and Purpose of International Law. Insights from the Theory and Practice of Enforcement. Oxford, 2011.
40 Kant, Immanuel. Metaphysics of Morals/Metaphysik der Sitten, AA 231.
41 See Kähler, Lorenz. Begriff und Rechtfertigung abdingbaren Rechts. Tübingen, 2012.
42 On the one hand: Weber, Max. Wirtschaft und Gesellschaft. Tübingen 1985, p. 183.

But some legal theorists assume that law is conceptually necessarily connected with coercion/force/sanctions.[43] How can that be? First some of them do not hold this for single norms, but for the whole normative system of law. E.g. Hans Kelsen in a first step assumes that all realizations of law are necessary an order or part of an order. Then he defines "order" in a second step in a very peculiar way: "Order" is a system of norms whose unity is constituted by all their norms having the same foundation of validity (Geltungsgrund).[44] And in a third step Kelsen assumes that legal orders are always connected with coercion/force/sanctions. An outcome is Kelsen's well-known monism on international law.

I have to admit that I doubt all these three steps. I think that law (in the aforementioned sense) as mediation between possibly contrary/disparate, conflicting concerns can be also a singular act which is not part of an order, e.g. a singular treaty like a peace treaty, a singular judicial judgment or a singular political decision with formal character. But even if singular legal acts are part of an order there is no a priori reason that this order needs one foundation of validity. Take the German legal order: We have besides the people of the Federal Republic also the peoples of the singular states and local communities as source of legitimization of law. And also the third step is in my view questionable. In light of the weakness and partial badness of the human character, it might be very useful to connect law with coercion. But this is an empirical mean to reach some degree of effectivity, not an a priori conceptual necessity of all law in all places and times. The necessary aim of law, the mediation between possible, conflicting concerns does not conceptually necessarily require sanctions. And also the above mentioned four necessary means of law (categoriality, externality, formality, immanence) do not necessarily require sanctions.

Most advocates of the necessity of sanctions of law hold a sceptical and/or naturalistic theory of commands and obligations as their mental results. They assume that commands/obligations need necessarily sanctions to obtain binding force. And because law needs necessary obligations henceforth it needs also necessary sanctions. E.g. Austin states: "A command is dis-

43 On the other Hand: Weber, Wirtschaft und Gesellschaft, p. 17f.; Hobbes, Leviathan, chap. 26; de Spinoza, Tractatus politicus, II, 9; Austin, Province of Jurisprudence Determined, p. 24; Kreuzbauer, Günther. Die Norm im Völkerrecht. Eine rechtsphilosophische und rechtstheoretische Untersuchung. Wien, 2006, p. 150f; Röhl, Klaus F./ Röhl, Hans Christian. Allgemeine Rechtslehre. 3rd ed., Köln, 2008, pp. 190, 201, 229. But on p. 222 they state that a sanctioning is only typical, not necessary.

44 Kelsen, Reine Rechtslehre, p. 32.

tinguished from other significations of desire, not by the style in which the desire is signified, but by the power and the purpose of the party commanding to inflict an evil or pain in case the desire be disregarded. If you cannot or will not harm me, in case I comply not with your wish, the expression of your wish is not a command, although you utter your wish in imperative phrase."[45]

But this thesis clearly mixes up linguistic, psychological and social issues. A wish is not necessarily communicated to others. If it is communicated to others, there can be two possibilities: (1) it can be purely descriptive concerning my future plans, e. g. when I tell a friend that I wish to finish my book, and do not mean/imply that I want some help from him. (2) If I ask my friend to help me with the book, this speech act is clearly distinguished from the mere wish. It is a request, plea or petition. I do not only describe my original wish/future plan to finish the book, but also my additional/second wish that he should help me. Decisive for such a request, plea or petition is that I ask my friend for agreement. He can say "yes" or "no".

What is then a command? In the case of a command, there is some additional imperative element, which comes on top of the description of the two wishes: he is necessitated. He cannot say "yes" or "no". We already mentioned in 7. 1. the categorical character of obligations. Commands do not have the concrete agreement of those obligated as a necessary condition.

As adult humans are independent individuals, it is clear that commands negate their own freedom of decision. These commands need therefore some justification. But this justification is not necessarily power or the possibility of harm. It can also be e. g. superior experience or the necessity to come quickly to an unanimous decision without lengthy discussion. Imagine a group of mountaineers which is composed of an experienced guide and some inexperienced participants. Before the tour, they can agree that all will follow the commands of the guide. If the guide issues a command to the group in a certain situation there is no room for disagreement. Thus, all necessary conditions of a command are fulfilled. And this holds independently of any power of the guide to exert any sanctions on the members of the group. Normally a tour guide has no power to inflict such sanctions. In the case of a community which issues law we face a similar necessity to come to an unanimous decision. And we can assume as a general agreement that the representatives of a group are allowed to issue such commands. Think of the commands of a religious group towards its members. It is not necessary that there exist any sanctions to back these commands. So commands

45 Austin, Province of Jurisprudence Determined, p. 21.

are justified and can be exerted without the addition of sanctions. Although, they might be very ineffective, if no sanction is added.

In order to better understand the effects of commands, it is necessary to look more closely at obligations: Obligations are comprised of three necessary elements: (1) a necessity of (2) an action which (3) evolves out of some meaningful act and not only out of natural forces.[46] Here we see why the addressee of a command cannot – according to the issuer – say "yes" or "no". The issuer creates with his speech act the meaning of necessity. But nothing in these elements requires sanctions, force or coercion.

In intersubjective contexts, which are necessary for law, such an obligation is created by an imperative speech act. This speech act does not require a sanction or coercion to be imperative. It just needs a locutionary or illocutionary act which is commanding, that is, creating the meaning of necessity. Consequently, legal obligations do not require necessary sanctions to be legal obligations. Sanctions are only an additional, contingent mean to secure effectiveness.

Additionally, law does not only comprise obligations, but provides individuals and communities like nations with facilities that are power-conferring norms, e.g. the facility to produce valid contracts.[47] If they do not comply with the statutory provisions the result is not a "breach" or a "violation" of any obligation but the mere nullity or defeasibility of the contract. This nullity or defeasibility is not an addition to the basic obligation like the sanction is, but it is part of the power-conferring norm.[48]

One can sum up: Law in general and henceforth international law, which aims at attaining peace, can be law without force, coercion or sanctions.[49] Such law suffers only from an empirical drawback: In some cases it will not be very effective if it lacks such sanctions. Therefore, the conclusion is that law in general and also international law does not need sanctions as a conceptual necessity.[50] Sanctions are only useful to reach compliance. In this practical sense they can contribute to the security of law. So if we want to reach peace through law, sanctions might be in certain cases a useful means. But when we make law, it is open to us to use these means or not.

---

46 See von der Pfordten, Dietmar. On Rules, Norms and Commands, forthcoming.

47 Hart, Concept of Law, p. 27ff.

48 Hart, Concept of Law, p. 35.

49 See Delbrück, Jost/ Wolfrum, Rüdiger. Völkerrecht, p. 43. Against the necessity of coercion also: v. Arnauld, Andreas. Völkerrecht. Heidelberg, 2012, p. 4.

50 See for the same conclusion that sanctions are not a necessary part of law: Barkun, Michael. Law without Sanctions. Order in Primitive Societies and the World Community. New Haven, 1968, p. 60ff.; Henkin, Louis. How Nations Behave. Law and Foreign Policy. New York (NY), 1968, pp. 28, 46, 88-94.

*7.6 Effectiveness/Effectivity*

But what is the case with effectiveness/effectivity itself as a necessary property of law? Is it a necessary condition of the concept of law? There seems to be no one who holds this claim. But some hold a thesis which is quite similar, although weaker. For them it is not law or the concept of law itself which is necessarily connected to effectiveness/effectivity, but its *validity*.[51] In this doctrine effectivity is a necessary condition for a norm to become valid. This cannot be true, because shortly after the enactment there must be assumed validity without effectiveness. For all norms we assume obligatory force, but we cannot immediately estimate the compliance.

But according to this doctrine a legal norm or legal order can *lose its validity* after a certain period of time in the case of in-effectivity. So a legal norm or a legal system shall only remain valid if it is still effective after a certain period of time. E.g. Gustav Radbruch holds: A statute is only valid if in the majority of cases of its application, it can expect compliance.[52] And Hans Kelsen states quite similarly but without any quantification of the figure of compliance: A legal norm will not be considered as valid anymore if it remains permanently ineffective. Effectivity is therefore considered to be a condition for validity in such a sense that – beside the enactment – there must be some frequency of compliance, in order for the legal norm not to lose its validity.[53] In international law many assume similarly the *principle of effectivity*.[54]

The problem of this doctrine of validity being dependent on effectivity is – in the light of the necessary property/mean of security – its *vagueness* in two important respects:

Firstly it is not clear what percentage of compliance is necessary in order to keep a norm valid: e. g. 10, 20, 30, 50, 60%? Is it really the case that a norm becomes invalid if only a minority complies, as Radbruch assumes? In contrast we know tax law which has a low rate of compliance, but is still considered to be valid. So only a nearly total lack of compliance – say 90% and more non-compliance – can cause invalidity.

Secondly it is not clear *how long* the non-compliance must last until an ineffective norm loses its validity: a year, ten years, fifty years or hundred years? In Canon Law, Can. 26 states that a reasonable custom (Can. 24 § 2),

51 See Kreuzbauer, Norm im Völkerrecht., p. 147f.
52 Radbruch, Gustav. Einführung in die Rechtswissenschaft. 13th ed., Stuttgart, 1980, p. 13.
53 Kelsen, Reine Rechtslehre, pp. 11, 215ff.
54 Cf. Krieger, Heike. Das Effektivitätsprinzip im Völkerrecht. Berlin, 2000.

which is in use by a legal community (Art. 25), reaches validity against or beside the law after 30 years and if future customs are prohibited explicitly after 100 years.

In order to evade this total lack of security by the doctrine of invalidation referring to ineffectivity we need an additional normative element. Like customary law, which only becomes valid if a vast majority *endorses* it (opinio communis), norms which are ineffective do not lose their validity automatically, but if and only if a vast majority of humans and institutions *accept* this invalidation by ineffectivity. So the vanishing of validity must be acknowledged by a vast majority of humans and institutions. This is in a certain sense the *actus contrarius* to the initial enactment of the norm as its validation. Therefore e. g. a peace treaty or a peace order is and remains valid even in the case of factual ineffectiveness if a significant minority still considers it to be valid.

To sum up: Security in the limited sense of effectiveness/effectivity is neither a necessary condition of the concept of law nor a necessary condition for a norm to become valid. But nearly total in-effectivity, say 90% non-compliance or more, can together with non-acceptance by a vast majority, as a sort of *actus contrarius* to the validation by the original enactment, *cause invalidation* of the norm after a due period of time, say 30 years. The vastness of the majority and the length of time are themselves evaluative or normative questions, which can be decided either by enacted or customary law or by explicit or implicit convention. In German law there exists the customary law of "Ersitzung" (usucapion, lat. usocapio) of things. According to this formerly customary and now codified law the unlawful holder of a thing acquires the property after 10 years (movables, § 937 BGB) or 30 years (immovables, § 900 BGB) if he is in good faith, that is if nobody else claims the right. So the ineffectiveness of the claim for the right invalidates the claim after 10 or 30 years.

If there is no decision by law or explicit convention, which is mostly the case, we have to assume vast majorities (e.g. more than 90%) and long duration (10 years in minor and 30 years in major issues). This holds especially for international law with its cross-cultural and severe impacts on whole states and therefore on a huge amount of human beings. E.g. after an annexation the unlawful act remains unlawful as long as a significant amount of states does not acknowledge it. Law preserves peace and security by not legitimizing unlawful acts as long as there is no significant agreement to legalize the unlawful act.

# Do We Need a World State? The Prospects of Multi-level Global Governance for the Organization of Peace in the 21st Century

*Andreas Hasenclever and Annette Schramm*

## *1. Introduction*

The optimists at the end of the Cold War proofed wrong. Armed conflict does not cease to exist and security concerns still range high on national agendas. Time and again, we observe external powers to forcefully intervene into the domestic affairs of smaller states mandated or not by the United Nations Security Council. Moreover, whole regions such as the Middle East or Central Africa suffer from international frictions and enduring violence. Tensions are also rising in Asia, where the military build-up is as pronounced as in no other part of the world[1]. Even in Europe, power politics are no relics of the past: after the Russian seizure of the Crimean Peninsula in March 2014 the specter of war re-emerged in the Western public and NATO-Russia relations reached a new low in post-cold war history.

Confronted with the ongoing violence in many places of the world the age-old question of how best to promote international peace and security gained new currency. The answers provided by liberal scholars, who counted on the stabilizing effects of decentralized institutions, seem outdated. While traditional realists call for new hedging strategies and ask governments to invest in international alliances, others are convinced that time has come to relaunch the world state project. Accordingly, the still enduring anarchic condition of international politics must be overcome. The world needs a central authority with a monopoly on the legitimate use of force to stop war mongering, to provide reliable security guarantees, and to induce global disarmament. Without a world state, even good-minded governments could not escape the security dilemma because they lack the necessary trust in each other's reliability. Additionally, only a world state would be able to mobilize the necessary resources to end civil wars, to protect human

1 Holtom, Paul/ Bromley, Mark/ Wezeman, Pieter/ Wezeman, Siemon. Developments in Arms Transfers, 2012. In: SIPRI Yearbook. Armaments, Disarmaments and International Security. Oxford, 2013, 257.

rights in humanitarian crises and to implement the "responsibility to protect". Without a world state desperately needed public security goods will be constantly undersupplied and national governments will be hesitant to invest in peace-making and peace-building.

In the first part of our paper we discuss the prospects of a world state under current conditions. Our argument will be that time has not yet come for a central authority in global politics. On the one hand, governments are still reluctant to transfer sovereignty to the supra-national level. On the other hand, we simply do not know how to design a world state that would live up to the expectations motivating and legitimating its formation in the first place. What should a central authority look like that is able to pacify the planet? Moreover, the establishment of a world state could be an extremely bloody process by itself. As already noted by Jean-Jacque Rousseau at the end of his "Judgement of Monsieur l'Abbé de Saint-Pierre's Plan for Perpetual Peace" in the 18 century: The cure might be worse than the disease.

In the second part of our paper we will return to the liberal argument that international organizations might help governments and societies to avoid war and to promote peace. While international organizations do not dictate peace – states are always able to use force for the pursuit of their interests if they want – they do provide governments with strong incentives to abstain from violence under conditions of interdependence and a partly globalized world[2]. Understood in this way, international institutions are no guarantee against war but a way to strengthen peaceful relations. In the end and as always, all depends on the willingness of governments and societies to use these instruments. In our understanding, however, the same would hold true for a functioning world state. There are no technical solutions to the problems of war and peace and even a powerful and well-designed world state would only work if sufficiently supported by its constituency. If international and transnational actors do not succeed in establishing a working system of global and regional institutions for peace in the first place, why should they be able to create a world state?

2 Keohane, Robert O. Governance in a Partially Globalized World. Presidential Address, American Political Science Association, 2000. In: American Political Science Review, 2001, 95(1), 1-13; Zürn, Michael. Globalization and Global Governance. In: Carlsnaes, Walter/ Risse-Kappen, Thomas/ Simmons, Beth A. (Hrsg.). Handbook of International Relations. London, 2013, 401-425.

## 2. World State and Peace

### 2.1 The New Debate

Since the late 1990s and early 2000s the world state is back on the agenda of International Relations. Driven by new challenges ascribed to globalization and the need to promote new forms of international cooperation, political scientists, sociologists, economists and philosophers discuss a range of arguments for, and diverse pictures of, a possible world state. Normative arguments for the creation of a world state try to answer why a world state *should* be and what it should look like[3].On the other end of the spectrum authors focus on the inevitability of a future world state[4], arguing that a world state *will* come into existence, whether it is normatively desirable or not. Others point out that there *are* already existing forms of "world statehood"[5].

The problems that are hoped to be addressed through a world state are manifold and range from security threats such as weapons of mass destruction[6] or collective action problems such as climate change[7] to poverty and the democratic deficit of international institutions[8]. There are cosmopolitan[9] as well as communitarian[10] lines of argumentation for a world state and models range from a rather informal world parliament[11] to a world republic[12].

Despite the plethora of arguments and ideas of a world state most concepts are united in aiming for a weak[13] or minimal[14] version of a world

---

3 Höffe, Otfried. Demokratie im Zeitalter der Globalisierung. München, 1999; Held, David. Soziale Demokratie im globalen Zeitalter. Frankfurt, 2007.

4 Wendt, Alexander. Why a World State is Inevitable. In: European Journal of International Relations, 2003, 9(4), 491-542.

5 Albert, Mathias. Einleitung: Weltstaat und Weltstaatlichkeit: Neubestimmungen des Politischen in der Weltgesellschaft. In: Albert, Mathias/ Stichweh, Rudolf (Hrsg.). Weltstaat und Weltstaatlichkeit. Wiesbaden, 2007, 9-23.

6 Chase-Dunn, Christopher. World-state Formation: Historical Processes and Emergent Necessity. In: Political Geography Quarterl, 1990, 9(2), 108-130.

7 Craig, Campbell. The Resurgent Idea of World Government. In: Ethics & International Affairs, 2008, (22)2, 133-142.

8 Falk, Richard/ Strauss, Andrew. Toward Global Parliament. In: Foreign Affairs, 2001, 80(1), 212-220; Held, Soziale Demokratie im globalen Zeitalter.

9 Cabrera, Luis: Political Theory of Global Justice. A Cosmopolitan Case for the World State. London 2004.

10 Etzioni, Amitai: From Empire to Community. A New Approach to International Relations. New York, 2004.

11 Falk/Strauss, Toward Global Parliament.

12 Höffe, Demokratie im Zeitalter der Globalisierung.

13 Neyer, Jürgen. Globale Demokratie. Eine zeitgemäße Einführung in die internationalen Beziehungen. Baden-Baden, 2013.

14 Tinnevelt, Ronald. Federal World Government: The Road to Peace and Justice? In: Cooperation and Conflict, 2012, 47(2), 220-238.

state, which would be different from the unitary nation state. Nobody seriously tries to simply transfer the nation state to the world level with the complete abolition of existing states. A world state is rather envisaged as a multi-level project with subsidiarity and decentralization as basic principles[15]. However, there does not seem to be much agreement when it comes to actually defining this minimal world state and distinguishing it from other concepts. While Wendt for example suggests that there would be a central command for military actions[16], others such as Deudney[17] or Cabrera[18] argue that the world state would not necessarily have the monopoly on the legitimate use of force. The problem with a minimal and at the same time vague understanding of a world state is aptly described by Tinnevelt:

> "If we defend a decentralized and fully non-hierarchical arrangement of international relations – one in which states have a right to secede and retain the right to their military forces – are we then still arguing for some form of world government or state? Or are we merely supporting a system of global governance?" [19]

That the boundary between the idea of a world state and global governance becomes increasingly blurred is also evident in the concept of "world statehood" as put forward by Albert et al., who argue, "that in the end global governance can be conceptualized as the emergence of forms of inclusive statehood on a global level"[20]. While a broad understanding of the term "world state" might help to shed light on issues such as the diffusion of sovereignty, it is not helpful analytically as it cannot be distinguished from other forms of global governance. We therefore use "world state" in a narrow sense, referring to concepts that ascribe the monopoly on the legitimate use of force to a global authority[21].

---

15 Tinnevelt, Federal World Government, 225.

16 Wendt, Why a World State is Inevitable, 506.

17 Deudney, Daniel. Bounding Power. Republican Security Theory from the Polis to the Global Village. Princeton, N.J, Oxford, 2007.

18 Cabrera, Political Theory of Global Justice.

19 Tinnevelt, Federal World Government, 229-230.

20 Albert, Mathias/ Harste, Gorm/ Patomaki, Heikki/ Jorgensen, Knud E. Introduction: World State Futures. In: Cooperation and Conflict, 2012, 47(2), 148.

21 In consequence concepts such as federal republican world nuclear government by Deudney or Albert's et al. world statehood will not be considered in the following discussion.

## 2.2 World State and the Promise of Peace

Many authors defending a world state assume that it would bring about a more peaceful world if not world peace itself. However, the argument behind this assumption is often only briefly touched upon and hardly ever spelled out in more detail. A closer look at these possible peace mechanisms, however, makes the shortcomings and problems of the world state project visible.

There are three general arguments made in the literature linking the creation of a world state with peace. The first argument uses the existential threat posed by Weapons of Mass Destruction as starting point. Proponents of this position assert that as long as single states possess nuclear weapons, there will always be the danger of a global atomic war extinguishing mankind. This substantial threat can only be met by the formation of a world authority, so the argument goes[22]. International treaties or other forms of global governance to outlaw nuclear weapons can never be a guarantor that a state will not go berserk one day[23]. Furthermore, advocates of a world government are skeptical about the future stability of mutual deterrence that lasted throughout the Cold War:

> "It is not at all certain that international politics is destined to return to a stable bipolar order, such as prevailed during the second half of the Cold War, but even if this does happen, there is no guarantee that nuclear deterrence would work as well as it did during the second half of the twentieth century. [...]As long as interstate politics continue, we cannot rule out that in some future conflict a warning system will fail, a leader will panic, governments will refuse to back down, a third party will provoke a response—indeed, there are any number of scenarios under which deterrence could fail and thermonuclear war could occur."[24]

The logic consequence then is to install some kind of world authority which can stop the proliferation of nuclear weapons, veto their use by individual states and promote national denuclearization. According to Chase-Dunn[25] such a world institution needs armed forces, strong enough to defeat any national army, and complete authority over the production of weapons of mass destruction (WMD). Or to put it differently, any viable control of nuclear weapons entails a world state with military supremacy. Deproliferation on

22 Chase-Dunn, World-state Formation; Craig, The Resurgent Idea of World Government; Etzioni, From Empire to Community.
23 Chase-Dunn, World-state Formation, 120; Craig, The Resurgent Idea of World Government, 138.
24 Craig, The Resurgent Idea of World Government, 136.
25 Chase-Dunn, World-state Formation, 120-121.

the global level would additionally avert the danger of WMDs getting in the hands of terrorists[26].

While this first argument focuses on nuclear weapons as threat to peace, Wendt makes his point by looking at struggles for recognition that follow from the logic of anarchy. In order to have an identity, states, analogously to individuals, need to be recognized in differentiation to another actor. This recognition, defined by Wendt[27] as "thin" recognition, will always remain unstable unless a world state is formed and anarchy is overcome. Wendt imagines 5 stages of world state formation, with the first being a Hobbesian natural condition that turns into a society of states (stage 2) when states start to recognize each other. The society of states then turns into a world society in phase 3. This stage is characterized by the recognition of individuals and their rights vis-à-vis the nation-state and the rule of non-violent behavior among states and individuals. However, a concept of solidarity that would prescribe states to help one another in case of an attack is only introduced in stage 4. This system of collective security however remains voluntary and the states would maintain their full sovereignty. Accordingly the system is still unstable. Real recognition is only possible when it is actually enforceable. This step follows in stage 5, the creation of a world state which owns the monopoly on the legitimate use of force[28].The five stages seem to gradually reduce the gravity of the problem of mutual recognition, until it is completely resolved in stage 5. Remaining incidences of violent conflict would be regarded as crime and "be domesticated by enforceable law"[29]. Following Wendt's reasoning a world state would be more peaceful than the current system, as the struggle for "thin" recognition, in the sense of simply being an independent actor, would end and remaining conflicts that might be fought for "thick" recognition, referring to the desire to be acknowledged for a particular role, would become manageable[30]. Summing up the argument, a world state would create a more peaceful world through managing and putting an end to struggles for recognition.

The third line of argumentation focuses on international legalization and global jurisdiction as a way to world peace. Höffe's[31] distinguished sketch for a world republic is derived from the moral imperative to secure the universal rule of law. Central to Höffe's model of a subsidiary, federal world

26 Etzioni, From Empire to Community, 119.
27 Wendt, Why a World State is Inevitable, 510-516.
28 Wendt, Why a World State is Inevitable, 517-525.
29 Wendt, Why a World State is Inevitable, 528.
30 Wendt, Why a World State is Inevitable, 511-512, 528.
31 Höffe, Demokratie im Zeitalter der Globalisierung.

state is the conceptualization of both, states as well as individuals, as juristic persons with their own rights. The courts of the world republic would oversee international law, regulating relations between states, and global civic law, focusing on every individual's rights vis-à-vis the nation state and the world republic. This global citizenship would complement existing national civic law and guarantee the respect for human rights. While the national citizenship concerns state-specific regulations such as welfare services or possibilities for participation, the global civic law grants the same basic rights to everyone. Global courts would have the task to review laws of nation states but also decide in cases concerning individuals, always adhering to the principle of subsidiarity. In consequence there would also be a global criminal law which would secure peace between nation states and which would have three functions for the protection of global citizenship: First, it would prescribe cooperation between nation states in order to fight transnational crime. Second, there would be a global criminal court responsible for certain types of crime and overruling national courts in case of an appeal. Third, global criminal law would establish and monitor basic standards for national criminal law. If necessary, law would be enforced by a global police force[32]. In the end the world republic would spread the rule of law and democracy all over the globe and achieve a state of worldwide justice[33].

A slightly different argument can be made from the standpoint of the democratic peace tradition: The more democracies there are the more peaceful the world will be. A democratic supranational authority would help to spread democracy throughout the world, which would in consequence lead to world peace[34]. Although these are two distinct arguments, both hold the view that peace between but also within non-sovereign states becomes possible through a worldwide rule of law and spread of democracy.

In essence these three lines of argumentation can be traced back to three different schools of thoughts in International Relations and their diagnosis for war and peace. The nuclear-weapons argument follows a realist line of thinking, in which the security dilemma among states cannot be resolved unless there is a world-wide authority guaranteeing the security of every single nation-state. Not surprisingly one can find this idea in classical realist writing of Morgenthau and Niebuhr, who however were skeptical about the realization of such a global authority[35]. In Wendt's social constructivist

32 Höffe, Demokratie im Zeitalter der Globalisierung, 353-370.
33 Höffe, Demokratie im Zeitalter der Globalisierung, 426-427.
34 Tännsjö, Torbjörn. Global Democracy. The Case for a World Government. Edinburgh, 2008, 19-29.
35 Craig, The Resurgent Idea of World Government, 134.

argumentation for a world state the global authority has a similar role: an ultimate guarantor for the mutual recognition of nation-states. The third line of argumentation picks ideas from liberal thinking: Both democracy as well as the rule of law are regarded as necessary conditions to ensure peace. Their global realization will therefore lead to global peace.

While these three lines of argumentation look promising at first sight, their weaknesses become visible when considering their implementation and the consequences. First, a potential world state would not be able to solve the problems which lead to violent conflict today. Second, the existence of a world state might lead to higher levels of violence and be even less peaceful than the world today due to violent conflicts that would be fought for the establishment of a world authority and the risk of the world state turning into a tyranny.

### *2.3 The Limits of the World State Idea*

Looking at armed conflict data it becomes clear that the great majority of present wars are fought within states[36]. As both Wendt and Höffe envisage a world state in which nation states would still exist, it remains unclear how civil wars would be prevented or stopped. Wendt's rather vague remarks that a world state would not need to have a collective army or police force, "[as] long as a structure exists that can command and enforce a collective response to threats"[37], make us wonder what this "structure" would look like. Thinking about this structure Wendt dismisses the idea of a world government in favor of a deliberative way of decision making. He, however, does not give any more details about what the rules for the "deliberation" would be, or how it could be ensured that decisions would not be dominated by militarily or economically powerful states. As Maus[38] rightly points out, a global social contract would not be between "equal" and "free" actors, fueling the fear that a "minimal" world state such as pictured by Wendt would rather lead to a world hegemony by one ore a few states.

Höffe's model of a world state goes further than Wendt's account. Not only does he develop an elaborate system of a world judiciary he also plans for a world legislative and a world executive body, which would also entail

36 Themner, Lotta/ Wallensteen, Peter. Armed Conflicts, 1946-2011. In: Journal of Peace Research, 2012, 49(4), 565-575.

37 Wendt, Why a World State is Inevitable, 506.

38 Maus, Ingeborg. From Nation-State to Global State, or the Decline of Democracy. In: Constellations, 2006, 13(4), 465-484.

a world police. While Höffe's concept might be less prone to fall prey to some powerful states it underestimates the requirements for a worldwide police system. All existing state militaries would have to cede their competences to a worldwide force alongside technological capacities which are closely linked to economic benefits. As the consequences of this transfer are far-reaching Lutz-Bachmann[39] is skeptical about the willingness of states to simply give up these capabilities. It remains unclear what a global security system would have to look like to be feasible. Trying to imagine a global security sector already shows part of the complexity a world state would have to deal with. As Maus outlines the same issue concerns global democratic institutions and their design:

> "Here the question is what, for example, the right to petition or to demonstrate could mean vis-à-vis a world parliament. In both cases, it is a matter of the right to impose information on the representatives (even if its use is left up to political elites). Mass petitions or mass street protests have at least a chance of putting an issue on the political agenda. It is not obvious, however, where the coercive character of transmitting information to a world parliament would lie: while messages clog the offices of a national parliament, electronic missives to a world parliament would be easier to ignore – not to mention the information overload which, in itself, a global right of petition would obviate."[40]

Apart from the high complexity world democratic procedures and institutions would contain, it remains unclear how or why a world parliament should do a better job in solving substantial problems than national parliaments[41].

In addition to the enormous complexity a functioning world state would have to face, the discussion about its formation is often predetermined by a certain image of "the state". In this view democratic state institutions are seen as a panacea to deal with all sorts of problems especially when it comes to security issues. However, in many parts of the world the state is neither a guarantor for security nor perceived as a positive concept[42]. To apply the concept of state to the global level and to expect that a world state could cope with rebel groups, terrorism and organized crime, issues where many nation states today fail, then seems overly simplified and even naïve.

---

39 Lutz-Bachmann, Matthias. Weltweiter Frieden durch eine Weltrepublik? Probleme internationaler Friedenssicherung. In: Lutz-Bachmann, Matthias/ Bohman, James (Hrsg.): Weltstaat oder Staatenwelt? Für und wider die Idee einer Weltrepublik. Frankfurt am Main, 2002, 32-45.

40 Maus, From Nation-State to Global State, 473.

41 Maus, From Nation-State to Global State, 481.

42 Neyer, Globale Demokratie, 230.

## 2.4 Dangers of a World State

Even if we could think of a world state design that would be able to take into consideration all these complexities it still remains unclear how it would come about. In thinking about the proposal for a (European) world state of Abbé de Saint-Pierre, Jean-Jaques Rousseau stayed skeptical about its implementation. While he acknowledged that such a plan for perpetual peace would be beneficial to everyone, he believed that its realization would be extremely violent and in the end do more harm than good[43].

Looking at current ideas about *how* a world state would be created Rousseau's apprehension still seems justified. Carneiro[44] for example believes that the most likely way a world state will develop will be through an American hegemony. The global military domination of the US would eventually be followed by political institutions and a world state would materialize. In a similar vein both Tönnies[45] and Etzioni[46] see the worldwide war on terror led by the US-government as a first step in the direction of the collectivization of security issues and in the long run the creation of a global authority. In this view the creation of a world state does not come about peacefully but rather through domination.

Höffe[47] is more careful when describing the establishment of his world republic. He cautions that the process must not destroy existing democracies and national improvements towards rule of law. His starting point for the development of a world state is a confederation of democratic states, which will attract authoritarian regimes culturally and economically. However, this confederation has to be able to defend itself as well as to intervene in repressive states in order to protect human rights. The development of the world state through the attractiveness of the confederation as well as its ability to defend and even intervene into other states, raises a chain of questions: What happens if the expectation of the voluntary accession of authoritarian regimes does not materialize? Will the interventions by the confederation become more frequent? What happens if they encounter resistance? And when should the confederation intervene? Brock warns that norm enforcement can in itself lead to lawless violence when colliding with

43 Rousseau, Jean-Jacques. Sozialphilosophische und politische Schriften. München, 1981, 404.

44 Carneiro, Robert L. The Political Unification of the World: Whether, When, and How—Some Speculations. In: Cross-Cultural Research, 2004, 38(2), 173.

45 Tönnies, Sibylle. Cosmopolis now. Auf dem Weg zum Weltstaat. Hamburg, 2002.

46 Etzioni, From Empire to Community.

47 Höffe, Demokratie im Zeitalter der Globalisierung, 427-428.

other norms[48]. However, it seems like the process of world state creation would entail many norm collisions which can be used to excuse the use of force. In this view the process of world state creation is an extremely conflictive process that would most likely lead to an exacerbation of violent conflict.

In the end it might not even play that big of a role if a world state is supposed to be created through domination or voluntarily. Once the process encounters serious resistance, it will easily turn violent. As long as these fears cannot be convincingly accommodated we should not start to work towards a world state.

Another risk of the world state, once it has been created, can be found in Kant's writing: the danger of despotism. Although Kant does not dismiss the idea of a world republic right away he later discards it in favor of a federation of sovereign states[49]. The fear that a world state would be so powerful that it would turn into a tyrannical omnipresent state is regarded as a justified one by both opponents and proponents of world state ideas. Proponents answer to these fears in three ways: Firstly, by insisting on the new dimension threats of our time have taken. The world of Kant neither knew nuclear weapons nor international terrorism. In face of these new existential threats some advocates of a world state seem to be willing to take the risk of a world tyranny[50]. Secondly, it is argued that a world state would not have to deal with any outside threats and would therefore have no grounds for legitimizing the use of repression inside. Consequently a world state would not be despotic[51]. These two arguments show a world in which security threats will disappear with the installation of a world state. However, one needs to question the assumption that this state of "total security" would ever materialize. Would it really not be possible for groups to get hold of nuclear weapons? Would there not still be enough possibilities to fight over the distribution of resources and welfare?

A third way in which advocates answer to the "tyranny" objection is by designing "minimal" world states. These are typically characterized by the principles of federalism and subsidiarity and only ascribe "minimal" com-

---

48 Brock, Lothar. Innerstaatliche Kriege und internationale Gewaltanwendung seit dem Ende des Ost-West-Konflikts: Indiz für die Emergenz oder das Ausbleiben von Weltstaatlichkeit? In: Albert, Mathias/ Stichweh, Rudolf (Hrsg.). Weltstaat und Weltstaatlichkeit. Wiesbaden, 2007, 178.

49 Kant, Immanuel: Zum ewigen Frieden. Ein philosophischer Entwurf (Herausgegeben von Rudolf Malter). Stuttgart, 2005, 16-20.

50 Craig, The Resurgent Idea of World Government, 141.

51 Craig, The Resurgent Idea of World Government; Deudney, Bounding Power.

petences to a global night-watchmen state. However, as Tinnevelt[52] points out, these models have high expectations about the capacities of a world authority while at the same time underestimating the consequences. If a world state is to grant peace and security, and in many models be legitimized through some democratic procedures, it will entail not just different institutions but also far reaching competences. If one takes for example Höffe's idea of world courts which can decide about breaches of international and global civic law, their decisions still need to be enforced. This capacity of enforcement – in Höffe's case by a world police – gives the world authorities considerable power over nation states and local groups. While this power may not be a problem as long as a consensus about the leading norms and rules of a world republic exists, but it would turn into one if conflicts about the layout of the world authorities break out. What if e.g. a regional coalition of states or peoples has a very different idea about how to organize the world republic than other regions? Not only would a struggle over power break loose, but there would be the danger of a group of states or peoples to impose their will on others. In other words: A worldwide tyranny does not become so unlikely. In the end the "minimal" world state seems like a slippery slope towards a bigger omnipresent world state.

The open questions and doubts we have about existing world state models are too grave to even consider these models as viable peace plans. Furthermore, we agree with Neyer[53] that a strong focus on world state concepts, which certainly will not materialize in the near future, keeps us from developing the necessary short- and medium term solutions to current real-world problems. At times a world state seems like the easy way out of international anarchy; however, this view overlooks the many ways in which global spaces are already organized despite a missing global authority. Following Jack Donnelly[54] or Volker Rittberger and his colleagues[55] states do no longer live under conditions of anarchy in a strict sense but are moving into a heterarchical system where international as well as transnational actors try to coordinate their interactions within an ever growing network of interlinking, and by times competing, institutions. From this perspective it does not make sense to assess the potential merits of a world state in comparison to an idealized state of anarchy. What we should look at are the

52 Tinnevelt, Federal World Government, 225.

53 Neyer, Globale Demokratie, 223.

54 Donnelly, Jack. Rethinking political structures. From 'ordering principles' to 'vertical differentiation' – and beyond. In: International Theory, 2009, 1(01), 49-86.

55 Rittberger, Volker/ Zangl, Bernhard/ Kruck, Andreas. Grundzüge der Weltpolitik. Theorie und Empirie des Weltregierens. Wiesbaden, 2010.

dynamics, prospects and potential shortcomings of multi-level governance in an emerging global society. Therefore, we now turn to multi-level global governance and the contributions of international organizations to peace and security as a viable alternative to the world state.

## *3. Multi-level Global Governance and Peace*

### *3.1 The Emergence of Multi-level Global Governance*

According to Michael Zürn

> "global governance refers to the entirety of regulations put forward with reference to solving specific denationalized problems or providing transnational common goods. The entirety of regulations includes the processes by which norms, rules, and programs are monitored, enforced, and adapted, as well as the structures in which they work."[56]

As such, global governance transcends the traditional Westphalian order of international politics which can be no longer conceived of as interdependence management by national governments[57]. The so-called "executive multilateralism" which dominated international relations after World War II and where sovereign states were the crucial political actors is outdated[58]. New actors such as NGOs, transnational firms, or subnational units have entered the global public space. They created boundary-crossing coalitions to manage common challenges and to pursue shared interests. In doing so, they seek to get their voices heard by governments and to influence decision-making processes at different political levels – be they global, regional, national or local.

As a result, a dense network of local, national, regional and global relations with a multitude of nodes emerged within which a diversity of public and private agents tries to coordinate their behavior in mutually beneficial

56 Zürn, Michael. Globalization and Global Governance. In: Carlsnaes, Walter/ Risse, Thomas/ Simmons, Beth A. Handbook of International Relations. London, 2013, 408.

57 Barnett, Michael/ Sikking, Kathryn. From International Relations to Global Governance. In: Reus-Smit, Christian/ Snidal, Duncan (Hrsg.). The Oxford Handbook of International Relations. Oxford, 2008, 63; Keohane, Robert O./ Nye, Joseph S. Introduction. In: Nye, Joseph S./ Donahue, John D. (Hrsg.). Governance in a Globalizing World, Cambridge, Mass., Washington, D.C.,Visions of Governance for the 21st Century, 2000, 25-26.

58 Rittberger et al., Grundzüge der Weltpolitik; Donnelly, Rethinking political structures.

ways[59]. While they evidently often fail to do so and while not all coordinated activities serve public interests, we do observe the development of an ever growing body of public institutions at various levels that are created to help an emerging global society to govern itself[60].

According to Nicole Deitelhoff and Christopher Daase[61], Christina Kreuder-Sonne and Bernhard Zangl[62] and Michael Zürn[63] many of these institutions now form "islands of authority" in international relations. These islands tend to operate according to bureaucratic routines. They challenge the consensus principle that traditionally governed international relations and they have gained a degree of autonomy and discretion which makes them at least partially independent political powers. While the "islands of authority" are still far away from a "world state" they nevertheless represent irreducible parts of an emerging post-Westphalian order where de-centralized multi-level governance systems start to structure more and more international issue areas. Cases in point would be the World Trade Organization, the World Bank or the International Health Organizations. Here governments have delegated decision-making power to supra-national bodies such as the Dispute Settlement Body of the WTO which in turn depend on the cooperation of political as well as societal actors at the national and at times local level for implementation. While only the Security Council, for instance, is in the position to impose binding obligations on member states in matters of peace and security, the implementation of Security Council resolutions is nevertheless deeply affected by member states willingness to comply with its rulings. Or to put it differently, supra-national and national bodies are moving into a mutual hostage relationship. Governments are as

59 Mitrani, Mor. Global Civil Society and International Society: Compete or Complete? In: Alternatives: Global, Local, Political, 2013, 38(2), 172-188; Schäferhoff, Marco/ Campe, Sabine/ Kaan, Christopher. Transnational Public-Private Partnerships in International Relations: Making Sense of Concepts, Research Frameworks, and Results. In: International Studies Review, 2009, 11(3), 451-474.

60 Dryzek, John S. Global Civil Society: The Progress of Post-Westphalian Politics. In: Annual Review of Political Science, 2012, 15, 101-119; Ruggie, John G. Reconstituting the Global Public Domain – Issues, Actors, and Practices. In: European Journal of International Relations, 2004, 10(4), 499-530.

61 Daase, Christopher/ Deitelhoff, Nicole. Jenseits der Anarchie: Widerstand und Herrschaft im internationalen System. In: Politische Vierteljahresschrift, 2015, 56(2), 299-318

62 Kreuder-Sonnen, Christina/ Zangl, Bernhard. Which post-Westphalia? International organizations between constitutionalism and authoritarianism. In: European Journal of International Relations, 2015, 21(3), 568-594.

63 Zürn, Michael: Global Governace as Multi-level Governance. In: Enderlein, Henrik/ Wälti, Sonja/ Zürn, Michael (Hrsg.). Handbook on Multi-level Governance. Cheltenham, 2010, 80-99.

dependent on the autonomous operation of international institutions as international institutions depend on the cooperation of governments.

As evident at various international sites the emergence of multi-level global governance is a highly conflictive and non-linear process. Powerful actors try to protect their vested interest by developing, and reforming, an ever closer network of interlocking, and at times interblocking, institutions. In turn, these institutions increasingly provoke a countermovement in different parts of the world. These protest movements seek to scandalize the way the world is governed by big government and big money, and they seek to regain political agency by coordinating their activities and by connecting them to international public spaces. Overall, therefore, we witness a still open, but certainly not unstructured, process of institution-building at different political levels and across a wide spectrum of public and private actors to better coordinate their cross-national interactions and to develop sufficiently stable behavioral expectations for mutually beneficial exchange and common problem solving. According to Michael Zürn[64], multilevel governance with all of its prospects and shortcomings is a fact of life and will become "the *condition politica* of the twenty-first century."

### *3.2 International Organizations in Global Governance*

International organizations are a crucial component of the emerging post-Westphalian order[65]. States create and maintain international organizations such as the Food and Agriculture Organization, the United Nations or the World Trade Organization to deal with common challenges in specific issue areas. The FAO is supposed to improve global food security, the United Nations to promote peace and international cooperation, and the World Trade Organization to encourage free trade. Furthermore, states transfer issue-area specific authority to these organizations[66]. For this purpose international organizations dispose of their own staff and budget. They are tasked with collecting and disseminating problem-specific information, they assist member states to devise appropriate solutions, and they often monitor the

64 Zürn, Global Governace as Multi-level Governance, 82.

65 Karns, Margaret P./ Mingst, Karen A. International Organizations. The Politics and Processes of Global Governance. Boulder, Colo, 2010; Rittberger, Volker/ Zangl, Bernhard: International Organization. Polity, Policy and Politics. Houndmills, 2006.

66 Barnett, Michael/ Finnemore, Martha. The Power of Liberal International Organizations. In: Barnett, Michael N./ Duvall, Raymond (Hrsg.). Power in Global Governance. Cambridge, UK, New York, 2005, 161-184.

implementation of common policies. By doing so international organizations socialize member states into a particular mode of global policy making[67]. Information is channeled through a bureaucratic system, evidence is provided according to established standards, and decisions are taken with at least some respect to the available facts and commonly agreed-upon principles and norms. In fact, international organizations support a culture of rationalized governance which avoids explicit external sanctions, builds on reasonable compromises, and internalizes the costs of deviant behavior. Member states know that they risk the break-down of cooperation if they do not stick to the rules as decided within international organizations.

While it is evident that member states occasionally choose to pay the material and reputational losses that come with the violation of international standards and while it is also evident that the proliferation and diversification of international organization does not match the global demand for cooperation in times of rapid globalization, there is a clear and consistent albeit imperfect trend towards more global multi-level governance[68]. States do delegate authority to international organizations and pool sovereignty in various supra-national decision-making bodies. What is more, they increasingly accept majoritarian decision making. According to Zürn

> "roughly two-thirds of all international organizations with the participation of at least one great power have the possibility to decide by a majority of votes by states."[69]

States also increasingly accept tight controls on the implementation of international policies. On the one hand, the monitoring of rule compliance is delegated to independent actors such as expert bodies or NGOs. On the other hand, we see a rise of binding dispute settlement procedures associated with international organizations. In fact, the trend toward the judicalization, if not legalization, of international politics seems to be unabated[70]. The

67 Barnett/ Finnemore, The Power of Liberal International Organizations; Hurd, Ian. International Organizations. Politics, Law, Practice. Cambridge, 2009.

68 Keohane, Governance in a Partially Globalized World; Zürn, Michael/ Binder, Martin/ Ecker-Ehrhardt, Matthias. International Authority and Its Politicization. In: International Theory, 2012, 4(1), 69-106.

69 Zürn, Globalization and Global Governance, 409; apparently, governments are more inclined to accept majority voting with growing membership size of international organizations according to Blake, Daniel J./ Lockwood Payton, Autum. Decision Making in International Organizations: An Interest Based Approach to Voting Rule Selection. Paper prepared for the Research in International Politics Workshop, Ohio State University. 2009, 23.

70 Simmons, Beth A. International Law. In: Carlsnaes, Walter/ Risse-Kappen, Thomas/ Simmons, Beth A. (Hrsg.). Handbook of International Relations. London,

same holds true for the transnationalization of international organizations. As pointed out by Thomas Risse[71] and Volker Rittberger et al.[72] international organizations tend to become more and more inclusive. Even though non-state actors do hold equal powers as governmental actors in only very few instances such as the International Labour Organization, most international organizations have found ways for a less formal but nevertheless effective participation of NGOs or transnational firms in their activities.

The emergence of global multi-level governance is a real but uneven process. In terms of institutional density and institutional effectiveness Western Europe and the Americas clearly outperform other World regions[73]. But the trend of pooling and delegating political authority within and towards international organizations is ongoing in Asia, Africa and the Arabic world as well. Given the proliferation of global and regional challenges such as climate change, the stabilization of markets, or the systematic violation of human rights governments do start to devise institutional solutions and to engage in multi-level global governances processes. This does not mean, however, that the world is automatically moving towards a well-ordered global society. The shortcomings and failures of international organizations to effectively address the problems that led to their creation and modification in the first place are obvious. The same holds true for the still persistent reluctance of many governments to consistently accept the authority of regional and global institutions. The context of policy-making under the conditions of the 21st century, however, has already dramatically – even if unevenly – changed and this change has clear consequence for the peace and security at the international as well as the national level.

### *3.3 International Organizations for Peace*

Liberal scholars have long argued that international organizations promote peace and security among nations. If managed appropriately they help states to avoid costly war and to find viable compromises to their conflicts.[74]

---

2013, 361; Zürn, Globalization and Global Governance, 410.

71 Risse, Thomas. Transnational Actors and World Poitics. In: Carlsnaes, Walter/ Risse-Kappen, Thomas/ Simmons, Beth A. (Hrsg.). Handbook of International Relations. London, 2013, 426-452.

72 Rittberger et al., Grundzüge der Weltpolitik.

73 Pevehouse, Jon C./ Timothy Nordstrom/ Kevin Warnke. The COW-2 International Organizations Dataset Version 2.0. In: Conflict Management and Peace Science, 2004, 21(1), 101-119.

74 It should be noted, however, that international organizations under certain conditions might also increase the risk of war. David A. Lake for instance showed

Realists, by contrast, remain skeptical[75]. They do not believe in the future of multi-level governance and they consider international organizations to be fine weather phenomena only. In cases of serious international conflict international organizations simply lack the necessary means to deter the use of force if states hold this to be in their national interest. Consequently, governments cannot and will not rely on international organizations for the protection of their security. Governments know that they are persistently operating under conditions of a self-help-system and they will resort to traditional forms of balancing and power politics as long as the shadow of anarchy is hanging over them. In the following we will first present the liberal argument for the peace-promoting effects of international organizations in some detail. In a second step we will muster the available empirical evidence to counter the Realist skepticism and support the liberal claim that peace and security can be promoted by international organizations.

### *3.3.1 The Liberal Argument*

For liberals wars are a social catastrophe and should be avoided. Wars signal the breakdown of law and order and go along with death and destruction. As a rule, not only fighters are victimized on the battlefield, but entire societies suffer. The number of non-combatants dying from the direct and indirect consequences of war such as economic shortages, famines, displacement or disrupted health care and social security systems by far exceeds military casualties. Even though a complete theory of war is still lacking, a number of factors are now known which affect the risk of war[76]. Basically, governments choose war if they come to the conclusion that the use of force is the best way to achieve their goals. If they expect military defeat or see more cost-efficient options, they will not take up arms. In this context, liberal

---

that the creation of NATO was reciprocated by the formation of the Warsaw Pact. More generally, exclusive international institutions – most of all highly institutionalized alliances – may intensify the security dilemma and promote instability; Lake, David A. Beyond Anarchy. The Importance of Security Institutions. In: International Security, 2001, 26(1), 129-160.

75 Gowa, Joanne. The Democratic Peace After the Cold War. In: Economics & Politics, 2011, 23(2), 153-171; Mearsheimer, John J. The Tragedy of Great Power Politics, New York, 2001; Waltz, Kenneth N. Structural Realism after the Cold War. In: International Security, 2000, 25(1), 5-41.

76 Fearon, James. Rationalist Explanations for War. In: International Organization, 1995, 49(3), 379-414; Levy, Jack S./ Thompson, William R. Causes of War. Chichester, West Sussex, 2010; Vasquez, John A. The War Puzzle Revisited. Cambridge, 2009.

scholars argue that international organizations help political actors to avoid war in multiple ways.

First of all, international organizations might support states to manage the security dilemma[77]. They can provide governments with clear behavioral standards for non-offensive behavior, they can introduce confidence and security measures, and they can increase military transparency. As a consequence, member states are in a position to detect unfriendly intentions early enough to take countermeasures for the protection of their national interests, which in turn minimizes the incentives for aggressive policies in the first place. Additionally, international institutions such as the Security Council of the United Nations or the International Atomic Energy Agency might offer conflicting parties reliable security guarantees which they need to escape the security dilemma. Without security guarantees, parties to a conflict often find it hard to develop enough trust in the benevolence of the other side to forego short term military advantages. If not accommodated, this missing trust can in turn further destabilize international relations.

Moreover, international organizations help states to deal with issue-area specific conflicts. For this purpose, they provide member states with a set of principles, norms and dispute settlement mechanisms designed to resolve contentious cases[78]. International organizations also bring high-level officials into regular contact and often monitor member states' behavior. By doing so, international organizations considerably increase the available information to assess each other's policy preferences which in turn enlarges the bargaining range and improves the prospects of negotiated settlements in cases of disputes. By increasing the likelihood of issue-area specific peaceful solutions international organizations tend to isolate conflicts and to decrease the risk of an all overarching "us-versus them" confrontation which typically proceeds a war[79].

Finally, international organizations not only diffuse the security dilemma and facilitate the peaceful settlement of conflicts but they also raise the

---

77 Müller, Harald. Security Cooperation. In: Carlsnaes, Walter/ Risse-Kappen, Thomas/ Simmons, Beth A. (Hrsg.). Handbook of International Relations. London, 2013, 607-634; Rittberger/ Zangl, International Organization.

78 Boehmer, Charles/ Gartzke, Eric/ Nordstrom, Timothy. Do Intergovernmental Organizations Promote Peace? In: World Politics, 2004, 57(1), 1-38; Rittberger, Volker/ Zürn, Michael. Towards Regulated Anarchy in East-West Relations. In: Rittberger, Volker (Hrsg.). International Regimes in East-West Politics. London, New York, 1990, 9-63.

79 Vasquez, John A. What Do We Know About War. In: Vasquez, John A. (Hrsg.): What Do We Know about War? Lanham, 2000, 335-370.

opportunity cost of war[80]. States know that they need multilateral organizations to successfully manage interdependence and globalization. Without them they would be much worse off and could not appropriately protect the welfare of their societies. Since the use of force always tends to destroy mutually beneficial relations, governments would think twice before returning to military means to promote their interests[81].

### *3.3.2 The Empirical Findings*

As already stated before, the strong liberal expectations on the peace-promoting effects of international organizations are met with an equally strong skepticism by realist scholars. For them international organizations closely mirror great power interests. As long as these interests are in harmony, peace prevails and international organizations work. Under conditions of anarchy, however, great power harmony is the exception and serious conflict cannot be avoided for long. As soon as serious conflict re-emerges, however, international institutions will lose their viability and will take a back seat in international politics again. As Randal Schweller has put it: "Binding institutions either work best when they are needed least or simply do not work at all."[82]

Recent empirical research, however, strongly suggests that international organizations have a life of their own and that they positively impact on international peace even if we control for power differences. First of all, international organizations may directly help states to avoid or settle interstate armed conflict. A number of studies found for instance that well-institutionalized regional security organizations significantly reduce the risk of militarized interstate disputes among member states[83]. Particularly effective in

80 Mansfield, Edward D./ Pevehouse, Jon: Trade Blocs, Trade Flows, and International Conflict. In: International Organization, 2000, 54(4), 775-808.

81 Keohane, Robert O. After Hegemony. Cooperation and Discord in the World Political Economy. Princeton, N.J. 1984; Chayes, Abram/ Chayes, Antonia H. The New Sovereignty. Compliance with International Regulatory Agreements. Cambridge, Mass, 1998

82 Schweller, Randall L. The Problem of International Order Revisited. In: International Security, 2001, 26(1), 163.

83 Boehmer et al., Do Intergovernmental Organizations Promote Peace?; Hansen, Holley E./ McLaughlin Mitchell, Sara/ Nemeth, Stephen C. IO Mediation of Interstate Conflicts: Moving Beyond the Global versus Regional Dichotomy. In: Journal of Conflict Resolution, 2008, 52(2), 295-325. Shannon, Megan. Preventing War and Providing the Peace? International Organizations and the Management of Territorial Disputes. In: Conflict Management and Peace Science, 2009, 26(2), 144-163.

this regard are international organizations with binding dispute settlement mechanisms[84]. Moreover, Brandon Kinne[85] showed that shared membership in well-institutionalized intergovernmental organizations promotes strong network ties which increases trust among governments enabling them to find negotiated conflict solutions. These strong network ties can also be mobilized by third parties from within common organizations to mediate between conflicting states[86]. The increase in common membership ties then clearly decreases the risk of armed conflict in international politics. Additionally, in cases where an armed conflict cannot be prevented common membership ties in international organizations tend to reduce the duration of militarized disputes:

> "International organizations can help their members overcome bargaining obstacles that prolong conflict, allowing states to more quickly reach agreements and end disputes. Our analyses reveal that joint IO membership indeed decreases the duration of conflict."[87]

Secondly, international organizations create an environment that indirectly prevents states from escalating conflicts by promoting trade and democracy and by terminating international rivalries. For instance, Edward Mansfield and Jon Pevehouse[88] found that preferential trade agreements significantly reduce the risk of militarized interstate disputes. Similarly, Yoram Haftel showed that regional trade arrangements not only stimulate economic exchange but also go along with regular meetings of high-level officials which "provide member-states with valuable information regarding the interests and resolve of their counterparts."[89] With the help of these information gov-

---

84 Hansen et al., IO Mediation of Interstate Conflicts; McLaughlin Mitchell, Sara/ Hensel, Paul R. International Institutions and Compliance with Agreements. In: American Journal of Political Science, 2007, 51(4), 721-737.

85 Kinne, Brandon J. IGO Membership, Network Convergence, and Credible Signaling in Militarized Disputes. In: Journal of Peace Research, 2013, 50(6), 659-676.

86 Dorussen, Han/ Ward, Hugh. Intergovernmental Organizations and the Kantian Peace: A Network Perspective. In: Journal of Conflict Resolution, 2008, 52(2), 189-212.

87 Shannon, Megan/ Morey, Daniel/ Boehmke, Frederick J. The Influence of International Organizations on Militarized Dispute Initiation and Duration. In: International Studies Quarterly, 2010, 54(4), 1138.

88 Mansfield, Edward D./ Pevehouse, Jon. Institutions, Interdependence, and International Conflict. In: Schneider, Gerald/ Barbieri, Katherine/ Gleditsch, Nils P. (Hrsg.). Globalization and Armed Conflict. Lanham, 2003, 233-250.

89 Haftel, Yoram Z. Designing for Peace. Regional Integration Arrangements, Institutional Variation, and Militarized Interstate Disputes. In: International Organization, 2007, 61(1), 217.

ernments are able to find negotiated solutions to their disputes. Moreover, it is a well-established finding in International Relations that democracies do not fight wars against each other and that they are only very rarely engaged in smaller armed conflict[90]. Interestingly, regional organizations are found to be positively related with the democratization of member states[91]. And in contrast to the often voiced concerns that international organizations tend to undermine national democracy, Robert Keohane, Stephen Macedo and Andrew Moravcsik showed that multilateral institutions can enhance domestic democracy in a number of ways:

> "Involvement with multilateral institutions often helps domestic democratic institutions restrict the power of special interest factions, protect individual rights, and improve the quality of democratic deliberation while also increasing capacities to achieve important public purposes."[92]

While these positive effects of multilateral institutions on domestic democracy have to be weighed against the often observed empowerment of national executives at the expense of national parliaments it should be clear that international organizations, at least under certain conditions, contribute to the proliferation of democracy, which in the end should lead to a pacification of international politics. Finally, international organizations facilitate the termination of international rivalries[93]. International rivalries are characterized by reciprocal enemy images which significantly increases the likelihood of conflict escalation. In these contexts, international organizations have the potential to transform enemy images. They open learning spaces by bringing parties into closer contact and by promoting small-step cooperation projects.

Moreover, there is not only strong evidence that international organizations help states to settle their conflicts without resort to arms and to maintain peace, international organizations are also found to play a role in the prevention of domestic conflict and in restoring peace after civil wars.

90 Russett, Bruce M./ Oneal, John R. Triangulating Peace. Democracy, Interdependence, and International Organizations. New York, 2001.

91 Pevehouse, Jon C. Democracy from the Outside-In? International Organizations and Democratization. In: International Organization, 2002, 56(3), 515-549.

92 Keohane, Robert O./ Macedo, Stephen/ Moravcsik, Andrew. Democracy-Enhancing Multilateralism. In: International Organization, 2009, 63(1), 2.

93 Hasenclever, Andreas/ Weiffen, Brigitte. International Institutions are the Key: A New Perspective on the Democratic Peace. In: Review of International Studies, 2006, 32(4), 563-585; Prins, Brandon C./ Daxecker, Ursula E. Committed To Peace: Liberal Institutions and the Termination of Rivalry. In: British Journal of Political Science, 2008, 38(01), 19-43.

Johannes Karreth and Jaroslav Tir made a convincing case that a state's membership in larger numbers of so-called highly structured international organizations such as the International Atomic Energy Agency (IAEA), the Inter-American Development Bank or the Southern African Customs Union IMF "significantly reduces the likelihood that a domestic conflict on its territory will escalate to a civil war, primarily by increasing the likelihood of settlement." [94] Additionally, Scott Sigmund Gartner found that "mediation by regional organizations has positive effect on settlement durability."[95] This effect has for a long time not been recognized in research because regional organizations tend to mediate particularly intractable conflicts and this selection effect had not been controlled for. Finally, it is a well-established finding in peace and conflict research that multilateral peacekeeping missions by the United Nations or other regional organizations significantly reduce the risk of civil war recurrence[96]. While this does not mean that peacekeeping missions are in most cases sufficiently well-designed to not only keep a negative peace but to move a post-conflict society from a divided past into common future, the negative impact of peacekeeping missions on the probability of a new civil war is clear and persistent. International organizations, therefore, can effectively support peace consolidation processes in ar-torn societies even though the current practice evidently is far from perfect and a lot can be done to improve the responsiveness of peacekeeping missions to local contexts[97].

Overall, the available empirical evidence gives strong support to the liberal expectation that international organizations make a difference and help governments to maintain peace both among and within nations. Additionally, international organizations proofed to be valuable for the restoration of peace after the outbreak of violence. While the deficits in international peace-keeping and peace-making are still more than evident, the problems lie not so much in the institutional environment of international affairs but in the lack of political will and political imagination on the part of im-

94 Karreth, Johannes/ Tir, Jaroslav. International Institutions and Civil War Prevention. In: The Journal of Politics, 2013, 75(1), 97.

95 Gartner, Scott S. Signs of Trouble: Regional Organization Mediation and Civil War Agreement Durability. In: The Journal of Politics, 2011, 73(2), 387.

96 Doyle, Michael W./ Sambanis, Nicholas. Making War and Building Peace. United Nations Peace Operations. Princeton, N.J. 2006; Mason, David T./ Gurses, Mehmet/ Brandt, Patrick T./ Michael Quinn, Jason. When Civil Wars Recur: Conditions for Durable Peace after Civil Wars. In: International Studies Perspectives 2011, 12(2), 171-189.

97 Paris, Roland. Saving Liberal Peacebuilding. In: Review of International Studies, 2010, 36(2), 337-365.

portant member states to use the available instruments and resources. This would not change with the establishment of a world state. What is needed, by contrast, is a growing public awareness of the potential of multi-level global governance and strong pressure by social movements on national governments to use this potential for the promotion of peace and stability. To put in a nutshell: Existing international organizations are far from perfect; however, they are the best option we have and we should try to improve them. This would also imply to increase the accountability of international organizations towards the affected societies and to dramatically improve their legitimacy by better integrating the voices and concerns of the Global South.

## *4. Conclusion*

Today the question of peace and how it can be achieved between and within nations is as relevant as ever. Activists and academics alike are in an ongoing search for the appropriate instruments to cope with inter-state conflicts and domestic violence. In this context, some pin their hopes on the idea of a world state. At first sight this thought seems logical: If international anarchy is the main barrier to peace, creating a world sovereign seems to be the obvious answer. However, in the same way as the realist idea of international anarchy paints an overly simplistic picture of global politics, conceptions of a world state underestimate the complexity of the international field. Both, international anarchy and the world state, are located at the ends of a continuum in the way of thinking about the international system: While a focus on international anarchy tends to dismiss the operation of international institutions, the call for a world state overestimates the feasibility of a global central authority. Somewhere in the middle lies the idea of multi-level global governance, which in our understanding is better suited to understand the complexity of contemporary international politics and the prospects for peace in a world with a multitude of actors such as states, international organizations, transnational corporations and non-governmental organizations.

We refute the concept of the world state on the principle of prudence. We do not see how a world state could better deal with the global challenges than national governments or existing international organizations. Today most violent conflicts take place within states and it remains unclear how a world state should be able to address and solve them. Furthermore, the creation of a world state would most likely be a very conflictive process.

At the same time, the danger of a world tyranny cannot be ruled out. Taken together these doubts lead us to caution against the pursuit of the world state project. It could in the end create more bloodshed then it hoped to avert.

Instead of following the world state agenda we propose to take a closer look at existing forms of multi-level global governance and the ways in which they foster peace. Following the liberal argument we believe that international organizations can support the settlement of conflicts in various ways, for instance by alleviating the security dilemma, by providing dispute settlement mechanisms, or through the promotion of conflict mediation. More indirect peace effects stem from socializing effects of international organizations on member states, for example by promoting democracy or reducing interstate rivalries. Last but not least empirical evidence shows that international organizations time and again help to settle armed intra-state conflicts and to reduce the risk of renewed civil war. Nonetheless, the organization of peace by multi-level global governance evidently has its own shortcomings that must be addressed in the future. Chief among them is the lack of political will by governments. Additionally, most international organizations suffer from a pronounced democratic deficit and privilege the interest of OECD-Countries at the expense of the legitimate concerns of the Global South. Consequently, they tend to mirror rather than to overcome the unequal distribution of power and welfare in the international system.

In the end, there is no easy answer to the question of how best to advance world peace under conditions of conflicting political interests and a strong proliferation of public as well as private actors in global politics. As history has shown time and time again, states and rebels go to war if they want to, and no international organization is in the position to stop them. However, international organizations can reduce the incentives for war, they can enable states and potential rebels to look for viable alternatives to the use of force, and they can support states and rebels to return to the negotiation table after war has broken out. While international organizations are certainly far away from guaranteeing a robust global peace, the same would hold true for a world state. We are, therefore, best advised to put our bet on the political, economic and social dynamics that drive states into multi-level global governance and to try to shape multi-level global governance in a way that enhances the prospect of peace within and among nations. For this purpose it is necessary to realistically assess the contributions of international organization to global peace and security and not to simply ignore them for the sake of a seemingly more effective alternative such as the balance-of-power politics or the formation of a world state.

# Global Governance vs. Global Government Political Philosophy in Times of Globalisation

*Michael Reder*

## *1. Introduction: 'First Globalisation' and Global Governance*

Some historians call the 15th and 16th century the 'First Globalisation'.[1] This time is characterised by a lot of developments that are similar to the globalisation processes during the last two decades: In the Renaissance, many new transport routes were explored and a new trade system was established. At the same time, significant academic and technical revolutions changed the everyday life as well as whole world views (e.g. printing press or heliocentric worldview). With regard to politics, this period is marked by dramatic changes, such as the severe challenges to/ upheavals against both imperial and papal power (cf. Reformation). Those developments were mirrored in fundamental social change (cf. agrarian disturbance) that took place simultaneously. Eventually, those parallel moments of change lead to a rearrangement of the political system and new relationships between different social actors,[2] which also gave rise to new questions for philosophy. Main philosophical questions of the Renaissance were the rediscovery of ancient ideals like the individual and intellectual perfection of man and the ideal of equality. Religion, however, lost its former position in society and had to partially give up its claims to absoluteness.

During this so-called 'First Globalisation', authors like Nicholas of Cusa reacted to these challenges with a new theoretical framework. In particular, he contributed to the field of epistemology by exploring new ways of interpreting human knowledge, which some philosophers interpret as a cornerstone to modern philosophy in general.[3] According to Cusa, final objective knowledge about the unity of reality is not possible due to basic epistemo-

1 Cf. Osterhammel, Jürgen/ Peterson, Nils. Geschichte der Globalisierung. Dimensionen, Prozesse, Epochen. München, 2003; Wallerstein, Immanuel. The Modern World-System I. New York (NY), 1974.

2 Landes, David S. The Wealth and Poverty of Nations: Why Some Are So Rich and Some So Poor. New York, 1998.

3 Rombach, Heinrich. Substanz, System, Struktur. Die Ontologie des Funktionalismus und der philosophische Hintergrund der modernen Wissenschaft. 2nd ed., Freiburg/ München, 1981.

logical limits. Consequently, he emphasises the moment of 'not knowing' – rather than knowing – when trying to grasp the Absolute. Man can thus only think paradoxically about the Absolute. "Quia igitur est omnia absolute maximum absolute quae esse actu possunt taliter absque quaecumque oppositione, ut in maximo minimum coincidat, tunc super omnem affirmationem est pariter et negationem."[4] In this sense, Cusa also pointed to the limits of both the non-contradiction principle and the principle of the 'unity of opposites' as it had been used in the tradition of negative theology.[5]

Starting from this epistemology, Cusa developed a relational ontology. The central figure of thought is the dialectical relation between the processes of enfolding and unfolding. The world is the unfolding of the infinite unity. The unity of the world should not be understood in the sense of a numerical unity, but on another level: it is the source and ground of all being.[6] If every part of the world is unfolded from this unity, any being is always in a dynamic relation with every other being. The individual beings can therefore not be separated from the relations, in which they are involved, but understood only in their relationality to the whole world.

Summarizing his ideas, three main characteristics of Cusa's theory seem to be important concerning the debate about the 'First Globalisation': First, Cusa interprets the world as a network. Therefore, he develops an ontology based on relations as central category. This is not only a philosophical theory, but also a reaction to the so-called 'First Globalisation'. This development leads philosophers like Cusa to the conclusion that the world should be understood as a network of complex and dynamic relations. Globalisation is an increase of such relations. Secondly, by establishing a negative epistemology, Cusa reflects on the limits of knowledge as a whole. In a similar vein as his ontology, this could also be interpreted as a reaction to the global dynamics of his times. As the social world was experienced as a complex network of different actors and relations between multiple cultures and religions, theorists like Cusa realised that knowledge itself should be interpreted as limited. Finally, Cusa also worked on a modern theory of communication as a consequence of these two insights. Because all people are part of a relational structure, they should become aware of this relatedness, the most promising way to which leads via communication.

Today's globalisation has a lot in common with the 'First Globalisation' of the 15$^{th}$ and 16$^{th}$ century. Globalisation during the last two decades is also

4 Nicholas of Cusa. De docta ignorantia (Buch I). 4th ed., Hamburg, 1994, N. 12.
5 Cf. Reder, Michael/ Inthorn, Julia. Philosophie und Mathematik bei Cusanus. Eine Verhältnisbestimmung von dialektischem und binärem Denken. Trier, 2005.
6 Cf. Nicholas of Cusa. De docta ignorantia (Buch II). 3rd ed., Hamburg, 1999.

a fundamental transformation process. Just as much as during the 'First Globalisation', new political structures and institutions have emerged in the last years, especially on the regional and global scale. It is also characterised by innovations in transport systems or technical and communication systems. Last but not least, globalisation is an economic process, e.g. concerning increasing growth rates of world trade and a deepening of global interdependencies. Therefore, Desai argues that global dynamics are "computers plus deregulated capital."[7]

A lot of new theories have been developed during the last two decades in order to explain or understand these global transformations. Within this discourse on globalisation, global governance emerged as one of the most famous and influential paradigms. The historic starting point of the debate on global governance is to be found in the 1980s. At the end of this decade, a group of experts started to analyse global dynamics and to reflect on new forms of governance.[8] In the subsequent academic discourse on global governance from 1990 until today, theorists from several disciplines took key roles, e.g. Rosenau,[9] Held[10] or Nuscheler.[11] Despite major differences between those approaches, their common goal is to provide convincing theories that allow for an understanding of the current global transformations and their dynamics.[12] The focus of global governance theories is to describe complex mechanisms of social and political influence beyond the traditional mechanism of the nation state. This is why the paradigm is called global governance and not global government. Global governance is commonly defined as "the sum of the many ways individuals and institutions, public and private, manage their common affairs. It is a continuing process through which conflicting or diverse interests may be

7 Desai, Meghnad. Globalisation. Neither Ideology nor Utopia. In: *Cambridge Review of International Affairs*, 2000, vol. 14, no. 1, p. 29.

8 Cf. The Commission on Global Governance. Our Global Neighbourhood. Oxford, 1995.

9 Cf. Rosenau, James. Along the Domestic-Foreign Frontier. Exploring Governance in a Turbulent World. Cambridge, 1997; Rosenau, James. Distant Proximities. Dynamics beyond Globalization. Princeton (NJ), 2003.

10 Cf. Held, David. Democracy and the Global Order. From the Modern State to Cosmopolitan Governance. Stanford, 1995; Held, David/ McGrew, Anthony (Eds.). Governing Globalization. Power, Authority and Global Governance. Cambridge, 2002.

11 Cf. Nuscheler, Franz (ed.). Entwicklung und Frieden im 21. Jahrhundert. Zur Wirkungsgeschichte des Brandt-Berichts. Bonn, 2000; Nuscheler, Franz. Global Governance, development, and peace. In: Paul Kennedy, Dirk Messner, Franz Nuscheler (Eds.). Global trends and global governance. London, 2002, pp. 156-183.

12 Cf. Reder, Michael. Global Governance. Philosophische Modelle von Weltpolitik. Darmstadt, 2006.

accommodated and co-operative action may be taken. It includes formal institutions and regimes empowered to enforce compliance as well as informal arrangements that people and institutions either have agreed to or perceive to be in their interest."[13]

Going more into detail, two different approaches of global governance can be distinguished. The first type describes global structures. The focus of these theories is to provide a neutral analysis of global dynamics and transformations. Some authors take one step further and develop political solutions for various global challenges the international community is facing. Thus, this second type of global governance is a normative approach that elaborates normative guidelines and policy options. In this latter perspective, the main normative and political goal of global governance is a just and peaceful world.[14] Peace is understood in a comprehensive way as the establishment of cooperative structures and institutions in different political fields. According to this strand of global governance research, working together in common institutions is the way in which peace can be maintained in the perspective of a normative approach of global governance.

Having sketched some introductory thoughts on global governance, I will now turn to reconstructing the key elements of the global governance paradigm. As a result of comparing different theories, the central dimensions of this paradigm seem to be (1) the analysis of the proliferation of global actors, (2) the interpretation of dynamic global relations and (3) the concept of governance with its normative foundations.

## *2. Basic Elements of Global Governance*

### *2.1 Proliferation of Global Actors and the Importance of Global Relations*

In the perspective of global governance, the proliferation of global actors is one of the main characteristics of the processes taking place in the context of globalisation. Before 1989, during the era called internationalisation, the analysis of global actors did not go beyond nation states and international institutions. After 1989, however, a variety of new actors entered the global stage and thus became important in theories about globalisation. First and foremost, a proliferation of NGOs could be observed. NGOs work on dif-

13 Commission on Global Governance, Global Neighbourhood, p. 2.

14 Cf. Höffe, Otfried. Democracy in an age of globalisation. Dordrecht, 2007.

ferent level – ranging from the local to the global – and in various social and political fields. An example of their activity is the important role they play in the UN system where they actively participate in political deliberation processes, e.g. if new strategies for sustainable development are set up. Secondly, the number of transnational co-operations increased dramatically. Both through their economic activity all around the world and their political commitment in different institutions, their influence became ever more important in global governance processes. Thirdly, different cultural actors such as world religions,[15] but also sports organisations are part of this proliferation.

From the perspective of global governance, one central problem is that traditional political theories are not able to describe this proliferation of global actors in a satisfying way. With their (liberal) focus on the nation state and its sovereignty, they have a blind spot when it comes to different actors of civil society or socio-cultural actors (e.g. religions). This is what motivated Rosenau to establish a new theoretical category in the study of global governance, namely his 'spheres of authority'. As Rosenau argues, "[this] disaggregation of power into myriad spheres of authority (SOA) is the central tendency in world affairs."[16]

This category allows for a better understanding of the proliferation of global actors as parts of complex and dynamic global networks. "[The] new [global governance] ontology requires us to focus on those political actors, structures, processes, and institutions that initiate, sustain, or respond to globalizing forces as they propel boundary-spanning activities and foster boundary-contracting reactions."[17] In the centre of global spheres, we still find actors understood in a traditional way (e.g. a person, an organisation or an institution). The main characteristic of these actors is that they are able to exert authority in global issues and that this authority is accepted by others. This authority, however, should not be thought of as a static feature of actors. Much rather, it is constructed and reconstructed through the *acceptance* of an actor's authority by the people. The spheres of authority "can differ in form and structure dependent on the degree to which their relational foundations

15 Cf. Reder, Michael. Religion in the Public Sphere: The Social Function of Religion in the Context of Climate and Development Policy. In: Dieter Gerten, Sigurd Bergmann (Eds.). Religion in Environmental and Climate Change. Suffering, Values, Lifestyles. New York (NY), 2012, pp. 32-45.

16 Rosenau, James. Governing the Ungovernable: The Challengeof a Global Disaggregation of Authority. In: *Regulation & Governance*, 2007, no. 2, p. 88.

17 Rosenau, James. Toward an Ontology for Global Governance. In: Martin Hewson, Timothy Sinclair (Eds.). Approaches to Global Governance Theory. New York (NY), 1999, p. 295.

are hierarchical arrays."[18] In this perspective, spheres of authority could be the World Bank and The Olympic Committee or even al-Qaida.

What is key to Rosenau's perspective is that authority and thus the influence of these spheres is not (only) dependent on their position in the socio-political order: Any actor could claim authority that might be limited, but not necessarily ineffective. Therefore, global actors cannot simply be understood as being ordered in a clearly structured power hierarchy. „Hierarchy involves power and the relative capability of actors, and we are so accustomed to positing pecking orders in these terms that it will not be easy to come to grips with an disaggregated array of actors whose power is limited to a particular expertise or set of issues, thus rendering them essentially autonomous and not dependent on where they stand in a pecking order."[19] A main purpose of Rosenau's contribution is thus to tackle the bias toward traditional actors in the analysis of in global affairs. As soon as actors are depicted as spheres of authority, the range of observable objects in global governance is broadened and any actor with claims to global authority that are accepted by others can be part of the analysis.[20]

Starting from the proliferation of global actors (or spheres of authority), global governance theories focus on the complex relations between different spheres of authority. These relations exist horizontally as well as vertically, which is why these relations do not only exist on the regional level, but also through the different levels. This is why global governance is called a multi-level system. Taking into account local, national and regional as much as global relations, the analytic aim of global governance is to integrate all these different levels into one political system. One famous example for such a multi-level process was the Agenda 21 process as follow up of the Rio Summit 1992.

One particularly relevant consequence of this multilevel approach is that the concepts of national boundaries and sovereignty become less important. As Rosenau puts it, "it has come to be widely understood in our emergent era

18 Rosenau, Ontology for Global Governance, p. 295.

19 Rosenau, Ontology for Global Governance, p. 297.

20 Obviously, the so-called "spheres of authority" are not the only category which was set up within the global governance paradigm. Other authors focus on "networks" as basic category (cf. Messner, Dirk. The Network Society. Economic Development and International Competitveness as Problems of Social Governance. London, 1997), others again on "world systems" (cf. Willke, Helmut. Atopia. Studien zur atopischen Gesellschaft. Frankfurt, 2001; Willke, Helmut. Heterotopia. Studien zur Krise der Ordnung moderner Gesellschaften. Frankfurt, 2003). What all theories have in common, though, is their emphasis on the proliferation of global actors as the center piece of the global dynamics we are witnessing.

that the boundaries separating domestic and foreign affairs are no longer firm and have, instead, been eroded and become porous, being transgressed by a variety of diverse types of actors and issues.“[21] Hence, some authors pointed to the need of a new ontology for the theories that seek to explain or understand these transformations. According to this assessment a new global governance ontology should focus on relations, not substances (like the nation state as a substantial actor or unit). The world – and this is again an argument of Nicholas of Cusa – should be understood as a dynamic relational network.

Let me summarise: In the perspective of the debate on global governance ontology, the proliferation of global actors and the relations between the different spheres of authority are the main characteristics of the globalisation processes as we know them today. Given that such developments can no longer be grasped within in the hitherto existing ontological frameworks, one of the main tasks of the global governance discourse is to provide a way of reflecting on social structures while acknowledging the limits of knowledge about multilevel and dynamic relations. Therefore, authors who contribute to this discourse try to explore ways "of eschewing the scientific procedure of designating independent and dependent variables, [instead] replacing it with a method that maintains a sensitivity to the interactive complexity of global order by relentlessly estimating how a shift in one set of dynamics may affect each of the other two sets and feedback as a stimulus to reinforcing or further shifting the original change."[22]

The conceptions of *heterotopy* (H. Willke) or *fragmegration* (J. Rosenau) are two examples of such endeavours, which illustrate two different important approaches in the current academic debate. The etymological innovation of the theoretical concept of *fragmegration* accounts for the insight that the processes of fragmentation and integration are closely interrelated or, put differently, that the social and political processes of aggregation and disaggregation are interacting rapidly and simultaneously. Compared to traditional concepts like liberalism or political realism, the concept of *fragmegration* avoids a reductionist view on global dynamics that highlights either one or the other of these to processes, but understands and reflects them as interrelated at the outset. "(…) (T)he virtue of a fragmegration concept is that it offers branching alternatives (…) which enable the theorist to anticipate the paths actions and systems will follow as a consequence of prior developments (or decisions). Instead of attributing common goals to actors,

21 Rosenau, Domestic-Foreign Frontier, p. 32.

22 Rosenau, James. Governance, Order, and Change in World Politics. In: Ernst-Otto Czempiel, James Rosenau (Eds.). Governance without Government. Order and Change in World Politics. Cambridge, 1992, p. 18.

in other words, such a perspective uses the tensions between fragmentation and integration as a basis for narrowing likely outcomes and excluding a wide range of other outcomes, depending on which set of tensions prevails when globalizing and localizing dynamics interact."[23]

While Rosenau's approach offers an analytical perspective that uncovers the intertwined character of integration and fragmentation, Willke's concept of *heterotopy* expresses another complexity of global governance processes: the interrelation order of global disorder.[24] "Heterotopy [therefore] designates an ideal type of social order that aims at globality and seeks to establish governance on the basis of federality and subsidiarity in a partially globalised world while at the same time accepting the frightening heterogeneity of global contexts."[25] Willke interprets disorder not as a lack,[26] but as part of a complex global structure. Subsidiarity and federality as two effective "forms of self-regulation of complex social systems"[27] could help in the actualisation of the idea of a global order that accepts disorder and interprets it as an integral part.

### *2.2 Normative Foundation and Concept of Governance*

While theoretically coping with the proliferation of global actors is mainly a question of adequate description and analysis, another focus of global governance concerns the question of how different formal and informal actors mutually influence each other beyond traditional mechanisms of *government* (in the nation state). Reflecting on this second basic element of global governance leads us to the political and ethical dimension of global governance. At a first glance, the distinction between global governance and global government seems to be a merely political one. A closer look however, reveals that it is also a philosophical, more precisely an ethical distinction. Therefore, it seems to be important to reflect shortly on political philosophy in general and its consequences for the global governance discourse.

---

23 Rosenau, Domestic-Foreign Frontier, p. 45.

24 Cf. Willke, Heterotopia.

25 Willke, Heterotopia, p. 11 (translation M.R.; German original: „Heterotopia meint die idealtypische Ordnung einer Gesellschaft, die auf Globalität zielt und in einer partiell globalisierten Welt Gouvernanz auf der Basis von Föderalität und Subsidiarität zu verwirklichen sucht, sich dabei aber der erschreckenden Heterogenität globaler Kontexte stellt").

26 Cf. Willke, Heterotopia, p. 48.

27 Willke, Heterotopia, p. 63 (translation M.R.; German original: „Formen der Selbststeuerung komplexer Sozialsysteme").

Approaches to political philosophy can roughly be divided into two traditions, one going back to Kant (e.g. Rawls), the other to Hegel (e.g. Honneth). Whereas theories in the tradition of Kant are based on a clear fact-value distinction and the assumption of an (abstract) reason of morality, theories in the tradition of Hegel integrate morality and ethical life and focus on the variety of social, political and cultural practices as starting point of philosophical reflection. As opposed to the Kantian tradition that understands law as an implementation of morality through a single political actor, the state, philosophers indebted to Hegel emphasise the heterogeneous social and political dynamics that have to be improved over time. This is why theories in the tradition of Hegel typically point to the diversity of values that, embedded in cultural practices, constitute morality. With this latter conceptualisation, it goes hand in hand that political strategies are not merely accepted because of an abstract reason but rather because they are incorporated in social life and heterogeneous cultural practices. In this perspective, it follows that philosophical reflections should be closely connected to such practices, which allows for moral principles to be grounded in and connected to social reality and therefore claim universal validity. As existing forms of social practices and the respective embedded moral norms are plural and diverse, theories in the tradition of Hegel – such as pragmatism – concentrate on the complementarity of existing different moral belief systems, assuming that humans always strive for practical coherence between different norms and convictions in their everyday life.[28].

Such arguments are famously advocated by Axel Honneth in his interpretation of Hegel. Honneth argues that our normative reflections should always be grounded in a detailed analysis of society, including the different social and normative practices to be found there. In the tradition of Hegel's philosophy of right, the aim should be "[to analyze] current institutions and practices according to their normative merit, in the order of their importance for the social embodiment and realization of socially legitimate values".[29] By doing so, Honneth rejects a clear distinction between facts and values as well as a focus on abstract moral principles. Instead, he emphasises the concrete potential of mutual recognition in the spheres of *Sittlichkeit*. As Axel Honneth argues, starting ethical reflection from social practices does not equal an acceptance of any existing practice. In fact, a critical recon-

28 Cf. Nida-Rümelin, Julian. Economic Rationality and Practical Reason. Dordrecht, 1997.

29 Honneth, Axel. A Theory of Justice as an Analysis of Society : Preliminary Remarks on a Research Program. In: Soeffner, Hans-Georg (ed.). Unsichere Zeiten, Herausforderungen gesellschaftlicher Transformation. Wiesbaden 2010, p. 711.

struction has to analyse and discuss the 'moral' potential of such practices and inquire the ways in which they could be improved in consideration of the fundamental ideas underlying them (cf. Honneth 2008). Obviously, such an analysis from a pragmatic point of view first has to identify what kind of practices it can grasp at all on a theoretical level. Of course, Honneth focuses on societies in their national borders. This, however, does not preclude an expansion of his perspective to a global level. We should then go about asking which social and normative practices are important in the global sphere of *Sittlichkeit*.

Theories of global government mostly claim to stand in a Kantian tradition, although Kant himself was in favour of a federalism of states as he argued in his work *Zum Ewigen Frieden*[30]. The key argument of global government approaches goes as follows: If constitutional democracy is the most reasonable form of government, and if globalisation processes lead to an infringement and a limitation of democratic governance within the nation state, then we have to establish a democratic government on the global level, too. Otfried Höffe's concept of a federal world republic is certainly one of the most famous elaborations on this argument.[31] In order to achieve peaceful and just coexistence on a global scale, a democratic government is the *conditio sine qua non*.[32] Despite his arguments in favour of subsidiarity and federalism as integral elements of the world republic, Höffe in the end sticks to a traditional set of governing instruments, especially rights and democratic power, as they had been developed for the context of the nation state. "Right culminates in world right and the public safeguarding of rights culminates in the task of a subsidiary and federal world republic."[33]

While (normative) global governance theories do agree with the political goal of global government, a just and peaceful world, they differ with respect to their conceptualisation of the various global actors, taking their different potentials of self-governance and governing others as a point of departure. On that basis, they argue for multi-level and multilateral forms of governing social processes, a structural understanding of power and a

30 Kant, Imanuel. Zum Ewigen Frieden. Ein philosophischer Entwurf. In: Kants Werke. Band VIII (hrsg. Königlich Preußische Akademie der Wissenschaften im Jahr 1923). Berlin, pp. 341-386.

31 Cf. Höffe, Democracy; Höffe, Otfried. *Kant's Cosmopolitan Theory of Law and Peace*. Cambridge, 2006; Höffe, Otfried. Some Kantian Reflections on a World Republic. In: Kantian Review 1998, vol., pp. 51-71.

32 I neglect at this point the difference between theories arguing for a government of a world state and those who are in favour of a federal world republic including an global government.

33 Höffe, *Kant's Cosmopolitan Theory, p.* 203.

concept of political influence underlying their theories. Rights and the traditional governance mechanisms of the nation state are only one part of the complex set or governing mechanisms that global governance seeks to describe and/or to promote. Both global governance and global government are thus goal-orientated political concepts based on a normative reflection. Yet, government theories rather focus on political activities by formal authorities and institutions, whereas governance "refers to activities backed by shared goals that may or may not derive from legal and formally prescribed responsibilities and that do not necessarily rely on police powers to overcome defiance and attain compliance. Governance, in other words, is a more encompassing phenomenon than government."[34]

What distinguishes global government and global governance is the different understanding of power. Whereas government orientated approaches focus on traditional power (similar to the power of the nation state), global governance theorists follow a structural understanding of power. "Power is in the 21st century is no longer based on controlling of large territories and only secondarily on the threat of violence or the amount of defence budgets, but primarily on the strategic, organizational, knowledge-based and focused on co-operative problem-solving skills in order to manage complex interactions, to organize cooperation and to reform structures actively and goal-oriented."[35] Power in the sense of global governance is not the 'traditional power' connected to a territory or to the army as a guardian of peace. Instead, it picks up the concept of power as propounded by Hannah Arendt: the power to cooperate in dynamic constellations and to act together across institutional arrangements. Mutual learning processes in such cooperative networks are one of the key concerns of global governance, especially the normative approaches. Governance is "the postmodern power par excellence. (…) The reference to structural power, the meta-power, is the best and most promising strategy in the *Gesellschaftswelt*."[36]

---

34 Rosenau, Governance, Order, and Change, p. 4.

35 Messner, Dirk. Globalisierungsanforderungen an Institutionen deutscher Außen- und Entwicklungspolitik. In: *Aus Politik und Zeitgeschichte*. 2001, Jg. 51, Nr. 18/19, p. 29 (translation by M.R. ; German original: „Macht basiert im 21. Jahrhundert also nicht mehr auf der Beherrschung großer Territorien und nur sekundär auf Gewaltandrohung oder der Höhe des Rüstungsetats, sondern primär auf der strategischen, organisatorischen, wissensbasierten und auf gemeinsame Problemlösung ausgerichteten Kompetenz, komplexe Interaktionen zu steuern, Kooperationen zu organisieren und durch Strukturbildung die Richtung des Wandels aktiv und zielorientiert (mit) zu gestalten").

36 Czempiel, Ernst-Otto. Kluge Macht. Außenpolitik für das 21. Jahrhundert. München, 1999, p. 96.

Against this background, global governance theories have a lot of reservations concerning global government. Let me summarize some of these sceptical objections: First, these theories reject the idea that the analytical framework of the nation state is adequate for the construction of global governance. Even more, analogy between nation state and global governance is misleading because the social context and political dynamics differ. "The theoretical responses to this constitutionalization of a supranational world power, however, have been entirely inadequate. Instead of recognizing what was really new about these supranational processes, the vast majority of juridical theorists merely tried to resurrect anachronistic models to apply to the new problems. To a large extent, in fact, the models that had presided over the birth of the nation-state were simply dusted off and reproposed as interpretive schema for reading the construction of a supranational power."[37] Furthermore, theories of global government often imply an old and insufficient understanding of statehood. Although the state is still an important political actor, it is witnessing through enormous changes. Today, the state is no longer exclusively a sovereign actor (or a monopolist of authority), but is becoming more and more a network manager (or a manager of political authority).[38]

Secondly, global governance argues that global government mechanisms must be grounded in a strong understanding of global community – which is still absent from (global) reality. The concept of the nation state was founded on an "imagined community"[39] that, for instance, shares common values and a common language. The world as a whole does not share these practices. As a consequence, global government mechanisms will only 'hover' above the people. The title of a review of Höffe's book about democracy in the age of globalisation was 'well done!'[40] Well done, because of the plausibility of the abstract reason for a word republic – but not convincing because a specified political concept (that of Germany) was just put on the global scale and cultural plurality was not understood as an integral part of, not even adequately mirrored / represented in a global government. "Global unity in the sense of a unitary global government is equally impossible

37 Negri, Antonio/ Hardt, Michael. Empire. Cambridge/ London, 2000, pp. 6f.

38 Genschel, Philip/ Zangl, Bernhard. State Transformations in OECD Countries: Towards the State as a Manager of Political Authority. In: *Annual Review of Political Science*, 2014, no. 17, pp. 337-354.

39 Anderson, Benedict R. Imagined Communities. Reflections on the Origin and Spread of Nationalism. London, 1991.

40 Cf. Günther, Klaus. Alles richtig! Otfried Höffes Entwurf einer subsidiären und föderalen Weltrepublik auf der Basis des Allgemeinmenschlichen. In: *Rechtshistorisches Journal*, 2000, no. 19, pp. 232-252.

and undesirable."[41] Thirdly, global governance theories emphasise a lot of practical problems of a world government, e.g. practicability, transparency, bureaucracy.[42]

The ambitions of global government and global governance are more or less the same: a just and peaceful world in which sustainable solutions to the overwhelming global challenges from climate change to poverty and terrorism can be found. And both theories try to provide an alternative to political realism as their famous counter-player. But the strategies to reach these goals are quite different. Whereas theories of global government try to set up an ideal political mechanism which is grounded in an abstract reason, global governance turns the argumentation on its head. Global governance theories (in the tradition of Hegel) start from the variety of social, political and cultural practices that already exist. These practices could be understood as established forms of communicative cooperation and governance. In a second step, these practices of mutual influence are transformed into a multilevel and multilateral institutional design in which as many actors – spheres of authority – as possible should be integrated.

### *2.3 Three examples: state, civil society and international law*

After reflecting on the concept of global governance and its normative foundations, I would like to briefly touch upon three political implications of global governance, namely the re-definition of the state, the focus on civil society and a re-interpretation of international law. These exemplary spotlights should help us understand the various political consequences of the global governance paradigm.

On the political level, global governance is arguing for both a new understanding of the state as a manager of complex networks[43] and the constructive role of civil society in global processes. The nation state is one actor among others in the global governance system. In addition, global governance theories argue that the traditional nation state is unable to cope with the global challenges in a sufficient way on its own. Or, as James Rosenau put it, states do not "seem able to fully withstand the consequences of an ever more turbulent world (…) Thus, while states may not be about to exit

41 Willke, Helmut. Smart Governance. Governing the Global Knowledge Society. Frankfurt/New York (NY), 2007, p. 109.

42 Cf. Reder, Michael. Global Governance, pp. 197-199.

43 Cf. Messner, Dirk (ed.). Die Zukunft des Staates und der Politik. Möglichkeiten und Grenzen politischer Steuerung in der Weltgesellschaft. Bonn, 1998.

from political stage, and while some may even continue to occupy the centre of the stage, they do seem likely to become increasingly ineffective as managers of their own affairs."[44] In the words of Willke, the state should itself have an interest in promoting a complex model of context management in which the dynamics inherent to different actors and social systems would not only be accepted, but used for governing processes. Global governance depends on these forms of self-governance simply because there is no world government that could substitute their role.[45] In this sense, "[t]he role embraced by the pro-active state is then to be understood as a correlate of a society in which a variety of autonomous, self-referential systems cause changes by changing themselves, but not by enforcing changes on other systems by means of external interventions."[46] It is precisely because of these changes that global governance is sceptical towards adapting the concept of the nation state on the global scale.

Secondly, civil society plays an important role in all global governance approaches, no matter which theoretical position they take up. In concepts of world government, e.g. in Höffe's concept of a federal word republic, the constructive role of civil society concerning global challenges is downplayed in some accounts it is even sidelined. Global governance theories, in contrast, emphasise that actors of civil society fulfil constructive functions in political processes. Three examples are pertinent here: First, NGOs take over the so-called 'early warning' function concerning new global problems. Secondly, NGOs are part of the UN-system and its deliberative processes. And finally, some NGOs analyse global challenges as a kind of academic think tanks in order to become a global sphere of authority and to influence global processes.

This is why the academic efforts of capturing the role of NGOs in global governance have been complex. For the purpose of analysing global NGOs systematically despite their complexity and heterogeneity, Rosenau, for instance, developed a 12-membered scheme (e.g. essential structures, membership degree of performance, scope or resources).[47] Another example is

44 Rosenau, James. Changing States in a Changing Word. In: Commission on Global Governance (Eds.). Issues in Global Governance. Papers written for the Commission on Global Governance. London, 1995, pp. 284f.

45 Willke, Smart Governance, 57.

46 Willke, Helmut. Ironie des Staates. Grundlinien einer Theorie des Staates polyzentrischer Gesellschaft. 2nd ed., Frankfurt/M., 1996, p. 143 (translation M.R., German original: „Die Form des aktiven Staates ist dann zu verstehen als Korrelat einer Gesellschaftsform, in der eine Vielzahl autonomer, selbstreferentieller Systeme Veränderungen bewirken, indem sie sich selbst ändern, nicht aber, indem sie anderen Systemen durch externe Interventionen Veränderungen aufzwingen").

47 Rosenau, Domestic-Foreign Frontier, p. 328.

the approach put forward by Meghnad Desai who points to the importance of the sceptical attitude global civil society embraces towards capitalism, thereby playing a critical role in global governance. „It was in devising defensive responses to this new situation that civil societies began to form in many countries. Until then, there had been a unity between the state and the people (…). Now the people had to articulate their voices against the state, even their own state.“[48] The critical perspective of the (global) civil society on capitalism is taking place at two friction points. "At one point, society is reacting to market encroachment on both personal and public spaces: consumerism, atomisation, the erosion of public services, and nation state models of democracy. At the other, society is reacting to socio-economic consequences of capitalism such as poverty, inequality, and instability.“[49]

These positive takes on (global) civil society, however, should not make us blind for the problems that such a focus entails. Theories of global government pointed out such critical aspects, e.g. the lack of legitimacy in cases where NGOs play an important part in deliberative processes, or their tendency to scandalise individual problems of small groups in order to push them on the political agenda. And last but not least, the power asymmetry between NGOs from the global North on the one, and from the global South has often been criticised. Yet, even though all these arguments are convincing, they are no principal objections against the social importance of civil society itself. From the perspective of the global governance paradigm, civil society is one important social, political and cultural practice which should be an integral part of the global governance system – otherwise the political system will lose its connection to the people and their social life.

The third aspect that should be reflected exemplarily is the interpretation of international law within the global governance discourse. Whereas theories of global government often focus on the unity of law, global governance approaches interpret the heterogeneity of international law as one of its advantages. In that perspective, the hybrid and procedural character of international law is emphasised. Hence, the leading concept of international law should not be unity, but plurality and variety, as Willke pointed out. "I suppose that this expansion and differentiation of law makes the conversion of the unity of the legal system from unity to the difference of unity and diversity necessary. The idea behind the law should no longer be sought in the

48 Desai, Meghnad/ Said, Yahia. The New Anti-Capitalist Movement. Money and Global Civil Society. In: Helmut Anheier, Marlies Glasius, Mary Kaldor (Eds.). Global Civil Society. Oxford, 2001, p. 57.

49 Desai/ Said, New Anti-Capitalist Movement, p. 64.

production of order, but in the competence to deal with disorders orderly."[50] Therefore, the competence of international law is monitoring heteronomy.

What global governance theories suspect is that global government approaches want to establish a homogeneous international law. In their view, however, such a homogeneous law not only creates a lot of pragmatic problems but also, and even worse, cannot integrate the different social, political and cultural traditions and legal practices. The plurality of different legal forms and practices, then, is not a problem, but an advantage – this is the central argument of global governance.

## *3. Conclusion: Global governance and democracy to come*

Let me come back to the globalisation of the 15$^{th}$ century and point out some similarities between the discourse about global governance and the approach of Nicholas of Cusa as a reaction to the social change in those times. I want to argue that, within the discourse about globalisation in general and within the discourse about global governance in particular, three characteristics could be mentioned as Nicholas of Cusa has done before me: (a) Global governance approaches often interpret the world as a network: everything is connected with each other. These connections or relations are the main characteristic of global processes. (b) Secondly, facing the tremendous complexity of global processes, a lot of approaches emphasise the limits of knowledge about global dynamics. Authors like Safranski[51] and Toulmin[52] argue in their books about globalisation and cosmopolitism that we should be aware of the limits of knowledge, especially in times of an ever-increasing popularity of rationalistic interpretations of global structures. (c) Thirdly, authors of the global governance discourse concentrate on communication and its cooperative effect (e.g. Dirk Messner). Of course, Jürgen Habermas and his reflections on communicative action and its consequences for democracy in times of globalisation play an important role in that discourse.[53] And even though it may seem surprising, Nicholas of Cusa's theory of communication has some similarities with this discursive approach.

---

50 Willke, Heterotopia, p. 112.

51 Cf. Safranski, Rüdiger. How much globalisation can we bear? Hoboken, 2006.

52 Cf. Toulmin, Stephan. *Cosmopolis.* The Hidden Agenda of *Modernity*. New York (NY), 1990.

53 Cf. Habermas, Jürgen. The Postnational Constellation. Cambridge, 2001.

One main advantage of global governance seems to be that this paradigm sheds light on the relational structure of global processes instead of reaffirming the substantial character of the actors like the nation state. The interconnectedness between the different spheres of authorities is one of the key elements of global governance. This relational focus goes together with an epistemological caution, reminding us that the knowledge about this relational process is always limited: There is no such thing as a comprehensive objective or rationalistic knowledge about all aspects of global dynamics. But this does not mean that global governance is a sceptical, let alone a particularistic approach. The goal of global governance is a just and peaceful world and therefore it implies a universalistic conception. But referring to the tradition of Hegel, this paradigm tries to integrate the cultural, social and political differences as essential part of globalisation and governing global dynamics. Hence, the plurality of social and political practices, a multilevel system of cooperation and a concept of structural power are the decisive building blocks of global governance.

Of course, when comparing global government and global governance, some limitations of global governance could be identified. Main limits of global governance are e.g. the lack of democratic legitimation and the deficient coherence between governance mechanisms. The advantage of global government, i.e. its claim to a homogeneous democratic framework, seems to be the great weakness of global governance. But is global governance really necessarily undemocratic? I do not think so. Globalisation is a challenge for our interpretation of democracy – both on the national and the global level. We need an alternative understanding of cosmopolitan democracy that does not conceptualise political processes in the traditional ways. Instead, what should be developed and explored is a cosmopolitan understanding of democracy that accepts plurality as an everlasting challenge to world society and promotes an understanding of democracy as a responsibility to bear and a task to fulfil by every citizen every day. This conception of cosmopolitan democracy in the perspective of global governance could be understood as a *democracy to come*, a notion coined by Jacques Derrida after the attacks of 9/11.[54] "All decisions made in the name of the Rights of

54 Such a *cosmopolitan democracy to come* could be grounded on the *human rights* as one established global practice. In the tradition of global governance, human rights are a political, normative and legal practice, which the global community has already agreed upon, seeking to provide answers to the many-faceted experience of injustice. From this standpoint, ethical measures for the future of global governance are determined with reference to concrete political and legal practices. Cf. Reder, Michael. Climate Change and Human Rights. In: Ottmar Eden-

Man are at the same time alibis for the continued inequality between singularities, and that we need to invent other concepts than state, superstate and citizen for this new International. The democracy to come obliges one to challenge instituted law in the name of an indefinitely unsatisfied justice, thereby revealing the injustice of calculating justice whether this be in the name of a particular form of democracy or of the concept of humanity. This democracy to come is marked in the movement that has always carried a present beyond itself, makes it inadequate to itself."[55]

hofer et al. (Eds.). Climate Change, Justice and Sustainability. Linking Climate and Development Policy. New York (NY)/ London, 2012, pp. 61-71.

55 Derrida, Jacques. Nietzsche and the Machine (Interview with Richard Beardsworth). In: *Journal of Nietzsche Studies*, 1994, no. 7, pp. 60.

# Global Public Authority in Today's International Economic Legal Order: Towards Substantive and Institutional Convergence à la Pacem in Terris?*

*Karsten Nowrot*

## *1. Introduction: (International) Economic Dimensions of a Positive "Peace on Earth"*

References and considerations with regard to developments in the economic sphere – including the international economic order and its structural as well as legal features – undoubtedly play a rather prominent role in *Pacem in Terris*, the well-known papal encyclical promulgated already more than fifty years ago on 11 April 1963. To mention only a few more or less randomly chosen examples, Pope John XXIII elaborates on the existence and specific expressions of economic human rights like the individual entitlement to work, to adequate working conditions as well as the right to property,[1] and he also highlights the progressive emancipation of the "working classes" as manifested in their increasingly notable participation in socio-economic as well as political affairs.[2] Furthermore, the papal encyclical stresses the inherent responsibilities of governments to promote economic progress as well as the development of "such essential services as the building of roads, transportation, communications, water supply […]", while also re-emphasizing that the respective steering activities in the economic realm should not deprive the individual citizens of their freedom of action in economic matters.[3]

---

* The present contribution was written during a research stay as visiting professor and Global Challenge Visiting Scholar 2015 at Seoul National University School of Law in summer 2015. The author is most grateful for the tremendous support he received from his Korean colleagues and the inspiring academic environment at Seoul National University School of Law.

1 *Pacem in Terris*, Encyclical of Pope John XXIII, promulgated on 11 April 1963, paras. 18-22, available under: <www.papalencyclicals.net/John23/j23pacem.htm> (20 July 2015).

2 *Pacem in Terris* (note 1), para. 40.

3 *Pacem in Terris* (note 1), paras. 64-65; see also already *Mater et Magistra*, Encyclical of Pope John XXIII, promulgated on 15 May 1961, paras. 54-56, available under: <www.papalencyclicals.net/John23/j23mater.htm> (20 July 2015).

With a view to respective developments in the international economic system, *Pacem in Terris*, *inter alia*, praises the "beneficial results" of transnational cooperative activities in the economic sphere, stresses the necessity of additional efforts to facilitate the transboundary circulation of goods, capital and manpower, but also again calls on the industrialized states to provide every kind of assistance to developing countries in order to enable them to benefit from the global welfare effects of international business transactions and thus to foster their own economic development.[4] Finally, also quite noteworthy in the present context is the perception included in this 1963 papal encyclical that as a result of the increasing "exchange of goods", "the interdependence of national economies has grown deeper, one becoming progressively more closely related to the other, so that they become, as it were, integral parts of the one world economy",[5] thereby in fact asserting processes of economic globalization the peculiarities and consequences of which have started to attract major scholarly attention only more than three decades later.[6]

At least at first sight, these frequent references to the (international) economic sphere might appear surprising to some observers, considering the fact that the primary focus of this papal encyclical is obviously the maintenance of global peace and security. In order to explain this notable feature of *Pacem in Terris*, at least two main aspects are worth highlighting. First, it seems useful to briefly recall that the perception of transboundary economic relations as a central factor contributing to the promotion of solidarity as well as amity between different peoples and thus also fostering peaceful relations among them has a long tradition in Christian theology as well as in philosophical thinking. On the one hand, already the early Christian tradition was, albeit not undisputed, also shaped by the belief that international trade and the exchange of goods could be attributed to the divine intervention of God who thus deliberately intended to promote commerce first and foremost with the aim to promote peaceful cooperation among men.[7] This understanding finds its probably most well-known manifesta-

4 *Pacem in Terris* (note 1), paras. 98, 101 and 121-123; see also already, e.g., *Mater et Magistra* (note 3), paras. 164 *et seq.*

5 *Pacem in Terris* (note 1), para. 130.

6 For an early notable analysis from the perspective of legal scholarship see, e.g., Delbrück, Jost. Globalization of Law, Politics, and Markets. In: *Indiana Journal of Global Legal Studies*, 1993, p. 9.

7 See thereto, e.g., Maneschi, Andrea. Comparative Advantage in International Trade – A Historical Perspective. Cheltenham, 1998, p. 26 et seq.; Irwin, Douglas A. Against the Tide – An Intellectual History of Free Trade. Princeton, 1998, p. 15 et seq.

tion in the following statement of the fourth-century Greek pagan Libanius who declared in his *Orations* (III): "God did not bestow all products upon all parts of the earth, but distributed His gifts over different regions, to the end that men might cultivate a social relationship because one would have need of the help of another. And so He called commerce into being, that all men might be able to have common enjoyment of the fruits of earth, no matter where produced."[8] This notion was not only frequently relied upon by Christian theologians like St. Basil, St. John Chrysostom, Theodoretus, St. Ambrose, Henri de Langenstein as well as Giovanni Botero.[9] Rather, it might be appropriate in the present context to stress that also for example one of the proverbial fathers of modern public international law, Hugo Grotius, cited this statement in his groundbreaking work *De Jure Belli ac Pacis* first published in 1625.[10] On the other hand, in the realm of philosophy one only needs to draw renewed attention to Immanuel Kant's famous finding on the incompatibility of the so-called "commercial spirit" and war in his 1795 essay "Perpetual Peace"[11] to illustrate the significant influence exercised by this perspective on modern discourses over the conditions conducive to "peace on earth".

The second main reason for a notable presence of economic considerations relates to the wider notion of peace underlying *Pacem in Terris*. Already the subtitle of this papal encyclical, emphasizing the establishment of peace in "truth, justice, charity and liberty", clearly indicates that it does not adopt the narrow understanding of a so-called "negative peace" as exclusively characterized by the absence of international armed conflicts. Rather, as also illustrated by its extensive elaborations on human rights, non-discrimination, rights of minorities and social justice,[12] "peace on earth" is based on a wider notion of peace.[13] It is thus the perception of the need for a "positive peace" that is a central element in Pope John XXIII's concept of international peace and security, understood as also encom-

8 Cited after: Viner, Jacob. The Role of Providence in the Social Order – An Essay in Intellectual History. Princeton, 1972, p. 36-37.

9 See Viner (note 8), 37-38.

10 Grotius, Hugo. De Jure Belli ac Pacis Libri Tres, translated by Francis W. Kelsey, Oxford, 1925, Book II, Chapter II, XIII, 5.

11 Kant, Immanuel. Perpetual Peace – A Philosophical Essay, translated with introduction and notes by M. Campbell Smith, London, 1903, p. 157.

12 See, e.g., *Pacem in Terris* (note 1), paras. 9 et seq., 86 et seq.

13 On this perception see also, e.g., Minnerath, Roland. Pacem in Terris. *Quid Novi*? In: The Global Quest for *Transquilitas Ordinis*. Pacem in Terris – Fifty Years Later, Pontifical Academy of Social Sciences, Acta 18, 2013, p. 31, available under: <www.pass.va/content/dam/scienzesociali/pdf/acta18/acta18-minnerath.pdf> (20 July 2015).

passing, *inter alia*, the protection of human rights and the environment as well as the creation of conditions for social justice and economic welfare.[14] These considerations do not only serve as another explanation for the frequent references to the economic sphere in the papal encyclical. Rather, from an overarching perspective, they also reveal that *Pacem in Terris* can indeed be regarded as a kind of forerunner of the perception, today rightly subscribed to by most international legal scholars, that in order to actually realize peace through law in a sustainable manner, public international law must first and foremost also be seen and progressively developed as a value-oriented legal order,[15] with the pacification of international relations thus being dependent not only on a more or less comprehensive prohibition on the use of force but also on the effective promotion of other interests such as economic prosperity.

In light of these inherently also (international) economic dimensions of a positive "peace on earth", it seems justified to evaluate whether some of the central conceptual ideas as developed and argued for in *Pacem in Terris* have now, viewed from the perspective of more than fifty years after its promulgation, in fact found their manifestation in the normative structure of today's global economic order. And indeed, such an analytical approach appears also potentially quite promising considering the fact that international economic law can no longer be described as – to take recourse to a recent ironic characterization – a kind of "ugly duckling" within the broader framework of public international law.[16] Quite to the contrary, some of its regulatory areas such as world trade law and more recently certainly also the international normative framework on the protection of foreign investments have in particular since the 1990s emerged as some of the most dynamic and

14 Thereto as well as generally on the distinction between the notions of "negative" and "positive" peace see for example also Bailliet, Cecilia M./Larsen, Kjetil M. Introduction: Promoting Peace through International Law. In: Cecilia M. Bailliet, Kjetil M. Larsen (Eds.). Promoting Peace Through International Law. Oxford, 2015, p. 1 (2 et seq.); Wolfrum, Rüdiger. Article 1 UN Charter. In: Bruno Simma *et al.* (Eds.). The Charter of the United Nations – A Commentary. Vol. I, 3rd ed. Oxford, 2012, paras. 8 et seq.

15 Delbrück, Jost. Peace Through Emerging International Law. In: Jost Delbrück, Die Konstitution des Friedens als Rechtsordnung, edited by Klaus Dicke *et al.*, Berlin, 1996, p. 275 (283).

16 Ziegler, Andreas R. International Economic Law: Still the Ugly Duckling of Public International Law? In: Marise Cremona *et al.* (Eds.). Reflections on the Constitutionalisation of International Economic Law – Liber amicorum for Ernst-Ulrich Petersmann. Leiden, 2014, p. 227 (241) ("It has grown into a young (at least to some, magnificent) swan [...].").

practically important components of the international legal order.[17] The famous saying by John H. Jackson that any attempt to follow the development of international economic law "is like trying to describe a landscape while looking out the window of a moving train – events tend to move faster than one can describe them" serves as an indication for this rightly held view.[18] Since the "law, institutions, and practices of international economic law" are thus now not infrequently perceived as "often advancing more quickly than other areas of international law",[19] it could – most certainly rebuttably – be presumed that also the structural concepts advanced in the papal encyclical, prominently among them the quest for a global public authority, have been first and foremost implemented in this transnational legal regime.

Against this background, the present contribution intends to approach this research issue in three steps, thereby following those main lines of argumentation presented in *Pacem in Terris*[20] that are of particular relevance in the present context. The first section addresses the question whether the current international economic legal order can validly be regarded as a value-oriented normative regime in the sense of its substantive norms focusing on the realization of global public interest concerns and thus on the promoting of objectives that, taken together, can be qualified as something like a universal common good (2.). Subsequently, in the second part an assessment will be given of the position enjoyed by (individual) states in the international economic system with particular emphasis on the perception of their diminished steering capacity as a result of the processes of economic globalization (3.). Based on the findings made in these two sections, the third and final part presents – from the perspective of today's international economic legal order – some systemizing thoughts on the current presence of as well as future prospects for an emerging global public authority in the sense of *Pacem in Terris* (4.).

17 On this perception see also, e.g., Bungenberg, Marc. Towards a More Balanced International Investment Law 2.0? In: Christoph Herrmann, Bruno Simma and Rudolf Streinz (Eds.), Trade Policy Between Law, Diplomacy and Scholarship – Liber amicorum in memoriam Horst G. Krenzler. Heidelberg, 2015, p. 15 (35).

18 Jackson, John H. Legal Problems of International Economic Relations. St. Paul, 1977, p. XV.

19 McRae, Donald. International Economic Law and Public International Law: The Past and the Future. In: *Journal of International Economic Law*, 2014, p. 627 (637).

20 Generally on the three-step analysis and lines of argumentation presented in *Pacem in Terris* see, e.g., also already Justenhoven, Heinz-Gerhard. Frieden durch Recht – Zur Relevanz des internationalen Rechts in der Friedensethik der katholischen Kirche. In: Mariano Delgado, Adrian Holdegger and Guido Vergauwen (Eds.). Friedensfähigkeit und Friedensvisionen in Religionen und Kulturen. Stuttgart, 2012, p. 259 (266 and 276).

### 2. Substantive Contribution to the Realization of the Universal Common Good: Evolving Value-Orientation of the International Economic Legal Order

The first central proposition made by Pope John XXIII and being of considerable relevance in the present context is the necessity to promote the universal common good as the fundamental overarching task of the various cooperative interactions by states in the international system, including their respective participation in the global law-making as well as law-enforcement processes.[21] This expectation essentially rests on a combination of two lines of reasoning. First, it is the solemn duty of all state organs – in fact even the very reason for their existence – to promote the common good of the political community,[22] a crucial characteristic feature of which is the human-orientedness of its realization processes that also comprises the protection of individual human rights.[23] Second, the public interests of a particular political community cannot be identified as well as achieved in isolation but always also have to take into account and thus bear a close relationship to the common good of mankind as a whole (and vice versa). Consequently, this relationship of reciprocal interdependence requires the promotion of a universal common good that bears in mind the interests of individuals as well as of the different peoples.[24]

In this regard, it seems worth to draw attention to the frequently highlighted perception that the international legal order as a whole has undergone quite substantial changes over the past few decades. While previously comprising basically a set of rules, often merely of a procedural nature, having the purpose to limit and guide states as the sole subjects of international law in their interactions with each other,[25] the international legal order has more recently extended its scope of application to regulatory areas that were previously thought to be in the exclusive domain of each country. By

21 See for example *Pacem in Terris* (note 1), para. 132; see thereto also Justenhoven, Heinz-Gerhard. Internationale Schiedsgerichtsbarkeit. Stuttgart, 2006, p. 57 et seq.

22 *Pacem in Terris* (note 1), para. 54.

23 *Pacem in Terris* (note 1), paras. 55 et seq.; see thereto, e.g. Justenhoven (note 20), p. 266. Generally on the necessary human-orientedness of the realization of the common good see also Nowrot, Karsten. Das Republikprinzip in der Rechtsordnungengemeinschaft. Tübingen, 2014, p. 448 et seq.

24 *Pacem in Terris* (note 1), paras. 98-99.

25 For such a description of this traditional understanding of international law see for example Zemanek, Karl. The Legal Foundations of the International System. In: *Recueil des Cours*, 1997, Vol. 266, p. 9 (112); Zacher, Mark W. The Decaying Pillars of the Westphalian Temple: Implications for International Order and Governance. In: James N. Rosenau, Ernst-Otto Czempiel (Eds.). Governance without Government: Order and Change in World Politics. 1992, p. 58 (59 et seq.).

transforming into what has already been called a "comprehensive blueprint for social life" and the evolution of a "world (internal) law" or "humanity law",[26] the international legal order is more and more independent of the will and interests of individual states.[27] Rather, its substantive norms are increasingly focusing on the promotion as well as protection of global public goods and thus on the realization of international community interests.[28]

These observations made with a view to the normative structure of the international system as a whole are also applicable to one of its sub-systems, the global economic system and its respective legal order. Aside from taking recourse to the topos *quidquid de omnibus valet, valet etiam de quibusdam et singulis*, there is also a growing explicit recognition that the normative framework of the transnational economic legal regime is more and more shaped by law-making as well as law-enforcement processes that first and foremost also take into account the need to foster and protect global community interests such as the protection of human rights and the environment or the promotion of good governance, public health as well as core labor and social standards.[29] This increasing orientation of international economic law and its primary steering subjects towards the realization of

26 See Tomuschat, Christian. International Law: Ensuring the Survival of Mankind on the Eve of a New Century. In: *Recueil des Cours*, 1999, Vol. 281, p. 9 (63); Delbrück, Jost. Prospects for a 'World (Internal) Law?': Legal Developments in a Changing International System. In: *Indiana Journal of Global Legal Studies*, 2002, p. 401; and Teitel, Ruti G. Humanity's Law. Oxford, 2011, p. 3 et seq., respectively.

27 See, e.g., Tomuschat, Christian. Obligations Arising for States Without or Against their Will. In: *Recueil des Cours*, 1993, Vol. 241, p. 195; Nowrot, Karsten. Global Governance and International Law. Halle/Saale, 2004, p. 15.

28 On this perception see, e.g., ICJ, *Case Concerning the Gabčíkovo-Nagymaros Project* (Hungary v. Slovak Republic), Separate Opinion of Vice-President Weeramantry, ICJ-Reports 1997, p. 88 (118) ("We have entered an era of international law in which international law subserves not only the interests of individual States, but looks beyond them and their parochial concerns to the greater interests of humanity and planetary welfare."); Simma, Bruno. From Bilateralism to Community Interest in International Law. In: *Recueil des Cours*, 1994, Vol. 250, p. 217 (229 et seq.).

29 See thereto for example Petersmann, Ernst-Ulrich. International Economic Law in the 21st Century – Constitutional Pluralism and Multilevel Governance of Interdependent Public Goods. Oxford, 2012, p. 43 et seq.; Petersmann, Ernst-Ulrich. Narrating "International Economic Law": Methodological Pluralism and Its Constitutional Limits. In: *Heidelberg Journal of International Law*, 2014, p. 763 (777 et seq.); Tietje, Christian. Begriff, Geschichte und Grundlagen des Internationalen Wirtschaftssystems und Wirtschaftsrechts. In: Christian Tietje (Ed.). Internationales Wirtschaftsrecht. 2nd ed., Berlin, 2015, p. 1 (63 et seq.); Nowrot, Karsten. Die Transnationale Verantwortungsgemeinschaft im Internationalen Wirtschaftsrecht – Strukturelle Ausgestaltung der normativen Gemeinwohlverwirklichung im internationalen Wirtschaftssystem unter den Bedingungen von Globalisierung und Konstitutionalisierung. In: Christian Tietje, Karsten Nowrot (Eds.). Verfassungsrechtliche Dimensionen des Internationalen Wirtschaftsrechts. Stuttgart, 2007, p. 57 (59 et seq.).

something that indeed could be characterized as a universal common good is for example supported by the ongoing discussion about the possibility of qualifying certain normative ordering principles of the global economic system themselves – among them the principles of open markets and free trade as well as the always precarious stability of the international financial markets – as global public goods in the sense of international community interests,[30] a perception apparently also shared, *inter alia*, by the Pontifical Council for Justice and Peace in its note "Towards Reforming the International Financial and Monetary Systems in the Context of Global Public Authority" of 24 October 2011.[31]

Furthermore, the increasing value-orientation of the international economic legal order and consequently the growing trend towards a substantive convergence of the different regulatory areas of public international law applicable to or affected by the interactions in the international economic system is also clearly indicated by the fact that international economic law and its relevant governance actors are ever more confronted with the multifaceted challenge of how to address the normative relevance of non-economic concerns. It was in particular since the middle of the 1990s that the so-called "trade and ..." issues or linkages[32] gained importance and received increasing attention among legal scholars and practitioners alike. These overarching themes primarily address questions of whether and, in the affirmative, how to incorporate non-economic concerns like the protection of human rights, the environment and consumer interests, the promotion of sustainable development, public health, corporate social responsibility and cultural diversity as well as the enforcement of core labor and social standards into the normative structure of the international economic system; thereby

30 On these discussions see, e.g., van der Eem, Bram. Financial Stability as a Global Public Good and Private International Law as an Instrument for its Transnational Governance – Some Basic Thoughts. In: Horatia M. Watt, Diego P. Fernandey Arroyo (Eds.). Private International Law and Global Governance. Oxford, 2014, p. 293; Shaffer, Gregory C. Recognizing Global Public Goods in WTO Dispute Settlement: Who Participates? Who Decides? In: *Journal of International Economic Law*, 2004, p. 459 (462 et seq.); Dieter, Heribert. The Stability of International Financial Markets: A Global Public Good? In: Stefan A. Schirm (Ed.). New Rules for Global Markets – Public and Private Governance in the World Economy. Houndsmills, 2004, p. 23.

31 Pontifical Council for Justice and Peace, Towards Reforming the International Financial and Monetary Systems in the Context of Global Public Authority, Note released on 24 October 2011, para. 3 ("the importance of guaranteeing, in addition to other collective goods, the good of a free, stable world economic and financial system"), available under: <www.vatican.va/roman_curia/pontifical_councils/justpeace/documents/rc_pc_justpeace_doc_20111024_nota_en.html> (20 July 2015).

32 On this labelling see, e.g., Trachtman, Joel P. Institutional Linkage: Transcending "Trade and ...", In: *American Journal of International Law*, 2002, p. 77.

establishing linkages – or areas of substantive convergence – between different policy fields and corresponding areas of law that have previously largely existed and progressively developed in "splendid isolation" of each other.[33] The respective debates and the relevant case-law of dispute settlement bodies have initially, and indeed also until more recently, primarily focused on the multilateral legal order of the World Trade Organization (WTO); a normative regime that – contrary to the "fire-wall approach" dominating under the General Agreement on Tariffs and Trade (GATT 1947) – is no longer supposed to be interpreted in "clinical isolation from public international law".[34]

While the global trade law focus of this first phase of debates was first and foremost also fueled by respective well-known trade disputes like *US-Tuna* and *US-Shrimp* addressing the legality under the GATT/WTO legal regime of governmental measures aimed at the protection of dolphins and sea turtles,[35] it is today generally recognized that this regulatory issue is of equal relevance in other fields of international economic law. Among them are the activities of major international financial institutions like the International Monetary Fund (IMF) and the World Bank[36] as well as the ever-expanding realm of treaties establishing free trade zones and other regional economic integration agreements.[37] In addition, to mention just one further example, it is also in the field of international investment for a variety of reasons by now

---

33 Cottier, Thomas. Trade and Human Rights: A Relationship to Discover, In: *Journal of International Economic Law*, 2002, p. 111 (112).

34 WTO, *United States – Standards for Reformulated and Conventional Gasoline*, Report of the Appellate Body of 29 April 1996, WT/DS2/AB/R, p. 17. On the respective scholarly debates see, e.g., Andersen, Henrik. Protection of Non-Trade Values in WTO Appellate Body Jurisprudence: Exceptions, Economic Arguments, and Eluding Questions. In: *Journal of International Economic Law*, 2015, p. 383.

35 See for example GATT, *United States – Restrictions on Imports of Tuna*, Report of the GATT Panel of 3 September 1991, DS21/R – 39S/155 (unadopted); GATT, *United States – Restrictions on Imports of Tuna*, Report of the GATT Panel of 16 June 1994, DS29/R (unadopted); WTO, *United States – Import Prohibition of Certain Shrimp and Shrimp Products,* Report of the Appellate Body of 12 October 1998, WT/DS58/AB/R; as well as more recently WTO, *United States – Measures Concerning the Importation, Marketing and Sale of Tuna and Tuna Products*, Report of the Appellate Body of 16 May 2012, WT/DS381/AB/R.

36 See thereto for example De Sena, Pasquale. International Monetary Fund, World Bank and Respect for Human Rights: A Critical Point of View. In: *Italian Yearbook of International Law*, 2010, p. 247; Skogly, Sigrun I. The Human Rights Obligations of the World Bank and the International Monetary Fund. London, 2001, p. 4 et seq.

37 See, e.g., Waleson, Joshua. Corporate Social Responsibility in EU Comprehensive Free Trade Agreements: Towards Sustainable Trade and Investment. In: *Legal Issues of Economic Integration*, 2015, p. 143; Jinnah, Sikina / Morgera, Elisa. Environmental Provisions in American and EU Free Trade Agreements: A Preliminary Comparison and Research Agenda. In: *Review of European Community & International Environmental Law*, 2013, p. 324.

ever more recognized among governments of industrialized and developing countries, practitioners and scholars alike, that at the level of drafting agreements as well as in the realm of the respective formalized dispute settlement mechanisms for foreign investors, one of the central challenges lawmakers as well as international judges and arbitrators are faced with is to provide for a suitable and thus acceptable balance between the liberalization of transboundary investment relations as well as the legal protection of economic interest of private business operators and the domestic steering capacity or "policy space"[38] of states and other governmental actors to allow the latter to pursue the promotion and protection of further (non-economic) public interest concerns.[39] Furthermore, although investment arbitration tribunals are so far still comparatively reluctant to consider other areas of public international law when interpreting the provisions of bilateral investment treaties,[40] and despite occasional fervent pleas to the contrary in arbitral practice,[41] it was in

38 Tietje, Christian. The Future of International Investment Protection: Stress in the System? In: *ICSID Review*, 2009, p. 457 (461) ("The need for a 'policy space' for governments, i.e. autonomy in national policy-making without constraints by international law and particularly international investment protection law, is one of the most significant consequences of the proliferation of investment law and the fragmentation of international law in general. We are currently witnessing discussions about the necessary policy space in the area of foreign investment, on both the national and international levels.").

39 On these debates see for example Nowrot, Karsten. How to Include Environmental Protection, Human Rights and Sustainability in International Investment Law? In: *Journal of World Investment & Trade*, 2014, p. 612; Titi, Aikaterini. The Right to Regulate in International Investment Law. Baden-Baden, 2014, p. 53 et seq.; Vinuales, Jorge E. Investment Law and Sustainable Development: The Environment Breaks into Investment Disputes. In: Marc Bungenberg *et al.* (Eds.). International Investment Law. Baden-Baden, 2015, p. 1714, each with further references.

40 On this perception see also, e.g., Hirsch, Moshe. Investment Tribunals and Human Rights: Divergent Paths. In: Pierre-Marie Dupuy, Francesco Francioni and Ernst-Ulrich Petersmann (Eds.). Human Rights in International Investment Law and Arbitration. Oxford, 2009, p. 97 (106); Simma, Bruno / Kill, Theodore. Harmonizing Investment Protection and International Human Rights: First Steps towards a Methodology. In: Christina Binder *et al.* (Eds.). International Investment Law for the 21st Century – Essays in Honour of Christoph Schreuer, Oxford, 2009, p. 678 (679).

41 See more recently in particular *Bernhard von Pezold and Others v. Zimbabwe*, ICSID Case No. ARB/10/15 and *Border Timbers Ltd., Border Timbers International et al. v. Zimbabwe*, ICSID Case No. ARB/10/25, Procedural Order No. 2 of 26 June 2012, paras. 57 et seq. ("The Arbitral Tribunals agree in this regard with the Claimants that the reference to 'such rules of general international law as may be applicable' in the BITs does not incorporate the universe of international law into the BITs or into disputes arising under the BITs. [...] The Petitioners provided no evidence or support for their assertion that international investment law and international human rights law are interdependent such that any decision of these Arbitral Tribunals which did not consider the content of international human rights norms would be legally incomplete.").

particular in light of Article 31 (3) (c) of the 1969 Vienna Convention on the Law of Treaties (VCLT)[42] in principle always beyond reasonable doubt and has more recently been explicitly emphasized that also international investment agreements "cannot be read and interpreted in isolation from public international law and its general principles".[43]

Finally, it seems appropriate to emphasize that from the perspective of public international law, the value orientation of the international economic legal order can, with regard to the promotion and protection of global public goods, be normatively based on a systematic interpretation of the Articles 55, 56, and 103 of the United Nations Charter.[44] According to Article 103, the obligations of the members of this international organization under the Charter prevail over the obligations of these countries under any other international agreement. Contrary to its restrictive wording, this provision's scope of application – in light of its object and purpose – is not limited to other obligations stipulated in treaties, but also covers obligations deriving from any other international legal sources, among them customary international law and general principles of law.[45] These Charter obligations in the sense of its Article 103 also include the various duties to cooperate that are listed in Articles 55 and 56 of the United Nations Charter that, when read together, are intended to contribute to the realization of international community interests.[46] Consequently, in light of Article 103, the normative structure of the international economic legal order must also be interpreted in a way that gives effect to the obligations to promote and protect the global public goods as stipulated in the Articles 55 and 56 of the Charter; a regulatory approach that with regard to its underlying purposes could very well be qualified as contributing to the realization of the universal common good in the sense of *Pacem in Terris* within and through the framework of international economic law.

---

42 Vienna Convention on the Law of Treaties of 22 May 1969, 1155 UNTS 331.

43 *Phoenix Action, Ltd. v. The Czech Republic*, ICSID Case No. ARB/06/5, Award of 15 April 2009, para. 78.

44 See thereto also already Nowrot, Karsten. Transnational Corporations as Steering Subjects in International Economic Law: Two Competing Visions of the Future? In: *Indiana Journal of Global Legal Studies*, 2011, p. 803 (834 et seq.); Tietje (note 29), p. 65.

45 Generally thereto, e.g., Leiss, Johann R. / Paulus, Andreas. Article 103 UN Charter. In: Bruno Simma *et al.* (Eds.). The Charter of the United Nations – A Commentary. Vol. II, 3rd ed. Oxford, 2012, paras. 66 *et seq.*, with further references.

46 For a more comprehensive assessment of the obligations stipulated in these provisions see Stoll, Peter-Tobias. Article 55 (a) and (b) UN Charter. In: Bruno Simma *et al.* (Eds.). The Charter of the United Nations – A Commentary. Vol. II, 3rd ed. Oxford, 2012, paras. 10 et seq.; Riedel, Eibe / Arend, Jan-Michael. Article 55 (c) UN Charter. In: *ibid.*, paras. 8 et seq.; Stoll, Peter-Tobias. Article 56 UN Charter. In: *ibid.*, paras. 4 et seq., each with further references.

### 3. *Effective Guardians of the Universal Common Good?: The Changing Role of States as Steering Subjects in the International Economic System*

While the previous assessment has revealed, broadly in line with the expectations stated in the papal encyclical, certain indications for an increasing orientation of the international economic legal order towards the promotion of economic and non-economic global community interests on the basis of a growing convergence of substantive normative values, the question remains as to the suitable steering subjects to be entrusted with implementing the universal common good. In this connection, *Pacem in Terris* argues that whereas in the past the heads of state and government seemed to have been able to advance global public interest concerns "either through normal diplomatic channels, or through top-level meetings, or through conventions or treaties",[47] the international system as a whole is more recently undergoing profound changes. These developments, being not comprehensively elaborated on by Pope John XXIII, have resulted in a growing inability of states to contribute to the realization of the universal public good, even when acting through joint cooperative efforts.[48] In reaching this conclusion, the papal encyclical emphasizes that this incapability to effectively promote international community interests is not caused by an absence of "goodwill and initiative" but rather by a "lack of adequate power to back up their authority" and thus the result of a diminished steering capacity of states in the international system;[49] a perception that was for example more recently reiterated in the encyclical letters *Caritas in Veritate* by Pope Benedict XVI on 29 June 2009[50] and *Laudato Si'* by Pope Francis on 24 May 2015.[51]

47 *Pacem in Terris* (note 1), para. 133.

48 *Pacem in Terris* (note 1), paras. 134-135.

49 *Pacem in Terris* (note 1), para. 134.

50 *Caritas in Veritate*, Encyclical Letter of Pope Benedict XVI, promulgated on 29 June 2009, para. 37 ("Perhaps at one time it was conceivable that first the creation of wealth could be entrusted to the economy, and then the task of distributing it could be assigned to politics. Today that would be more difficult, given that economic activity is no longer circumscribed within territorial limits, while the authority of governments continues to be principally local."), available under: <http://w2.vatican.va/content/benedict-xvi/en/encyclicals/documents/hf_ben-xvi_enc_20090629_caritas-in-veritate.html> (20 July 2015).

51 *Laudato Si'*, Encyclical Letter of Pope Francis, promulgated on 24 May 2015, para. 175 ("The twenty-first century, while maintaining systems of governance inherited from the past, is witnessing a weakening of the power of nation states, chiefly because the economic and financial sectors, being transnational, tends to prevail over the political."), available under: <http://w2.vatican.va/content/francesco/en/encyclicals/documents/papa-francesco_20150524_enciclica-laudato-si.html> (20 July 2015).

When evaluating these propositions in light of the current regulatory reality in the global economic order and the respective scholarly discussions, one cannot but notice remarkable congruencies with certain effects, already for quite some time recurrently ascribed to the processes of globalization, on the changing role of the state as a primary steering subject of international economic law. The various phenomena of globalization, appropriately defined as the "denationalization of clusters of political, economic and social activities",[52] are frequently perceived as not only reinforcing each other, but in doing so also leading to an increasing loss by states of their previously held and virtually unchallenged ability to channel and control the respective processes in pursuance of the promotion of the common good even if they take place on their own territory.[53] This diminished steering capacity of states has first and foremost also been emphasized with regard to the transactions and other interactions taking place in the transnational economic system.[54] As a consequence, states are in the global economic realm ever more required to create and participate in formal as well as informal cooperative steering regimes with not just other states and international organizations,[55] but in particular also with increasingly influential non-state actors such as business associations, multinational enterprises, and representatives of civil society in order to provide an effective regulatory scheme for the socio-economic processes they are unable to control and channel when acting alone.[56]

---

52 Delbrück (note 6), p. 11.

53 On this perception see, e.g., Basedow, Jürgen. The Law of Open Societies. Leiden, 2015, p. 56 et seq.; Delbrück, Jost. Structural Changes in the International System and its Legal Order: International Law in the Era of Globalization. In: *Swiss Review of International and European Law*, 2001, p. 1; Tietje, Christian. Internationalisiertes Verwaltungshandeln. Berlin, 2001, p. 165; Hobe, Stephan. The Era of Globalisation as a Challenge to International Law. In: *Duquesne University Law Review*, 2002, p. 655 (656).

54 See thereto for example Jackson, John H. International Economic Law: Reflections on the "Boilerroom" of International Relations. In: *American University Journal of International Law and Policy*, 1995, p. 595 (603); Tietje (note 29), p. 65 et seq.; Strange, Susan. The Retreat of the State – The Diffusion of Power in the World Economy. Cambridge, 1996, p. 3 et seq.; Nowrot, Karsten. Steuerungssubjekte und -mechanismen im Internationalen Wirtschaftsrecht (einschließlich regionale Wirtschaftsintegration). In: Christian Tietje (Ed.). Internationales Wirtschaftsrecht. 2nd ed., Berlin, 2015, p. 67 (71 et seq.).

55 Specifically on the shortcomings of cooperative efforts that are confined to state actors see, e.g., Bayne, Nicholas. Current Challenges to Economic Diplomacy. In: Nicholas Bayne, Stephen Woolcock (Eds.). The New Economic Diplomacy – Decision-Making and Negotiation in International Economic Relations. Aldershot, 2003, p. 83 (94 et seq.).

56 With regard to the growing need for these kinds of cooperative regulatory efforts that also include various categories of non-state actors see for example Delbrück,

Despite this increasing loss of governance capacity on the side of state actors, it is not argued that they are no longer of importance in the international economic system or even about to 'wither away'. In principle, they most certainly still remain quite influential steering subjects on the international scene.[57] Nevertheless, under the influence of globalization, individual countries are more and more incorporated in a multi-layered scheme of global economic governance; and since the state "cannot any longer remain the overall dominating actor"[58] their position in these transnational regulatory processes and regimes is not even appropriately characterized as being *primus inter pares*. In light of, for example, the "diplomacy between states and transnational corporations [becoming often] more decisive for the future of peoples and of their governments than the diplomacy of states with other states",[59] it has thus rightly been stressed by legal scholars that the need arises for a reconceptualized understanding of the sovereignty of these open and cooperative states in the sense that this traditional concept of international law "no longer consists in the freedom of states to act independently, in their perceived self-interest, but in membership in reasonably good standing in the regimes that make up the substance of international life".[60]

---

Jost. Transnational Federalism: Problems and Prospects of Allocating Public Authority Beyond the State. In: *Indiana Journal of Global Legal Studies*, 2004, p. 31 (32 et seq.); Tietje (note 29), p. 66; Jackson, John H. Sovereignty-Modern: A New Approach to an Outdated Concept. In: *American Journal of International Law*, 2003, p. 782; Reinisch, August. Governance Without Accountability? In: *German Yearbook of International Law*, 2001, p. 270 (271 et seq.).

57 See thereto, e.g., Schachter, Oscar. The Decline of the Nation-State and its Implications for International Law. In: *Columbia Journal of Transnational Law*, 1997, p. 7 (22); Möllers, Christoph. Transnational Governance without a Public Law? In: Christian Joerges, Inger-Johanne Sand, and Gunther Teubner (Eds.). Transnational Governance and Constitutionalism. Oxford, 2004, p. 329 (330 et seq.); Nowrot (note 54), p. 75.

58 Hobe, Stephan. Individuals and Groups as Global Actors: The Denationalization of International Transactions. In: Rainer Hofmann (Ed.). Non-State Actors as New Subjects of International Law: International Law – From the Traditional State Order Towards the Law of the Global Community. Berlin, 1999, p. 115 (118).

59 Strange, Susan. States and Markets. 2nd ed., London, 1994, p. 62.

60 Chayes, Abram/Handler Chayes, Antonia. The New Sovereignty – Compliance with International Regulatory Agreements. Cambridge, 1995, p. 27; see also, e.g., Slaughter, Anne-Marie. Disaggregated Sovereignty: Towards the Public Accountability of Global Government Networks. In: David Held, Mathias Koenig-Archibugi (Eds.). Global Governance and Public Accountability. Malden, 2005, p. 35 (64); Delbrück, Jost. The International Obligation to Cooperate – An Empty Shell or a Hard Law Principle of International Law? In: Holger P. Hestermeyer

The important role played in this regard also by non-state actors in the governance processes aimed at promoting the universal common good has for example been vividly described by the former Secretary-General of the United Nations, Kofi Annan, who stated already more than ten years ago in his Report titled "In Larger Freedom": "States, however, cannot do the job alone. We need an active civil society and a dynamic private sector. Both occupy an increasingly large and important share of the space formerly reserved for States alone, and it is plain that the goals outlined here will not be achieved without their full engagement."[61] To summarize, it is first and foremost the processes of globalization that have more recently led to a changing role of states in the international economic system and thus the evolution of a global economic legal order in which the "largest and most powerful states [still] can sometimes get their way through sheer exertion of will, but even they cannot achieve their principal purposes – security, economic well-being, and a decent level of amenity for their citizens – without the help and cooperation of many other participants in the system, including entities that are not states at all".[62]

### *4. Institutional Allocation of Global Public Authority in the International Economic Legal Order: Towards New Convergence or Increased Divergence?*

The conclusion drawn by Pope John XXIII from the necessity to pursue the universal common good on the one hand and the increasing inability of states to effectively fulfill this overarching task on the basis of traditional cooperative efforts on the other hand undoubtedly constitute the central innovative proposition made in *Pacem in Terris*,[63] namely the need to es-

*et al.* (Eds.). Coexistence, Cooperation and Solidarity – Liber Amicorum Rüdiger Wolfrum. Vol. I, Leiden, 2012, p. 3 (15).

61 In Larger Freedom: Towards Development, Security and Human Rights for All, Report of the Secretary-General, UN Doc. A/59/2005 of 21 March 2005, para. 20; see also more recently, e.g., Global Economic Governance and Development, Report of the Secretary-General, UN Doc. A/67/769 of 1 March 2013, paras. 63 et seq.

62 Chayes/Handler Chayes (note 60), p. 27; see in this connection also Tietje, Christian. Die Staatsrechtslehre und die Veränderung ihres Gegenstandes: Konsequenzen von Europäisierung und Internationalisierung. In: *Deutsches Verwaltungsblatt*, 2003, p. 1081 (1095 et seq.).

63 See, however, also concerning earlier proposals made in this regard by predecessors of Pope John XXIII, starting with related conceptual ideas advanced by Pope Leo XIII at end of the 19th century, Justenhoven, Heinz-Gerhard. Peace through a Public Global Authority in Papal Teaching from Leo XIII to John XXIII. In:

tablish a global public authority "endowed with a wideness of powers [...] which is in a position to operate in an effective manner on a world-wide basis"[64] with the aim to pursue international community interests, prominently including "the recognition, respect, safeguarding and promotion of the rights of the human person".[65] This conceptual idea has, at least on the level of theory and in particular in modern Catholic social teaching, proven to be quite influential and enduring, as for example evidenced by respective statements of Pope John Paul II,[66] Pope Benedict XVI,[67] Pope Francis[68] as well as the Pontifical Council for Justice and Peace.[69]

Thereby, probably also due to the tense and polarized situation at the height of the "Cold War", *Pacem in Terris* abstains from making detailed suggestions concerning the structural design of the envisioned global public authority.[70] Nevertheless, the papal encyclical indicates a number of requirements that have to be met in order for such an institutional setting to be considered effective and, from the perspective of the members of the international community, at the same time also acceptable for the realization of the universal common good. Among these prerequisites listed by Pope John XXIII and his successors are, *inter alia*, the endowment with effective competences to ensure compliance with its decisions, a global reach of its powers, impartiality, observance of the principle of subsidiarity and

Heinz-Gerhard Justenhoven, James Turner (Eds.). Rethinking the State in the Age of Globalisation – Catholic Thought and Contemporary Political Theory. Münster, 2003, p. 167.

64 *Pacem in Terris* (note 1), para. 137.

65 *Pacem in Terris* (note 1), para. 139.

66 See in particular *Pacem in Terris*: A Permanent Commitment, Message of Pope John Paul II for the Celebration of the World Day of Peace, 8 December 2002, paras. 5-6, available under: <http://w2.vatican.va/content/john-paul-ii/en/messages/peace/documents/hf_jp-ii_mes_20021217_xxxvi-world-day-for-peace.html> (20 July 2015). See also for example already in this regard, albeit without an explicit reference to a global public authority, *Sollicitudo Rei Socialis*, Encyclical Letter of Pope John Paul II, promulgated on 30 December 1987, para. 43 ("In the opinion of many, the international organizations seem to be at a stage of their existence when their operating methods, operating costs and effectiveness need careful review and possible correction. Obviously, such a delicate process cannot be put into effect without the collaboration of all. This presupposes the overcoming of political rivalries and the renouncing of all desire to manipulate these organizations, which exist solely for the common good."), available under: <http://w2.vatican.va/content/john-paul-ii/en/encyclicals/documents/hf_jp-ii_enc_30121987_sollicitudo-rei-socialis.html> (20 July 2015).

67 *Caritas in Veritate* (note 50), para. 67.

68 *Laudato Si'* (note 51), para. 175.

69 Pontifical Council for Justice and Peace (note 31).

70 Justenhoven (note 21), p. 61 et seq.

the international rule of law, and the free consent of all states serving as the necessary basis for its establishment and the respective transfer of powers.[71]

The analysis made in the preceding two sections has shown certain indications that the propositions made in *Pacem in Terris* with regard to, first, the need for a value-oriented normative structure of the international system and, second, the growing loss by states of their steering capacity are indeed increasingly reflected in the regulatory reality of the international economic legal order.[72] Quite to the contrary, already the fact that Pope John XXIII's successors continue advocating the creation of a global public authority to this day might very well be considered as supporting the conclusion that this central vision itself – in the words of Pope John Paul II – "has not yet been entirely achieved",[73] neither with regard to the international system and its legal order in general nor in the realm of international economic law in particular. In order to illustrate this finding from the perspective of the last-mentioned legal regime, it seems appropriate to start off by drawing attention to the widely shared perception that the United Nations, in principle not unjustifiedly considered by Pope John XXIII as a potentially promising candidate for the emergence of a global public authority in the sense of *Pacem in Terris*,[74] have over the decades most certainly undertaken numerous activities aimed at addressing various issues of the international economic system and its legal order, in particular through the Economic and Social Council (ECOSOC), but also for example via respective sub-organs established by the General Assembly such as the United Nations Conference on Trade and Development (UNCTAD) and the United Nations Commission

71 See *Pacem in Terris* (note 1), paras. 138 et seq.; as well as for example *Caritas in Veritate* (note 50), paras. 67; *Laudato Si'* (note 51), para. 175; Pontifical Council for Justice and Peace (note 31), para. 3. See thereto also Justenhoven (note 21), p. 58 et seq.; Justenhoven (note 20), p. 267 et seq.

72 See *supra* parts 2. and 3.

73 *Pacem in Terris*: A Permanent Commitment (note 66), para. 5. Generally on the respective conceptual ideas developed and advocated by Pope John Paul II in this regard, see Justenhoven, Heinz-Gerhard. The Peace Ethics of Pope John Paul II. In: Heinz-Gerhard Justenhoven / William A. Barbieri (Eds.). From Just War to Modern Peace Ethics. Berlin, 2012, p. 313 (333 et seq.).

74 *Pacem in Terris* (note 1), paras. 142 et seq.; see also in this regard for example *Pacem in Terris*: A Permanent Commitment (note 66), para. 5 ("John XXIII looked with hope and expectation to the United Nations Organization"); Justenhoven (note 20), p. 272; Minnerath (note 13), p. 35. For a more recent confirmation of this view see, e.g., Pontifical Council for Justice and Peace (note 31), para. 3 ("It would seem logical for the reform process to proceed with the United Nations as its reference because of the worldwide scope of the UN's responsibilities, its ability to bring together the nations of the world, and the diversity of its tasks and those of its specialized Agencies.").

on International Trade Law (UNCITRAL).[75] Despite all these efforts, however, probably almost general agreement exists that the United Nations in general and ECOSOC in particular have for a variety of reasons ultimately not proven to be an effective steering authority in the international economic system.[76] Rather, the institutional structures of the global economic legal order have in fact so far not only evolved largely outside the realm of the United Nations[77] but also in more or less distinctly separate normative regimes, prominently among them world trade law, the transnational legal framework on the protection of foreign investments and the international financial and monetary system.[78]

With regard to the last-mentioned regime, it is well-known that the World Bank and the IMF were already established prior to the creation of the United Nations at the Bretton Woods conference in July 1944. Although it was originally envisioned to integrate these Bretton Woods institutions into the system of the United Nations with their activities intended to be supervised by ECOSOC, these plans were never implemented in practice. Quite to the contrary, the IMF as well as the World Bank subsequently "es-

75 Generally on the activities of the United Nations in the realm of international economic law see, e.g., Stoll (note 46), paras. 28 et seq.; Tietje (note 29), p. 27 et seq.; Fortin, Carlos. United Nations Conference on Trade and Development (UNCTAD). In: Rüdiger Wolfrum (Ed.). Max Planck Encyclopedia of Public International Law. January 2013, paras. 1 et seq., available under: <www.mpepil.com/> (20 July 2015); Zumbansen, Peer / Panezi, Maria. United Nations Commission on International Trade Law (UNCITRAL). In: Rüdiger Wolfrum (Ed.). Max Planck Encyclopedia of Public International Law. June 2007, paras. 1 et seq., available under: <www.mpepil.com/> (20 July 2015), each with further references.

76 On this perception see more recently Charnovitz, Steve. The Field of International Economic Law. In: *Journal of International Economic Law*, 2014, p. 607 (624) ("ECOSOC has not been a successful coordinating institution"); Stoll, Peter-Tobias. World Trade Organization (WTO). In: Rüdiger Wolfrum (Ed.). Max Planck Encyclopedia of Public International Law. October 2014, para. 97 ("hardly fulfilled its expectations"), available under: <www.mpepil.com/> (20 July 2015); as well as already, e.g., Stewart, Frances / Daws, Sam. An Economic and Social Security Council at the United Nations. QEH (Queen Elizabeth House) Working Paper No. 68, Oxford, March 2001, p. 4, available under: <www3.qeh.ox.ac.uk/RePEc/qeh/qehwps/qehwps68.pdf> (20 July 2015).

77 See thereto also for example Stoll (note 46), para. 106 ("States have chosen to deal with economic matters outside the UN in other multilateral forums – like the WTO – in small groups – such as the G-20 – and at regional or bilateral levels.").

78 For the view that these three fields of international economic law constitute the core regimes of the current public international law rules governing transboundary economic relations see also, e.g., Herdegen, Matthias. Principles of International Economic Law. Oxford, 2013, p. 7 et seq.; Krajewski, Markus. Wirtschaftsvölkerrecht. 3rd ed., 2012, p. 4 and 10 et seq.

tablished a rather reluctant position towards the UN".[79] Furthermore, since the 1970s the governance structure of the international financial architecture underwent considerable modifications, a process that let to growing institutional fragmentation. In the first three decades following the end of World War II, the international legal regime dealing with monetary and financial issues was primarily shaped by the activities of international governmental organizations like the World Bank and the IMF. In particular as a consequence of an increase in the intensity of globalization of financial markets since the end of the 1960s, however, a governance framework parallel to the Bretton Woods institutions was subsequently created in order to deal with the regulatory challenges arising from these novel developments. This newly emerging global regime on financial markets primarily comprised – and also still as of today comprises – not of international organizations in the classical sense of public international law, but rather of a considerable number of informal governmental, intermediate and non-governmental institutions that are more recently frequently characterized as governance networks and whose coordinating and cooperating activities are, *inter alia*, aimed at developing global standards for this increasingly important area of transboundary financial transactions.[80] Among the various international standard-setting bodies in the form of regulatory networks are for example the Basel Committee on Banking Supervision, the International Organization of Securities Commissions (IOSCO), the International Accounting Standards Board (IASB) and the Financial Stability Board (FSB).[81]

---

79 Tietje, Christian. The International Financial Architecture as a Legal Order. In: *German Yearbook of International Law*, 2011, p. 11 (19).

80 See thereto, e.g., Eernisse, Arie C. Banking on Cooperation: The Role of the G-20 in Improving the International Financial Architecture. In: *Duke Journal of Comparative & International Law*, 2012, p. 239 (252) ("TRNs [transnational regulatory networks] – including the FSB, BCBS, IOSCO, and IASB – have come to dominate the field of international financial law"); Arner, Douglas W. / Taylor, Michael. The Global Financial Crisis and the Financial Stability Board: Hardening the Soft Law of International Financial Regulation? In: *University of New South Wales Law Journal*, 2009, p. 488 (489) ("Policy networks have been at the centre of the new forms of cooperation and coordination that nationally based regulatory agencies have used to adapt to the realities of the global financial system in the past thirty years, with international standard-setting bodies being at the core of their response.").

81 For further details on these regulatory institutions see Alexander, Kern / Dhumale, Rahul / Eatwell, John. Global Governance of Financial Systems – The International Regulation of Systemic Risk. Oxford, 2006, p. 37 et seq.; Manger-Nestler, Cornelia. Impacts of International Law on the Restructuring of the Global Financial System. In: *Max Planck Yearbook of United Nations Law*, 2011, p. 165 (187 et seq.); Nowrot, Karsten. Evolving Hierarchies in Transnational Financial Networked Governance: The Relationship between the International Accounting Standards

The international normative framework governing the protection of foreign investments presents itself as even more fragmented and considerably less institutionalized.[82] Aside from a number of global institutions devoted to specific aspects of international investment law like the Multilateral Investment Guarantee Agency (MIGA)[83] and the International Centre for Settlement of Investment Disputes (ICSID),[84] the public international law "backbone" of this legal regime is basically made up of a fragmented landscape of at present already more than 2900 bilateral investment treaties as well as almost 350 other investment agreements, among them in particular regional trade agreements with investment chapters.[85]

Finally, when turning to the realm of world trade law, we undoubtedly find – despite the failure of the International Trade Organization (ITO) conceived to supplement the Bretton Woods institutions in providing a comprehensive regime governing international trade relations on the basis of the 1948 Havana Charter[86] – currently a degree of centralization and institutionalization that clearly surpasses the respective developments and outcomes in the area of international investment law. Although certain tendencies aimed at establishing organizational structures already took place under the GATT 1947, this is first and foremost due to the creation of the World Trade Organization (WTO) in 1995 as the central intergovernmental institution of the multilateral trading system. Despite being frequently and rightly regarded as a major achievement in this sub-system of the international economic

---

Board, the Financial Stability Board and the G-20. In: Mark Fenwick, Steven Van Uytsel and Stefan Wrbka (Eds.). Networked Governance, Transnational Business and the Law. Berlin, 2014, p. 231 (240 et seq.), each with further references.

82 See in this connection also Dolzer, Rudolf / Schreuer, Christoph. Principles of International Investment Law. 2nd ed., Oxford, 2012, p. 11 ("At present, a comprehensive multilateral solution to investment issues is not in sight. It remains to be seen whether the international community will continue to develop its patchwork approach to foreign investment or whether the advantages of more global homogeneity will eventually be accepted.").

83 See Salacuse, Jeswald W. The Three Laws of International Investment: National, Contractual, and International Frameworks for Foreign Capital. Oxford, 2013, p. 266 et seq.

84 See thereto, e.g., Schreuer, Christoph *et al.* The ICSID Convention – A Commentary. 2nd ed., Cambridge 2009.

85 UNCTAD, World Investment Report 2015: Reforming International Investment Governance, 2015, p. 106.

86 For a more comprehensive evaluation see Sacerdoti, Giorgio. Havana Charter (1948). In: Rüdiger Wolfrum (Ed.). Max Planck Encyclopedia of Public International Law. June 2014, paras. 1 et seq., available under: <www.mpepil.com/> (20 July 2015); Lowenfeld, Andreas F. International Economic Law. 2nd ed., Oxford, 2008, p. 23 et seq.

legal order, in particular also in light of its dispute settlement mechanism,[87] it cannot be denied that the WTO at present also faces a number of challenges that can be attributed to internal as well as external factors. In order to illustrate this proposition, one only needs to refer, from an internal perspective of the WTO, to the difficult task of successfully completing the Doha Development Round of trade negotiations initiated in November 2001[88] and the often perceived need for organizational reforms of this institution with regard to, *inter alia*, the dominant mode of decision-making by consensus[89] to illustrate this proposition.

Prominent among the notable external factors is the ongoing rise of regionalism in the international economic system. In particular since the middle of the 1990s, for a variety of reasons numerous treaties establishing free trade zones and other regional economic integration agreements have been successfully concluded or are currently under negotiation. Whereas within the time frame of close to fifty years under the former GATT 1947, from the beginning of 1948 until the end of 1994, only a total number of 107 regional trade agreements and accessions thereto where notified by contracting parties under Article XXIV:7 GATT 1947,[90] as of 7 April 2015, already some 612 respective notifications have been received by the WTO. These figures correspond to a total of 449 regional trade agreements, of which 262 treaties are at present in force.[91] As a result, the number of regional trade agreements

87 On this perception see also, e.g., Hughes, Valerie. The Institutional Dimension. In: Daniel Bethlehem *et al.* (Eds.). The Oxford Handbook of International Trade Law. Oxford, 2009, p. 269 (294) ("WTO dispute settlement institutions have proved to be the success story of the WTO").

88 Concerning the Doha Development Round see, e.g., Muzaka, Valbona / Bishop, Matthew L. Doha Stalemate: The End of Trade Multilateralism? In: *Review of International Studies*, 2015, p. 383; Herwig, Alexia. The WTO and the Doha Negotiations in Crisis? In: *Netherlands Yearbook of International Law*, 2013, p. 161; see also for example the respective appraisal by Fabbricotti, Alberta. Economic Organizations and Groups, International. In: Rüdiger Wolfrum (Ed.). Max Planck Encyclopedia of Public International Law. October 2014, para. 71 ("Notwitstanding the many attempts to bring back the Doha Round no real progress was made thereafter. To date, the Doha Round is still ongoing, but with little chance of success."), available under: <www.mpepil.com/> (20 July 2015).

89 See thereto as well as on other reform proposals more recently Cottier, Thomas. The Common Law of International Trade and the Future of the World Trade Organization. In: *Journal of International Economic Law*, 2015, p. 3 (12 et seq.), with further references.

90 See WTO, *Turkey – Restrictions on the Imports of Textile and Clothing Products*, Report of the Panel of 31 May 1999, WT/DS34/R, para. 2.3.

91 On these data as well as continuously updated information on this issue see the respective information provided by the WTO on its website available under: <http://www.wto.org/english/tratop_e/region_e/region_e.htm> (20 July 2015).

has increased more than four-fold in the last two decades.[92] In order to illustrate the overall significance and consequences of these developments, let it initially suffice to draw attention to the fact that already as of today the overwhelming majority of the at present 161 WTO members – notable exceptions being for example Mauretania, the Democratic Republic of Congo and Mongolia – is party to at least one regional trade agreement; and most of them have concluded considerably more than one of these types of arrangement. Already towards the end of the previous decade, the average WTO member had concluded regional trade agreements with roughly fifteen other countries.[93] From the perspective of the international trade law regime as a whole, this rise of regionalism is commonly seen as a shift away from multilateralism and institutional centralization as manifested in the WTO legal order, with the consequences of these processes of fragmentation being already for quite some time subject to intensive and controversial debates among popes,[94] scholars and practitioners alike.[95]

Against this background, one can in principle agree with the recent finding made by Peter-Tobias Stoll that the international economic legal order as a whole as well as its major public international law sub-systems "consist[…] of a number of separate institutions, regimes, and agreements, which are poorly coordinated";[96] and thus comprise a regulatory and organizational structure that does not even remotely resemble the global public

92 See on this finding already WTO, World Trade Report 2011, The WTO and Preferential Trade Agreements: From Co-Existence to Coherence, 2011, p. 3.

93 Freund, Caroline / Ornelas, Emanuel Ornelas. Regional Trade Agreements. World Bank Policy Research Working Paper 5314, May 2010, p. 2; Bungenberg, Marc. Preferential Trade and Investment Agreements and Regionalism. In: Rainer Hofmann, Stephan W. Schill and Christian J. Tams (Ed.). Preferential Trade and Investment Agreements – From Recalibration to Reintegration. Baden-Baden, 2013, p. 269 (270).

94 For an early assessment in this regard by Pope John Paul II see *Sollicitudo Rei Socialis* (note 66), para. 43 ("In this respect I wish to mention specifically: the reform of the international trade system, which is mortgaged to protectionism and increasing bilateralism; […].").

95 The contributions on the vertical relationship between the WTO legal order and regional trade agreements are by now more than legion. See for example Bhagwati, Jagdish. Termites in the Trading System: How Preferential Agreements Undermine Free Trade. Oxford, 2008; Nowrot (note 54), p. 136 et seq.; Kyle W. Bagwell / Petros C. Mavroidis (Eds.). Preferential Trade Agreements – A Law and Economics Analysis. Cambridge, 2011; Senti, Richard. Regional Trade Agreements: 'Stepping Stones' or 'Stumbling Blocks' of the WTO? In: Marise Cremona *et al.* (Eds.). Reflections on the Constitutionalisation of International Economic Law – Liber amicorum for Ernst-Ulrich Petersmann. Leiden, 2014, p. 441, each with numerous further references

96 Stoll (note 76), para. 97.

authority as envisioned in *Pacem in Terris*. Moreover, respective conceptual ideas aimed at establishing a single universal steering institution for the realm of international economic governance like the more recent proposal to create a Global Economic Coordination Council made by the Commission of Experts of the President of the United Nations General Assembly on Reforms of the International Monetary and Financial System (Stiglitz Commission) in its report of 21 September 2009[97] had until now no – and are also in the foreseeable future likely to have, if at all, little – chance of being accepted by the international community.[98] Nevertheless, and leaving for the moment aside this from the perspective of modern Catholic social teaching and peace ethics rather unsatisfactory "state of play", two additional aspects seem to be worth highlighting in the present context in order to indicate some more recent structural developments in connection with the realization of global community interests in the international economic legal order.

The first notable development concerns the rise of the intergovernmental Group of 20 (G-20) in international economic governance. The G-20 was originally established in the aftermath of the Asian financial crisis of the late 1990s at the initiative of the G-7 finance ministers and central bank governors in September 1999.[99] Its membership comprises of nineteen countries – Argentina, Australia, Brazil, Canada, China, France, Germany, India, Indonesia, Italy, Japan, the Republic of Korea, Mexico, Russia, Saudi Arabia, South Africa, Turkey, the United Kingdom and the United States of America – as well as the European Union. In addition, the G-20 maintains close relations with a number of international economic organizations, among them the IMF, the World Bank, the WTO, the Organisation for Economic Co-operation and Development (OECD) and the International Labour

97 Report of the Commission of Experts of the President of the United Nations General Assembly on Reforms of the International Monetary and Financial System, 21 September 2009, p. 87 et seq., available under: <www.un.org/ga/econcrisissummit/docs/FinalReport_CoE.pdf> (20 July 2015); see thereto also Ocampo, José A. / Stiglitz, Joseph E. From the G-20 to a Global Economic Coordination Council. In: *Journal of Globalization and Development*, 2011, available under: <www.degruyter.com/view/j/jgd.2011.2.issue-2/issue-files/jgd.2011.2.issue-2.xml> (20 July 2015); Schröder, Frank / Stetten, Jürgen. Mythos Weltwirtschaftsrat. In: *Vereinte Nationen*, 2010, p. 104.

98 See in this regard also, e.g., Tietje (note 79), p. 45.

99 For a more detailed account of the origins and subsequent activities of the G-20 see for example Norton, Joseph J. NIFA II or 'Bretton Woods II'?: The G-20 (Leaders) Summit Process on Managing Global Financial Markets and the World Economy – Quo Vadis? In: *Journal of Banking Regulation*, 2010, p. 261 (275 et seq.); Manger-Nestler (note 81), p. 212 et seq.; Eernisse (note 80), p. 241 et seq.

Organisation (ILO). In the first nine years of its existence, this governance network only met in the form of the G-20 finance ministers and central bank governors. Respective proposals to upgrade the so-called "G-20 Finance" to something like an "L20" ("Leaders 20") received little political support in the beginning and the middle of the previous decade.[100] Rather, it was only in reaction to the global financial crisis of 2008 that the G-20 heads of state and governments convened for the first time at the Washington D.C. summit in November 2008. Since then, eight more G-20 summits have so far taken place, with this intergovernmental network already from September 2009 being considered by its members as "the premier forum for our international economic cooperation".[101]

And indeed, the role and functions now assumed by the G-20 are not only to be regarded as the most important institutional development evolving from the recent global financial crisis.[102] Far beyond its central position in the international financial architecture, this transnational governance regime has more recently emerged as "the new global coordinating mechanism in economic and financial matters"[103] or – to mention but one further characterization – "the most important room for global economic governance".[104] In light of these findings and adopting a broader perspective, one can thus in principle agree with the observation more recently made by Jan Wouters and Thomas Ramopoulos that the "post-2008 G20 has changed the international economic institutional architecture and thereby global economic governance as we knew it. It has introduced an informal element together with overtly political – rather than technocratic – imperatives at the top of the interna-

100 Brouder, Alan. G8. In: Christian Tietje, Alan Brouder (Eds.). Handbook of Transnational Economic Governance Regimes. Leiden, 2009, p. 95 (114).

101 G-20 Leaders‘ Statement, The Pittsburgh Summit, 24-25 September 2009, para. 50, available under: <http://www.g20.org/documents/> (20 July 2015).

102 Tietje (note 79), p. 31. On the G-20's potential to contribute to the creation of a global public authority see also Pontifical Council for Justice and Peace (note 31), para. 4.

103 Arner, Douglas W. / Buckley, Ross P. Redesigning the Architecture of the Global Financial System. In: *Melbourne Journal of International Law*, 2010, p. 1 (24); see also Farrar, John H. / Parsons, Louise. Globalisation, the Global Financial Crisis and the Reinvention of the State. In: *Singapore Academy of Law Journal*, 2012, p. 367 (386) ("the lead player in the international conversation during and in the aftermath of the GFC [global financial crisis]").

104 Napolitano, Guilio. The Two Ways of Global Governance after the Financial Crisis: Multilateralism versus Cooperation among Governments. In: *International Journal of Constitutional Law*, 2011, p. 310 (316); see also, e.g., Brummer, Chris. Soft Law and the Global Financial System. Cambridge, 2012, p. 70 ("perhaps today's most visible body for international economic coordination").

tional system of economic governance".[105] Despite its undisputable shortcomings[106] and although it does for a variety of reasons not conform to the above-mentioned requirements listed by Pope John XXIII and his successors for the global public authority in the sense of *Pacem in Terris*, the G-20 appears – in the absence of viable alternatives – for the time being the only transnational governance network that is endowed with the required political authority to have the potential to emerge as the central gubernative regime[107] for the international economic legal order as a whole.[108]

While the rise of the G-20 can serve as an indication for certain processes of centralization and institutional convergence in global economic governance, a second development that should not be left unmentioned rather points in the opposite direction towards a tendency of increased organizational divergence in this transnational realm: the emergence and growing importance of private as well as intermediate regulatory regimes. In light of the increasing inability – and occasional reluctance – of states to pursue global community interests,[109] the steering processes aimed at identifying and implementing the universal common good in the international economic system are currently characterized by an ever-growing involvement of various types of non-state actors. Thereby, the former distinction between so-called "hard law" and non-binding regulatory instruments is increasingly blurred.[110] From an institutional perspective, these developments have

105 Wouters, Jan / Ramopoulos, Thomas. The G20 and Global Economic Governance: Lessons from Multi-Level European Governance? In: *Journal of International Economic Law*, 2012, p. 751 (764).

106 For a rather critical evaluation of this intergovernmental network see, e.g., Charnovitz, Steve. Addressing Government Failure through International Financial Law. In: Thomas Cottier, John H. Jackson, and Rosa M. Lastra (Eds.). International Law in Financial Regulation and Monetary Affairs. Oxford, 2012, p. 205 (218 et seq.); Zobl, Martin / Thuerer, Daniel / Alexander, Kern. Die Legitimation der G-20. In: *Archiv des Voelkerrechts*, 2013, p. 143; Manger-Nestler (note 81), p. 214 et seq.

107 See in this regard also Tietje (note 79), p. 40 and 43; Manger-Nestler (note 81), p. 202. On the term "gubernative" itself see for example Dann, Philipp. The Gubernative in Presidential and Parlamentary Systems. In: *Heidelberg Journal of International Law*, 2006, p. 1 (2 note 1) ("The notion of the "gubernative" is not very common, but captures more precisely than the notions of "executive", "government" or "administration" what is meant here. The notion is based on the distinction between the politically responsible leadership of the executive branch (the gubernative) and the hierarchically subordinated administration or bureaucracy. Both together form the executive branch. The term "government", which is often used to name the political pinnacle of the executive branch, is too vague, since it can also mean a l l branches of government and the process of governing.").

108 On this perception see, e.g., also already Tietje (note 79), p. 45.

109 See already *supra* part 3.

110 See thereto Tietje, Christian / Nowrot, Karsten. Laying the Conceptual Ghosts of the Past to Rest: The Rise of Philip C. Jessup's 'Transnational Law' in the Regula-

on the one hand let to the creation of a considerable number of regimes, often endowed with a quite elaborate and in part even federalized as well as parliamentarized organizational structure,[111] whose membership comprises public and private actors. The United Nations Global Compact, the Extractive Industries Transparency Initiative, the FSB and the Global Reporting Initiative serve as respective examples.[112] On the other hand, the last two decades also bore witness to the emergence of quite effective institutionalized private steering regimes like the Forest Stewardship Council, Fairtrade Labelling Organizations International, the Ethical Trading Initiative as well as the Marine Stewardship Council that were created by, *inter alia*, civil society organizations, transnational enterprises, business associations and trade unions without the involvement of state actors.[113] Although in particular these last-mentioned governance organizations do most certainly not have the competence to exercise public authority as traditionally understood, they nevertheless play an increasingly important role in the steering processes aimed at realizing community interests in the global economic system while at the same time obviously contributing to a growing institutional fragmentation in the international economic legal order.

---

tory Governance of the International Economic System. In: Christian Tietje, Alan Brouder, and Karsten Nowrot (Eds.). Philip C. Jessup's *Transnational Law* Revisited – On the Occasion of the 50th Anniversary of its Publication, Halle/Saale, 2006, p. 17 (22 et seq.), with numerous further references.

111 For a more comprehensive evaluation of these phenomena see Nowrot, Karsten. The New Governance Structure of the Global Compact – Transforming a "Learning Network" into a Federalized and Parliamentarized Transnational Regulatory Regime. Halle/Saale, 2005, p. 17 et seq.; Nowrot, Karsten. Towards 'Open' Transnational Administrative Networks: Emerging Structural Features. In: Olaf Dilling, Martin Herberg, and Gerd Winter (Eds.). Transnational Administrative Rule-Making – Performance, Legal Effects, and Legitimacy. Oxford, 2011, p. 255.

112 On these intermediate steering regimes see, e.g., Khan, Rahmatullah. Global Compact. In: Rüdiger Wolfrum (Ed.). Max Planck Encyclopedia of Public International Law. April 2011, paras. 1 et seq., available under: <www.mpepil.com/> (20 July 2015); Brouder, Alan. Extractive Industries Transparency Initiative. In: Christian Tietje, Alan Brouder (Eds.). Handbook of Transnational Economic Governance Regimes. Leiden, 2009, p. 849; Nowrot, Karsten. Global Reporting Initiative. In: *ibid.*, p. 117.

113 See thereto for example Blowfield, Mick. ETI: A Multi-Stateholder Approach. In: Rhys Jenkins, Ruth Pearson and Gill Seyfang (Eds.). Corporate Responsibility and Labour Rights. London, 2002, p. 184; Nowrot, Karsten. Forest Stewardship Council. In: Christian Tietje, Alan Brouder (Eds.). Handbook of Transnational Economic Governance Regimes. Leiden, 2009, p. 865; Brouder, Alan. Fairtrade Labelling Organizations International. In: *ibid.*, p. 75; Nowrot, Karsten. Marine Stewardship Council. In: *ibid.*, p. 705.

## *5. Conclusion*

The – necessarily selective – assessment undertaken in the present contribution with regard to the current presence of and future prospects for an emerging global public authority as proposed in *Pacem in Terris* in the international economic legal order largely confirms the perception more recently expressed by the Pontifical Council for Justice and Peace in its 2011 note "Towards Reforming the International Financial and Monetary Systems in the Context of Global Public Authority" that apparently "a long road still needs to be travelled before arriving at the creation of a public Authority with universal jurisdiction".[114] On the one hand, the analysis has revealed a number of developments that, first, serve as an indication for a growing orientation of the international economic legal order towards the realization of the universal common good in the sense of *Pacem in Terris* and, second, also largely validate Pope John XXIII's proposition concerning the increasing loss by states of their previously held steering capacity to pursue international community interests, even when acting through joint cooperative efforts. On the other hand, however, it has also been shown that the international economic legal order and its core sub-regimes not only remain in the state of intergovernmental institutional fragmentation so characteristic for the evolution of this transnational realm ever since the creation of the Bretton Woods institutions in the 1940s. Rather, except for the more recent rise of the G-20 (albeit for a variety of reasons with uncertain future prospects), the global economic system and its legal order are currently even shaped by processes of increasing organizational divergence due to, among others, the growing importance of regionalism as well as in particular also the emergence of numerous intermediate and private regulatory regimes. In sum, an institutional convergence à la *Pacem in Terris* is (almost) nowhere in sight in today's international economic legal order.

Nevertheless, in particular with a view to the last-mentioned growing involvement of non-state actors, it seems appropriate to recall that this development should not merely be perceived as contributing to an increasing fragmentation in the exercise of governance authority in the international economic system. Quite to the contrary, it is today ever more and rightly recognized that – in the absence of a global public authority – the inclusion of private actors in the regulatory processes, the transparency of the decision-making and value-realization processes being at the same time a prerequisite and a consequence of this participation, but also the responsibility

114 Pontifical Council for Justice and Peace (note 31), para. 3.

for the universal common good of all public and private actors involved as well as their respective accountability, have to be regarded as indispensable elements of the constitutional structure of an emerging transnational (economic) community oriented towards the realization of global public goods.[115] And in light of these findings, it should finally in the present context not be left unmentioned that these conceptual ideas can not only be presumed to be, at least in principle, in line with the overarching vision of *Pacem in Terris*, but first and foremost also correspond to the thoughts subsequently expressed by Pope John Paul II in his message for the celebration of the 2003 World Day of Peace titled "*Pacem in Terris*: A Permanent Commitment", who emphasized that "a new constitutional organization of the human family" does not require a centralized "global super-State" but a continuation of "processes already in place to meet the almost universal demand for participatory ways of exercising political authority, even international political authority, and for transparency and accountability at every level of public life".[116]

115 See thereto for example Klabbers, Jan / Peters, Anne / Ulfstein, Geir. The Constitutionalization of International Law, Oxford, 2009, p. 153 ("The concept of an international community suggests inclusiveness and therefore tends to favour rather than to hinder the inclusion of non-state actors."); *ibid.* 222 (on an emerging "general legal principle of openness" stipulating that "global governance fora are no longer presumed to be *a priori* closed"); *ibid.*, 250-251 ("business does not yet and should not acquire any legitimate expectation to participate in international law-making unless the business actors specifically demonstrate their commitment to the public interest"); as well as Nowrot (note 44), p. 836 et seq., with further references.

116 *Pacem in Terris*: A Permanent Commitment (note 66), para. 6.

# World Peace through International Adjudication?*

*Christian J. Tams*

> 'If all disputes could be resolved in the hushed calm of courtrooms rather than the swirling world of political cut-and-thrust, then civilization could be said to have taken a giant and noble forward stride.'[1]

## *1. Introduction*

Stephen Neff's introductory quote gives eloquent expression to a recurring theme of internationalist thought: the hope that, in a just and civilized world order, conflicts will be resolved, not only on the basis of law, but also before institutions tasked to apply rules of law, viz. impartial and independent international courts and tribunals. It juxtaposes the dangerous world of power politics ('swirling', and dominated by the 'cut-and-thrust') to the rational and civilized atmosphere (the 'hushed calm') of the courtroom. It evokes an image of wise arbiters of peace addressing the great challenges of mankind on the basis of international law and justice.

In line with this powerful image, the traditional approach has been to view international courts as instruments of war-prevention: 'going to court' was traditionally posited as a preferable alternative to 'going to war'. In fact, arbtiration and adjudication (or at least some rudimentary form of decision-making by an independent body) as a means of 'taming' inter-State relations were there from the beginning of the modern debates about international peace and security. Dispute settlement by an impartial body of sovereigns was a crucial means of containing conflict and avoiding war in the peace projects of William Penn and the Abbé de Saint-Pierre.[2] In his *Plan for a Universal and Perpetual Peace,* Jeremy Bentham justified his proposal for a Common Court of Judicature in the following terms: "Establish a common tribunal, the necessity of war no longer follows from difference of opinion. Just or unjust, the decision of the arbiters will save

* This chapter draws on research conducted during a fellowship Centre for Global Cooperation Research (Duisburg). I am grateful for the Centre's support.

1 St. Neff, *Justice Among Nations. A History of International Law* (2014), 346

2 *W. Penn, An Essay towards the Present and Future Peace of Europe (1693);* Ch.I. Castel de Saint-Pierre, *Projet pour rendre la paix perpétuelle en Europe* (1713).

the credit, the honour, of the contending party."[3] And around 150 years later, when an international court had become a reality, a delegate at the San Francisco Conference establishing the United Nations praised the creation of the International Court of Justice (ICJ) as a way of "substituting orderly processes for the vicissitudes of war and the reign of brutal force".[4]

A further seventy years on, the landscape of international adjudication has changed beyond recognition. International courts and tribunals – non-existent at the times of Penn, Saint-Pierre and Bentham; a rarity in 1945 – have mushroomed. A recent account puts the number of operative permanent international courts at "at least two dozen", and the number of binding judicial decisions rendered between 1990 and 2011 at a staggering 34,000.[5] International lawyers have begun to speak of the present era as an "age of adjudication", noting that recourse to courts and tribunals has become more common than ever before in the history of international relations.[6] And not just the numbers have changed. The change is qualitative as much as it is quantitative; it affects the functions of international adjudication as well. Courts today are not just dispute settlers; they are also law-makers, fact-finders, and instruments of governance.[7] But do they play a significant role in preserving world peace? Does Bentham's straightforward argument – "[e]stablish a common tribunal, the necessity of war no longer follows from difference of opinion"[8] – still hold appeal?

***

3 J. Bentham, *Plan for an Universal and Perpetual Peace* (Principles of International Law, Essay IV), in *The Works of Jeremy Bentham, Part VIII* (1839), 552.

4 See Doc. 913 /IV /1/74(1)(1945), in *United Nations Conference on International Organization* (UNCIO), vol XIII, at 393.

5 K.J. Alter, The Multiplication of International Courts and Tribunals after the End of the Cold War, in C.P. Romano/K.J. Alter/Y. Shany, *The Oxford Handbook of International Adjudication* (2014), 53, at 65 and 68. The numbers do not include non-permanent bodies engaged in dispute settlement, such as investment tribunals.

6 The title of a lecture by Judge Christopher Greenwood, at http://legal.un.org/avl/ls/Greenwood_CT.html.

7 The debate about the functions of international courts is still at an early stage. The terminology used in the text follows J.E. Alvarez, What Are International Judges For? in *Oxford Handbook of International Adjudication* (n. 5), 159. For influential accounts (often using other terminology) see e.g. Alter, *The New Terrain of International Law: Courts, Politics, Rights* (2014); and Kingsbury, International Courts: Uneven Judicialization in Global Order, in J. Crawford/M. Koskenniemi, *The Cambridge Companion to International Law* (2012), 203.

8 Bentham (n. 3).

These cursory remarks point to important changes in the role of international courts in international relations, and in our expectations of their influence on international affairs. The subsequent considerations explore these changes by tracing the history of international arbitration and adjudication over the past two centuries.[9] In line with the focus of the present collection, particular emphasis is placed on the role of the Catholic Church, on John XXIII's encyclical *Pacem in terris* as one of the Church's most influential 'peace through law' initiatives of the 20th century, and on the international struggle to overcome war and military conflict. As will be shown, the Papacy and the Holy See have taken a keen interest in international adjudication for most of the time, which, on occasion, has resulted in influential interventions. Yet their position, too, has undergone considerable change, reflecting the international community's changing perceptions of courts; and *Pacem in terris* is an instructive outlier.

To trace developments, the discussion follows a chronological approach, within which *general developments* concerning international courts and the *evolution of Catholic thought* on dispute settlement are distinguished.[10] For

9 The subsequent discussion does not systematically distinguish between the two main modes of binding dispute resolution, viz. *adjudication* before standing courts and *arbitration* (where the parties enjoy greater influence over the dispute settlement process, including by choosing the arbitrators). As is clear form section II.1., historically, arbitration precedes adjudication; and for a while (as noted in III.1.), the establishment of a standing international court was an important demand. However, since 1945, there has been a rapprochement; and from the perspective of dispute settlers, arbitral and adjudicative bodies are essentially characterized by their power to render binding decisions. For more on this see I. Brownlie, The Peaceful Settlement of International Disputes, Chinese Journal of International Law 8 (2009), 267, at 273-277.
For more on the early history of arbitration see J. Ralston, *International Arbitration from Athens to Locarno* (1929); H.S. Fraser, A Sketch of the History of International Arbitration, Cornell Law Quarterly, 11 (1926), 179; K.-H. Lingens *Internationale Schiedsgerichtbarkeit und Jus Publicum Europaeum 1648-1794* (1988). Instructive summaries can be found in M.E. O'Connell/L. VanderZee, The History of International Adjudication, in *Oxford Handbook* (n. 5), 42; C.G. Roelofsen, International Arbitration and Courts, in A. Peters/B. Fassbender, *The Oxford Handbook of the History of International Law* (2012), 145.

10 The subsequent discussion side-steps the (at times technical) debate about the respective roles of the Pope, the Holy See and the Vatican in the external relations of the Catholic Church. For reasons of convenience, references are mainly to the '(Catholic) Church', to the 'Papacy' and/or to individual popes. For a detailed assessment of the underlying legal issues see C. Rijngaert, The Legal Status of the Holy See, Goettingen Journal of International Law 3 (2011), 829; G. Arangio Ruiz, On the Nature of the International Personality of the Holy See, Revue belge de droit international 29 (1996), 354; G. Westdickenberg, The Holy See, in *Max Planck Encyclopedia of Public International Law* (www.mpepil.com).

reasons of convenience, the narrative distinguishes four stages in the on-going debate about the role of world courts: the *gradual re-emergence* of arbitration as a common method of dispute settlement from the end of the 18th century (section II.); the consolidation of this practice, coupled with efforts to make it compulsory, from the late 19th century onwards, in what might is described as an *idealistic turn* in dispute resolution (section III.); the *pragmatic turn* from the inter-War period, which envisioned a much more circumscribed role for international courts, and which continues to dominate debates (section IV.); and the more recent *re-vitalization,* characterized by the establishment of dozens of new courts and tribunals, but firmly wedded to the pragmatist understanding of their role (section V.). Needless to say, the distinction between four stages of development does not do justice to the continuous evolution of ideas: debates about world courts have been far too diverse to be neatly categorized into four 'eras', and the treatment in the following is impressionistic rather than comprehensive. Yet it is hoped that, by following a simplified structure, the subsequent discussion will succeed in accentuating important developments in the international community's perception of courts and tribunals as instruments of world peace.

## *2. New Beginnings: the Gradual Re-emergence of International Arbitration*

Where there is law, there are disputes. International law forms no exception: much of it has been forged in disputes about legal rights and duties. Yet international law is special in that, compared to other legal systems, courts and tribunals have historically played a relatively limited role in the process of settling international legal disputes. To be sure, from ancient times, the actors of international law have occasionally relied on impartial third parties for the settlement of their disputes; arbitration did indeed take place (in the words of an influential treatise published in the 1920s) 'from Athens to Locarno' (and has, since then, continued).[11] But submission to binding dispute settlement was always based on the consent of the parties; at no point in time were States legally required to accept adjudication or arbitration as a regular means of dispute settlement. What is more, during the formative age of contemporary international law – the 17th and 18th centuries – binding dis-

11 Ralston (n 9). See also O'Connell/VanderZee (n. 9), 42: "Formal processes of inter-group dispute resolution long pre-date the rise of modern international law in 1648."

pute resolution was very much in decline:[12] a system emphasising external sovereignty approached the notion of an impartial authority sitting in judgment over independent States with some caution. The cautious approach was overcome in the course of the late 18th and 19th centuries, during which international arbitration re-emerged as a useful means of dispute resolution.[13] The subsequent section traces this development and highlights how the Catholic Church responded to it.

### *2.1 General Developments*

While drawing on ancient practices, "[p]our voir surgir de manière définitive et précise les moyens de [règlement pacifique des différends] interétatiques tels qu'on les connaît aujourd'hui, il a fallu attendre l'émergence et la consolidation de l'Etat moderne et d'une société interétatique."[14] The Jay Treaty of 1794[15] is widely credited[16] to have ushered in the new era: concluded between two recent belligerents, Great Britain and the United States of America, it envisaged different arbitral mechanisms to address boundary disputes, claims by British merchants against U.S. nationals, and claims by U.S. citizens against Great Britain. These mechanisms and their frequent

12 Fraser (n. 9) speaks of an 'eclipse' (at 196), W. Grewe of a "nadir of international arbitration" (*The Epochs of International Law* (transl. by Byers), 2000, at 363); but that may be an exaggeration: contrast the accounts of Roelofsen (n. 9), 155-159, and (in greater detail) Lingens (n. 9). In Roelofsen's words: "In the 18th century, the idea of arbitration enjoyed a certain popularity but its actual practice was in decline. Even though there was no total eclipse of arbitration in diplomatic practice, the number of actual cases of arbitration from the 1730s on recorded in treaty practice is small" (159).

13 The process has been described in detail elsewhere. For reliable accounts see e.g. J.L. Simpson/H. Fox, *International Arbitration* (1959), ch. 1; L. Caflisch, Cent ans de règlement pacifique des différends interétatiques, Recueil des Cours 288 (2001), 245.

14 Caflisch (n. 13), 306.

15 Reproduced in: *Treaties and Other International Acts of the United States of America* (D. Hunter Miller, ed.), Vol. 2, Documents, 1776-1818, and in C.J. Tams/A. Tzanakopoulos, *The Settlement of International Disputes. Basic Documents* (2012), 3.

16 Ralston (n. 9) is emphatic: "the modern era of arbitral or judicial settlement of international disputes, by common accord among all writers upon the subject, dates from the signing on 19 November 1794 of Jay's Treaty between Great Britain and the United States" (at 191). But this claim – just as Fraser's point about the 'eclipse' of arbitration in the early modern era (n. 12) – is in fact quite controversial: deviating from the alleged 'common accord', Lingens (n. 9, 153) and Roelofsen (n. 9, at 160) emphasize commonalities between the Jay Treaty arbitration and earlier 18th century precedents. That said, the Jay Treaty was special because it marked the conscious use of arbitration to address claims (including by private individuals) relating to a prior major conflict, and because it resulted in a large number of decisions.

use[17] did much to help regularize the practice of arbitration, which, in the course of the 19th century, came to be seen as a useful, practical way of settling disputes – and acceptable even to States protesting their sovereignty, as it was not imposed, but remained based on their consent. In retrospect, the breadth of disputes considered arbitrable is quite remarkable: large numbers of inter-State treaties provided for arbitration over boundary disputes, many others set up institutions to deal with pecuniary claims (whether inter-State or claims by private citizens).

In all that, arbitration remained an unusual form of dispute resolution. Stuyt's prominent survey[18] lists circa 180 awards rendered in the century following the Jay Treaty, i.e. less than two per year. But it clearly became less uncommon; especially if the more numerous (yet typically smaller) claims addressed by claims commissions are taken into account.[19] And over time, the process of binding dispute settlement matured, and evolved.[20] Sovereign arbitration by heads of States or dignitaries – Kings, Queens, Tsars, Emperors, and on occasion even the Senate of Hamburg[21] – was gradually replaced by professionalized forms of arbitration, with lawyers taking (and not just preparing) decisions. Unreasoned decisions gave way to reasoned awards. Parties and arbitrators took greater pains to clarify the basis of decisions; decisions came to be rendered on the basis of some pre-identified body of law (as opposed to equity), and, in turn, contributed to the thickening of rules governing international claims. And finally, best practices of arbitral procedure (how to select arbitrators; how to deal with evidence, etc.) began to crystalize.

The experience with the *Alabama claims* of 1872,[22] another landmark, suggested that, in fact, sovereign States (including the powerful ones)

17 A point stressed by O'Connell/VanderZee (n. 9), who note that "[b]etween 1794 and 1804, 536 arbitral awards were made under the Jay Treaty, beginning with the St. Croix River Arbitration of 1798, which delineated much of the Canada–United States boundary" (44).

18 A. Stuyt, *Survey of International Arbitrations 1794-1989* (3d ed. 1990).

19 See R. Dolzer, Mixed Claims Commissions, in *Max Planck Encyclopedia of Public International Law* (www.mpepil.com), at para. 6-7.

20 The point is overlooked in quite a number of general accounts. See Simpson/Fox (n. 13) 1-12, for a clear summary.

21 See e.g. the two British-Portuguese disputes (1855, 1861) about indemnities and denial of justice, referred to in Stuyt (n. 18), at 52 and 69.

22 For the relevant documents see C. Parry (ed.), *Consolidated Treaty Series*, vol. 143, 145 (1969); Tams/Tzanakopoulos (n. 15), 5; and P. de Lapradelle, N. Politis, *Recueil des arbitrages internationaux*, vol. II (1923) 889. In the words of two commentators, "[t]his award – and, indeed, the arbitral process itself – energized the peace movement and motivated states to engage in arbitration to settle more disputes. The single most important fact about the Alabama Claims was the example of a great power voluntarily entering into arbitration with a weaker state over an

would accept the authority of international law, even where this came at a considerable price: grudgingly, no doubt, but relatively swiftly, the United Kingdom paid $ 15.5 million to the United States, to compensate damages caused by Confederate ships which the United Kingdom had failed to prevent. This sent a powerful signal, and one not lost on States: henceforth, there were calls to rely on arbitration, not only as a form of 'emergency treatment', resorted to once a dispute had arisen, but prospectively, by formulating arbitration treaties that would allow resort to arbitration in future disputes.[23] Arbitration had come of age.[24]

---

important issue and abiding by the result" (O'Connell/VanderZee, n. 9, 45). See further D.D. Caron, War and International Adjudication: Reflections on the 1899 Peace Conference, American Journal of International Law 94 (2000), 4, at 8-9; and, for many details, T. Bingham, The Alabama Claims Arbitration, International and Comparative Law Quarterly 54 (2005), 1; and

23 Caflisch (n. 13), 307. See further below, III.1.

24 A (fictitious) scene from August Strindberg's *The German Lieutenant* (which David Caron refers to in his account: n. 22, 9) illustrates the importance attached to the *Alabama* arbitration at the time. It involves the German Lieutenant von Bleichroden and his wife discussing politics with other guests in a hotel in Vevey on the Lake Geneva. While they converse, "the dark, steel-blue evening sky was cut through by a streak of light, and above the low-lying Savoy shore there rose a rocket of enormous size … before it exploded with a report which took two minutes to reach Vevey. Then there spread out something like a white cloud which assumed a four-cornered rectangular shape, a flag of white fire; a moment after there was another report, and on the white flag appeared a red cross. All the party sprang up and hastened into the veranda. 'What does that mean?' exclaimed Herr von Bleichroden, startled. No one could or would answer, for now there rose a whole volley of rockets as if discharged from a crater over the peaks of the Voirons, and scattered a shower of fire which was reflected in the gigantic mirror of the lake. 'Ladies and gentlemen!' said the Englishman, raising his voice, while a waiter placed a tray with filled champagne glasses on the table. 'Ladies and gentlemen!', he repeated, 'this means, according to the telegram which I have just received, that the first International Tribunal at Geneva has finished its work; this means that a war between two nations, or what would have been worse – a war against the future, has been prevented … The Alabama Question has been settled not to the advantage of America, but of justice, not to the injury of England, but for the good of future generations. Does our Spanish friend still believe that wars are unavoidable? When our French friend smiles again, let him smile with the heart and not with the lips only. To-day, as an Englishman, I ought to feel depressed, but I feel proud on account of my country, as an Englishman always does, you know; but to-day I have a right to be so, for England is the first European Power which has appealed to the verdict of honourable men, instead of to blood and iron. And I wish you all many such defeats as we have had to-day, for that will teach us to be victorious. Raise your glasses, ladies and gentlemen, for the Red Cross, for in this sign we will certainly conquer.'" (A. Strindberg, The German Lieutenant and other stories, 1915 (transl. by Field), at 64-65).

## 2.2 Evolution of Catholic Thinking

In the pre-modern practice of international dispute settlement, the papacy had played a significant role.[25] Papal mediation and arbitration resolved a considerable number[26] of disputes, from the mundane (protocol) to the dramatic (Tordesillas); this squared well with papal claims to act as supreme arbiter of Christendom. Yet the re-emergence of international arbitration during the late 18th and 19th centuries initially bypassed the Papacy, whose spiritual authority had waned and whose status as a territorial power was increasingly in doubt. Against this background, it is perhaps surprising that Pope Leo XIII succeeded in re-positioning the Papacy as a relevant actor in international dispute settlement relatively quickly after the capture of Rome and the extinction of the Papal States in 1870.

Leo's initiatives were at two levels.[27] First, he agreed to act as mediator or arbitrator in a number of inter-State controversies of the late 19th century. The German-Spanish dispute about control over the Caroline islands[28] is perhaps the most prominent of these. It saw the German Chancellor propose Papal arbitration to defuse a crisis, while Catholic Spain – wary not to give away too much power – insisted on mediation; it thus reflects the continuing authority of the Pope as well as the limits of the role accorded to him by States. In other disputes, notably in Latin America, the Pope did act as arbitrator, and on a number of occasions helped resolve low- or mid-level

25 For details see H.T. King Jr./M.A. Le Forestier, Papal Arbitration: How the Early Roman Catholic Church Influenced Modern Dispute Resolution, Dispute Resolution Journal 1997, 74; and cf. the comprehensive collection of materials in J Müller, *Das Friedenswerk der Kirche in den letzten drei Jahrhunderten: Die Diplomatie des Vatikans im Dienste des Weltfriedens seit dem Kongress von Vervins 1598* (1927) vol 1. Brief summaries are provided by Westdickenberg (n. 10), at para. 15; and Fraser (n. 9), 193-194.

26 Westdickenberg (n. 10) puts their number at "close to 100 until the end of the 19th century, possibly even more" (para. 15); but perhaps that is an aggregate figure comprising mediation and arbitration. Fraser (n. 9) is more cautious, speaking of "several instances of cases submitted to papal arbitrament"; he also notes that papal "[m] ediations were more common than arbitrations" (193-194 with footnote 56).

27 The subsequent account largely draws on H.-G. Justenhoven, *International Schiedsgerichtsbarkeit. Ethische Norm und Rechtswirklichkeit* (2006), 28 et seq. For further details see H.E. Cardinale *The Holy See and the International Order* (1976); and H.F. Köck, *Die völkerrechtliche Stellung des Heiligen Stuhls: Dargestellt an seinen Beziehungen zu Staaten und internationalen Organisationen* (1975).

28 See H.-N. Götz, Karolinen-Streit, in K. Strupp/H.-J. Schlochauer, *Wörterbuch des Völkerrechts,* vol. 2 (1961), 203.

conflicts.[29] And while all this remained ad hoc, and conditioned by State consent, it was in fact quite remarkable: by the end of the 19th century, when its authority was no longer grounded territorially, the Papacy once more had joined the ranks of eligible arbitrators: this indeed marked a "new beginning in Papal peace policy".[30]

Second, and perhaps as remarkably, even at a time of geopolitical marginalization, Leo XIII made clear his firm belief in the special mission of the papacy as an 'apostle of world peace'. As regards the peaceful settlement of international disputes, Leo, no doubt emboldened by his experience in concrete conflict settlement processes, considered the Papacy to be ideally suited to administer justice in inter-State disputes. An anecdote related by Justenhoven[31] illustrates this point: according to contemporary sources, after the conclusion of the Carolines dispute, Leo XIII presented the German Chancellor Otto von Bismarck – staunch protestant and Catholic nemesis during the German 'Kulturkampf' – with a medal describing himself as the 'arbiter of the world'.

Against this background, it does not come as a surprise that Leo XIII viewed the general developments described in the preceding section very favourably. Towards the end of the century, he enthusiastically welcomed Tsar Nicolas' initiative to convene a universal peace conference bringing together the nations of the world (which eventually was held in The Hague during 1899[32]). As is clear from his correspondence, Leo XIII saw this initiative as an opportunity to reassert for the Papacy a more active role in world peace politics: "We believe that it is a specific part of our task, not only to provide moral help to such undertakings, but also to cooperate in them actively: because their objectives are most noble by nature and intimately linked to our august ministry which, through the divine Founder of the Church and by virtue of age-old tradition, in some way includes the function of mediator for peace".[33] Yet, while the Hague Conference indeed pursued 'noble objectives', the States of the world were to give short shrift to Leo XIII's claims to 'cooperate in them actively'. Both of these aspects will be explored in the next section.

29 Epstein, *The Catholic Tradition of the Law of Nations* (1935; reprint 2008) lists the main disputes (at 473).

30 Justenhoven (n. 27), 30 („Neubeginn päpstlicher Friedenspolitik"). See further Rijngaert (n. 10), 849-850 ('widely solicited as a mediator' – perhaps an overstatement). Köck provides many details (n. 27, 459 et seq.).

31 Justenhoven (n. 27), 34.

32 See *infra*, III.1.

33 Letter to Queen Wilhelmina of 29 May 1899, reproduced in *Civitta Cattolica* 1900 XVII XII, 283.

### 3. Building the 'Invisible Palace of Law and Justice'[34]: the Idealist Turn in Dispute Settlement

Since its re-emergence during the 19th century, binding dispute settlement has remained part of international relations. However, its relevance has varied over time. The subsequent sections highlight the main 'ups' and 'downs', and they begin on a wildly optimistic note: towards the end of the 19th century, the ideas of arbitration and adjudication gained huge momentum. To a powerful 'legalist movement',[35] courts and tribunals were the obvious instruments of world peace, and arbitration and adjudication natural ways of resolving international conflicts in a civilized world society, which – having opted for binding dispute resolution – would no longer need to espouse war.

Developments during the two to three decades preceding World War 1 are little short of remarkable.[36] They witnessed unprecedented popular debates about – perhaps even obsession with – dispute settlement, arbitration and adjudication. Prior to the emergence of general world organizations, courts and tribunals were seen as central elements of a better world order. This was an 'idealist turn' of significance. Until the outbreak of World War 1, idealist sentiment dominated the day and led to significant advances in the cause of peaceful dispute resolution. And four years after the end of the war, the international community would eventually set up its first 'world court', the Permanent Court of International Justice, in The Hague. Yet by then, faith in international courts and tribunals as guardians of world peace had been shaken, many progressive internationalists began to embrace other projects, and the legalist movement for international arbitration and adjudication had begun to lose steam.

---

34 Cf. W. Schücking, *The International Union of the Hague Conferences* (1918), xi.

35 Terminology is not uniform. Others speak of the 'international arbitration campaign' or 'movement' (see e.g. Mazower, *Governing the World. The History of an Idea* (2013), at 83), but that risks ignoring the push for international adjudication and 'proper courts'.

36 For much more on the 'legalist movement' see the highly accessible accounts by Mazower (n. 35), 81 et seq.; and N. Hollander, *Elusive Dove. The Search for Peace During World War I* (2013), chapter 1 ('A Prelude for Peace); and further, C. Reid, Peace and Law. Peace Activism and International Arbitration 1895-1907, Peace & Change 2004, 527. The American approach – by far the most influential – was shaped by the work of W. Ladd (*Essay on a Congress of Nations for the Adjustment of International Disputes Without Resort to Arms,* 1840); it is covered in detail in F.A. Boyle, *Foundations of World Order. The Legalist Approach to International Relations,* 1898-1922 (1999); M.E. O'Connell, Arbitration and the Avoidance of War: the Nineteenth Century American Vision, in C.P. Romano, *The Sword and the Scales. The United States and International Courts and Tribunals* (2009), 30; and M.W. Janis, *The American Tradition in International Law. Great Expectations 1789-1914* (2004), 95 et seq.

### 3.1 General Developments

But what power the legalist movement possessed at the turn of the last century! In retrospect, one cannot but be amazed at the huge appeal of the concepts, which, barely a century earlier, had had to be rescued from near-obsolescence. Predictably, the emerging influential professional networks of international lawyers – the Institut de droit international and the International Law Association, both set up in 1873[37] – found the idea of orderly dispute resolution according to legal standards attractive and supported it. But beyond that, and much less predictably, from the late 19th century 'international arbitration' and, increasingly, 'international adjudication' became rallying cries for a wide range of heterogeneous pressure groups, among them pacifists, the Inter-Parliamentary Union, socialist movements, national leagues for the furtherance of peace, and – not least – religious associations and the Catholic Church.[38] These, and many more, formed a powerful legalist movement: no doubt a broad church, but firm in its faith in courts and tribunals as guardians of world peace and committed (more pragmatically) to increase their role in world affairs. This, to be sure, was but one of a number of progressive causes of the day; but around the turn of the last century, it was at the forefront of the internationalist struggle.[39]

In the two decades preceding the outbreak of the First World War, the legalist movement seemed to go from strength to strength. Its manifestos exuded growing confidence.[40] Its claims were espoused by universal peace

37 On both, and on the emergence of an international legal profession from the 19th century, see M. Koskenniemi, *The Gentle Civilizer of Nations* (2002), 11 et seq.

38 Janis (n. 36) underlines the limited influence of trained (international) lawyers: given how much debate about today's international courts has become "the erudite province of lawyers and judges", he notes that "it is easy to suppose that it was a juridical impulse that was principally responsible for their creation. However, to a surprising extent, the international courts of today were the work of nineteenth-century American Utopians by and large untrained in law" (at 95).

39 As Caron (n. 22) observes, "these [pacifist] movements could have chosen other strategies to promote peace" (and in fact they would during most of the 20th century); because this is so, "[the internationalists' focus on a permanent international court deserves attention" (at 8). Reid (n. 36) agrees that the focus on courts and tribunals was "deliberate and methodical" (at 543). The fact that the Inter-Parliamentary Union had initially been founded as an 'Inter-Parliamentary Conference on International Arbitration' reflects the prominence of international arbitration to the internationalist cause.

40 "The feasibility of arbitration as a substitute for war is now demonstrated" – this was the opening line of the 1895 Resolution adopted at the first Lake Mohonk Conference on International Arbitration. John Westlake's treatise on *International Law* (vol. 1, 1896) ended with the words: "[I]nternational arbitration is in the air. … It is

congresses. And advocates of international courts and tribunals – Asser, Fried, Root, Cramer, the Institut de droit international, Theodor Roosevelt – dominated the lists of Nobel Peace laureates.[41] By 1914, as noted by Mark Mazower, "the campaign for international arbitration" was "probably the single most influential strand of internationalism".[42] Alongside civil society groups, it included relevant political establishment figures (notably within the United States); and while it faced divisions between more utopian and more pragmatic camps, agreement on core demands remained strong: more binding dispute resolution would minimize tensions between States; as a consequence, it was necessary to increase the reach of treaties requiring States to accept arbitration and adjudication, and ideally to move from ad hoc arrangements to standing international courts.

Needless to say, the practical implementation of these proposals proved challenging. Yet, despite disappointments, vigorous lobbying by the legalist movement facilitated the consolidation and significant expansion of binding dispute settlement in the period up to 1914. The Hague Peace Conferences, the first universal conferences, shaped, at least to some extent, by "world society action"[43], saw States discuss proposals for compulsory dispute settlement. In the end, as is well known, the Conferences did not endorse proposals requiring States to accept arbitration as obligatory, but they reflected the broad support for the principle.[44] The 1899 Hague Convention for the Pacific Settlement of Disputes set up a mechanism for the smooth organization of arbitral proceedings (which it misleadingly called the 'Permanent

---

the season to raise our hopes, and do our utmost to try what the idea of international arbitration can accomplish" (at 368).

41 See http://www.nobelprize.org/nobel_prizes/peace/laureates/ for details, short biographies, and acceptance speeches.

42 Mazower (n. 35), 83, See also Reid (n. 36): "On the global level, turn-of-the-century peace advocates were unique because of their composition and their political foresight. Current and former members of American, British, French, Japanese, Chinese, and Italian governments eventually participated in these gatherings of arbitrationists, as did military personnel, clergy, labor, teachers, bankers, and journalists" (528). Janis (n. 36) notes that "by the turn of the century, British and US international law enthusiasts were exerting increasing influence over their governments (at 145).

43 I. Clark, *International Legitimacy and World Society* (2007), 71.

44 On the conferences (and their impact on dispute settlement) see e.g. B. Baker, Hague Peace Conferences (1899 and 1907), in *Max Planck Encyclopedia of Public International Law* (www.mpepil.com). For more on the first conference see Caron (n. 22); for details on the second see A. Eyffinger, A Highly Critical Moment: Role and Record of the Second Hague Peace Conference, Netherlands International Law Review 54 (2007), 197; and C.J. Tams, Die Zweite Haager Konferenz und das Recht der friedlichen Streitbeilegung, Friedens-Warte 82 (2007), 119.

Court of Arbitration' (PCA)[45]) and, recognized that "[i]n questions of a legal nature … arbitration is … the most effective, and, at the same time, the most equitable means of settling disputes which diplomacy has failed to settle".[46] Eight years later, at the second Hague Conference, a clear majority of States were willing to accept compulsory arbitration in all disputes not involving questions of vital interests, and only after "titanic debate",[47] a handful of States succeeded in blocking the adoption of a provision to this effect.[48]

At the bilateral and regional level, like-minded States went further. While the time may not have been ripe for a universal arbitration treaty, States concluded dozens of bilateral arbitration treaties that permitted the unilateral recourse to arbitration in the event of a dispute.[49] The Permanent Court of Arbitration, misnamed though it may have been, allowed for arbitral proceedings to be initiated relatively smoothly; and its record of its activities at the beginning of the 20th century reflects a growing willingness of States to submit to binding dispute resolution.[50] And where the Hague Peace Conference had been deadlocked over the establishment of permanent institutions, American States in 1907 set up the first proper international court, the Central American Court of Justice, competent to hear inter-State disputes as well as claims by private citizens.[51] An influential US-American *Handbook of International Law* published in 1910 gave expression to a wide-spread sentiment when noting that "in a single decade the advance made in centuries [had been] surpassed."[52] In the light of these developments, the inauguration of the Peace Palace in The Hague, on 28 August 1913, was perceived by many as another 'coming of age': built with

---

45 As has often been observed, the PCA was neither a 'court' nor 'permanent'. To which one may add that since the 1930s, it no longer 'arbitrates', but administers arbitrations organised outside the Hague Convention.

46 *Convention (I) on the Pacific Settlement of International Disputes* (1899), Article 20.

47 Eyffinger (n. 45), 219.

48 Tams (n. 45), 126-127. Two other courts proposed at The Hague never saw the light of day: the Court of Arbitral Justice and the International Prize Court. For details see Tams (n. 45), 127-129.

49 The United States entered into 22 such treaties during 1908 and 1909 (though with caveats for disputes involving vital interests): see Neff (n. 1), 329-330.

50 For a detailed survey see J.P.A. François, La Cour permanente d'arbitrage son origine, sa jurisprudence, son avenir' (1955 I) 87 Recueil des cours 457, at 479-522.

51 See American Journal of International Law 2 (1908) (Suppl.), 231 for the founding document, and further R. Riquelme Cortado, Central American Court of Justice (1907-1918), in Max Planck Encyclopedia of Public International Law (www.mpepil.com).

52 G.G. Wilson, *Handbook of International Law* (1910), at v. For more on the pre-1914 sentiment see Hollander (n. 36), 7-13.

American funds by European leaders, it reflected the consolidation of the arbitration movement and symbolized the power of the legalist movement.

Then came 28 June 1914 and exposed the hollowness of the structure. The July crisis in particular highlighted the limited practical impact of international arbitration treaties. Nations (including those who had come out in favour of compulsory dispute settlement) consciously shunned "the hushed calm of court rooms" and instead opted for the "swirling world of political cut-and-thrust".[53] Over the following four years of bitter warfare, they would come to rely on attrition tactics, unrestricted submarine warfare, chemical weapons, and genocidal violence. Arbitration, which, prior to 1914, had helped resolve low- and mid-level conflicts, proved powerless to stop a major global conflict from spiralling out of control.

This was not lost on statesmen and observers, and it led to an (under-appreciated[54]) re-assessment of the role of international courts and tribunals. When, driven by war fatigue and the growing awareness of the horrors of war, the leaders of the Allied and Associated Powers began to discuss the design of the post-war world order, international courts and tribunals no longer took centre stage in their visions. True, the inter-war period saw the creation of the first ever world court, the Permanent Court of International Justice. But even the grand rhetoric commemorating its inauguration[55] could not mask the fact that this was to be a different court than the supreme tribunal envisaged by the legalists. Unlike in 1907, when proposals to make

53 Cf. Neff (n. 1). As Matheson notes, "on the brink of the War in July 1914, the Tsar proposed tot he Kaiser that the dispute between Austria and Serbia about the assassination of Archduke [Franz] Ferdinand be submitted for arbitration in The Hague, but Austria was unwilling": M.J. Matheson, *International Civil Tribunals and Armed Conflicts* (2012), 19.

54 The following draws on St. Wertheim, The League of Nations: A Retreat from International Law?, Journal of Global History 7 (2012), 210. For much more on 'legalist' and 'anti-legalist' trends in the establishment of the post-WW1 order see D. Kennedy, The Move to Institutions, Cardozo Law Review 8 (1987), 841; condensed accounts can be found in Mazower (n. 35, 119-123); and J. von Bernstorff, *The Public International Law Theory of Hans Kelsen* (2010), 193-195.

55 See e.g. J. Scott Brown, Editorial Comment, 15 AJIL (1921), 55: "We should…fall upon our knees and thank God that the hope of ages is in process of realization". At the inaugural ceremony, the League of Nations Secretary General, Sir Eric Drummond, had even gone so far as to praise he Court's establishment as "the greatest and … most important creative act of the League … There have been various well-distinguished marks in the progress of mankind. The opening of the Court is not the least of these. Indeed, we believe and hope that it will prove the greatest. After all, the ideal to which I presume all men of goodwill look forward is that not only individual nations but the whole world shall be ruled by law" (PCIJ Reports 1922, Series D, No 2, at 320).

arbitration compulsory had enjoyed the support of Britain, France and the United States (to name but a few), this time the great powers ensured the world court would not possess automatic jurisdiction.[56] In practice, as will be explored in the next section, it was to be a court for low- and mid-level disputes.[57] And most importantly, the world court was designed to operate on the margins of the new world organization, the League of Nations: not part of the League's machinery for preserving peace and barely integrated in its (ill-fated) collective security system. The League's founders were idealist, too, but theirs was not the idealism of the legalists: not arbitration or adjudication but collective decision-making within international organizations, not the force of law but the strength of political action backed by public opinion, were to ensure the League's success.[58] Elihu Root's assessment of the League Covenant reflected a sense of disappointment at the 'relegation' of legalist thought in new post-war order: "Nothing has been done to provide for the reestablishment and strengthening of a system of arbitration or judicial decision … We are left with a program which rests the hope of the whole world for future peace in a government of men, and not of laws, following the dictates of expediency, and not of right."[59] And so, the post-war order brought about the long-sought establishment of a proper world court, but at the same time saw that court relegated to the margins of the newly established architecture of international security.[60] The idealist ap-

56 Rosenne notes that "there was a strong drive in the preparatory phase to endow the Court with compulsory jurisdiction over legal disputes"; however "[t]he Great Powers especially were firmly opposed to this and the [League] Council rejected the idea: Sh. Rosenne, Permanent Court of International Justice, in Max Planck Encyclopedia of Public International Law (www.mpepil.com) (at para. 30). The case for compulsory jurisdiction is set out in detail in the dissenting opinion of Judge *Cançado* Trindade in the *Case concerning the Application of the International Convention on the Elimination of All Forms of Racial Discrimination* (Georgia v. Russian Federation), ICJ Reports 2011, 239, at paras. 6-26.

57 See *infra,* IV.1.

58 Mazower (n. 35) speaks of "Woodrow Wilson's impatience with the entire legalist paradigm" (at 121).

59 Root to Henry Cabot Lodge, 19 June 1919, cited in Wertheim (n. XX), 228. See further J. Zasloff, Law and the Shaping of American Foreign Policy: From the Gilded Age to the New Era, New York niversity Law Review 78 (2003), 239, at 348-349: "Root's legalism, however, diverged sharply from Wilsonian diplomacy, a point obscured by frequent references to Wilson's 'legalism.' As Root noted, neither the Versailles Treaty nor the Fourteen Points called for international legal institutions (such as a world court) or compulsory arbitration of legal disputes; indeed, Wilson rejected the legal-political distinction that served as the essential framework of Root's thinking."

60 See von Bernstorff (n. 54), 195-196: "The Covenant … enshrined the primacy of politics over international law institutionally within the powerful organ of the

proach of the early 20th century was giving way to a much more pragmatic assessment of the role of international courts and tribunals in world affairs.

### 3.2 Evolution of Catholic Thinking

The papal contributions to debates about dispute settlement during this second stage of development remained discrete and occasionally significant; yet thinking on the proper role of the Pope in the universe of dispute settlement evolved significantly. As regards the practical dimension of dispute settlement, there was a good deal of continuity: as towards the end of the 19th century, the Papacy continued to be involved in the inter-State mediations and arbitrations, notably in Latin-American disputes where Catholic sentiment remained strong.[61] The disputes in question typically were not as significant as the dispute about the Caroline islands had been; yet in retrospect, they stand out as the Papacy's last active interventions in arbitral proceedings.[62]

As regards the Papacy's views on dispute settlement, there was a measure of continuity, too. Benedict XV in particular (1914-1922) was an ardent advocate of dispute settlement.[63] However, he did not cling to Leo XIII's naïve vision of the Pope as a natural 'arbiter of the world'. In fact, the gap between self-perception and reality had become very apparent during the end of Leo XIII's pontificate. While Tsar Nicolas had sought (and received) Leo's support for his Hague Peace Initiative, the actual Hague Peace Conference saw the 'apostle of peace' sidelined: at the instigation of Italy, the Papal delegation was excluded from the proceedings of this first universal

---

Council .. [but] failed to institutionalize the encompassing and compulsory judicial controls of political decisions demanded by the [legalist] internationalists." Giustini makes a similar point when noting that " The League of Nations system which followed the War did little to live up to these [legalist] expectations. It focused on the political rather than judicial settlement of disputes": A. Giustini, Compulsory Adjudication in International Law: The Past, The Present, and Prospects for the Future, Fordham International Law Journal 9 (1985), 213, at 224.

61 Köck (459 et seq.) provides details; Cardinale (89 et seq.) and Eppstein (n. XX, 473-474) list the main activities. In addition to concrete disputes, it may be worth noting that the 1905 Colombian-Peruvian Arbitration Agreement – one of the large number of bilateral arrangements making up the increasingly dense web of binding dispute settlement (*supra,* III.1.) – envisaged recourse to the Pope in all inter-State disputes (with a caveat for disputes involving questions of indepedencen and honour).

62 See *infra,* V.2. for brief comment on Pope John Paul's mediation in the *Beagle Channel* dispute.

63 Justenhoven provides details: n. 27, at 39-43. For more context see J.F. Pollard, *Benedict XV. The Pope of Peace* (1999).

conference convened to "see[k] the most effective means of ensuring to all peoples the benefits of a real and lasting peace".[64] Whereas Leo XIII had emphasized the trans-boundary reach of his mission and authority on numerous occasions, the nations of the world preferred to remain among themselves when spelling out the regime for avoiding and taming war.

The change in (self-)perception is very evident from Benedict XV's teachings. His famous Appeal of 1 August 1917 ('From the beginning')[65] urged States to accept mechanisms for the binding arbitration of disputes; as in earlier papal writings, orderly dispute settlement was seen as an alternative to war. However, arbitration to Benedict no longer was as panacea. In his encyclical *Pacem dei* of 1920, the focus is on a much more fundamental change in world affairs, viz. the establishment of an "association of nations", "one league … a sort of family of peoples, calculated both to maintain their own independence and safeguard the order of human society".[66] And as regards the Papacy's own role in dispute settlement, Benedict XV moved away from Leo XIII's far-fetched claims: the warring parties having ignored his pleas for peace, he accepted that a future system of dispute settlement would need to be based on the consent of States, and designed as a worldly institution. As aptly noted by Justenhoven, the Papacy's main role – as perceived by Benedict himself – henceforth would be to "spell out the ethical foundations of obligatory arbitration and urge States to establish it"[67] – but it could no longer claim to act as natural and supreme arbiter of the world. Towards the end of the 'idealist turn', a helpful sense of realism had set in.

## *4. Towards Pragmatism: International Courts and Tribunals on the Margins of World Politics*

By the 1920s, the main aspects of the modern system for the settlement of inter-State disputes had been established. Arbitration had matured into a recognized form of dispute settlement. The international community had set up mechanisms for the administration of arbitral proceedings and, from

64 Cf. the Russian Circular Note of December 1898, reproduced in J.B. Scott, The Proceedings of the Hague Peace Conferences, vol. 1 (1920), xv.

65 Available online e.g. at http://wwi.lib.byu.edu/index.php/Pope_Benedict_XV's_Peace_Proposal. For comment on Benedict XV's earlier initiatives see Pollard (n. XX), 112 et seq.

66 Benedict XV, Pacem, dei munus pulcherrimum, available at http://w2.vatican.va/content/benedict-xv/en/encyclicals/documents/hf_ben-xv_enc_23051920_pacem-dei-munus-pulcherrimum.html, at para. 17.

67 Justenhoven (n. 27), at 42 (translation by the author).

1922, possessed an operative, permanent, world court that could respond quickly if so requested. A large number of bilateral and regional agreements permitted recourse to arbitration over particular types of disputes, while treaties concluded after World War 1 (beginning with the Paris peace agreements and the arrangements for minority protection) envisaged proceedings before the Permanent Court of International Justice. These were significant steps forward; and yet, even by the 1920s, a more sober perspective on courts and tribunals was gaining ground. "[T]he profound and widespread nineteenth-century faith in the peacekeeping ability of an international court"[68] (still strongly felt during Hague Peace conference) was giving way to a pragmatic appreciation of the role of courts and tribunals: useful they were, no doubt, but less came to be expected from them.

The move towards pragmatism was not brought about by a 'one-off', momentous decision; it was perhaps rather a 'slide' – a process in the course of which a world court was 'operative', but played a much more modest role than envisaged by legalists. This 'pragmatic period', it is argued, lasted for around five decades, from the 1920s to the 1970s, when the world court, in the view of contemporary observers, "ha[d] fallen to perhaps its lowest position of international prestige".[69]

### *4.1 General Developments*

In the slide towards pragmatism, the experience of the newly established PCIJ was highly relevant. A world court had been established, but it hardly ever addressed disputes of world relevance. The move from arbitration to adjudication permitted for a more systematic evolution of international law, gradually moulded, as a by-product of litigation, in the jurisprudence of a permanent court.[70] However, the disputes submitted to the new world

68 Caron (n. 22), 9.

69 R.A. Falk, Realistic Horizons for International Adjudication, Virginia Journal of International Law 11 (1971), 314, at 315.

70 After little more than a decade of the PCIJ jurisprudence, Hersch Lauterpacht published a series of lectures, in monograph form, on the *The Development of International Law by the Permanent Court of International Justice* (1934); this marked the beginning of a never-ending stream of literature on the PCIJ's and ICJ's law-making potential. Writing in 2013, Ole Spiermann notes perceptively: "Obscure cases decided by the Permanent Court are household names, familiar to present generations of international lawyers, because they were, by chance, the first place for authoritative expression of various principles of general international law. Such statements of principle have found wide use far beyond their original context. As

court were, if anything, of lesser relevance than those submitted to arbitration before World War 1. This was not principally a problem of jurisdiction. Even in the absence of automatic, compulsory jurisdiction, during the 1920s and 1930s, States regularly agreed on compromissory clauses establishing the jurisdiction of the PCIJ over specific types of disputes.[71] Many States went one step further and accepted the Court's jurisdiction over *all* disputes under the so-called optional clause.[72] Still, the considerable potential for inter-State litigation was never realized.[73] States made sparing use of the Court, and for the bigger question of the day they relied on other means of dispute settlement (or preferred not to settle). Over the two decades of its existence, the Court rendered a total of 32 judgments and 27 advisory opinions (i.e. less than three decisions per year). Its sphere of activity remained decidedly European: in only *four* cases did non- European States appear, and in only *one* single case did a non-European State (Brazil) play a decisive role.[74] Its decisions, while generally well received, concerned a fairly limited set of issues, among them disputes about maritime incidents, the treatment of aliens and, notably, minority issues. Through its competent handling of these, the Court established itself – and it largely eclipsed the Permanent Court of Arbitration as the most prominent framework of inter-

---

such they have little to do with the actual life of the Permanent Court, except for confirming the ambition on the part of the Permanent Court to take an active role in the development of international law, at least in the 1920s" (Spiermann, The Legacy of the Permanent Court of International Justice – On Judges and Scholars, and Also on Bishops and Clowns, in C.J. Tams/M. Fitzmaurice, *Legacies of the Permanent Court of International Justice* (2013), 399).

71 Surveying developments, Jenks perceptively notes that "[f]rom the Geneva Arbitration Act of 1872 until 1930, there appeared to be long-term trend towards the acceptance of a larger measure of compulsory jurisdiction": C.W. Jenks, *Prospects of International Adjudication* (1964), 13. The 1928 Act for the Pacific Settlement of International Disputes (League of Nations Treaty Series, vol. 93, 344) was the most ambitious attempt to expand the PCIJ's jurisdiction; it marked the last major attempt to introduce compulsory arbitration or adjudication through a universal dispute settlement treaty, yet limited ratification numbers and far-reaching reservations affected its relevance: see Caflisch (n. 13), at 317-318. As Giustini notes (n. 60), "[n]o case was ever brought before the Permanent Court on the basis of the General Act" (at 228).

72 Under the 'optional clause', agreed as a substitute for proper compulsory jurisdiction during the drafting of the PCIJ Statute, States could voluntarily declare their willingness to accept the Court's jurisdiction over all disputes; during the 1920s and 1930s, this was regularly done (albeit with reservations). See C.J. Tams, The Contentious Jurisdiction of the Permanent Court, in Tams/Fitzmaurice (n. 70), 11, at 19-21; and, for a fuller treatment, V. Lamm, *Compulsory Jurisdiction in International Law* (2014), 12-32.

73 See Tams (n. 72), 21-28, for further comment.

74 Jenks provides many details: (n. 71), at 75-76.

national arbitration. But the PCIJ could hardly be said to intervene in matters of peace and war. In the words of Spiermann, "[i]n the political history of the League of Nations, the Permanent Court [was] but a footnote, partly because it did not address the main political issues of the day."[75]

If the world court – and international arbitration – played a limited role in questions of war and peace, then this was partly because other international actors had entered the stage. As is implicit in Spiermann's quote, the League of Nations was the new framework within which matters of peace and war were to be addressed. As the first world organization of general competence, the League established a system of collective security, set up permanent institutions and gradually built networks for international co-operation.[76] In the design of the inter-War period, collective security and institutional mechanisms for conflict resolution (but no longer courts) were envisaged as the real alternatives to war, gradually coupled with normative prescriptions against military force. As is well known, that, too, was rather naïve. Agreed outside institutional structures, rules against war (such as those of the Kellogg-Briand Pact) had little traction.[77] The existing institutional structure – the League – was meant to be a world organization, but never achieved universality.[78] The Covenant's collective security system was not designed to cope with the challenges of the 1930s.[79] Throughout, the League depended on the support of its member States, which very often was not forthcoming.

But an exclusive focus on its failures risks overlooking how much the 'League experience' shaped the international community's approach to the

75 Ole Spiermann, *International Legal Argument in the Permanent Court of International Justice. The Rise of the International Judiciary* (2005), 132.

76 For instructive summaries see I.L. Claude, *Swords into Plowshares* (4th edn., 1971), 42 et seq.; Y. Dinstein, *War, Aggression and Self-Defence* (4th edn., 2005), 80 et seq.; for a contemporary perspective cf. J.L. Brierly, International Law and Resort to Armed Force, Cambridge Law Journal 4 (1930-32), 308. The writer's own view is set out in C.J. Tams, League of Nations, in *Max Planck Encyclopedia of Public International Law* (www.mpepil.com), at paras. 24-29..

77 See League of Nations Treaty Series, vol. 94, 57, for the treaty text; and Dinstein (n. 76), 83-85, for comment.

78 Tams (n. 76), paras. 7-9.

79 Tams (n. 76), paras. 30-31. In the words of Inis L. Claude (n. 76), the League's collective security system (like "the French Maginot line") was the product of a "retrospective mentality" (at 46). Prescribing mandatory cooling-off periods and recourse to an international body, it might very well have prevented States from sleepwalking into another World War 1. But the challenges of the 1930s were not about sleepwalking into war. "The League, established to prevent the accidental war, was unable to cope with Hitler's deliberately plotted campaign of conquest" (ibid.).

prevention of war. After 1919, the maintenance of international peace and security has come to be seen as a project of collective security to be pursued within international organizations, with courts (unlike in the legalist project) limited to some form of associated role. And while concepts and strategies of collective security evolved over time, that basic division of roles – between an institutionalized "peace machinery"[80] on the one hand, and courts and tribunals on the other – would never be reversed. At the universal level, during the 1940s, when designing the new organization for the post-WW2 order, the Allied Powers insisted that the Charter would recognize their primary responsibility for the maintenance of international peace and security.[81] Correcting another 'design failure' of the League, the Charter banned resort to military force comprehensively.[82] Of course, the UN also was to have its court (in fact, one more integrated into the organization[83]); however, attempts to 'upgrade' its role into that of a true supreme court stood no realistic chance of success.[84] The world court's 'second incarnation', the International Court of Justice, was closely modelled on the Permanent Court. Its link with the UN's peace and security machinery was tenuous.[85] And its jurisdiction remained optional. States could submit disputes for judicial settlement, including in questions of peace and security,

80 The term is Jessup's: see Ph.C. Jessup, A Half-Century of Efforts to Subtitute Law for War, Recueil des Cours 99 (1960), 1, at 18.

81 See Claude (n. 75), 60 et seq.

82 According to Article 2(4) of the Charter, "[a]ll Members shall refrain in their international relations from the threat or use of force against the territorial integrity or political independence of any state, or in any other manner inconsistent with the Purposes of the United Nations." This is indeed, as Schrijver notes, the "backbone of the Charter system of collective security" (N. Schrijver, The Ban on the Use of Force in the UN Charter, in M. Weller, *The Oxford Handbook of the Use of Force in International Law* (2014),, 465, at 487).

83 Notably, the ICJ was to be one of the UN's principal organs (UN Charter, Article 7); the UN organs were authorized to seek advisory opinions (Article 96); the ICJ Statute became an integral part of the Charter (Article 92); and compliance with judgments a Charter obligation, which the Security Council could help enforce (Article 94).

84 In fact, the Inter-Allied Committee ('London Committee') had recommended to keep the Court out of the UN's political work: see American Journal of International Law 39 (1945), Supplement, 1.

85 While the Court is a principal organ oft he UN, the Charter does not provide it with jurisdiction to entertain disputes. Under its Article 36, the Security Council can "recommend appropriate procedures or methods of adjustment" and, in so doing, is meant to "take into consideration that legal disputes should as a general rule be referred by the parties to the International Court of Justice". Yet in the Court's first contentious case, seven ICJ judges clarified that Article 36 of the Charter did not form a self-standing basis of jurisdiction: see *Corfu Channel case,* Separate opin-

but they did not have to.[86] All this confirms Claude's assessment: "The United Nations has clearly contributed little to establishing the sanctity of the principle of judicial decision."[87]

Not surprisingly, during the first decades of its existence, the ICJ remained on the sidelines of world affairs, and had little involvement in questions of war and peace. The *Corfu Channel case* saw the Court pronounce on a British-Albanian maritime incident.[88] Otherwise, however – and notwithstanding the willingness of UN organs occasionally to use the ICJ as an 'in-house' lawyer renedering opinion of aspects of United Nations law – from Korea to Indochina to Biafra, "States remained reluctant to accept international adjudication of their conduct during wartime".[89] In fact, if anything, its role declined. Whereas most League members had not, in principle, been opposed to the idea of binding dispute settlement, Communist States were.[90] Newly-independent States emerging since the late 1950s viewed the world court with indifference or suspicion; after the 1966 *South West Africa* judgment, in which the Court, on dubious grounds, refused to entertain Ethiopia's and Liberia's legal challenge of South Africa's imposition of apartheid policies, many became openly hostile.[91]

---

ion of Judges Basdevant, Alvarez, Winiarski, Zoricic, De Visscher, Badawi Pasha, Krylov, ICJ Reports 1948, 32.

86 For a survey of attempts, during the San Francisco Conference, to move towards compulsory jurisdiction see *Cançado* Trindade (n. 56), at paras. 27-36. The UN's only subsequent attempt to sponsor a general dispute settlement treaty – the Revised General Act of 1949 – ended as a farce. As explored in section V.1., the trend has been (in the words of O'Connell and VanderZee) "from general to specialized compulsory jurisdiction" (n. 9, at 58).

87 Claude (n. 76), 234. For a similar observation see Giustini (n. 60), 229: "The Charter does not encourage international adjudication. Instead, it continues the focus on political settlement". D.W. Greig goes further: "The Charter is perhaps more of a discouragement than an incentive to judicial settlement. The dispute machinery of the Charter provides a new arena for diplomatic exchanges and the advancement of legal arguments without fear of a final determination upon their validity" (*International Law* (1976), 693).

88 This, admittedly, was a dispute involving military questions; and in retrospect, one can perhaps view *Corfu Channel* as an early example of ICJ 'conflict litigation' (on which more below, in section V.1.). But by the 1970s, it could equally be seen an isolated incident – the exception that proved the rule. And of course, like subsequent instances of conflict litigation, *Corfu Channel* raised serious compliance problems; it took around 45 years for Albania to honour the award.

89 Matheson (n. 53), 31.

90 See Giustini (n. 60), 243: "In general, the influence of the Soviet bloc has been strongly against the extension of the judicial function in international relations."

91 In 1960, Ethiopia and Liberia, the only two African States that had been members of the League of Nations, instituted ICJ proceedings, alleging that South Africa

Assessments of the ICJ's record during the first 25-30 years of its existence reflect a growing sense of pessimism, if not despair: Inis L. Claude criticized the "Politics of neglect",[92] which led States to withhold cases from the Court; an influential study published in 1976 bore the title "The International Court of Justice: An Analysis of a Failure".[93] Not everyone agreed with that overall verdict, yet even benevolent observers recognized that in relation to the questions of peace and security, the ICJ was not a relevant factor: "At present the Court has very little to do with the enforcement of peace", states Lissitzyn in an influential study prepared for the Carnegie Endowment.[94] (In fact, during the mid-1970s, the Court had nothing to do at all, as States had stopped referring disputes to it.) In Max Sørensen's assessment, the Court's role in world affairs was "relatively insignificant";[95] while Hersch Lauterpacht (perhaps the 20th century's most influential advocate of international courts) thought it "an exaggeration to assert that the Court has proved to be a significant instrument for maintaining international peace."[96] And according to a detailed German study published in the 1970s, the idea of 'arbitration instead of war' had gone "completely belly-up".[97]

These verdicts by contemporaries are perhaps too damning. With the benefit of hindsight, when looking at international arbitration and adjudication from a slightly broader perspective, one can make out signs of a re-orientation. Though not 'enforcing peace' (or stopping wars), courts and

---

had not fulfilled its duties under the South West Africa mandate granted to it by the League of Nations. After having initially upheld jurisdiction, the ICJ in 1966 dismissed the case, holding – with the narrowest of margins – that Ethiopia and Liberia had no standing to enforce the mandate provisions (see ICJ Reports 1966, 6). As Falk (n. 69) explains, the 1966 decision ran counter to the general view within the United Nations that South Africa was internationally accountable for its conduct in South West Africa: "For the ICJ to cast a shadow across this consensus, after so many years of pleadings and arguments, was to outrage the diplomats of black Africa, to disappoint almost every government in the world, and to give international adjudication an image, at once, hopelessly reactionary and cumbersome" (at 318).

92 I.L. Claude, Jr., States and the World Court: The Politics of *Neglect*, Virginia Journal of International Law 11 (1971), 344.

93 J. King Gamble/D. Fischer, *The International Court of Justice: An Analysis of Failure* (1976).

94 O.J. Lissitzyn, *The International Court of Justice: Its Role in the Maintenance of International Peace and Security* (1951), 103.

95 M. Sørensen, The International Court of Justice: its Role in Contemporary International Relations, International Organization 14 (1960), 261, 272.

96 H. Lauterpacht, *The Development of International Law by the International Court of Justice* (1958), 4.

97 H. von Mangoldt, *Die Schiedsgerichtsbarkeit als Mittel internationaler Streitschlichtung* (1974), 83 („hat totalen Schiffbruch erlitten").

tribunals even in the 'pragmatic phase' were mandated to address discrete legal issues relating to military conflicts. Two of these discrete functions deserve to be mentioned, as they were to provide blueprints for subsequent, more ambitious, initiatives. First, drawing on 19th century practice, arbitral tribunals were set up to hear claims by individuals for war-time losses.[98] In the aftermath of World War 1, this was a prevalent method of dealing with a particular set of consequences of the war; but after 1945, the practice seemed to fall out of favour: questions of reparation were largely dealt with through treaty arrangements.[99] Second, the international community had begun to rely on courts as instruments of international criminal justice. After cautious initiatives after World War 1, the tribunals of Nuremberg and Tokyo marked the first concerted attempts to hold individuals criminally accountable for their conduct during wartime.[100] This was a much more visible (and much more controversial) form of adjudication about military conflicts, which served a range of functions, from punishment to the recording of history. By the 1960s and 1970s, attempts to consolidate the post-WW2 *acquis* of international criminal justice[101] had clearly lost momentum; still, the examples of Nuremberg and Tokyo suggested that courts could perhaps adapt to perform new roles relating to war and peace.

But outside these discrete functions, relatively little remained of the ambitious legalist plans for world peace. The movement itself faded away relatively quickly.[102] Arbitration and adjudication remained relevant topics to international lawyers, but, after the 1920s, quickly ceased to be matters of general interest. Internationalist sentiment did not disappear, but embraced other causes, from the League in the 1920s (when national 'League associations' attracted large numbers of members[103]) to nuclear disarmament,

98 See Matheson (n. 53), 19-21; Neff (n. 1), 357-358.

99 Matheson (n. 53), 24-25.

100 Neff (n. 1), provides an instructive summary (at 397-400); Robert Cryer traces the impact of the trials of Leipzig, Nuremberg and Tokyo: *Prosecuting International Crimes* (2005), 31-48. For many details on the German position see C. Kress, Versailles – Nuremberg – The Hague: Germany and International Criminal Law, *The International Lawyer* 40 (2006), 15.

101 See notably UN General Assembly Resolution 95(I) (1946); International Law Commission, Principles of International Law recognized in the Charter of the Nürnberg Tribunal and in the Judgment of the Tribunal, Yearbook of the International Law Commission, 1950, vol. II, 374.

102 In Mazower's words, the legalist "movement['s] … success in the years before [Wrold War 1] was matched only by the marginalization that greeted it in the decades after it" (n. 35, at 83-84).

103 To give just one example, membership in the British League of Nations Union stood at circa 400,000 in 1931; in the words of a recent study, "the League inspired

self-determination and perhaps human rights after 1945. Ironically, the limited appeal of the legalist movement during the pragmatic era can be seen from the response to one of its most ambitious proposals, viz. Hans Kelsen's *Peace Through Law* project.[104] Published in 1944, at the height of debates about the post-WW2 order, this was a new attempt to prescribe an old medicine:[105] Kelsen proposed to found a new world organization built around a 'proper' world court, which would have jurisdiction over disputes relating to war and peace. To him, the decision to establish the world court on the margins of the League's "peace machinery"[106] was a fundamental mistake; like earlier generations of legalists, Kelsen felt that progress towards the "pacification of the world" had to be brought about by courts and tribunals with compulsory jurisdiction.[107] But what had seemed prophetic a few decades earlier, now failed to resonate: academic response among international lawyers was at best lukewarm;[108] and at San Francisco, the drafters of the Charter much preferred other methods of pacifying international relations. To them, as to one of Kelsen's reviewers, it simply seemed "an illusion to believe that it ever will be possible to transform world history into nothing but a court procedure".[109] As a consequence, "progress on the way to the

---

a rich and participatory culture of political protest, popular education and civic ritual, which took root in British society between the wars": H. McCarthy, *The British People and the League of Nations.* Democracy, Citizenship and Internationalism (2011), at p. x.

104 H. Kelsen, *Peace Through Law* (1944). For a clear analysis see von Bernstorff (n. 54), 193 et seq.

105 As Jochen von Bernstorff (n. 54) notes, Kelsen was essentially "reviving the Hague Movement's strategy of juridifying international relations through obligatory arbitration" (193).

106 Cf. Jessup (n. 80). In the words of Kelsen: "One of the most important, if not the decisive, causes [for the League's failure] is a fatal fault of its construction, the fact that the authors of the Covenant placed at the center of this international organization not the Permanent Court of International Justice, but a kind of international administration, the Council of the League of Nations": see H. Kelsen, *Law and Peace in International Relations* (1942), 151-152.

107 Kelsen was emphatic on this point: "As long as it is not possible to remove from the interested States the prerogative to answer this question [whether international law has been violated] and transfer it once and for allto an impartial authority, namely, an international court, any further progress on the way to the pacification of the world is absolutely excluded" (*Peace Through Law,* n. 103, at 13-14).

108 For a survey see J. von Schmädel, Kelsen's *Peace through Law* and its Reception by his Contemporaries, Hitotsubashi Journal of Law and Politics 39 (2011), 71. For a much more positive assessment of Kelsen's approach (and impact) see O'Connell/VanderZee (n. 9), 56-58.

109 J.L. Kunz, Book Review, American Journal of International Law 38 (1944), 673, at 678.

pacification of the world"[110] (which according to Kelsen required compulsory adjudication) could be sought through a range of different methods.

## 4.2 Evolution of Catholic Thinking

The same insight guided the Catholic Church during the long third stage of development: it, too, began to see courts and tribunals much more pragmatically, and as part of a comprehensive approach to international peace and security. In the first place, this can be seen in the declining attention paid to international arbitration and adjudication, which – compared to the late 19th and early 20th century – became topics of lesser relevance. Popes no longer acted as arbitrators in inter-State disputes. And to none of their successors did binding dispute settlement have the same importance as to Leo XIII and Benedict XV: there is, between the 1920s and 1970s, no equivalent to Benedict's peace appeal of 1917, or to Leo's reflections on the special mission of the Pope in dispute settlement.

Instead, the writings of successive 20th century popes reflect the increasing relevance of world organizations, which over time become the focus of Catholic peace ethics.[111] Concerns about the post-WW1 settlement tainted the Papacy's relationship with the League; but from the 1940s onwards, the United Nations became the subject of continuous engagement. Pius XII's Christmas messages broadcast during World War 2 emphasized the need to establish an effective international authority that would not repeat the mistakes of the League.[112] Just as the Charter's, so Pius' focus is on the prevention of war;[113] his reaction to the 1956 Soviet intervention in Hungary reflects growing disappointment at the UN's failure to respond effectively.[114] In assessing the performance of the UN, Pius accepts that the effective international order has to be grounded on State consensus and rules of international law, but derives from natural law an ambitious reform agenda comprising democratic freedoms and individual rights.[115]

110 Cf. Kelsen, *Law and Peace* (n. 106), 152.

111 Two books by R.J. Araujo and J.A. Lucal provide detailed surveys: see *Papal Diplomacy and the Quest for Peace: The Vatican and International Organizations from the Early Years to the League of Nations* (2004); and *Papal Diplomacy and the Quest for Peace: The United Nations from Pius XII to Paul VI* (2010).

112 See notably the 1942 and 1944 Christmas Messages, both in *Major Speeches of Pius XII,* at 62 and 85.

113 See the 1942 Christmas Message (n. 112), which emphasizes the need for a ban, and the possibility of effective collective action, against aggression.

114 Justenhoven (n. 27) provides details (at 50).

115 For details see Justenhoven (n. 27), at 43-51.

Given his critical engagement with questions of war, peace and international order, it is interesting how little international courts feature in Pius XII's teaching.[116] The Nuremberg and Tokyo tribunals prompted him to demand the establishment of a system of international criminal justice, as natural justice required the punishment of those responsible for grave crimes.[117] However, on inter-State arbitration and adjudication, he remains largely silent.[118] This approach – which stands in marked contrast to the interventions of Leo XIII and Benedict XV – can be taken to reflect the lessened importance accorded to courts and tribunals during the 'pragmatic period'.

John XXIII's encyclical *Pacem in terris*[119] affirms and completes this development. Heavily drawing on Pius XII's teaching, *Pacem in terris* was "a threshold encyclical ... that united in a single document the teachings of the Church on war and peace".[120] As is well known (and explored in other contributions to this volume), it marks a breakthrough in the Church's acceptance of individual rights as the basis of a human-centred global order and a milestone in its engagement with the United Nations. The encyclical sets out an ambitious vision for a universal political authority, which – as foreshadowed by Pius XII – must be based on the consent of all nations, able to influence world affairs effectively ('equipped with world-wide power'[121]), without interfering unnecessarily in the domestic affairs of its constituents.

116 In their book on papal diplomacy at the UN, Araujo and Lucal (n. 111) refer to articles, in the *Osservatore Romano* of 1942, by Professor Guido Gonella, which offer "more specific ideas about international institutions" and emphasize the need for an obligatory system of arbitration (at 9-10). In the view of Araujo and Lucal, Gonella's work "certainly had the approval of the Pope" (at 9).

117 See Address to the Sixth International Congress of Penal Law (1953), in The Catholic Mind, February 1954, 107. While endorsing the principle of international criminal justice, Pius XII emphasized the need for impartiality, and on that basis criticized the composition of the tribunals rendering justice at Nuremberg and Tokyo.

118 Justenhoven (n. 27, at 51) refers to Pius XII's 1956 address to the diplomatic corps, in which the pope expressed his hope "that the pressure of world opinion will curb resistance and foolish stubbornness, make it necessary everywhere to settle even the sharpest disputes amicably and force the acceptance of arbitration and compromise, through which many irreparable evils can be avoided" (see https://w2.vatican.va/content/pius-xii/en/speeches/1956/documents/hf_p-xii_spe_19560304_corpo-diplomatico.html). But the point is not explored.

119 John XXIII, *Pacem in terris*, at http://w2.vatican.va/content/john-xxiii/en/encyclicals/documents/hf_j-xxiii_enc_11041963_pacem.html. For comment on the encyclical's engagement with international law see O. Kimminich, Der völkerrechtliche Gehalt der Enzyklika *Pacem in Terris,* in A. Klose, *Frieden und Gesellschaftsordnung. Festschrift für Rudolf Weiler* (1988), 67; St. Verosta, Das Völkerrecht und die Vereinten Nationen in der Enzyklika *Pacem in Terris,* in R. Weiler/J. Weinbacher, *Die Friedensenzyklika Johannes XXIII. Pacem in Terris* (1974), 72.

120 Araujo/Lucal (n. 111), 73.

121 *Pacem in terris* (n. 119), para. 138.

According to John XXIII, the United Nations is the only credible framework within which such universal political authority can be exercized; yet to meet the needs of the world, it needs to evolve:[122] "It is therefore Our earnest wish that the United Nations Organization may be able progressively to adapt its structure and methods of operation to the magnitude and nobility of its tasks."[123]

There is no shortage of suggestions in *Pacem in terris* for the 'progressive adaptation' of the UN's 'structure and methods of operation', and for progressive reorganization of international society. The Universal Declaration of Human Rights is praised as "a step in the right direction", namely "toward the establishment of a juridical and political ordering of the world community".[124] To limit the likelihood, and potential impact, of war, John XIII was adamant that States must reduce "[t]he stockpiles of armaments which have been built up in various countries… Nuclear weapons must be banned. A general agreement must be reached on a suitable disarmament program, with an effective system of mutual control."[125] In their relations, States must ensure the "elimination of every trace of racial discrimination", refrain from interfering with the "vitality and growth of … ethnic minorities", and respect the right of refugees.[126]

Yet while engaging with many of the tropes and themes of internationalist thought, *Pacem in terris* has very little, and nothing specific, to say about international courts and tribunals. The encyclical's prescriptions concern substantive conditions of justice (of which the absence of war is one) and procedures for making peace more attainable. But the peaceful settlement of disputes is referred to only in the most general terms: "There may be, and sometimes is, a clash of interests among States, each striving for its own development. When differences of this sort arise, they must be settled in a truly human way, not by armed force nor by deceit or trickery. There must be a mutual assessment of the arguments and feelings on both sides, a mature and objective investigation of the situation, and an equitable reconciliation of opposing views."[127]

122 In the view of Araujo and Lucal (n. 111), the encyclical's references to he UN, "while not an unqualified endorsement, were a sincere expression of general support and hope for the institution" (at 75).

123 Pacem in terris, para. 145.

124 *Pacem in terris* (n. 119), para. 144.

125 *Pacem in terris* (n. 119), para. 112

126 *Pacem in terris* (n. 119), paras. 86 and 105 respectively.

127 *Pacem in terris* (n. 119), para. 93.

Compared to the clear language on nuclear disarmament and human rights, and to the firm views of John XXIII's predecessors on peaceful dispute settlement, this passage is of remarkable generality. It does not, of course, offer arguments against adjudication or arbitration. Presumably, recourse to international courts or tribunals would permit for the desired 'mature and objective investigation' of the dispute and ideally result in an 'equitable reconciliation of opposing views'. But the same could be said for 'truly human' negotiations in good faith, for UN or multilateral crisis diplomacy, and for other forms of settling disputes peacefully. There is, in short, nothing in *Pacem in terris* to recognize a special role of international arbitration or adjudication – neither in matters of war and peace, nor in relation to other categories of disputes. Four decades after the establishment of a world court, the Catholic Church's most ambitious world order scheme had fully accepted the turn to pragmatism: the universal political authority had little place for courts and tribunals.

## 5. *Re-Vitalization and Re-Orientation: the New Popularity of International Courts and Tribunals*

Fifty years after *Pacem in terris*, international courts are pursuing new, and different, horizons. As noted in the introduction, dozens of new courts and tribunals have been established and risen to relevance; they occupy "new terrains"[128] well beyond the expectations that would have seemed "realistic"[129] to observers writing in the 1960s or 1970s. WTO dispute settlement organs assess the legality of the EU's anti-GMO policies; the European Court of Human Rights scrutinizes British conduct during the occupation of Iraq; an ICSID tribunal hears argument on Germany's nuclear phase-out; while the Philippines pursues arbitral proceedings against China over maritime rights in the South China Sea. If numbers, and public interest, are relevant indicators, this indeed seems to be an 'age of adjudication'.[130] Yet from even the most eclectic of listings, it is clear that adjudication has not just been re-vitalized, but also adapted to meet new goals. The subsequent sections trace the parallel trends of re-vitalization and re-orientation, but they also highlight how, in crucial respects, things have not really changed that much.

128 Cf. the title of Karen Alter's influential study (n. 7).
129 Cf. Falk (n. 69).
130 Cf. Greenwood (n. 6)

### 5.1 General Developments

The most obvious development in dispute resolution over the past half-century is the "enormous growth of fora"[131] involved in binding dispute resolution. The growth had begun towards the end of the 'pragmatic phase', and it has picked up speed since 1989: at that point, there were six standing judicial bodies; to which nearly twenty courts and arbitral frameworks have been added since. As developments have been analysed elsewhere in detail,[132] it may be convenient to focus on the main trends, which, for reasons of convenience, can be summarized under three headings:

Specialization: The first trend has been one of functional specialization. Whereas debates during the first half of the 20th century focused on courts with potentially unlimited, general jurisdiction, the new courts tend to be specialized. Whereas the PCIJ and ICJ, just as arbitral tribunals established under the Hague system, could potentially address disputes covering international law in its entirety, more recent courts and tribunals have been established as guardians of particular treaty regimes.[133] This has made the landscape of international dispute settlement more diverse; systems of international adjudication and arbitration today are tailor-made to meet the demands of specialized sub-systems. It has also resulted in a very uneven degree of 'judicialization'. The "growth of fora"[134] is 'sector-specific' and has mainly concerned three distinct fields: human rights law, economic international and international criminal law. As in all moves towards specialization, courts and tribunals established in these fields come with the promise of increased expertise, which needs to be balanced against the risks of silo thinking.

Regionalization: Similarly, there has been a move from global towards regional dispute settlement bodies.[135] With the exception of the Central American Court,[136] the early courts were set up as universal institutions (even though the practical impact of this may have been limited in a global legal order dominated by European States). Since 1945, the move towards a

131 C.P.R. Romano, Progress in International Adjudication: Revisiting Hudson's Assessment of the Future of International Courts, in R. Miller/R.M. Bratspiess, *Progress in International Law* (2008), 431, at 435.

132 The following notably draws on Alter (n. 7); Alter, in *Oxford Handbook* (n. 5); Romano (n. 130); Kingsbury (n. 7); and Y. Shany, No Longer A Weak Department of Power? Reflections on the Emergence of a New International Judiciary, European Journal of International Law 20 (2009), 73.

133 Shany (n. 131), 80.

134 Romano (n. 130), 435.

135 Alter, in Romano/Alter/Shany (n. 5), 65.

136 *Supra*, III.1.

truly universal legal order has been matched (and to some extent balanced) by a return to regional law-making, which has also led to the establishment of regional courts. As with specialization, this has permitted groups of States to advance where universal solutions lacked general support; at the same time, it has accentuated differences between more and less judicialized areas of international law: in terms of numbers, Europe clearly leads the move towards courts and tribunals, with Africa and the Americas following, and Asia lagging behind.[137]

The rise of non-State actors: Finally, within the more diversified landscape of international dispute settlement, non-State actors have risen to prominence.[138] Until 1945, permanent institutions for international adjudication and arbitration were typically reserved to States.[139] Since then, and increasingly, binding dispute resolution has opened up and become more inclusive. Individuals are the natural claimants before human rights courts. Investment arbitration is driven by corporations. And since Nuremburg, the fact that "[c]rimes against international law are committed by men, not by abstract entities"[140] has been an article of faith for proponents of international criminal justice, which is justice imposed on individuals.

These developments have clearly strengthened the role of international courts and tribunals in international relations, to the point where commentators speak of a "paradigm change"[141] or (more ambivalently) of a "new tribunalism".[142] This shift ostensibly concerns the relevance of international adjudication and arbitration, which according to most intuitive parameters – numbers of decision; their impact on state governance; newspaper coverage; academic interest – has greatly increased. Beyond that, it also affects the roles played by them. International courts and tribunals still tend to become active once a dispute has been submitted to them. However, their impact on international relations seems to have shifted. In the words of Yuval Shany, "despite their frequent engagement in dispute set-

137 C.P.R. Romano speaks of "uneven geographical distribution": The Shadow Zones of International Judicialization, in *Oxford Handbook* (n. 5), 90, at 91.

138 Romano (n. 130), 437-438.

139 While the inter-State paradigm dominated, there were exceptions: the Central American Court of Justice was open to individuals, as would have been the International Prize Court. And claims commissions and tribunals were mixed from the beginning.

140 International Military Tribunal, Judgment and Sentences, in American Journal of International Law 41 (1947), at 223.

141 Alter (n. 7), 3.

142 Th. Skouteris, The New Tribunalism: Strategies of De-Legitimation in the Era of International Adjudication, Finnish Yearbook of International Law 17 (2006), 307.

tlement activities, the new courts are no longer primarily dispute-settling bodies … They appear to have assumed two other primary functions instead: norm-advancement and regime maintenance", which may involve "promoting a set of values such as human rights, or an end to impunity for international criminals", but also "strengthening the rule of law in some areas of international relations which have undergone, or are undergoing, a process of legalization".[143] In the process, courts to some degree have lost their innocence and become highly controversial – witness current European debates about investment arbitration and the African Union's concerns about the ICC as a political tool of Western States. At the same time, they have assumed fairly mundane functions such as controlling the interpretation and application of international rules within areas of regional economic integration.

Given all these fundamental changes, it is worth noting that, in the particular area under review in the present contribution, developments have been less dramatic. While the international community today 'deploys' courts and tribunals to perform a wide array of governance functions, the prevention of military conflict is usually not among them.[144] Put differently, the re-vitalization of international courts and tribunals is not a return to the 'idealistic approach' of old that had viewed arbitration and adjudication as alternatives to war. Even in the "era of adjudication", courts and tribunals typically deal with discrete aspects of military conflicts: more often than before, no doubt, but not systematically or at the forefront of international endeavours at conflict resolution.

The pursuit of international criminal justice is the most visible of these discrete aspects. Since the 1990s, the international community has built on the Nuremberg and Tokyo precedents and established a network of international and hybrid criminal tribunals competent to hold individuals accountable for atrocities usually committed during military conflict.[145] Equally re-

143 Shany (n. 131), at 81 and 83.

144 As Kingsbury notes, "[t]he issues being adjudicated … are largely those of a global legal order dominated by liberal interests": see Kingsbury (n. 7), 211. To illustrate, trade law issues can today be litigated, foreign intervention in civil wars only exceptionally; investors frequently have access to international tribunals, refugees tend not to.

145 Alter lists three properly international criminal tribunals (ICTY, ICTR, ICC) and a range of hybrid equivalents (in Oxford Handbook, n. 5, at 66-67). Romano (n. 130), 438-440, provides an instructive summary. It is worth noting that the jurisdiction of international criminal courts does not necessarily depend on whether crimes have been committed during armed conflict; but in practice, some nexus will typically exist.

vived has been the tradition of claims procedures set up in the aftermath of conflicts and crises.[146]

In addition to these established contributions, international courts and tribunals today address aspects of military conflicts from two novel angles. The first has to do with the rise of human rights law. Over the past decades, regional courts have begun to apply human rights to conflict situations, and to hold States to account over their conduct.[147] In so doing, they have overcome archaic divisions between the legal regimes for peace and wartime. Yet the practical challenge of identifying the precise reach of individual rights guarantees in crisis situations remains enormous.[148]

The second new trend is perhaps more remarkable. Since the 1980s, States have gradually become aware of the potential of submitting aspects of military conflicts to international courts and tribunals. States as diverse as Nicaragua, Bosnia, the Federal Republic of Yugoslavia, the Democratic Republic of the Congo and Georgia have sought judicial decisions against States involved, directly or indirectly, in military conflicts with them.[149] Such forms of 'conflict litigation' face enormous obstacles. Due to jurisdictional limits, international courts are hardly ever capable of addressing a conflict in its entirety;[150] typically they can only deal with a side-aspect of it (or eventually conclude that they lack jurisdiction).[151] What is more, proceedings can last for years and test the faith of States in courts.[152] Because of

146 See Matheson (n. 53), 87-90 (with brief comment on the two most prominent examples, the UN Compensation Commission established after the 1991 Gulf War and the Eritrea-Ethiopia Claims Commission).

147 See G. Oberleitner, *Human Rights in Armed Conflict* (2015) for a comprehensive account.

148 See N. Lubell, Challenges in Applying Human Rights Law to Armed Conflict, International Review oft he Red Cross 87/860 (2005), 737.

149 The clearest survey – covering both contentious cases and advisory opinions requested on aspects of military conflicts (notably the Israeli wall/security fence) – can be found in Matheson (n. 53), 33-62; also instructive is J. Crook, Adjudicating Armed Conflicts, in N. Klein, *Litigating International Disputes. Weighing the Options* (2014), 330.

150 To illustrate, in addressing the claims by Bosnia and Croatia against the Federal Republic of Yugoslavia, the ICJ could only pronounce on questions of genocide. See Matheson (n. 53), at 42-44.

151 This e.g. happened in the cases brought by Georgia against Russia (relating to the July war of 2008), by the Federal Republic of Yugoslavia against ten NATO member States (during the Kosovo campaign of 1999), and the Democratic Republic of the Congo against Rwanda (concerning the respondent's involvement in the second Congo war): see Matheson (n. 53), 44-45, 50-53 and 58-59.

152 For example, when warned about Nicaragua's institution of proceedings, the United States first amended and then revoked its optional clause declaration; while this did not prevent the ICJ from pronouncing on Nicaragua's claims, the United

these obstacles, international litigation is typically pursued alongside other methods of conflict resolution. Unlike in the legalist vision of a century ago, it is not an alternative to war, but one among many strategies employed by the claimant to minimize the negative consequences of conflicts.[153]

Still, the combined effect of these trends is that international courts and tribunals today engage with aspects of military conflicts almost on a regular basis.[154] Yet they (continue to) do so from very particular angles: they have become fora for (often retrospective) debates about matters of war and peace, tools for mobilising public opinion and recorders of history; they impose sanctions, enforce individual claims and occasionally rule on the legality of forcible State conduct. The prevention of wars is still largely outside their remit: the judicial role in crisis management remains "an auxiliary or supporting role".[155]

Judging from public debates, this is unlikely to change any time soon. Just as international courts have become specialized, so has the debate about them. Courts are appreciated and evaluated as integral parts of sectoral regimes: controversies surround the particularities of world trade panels, human rights courts or investment tribunals. There is no attempt to return to the times of general courts: the debate has moved "from general to specif-

---

States has since remained a more cautious ICJ participant; it also withdrew from the *Nicaragua* proceedings and refused to honour the damages ICJ's award. When the Federal Republic of Yugoslavia sued ten NATO member States during the 1999 Kosovo campaign, and amongst other claims relied on the Genocide Convention, this was decried as an abuse of process. By the same token, Israel (and a number of other States) were highly critical of the decision to request an ICJ advisory opinion on legal issues relating to the Israeli wall/security fence. For much more on these and similar challenges see Crook (n. 149); and C.D. Gray, The Use and Abuse of the International Court of Justice: Cases concerning the Use of Force after Nicaragua, European Journal of International Law 14 (2003), 867.

153 Gray (n. 152) succinctly summarizes the divergent perceptions on conflict litigation: "The large increase in the number of cases on the use of force taken to the ICJ in recent years can be interpreted in a variety of ways. Taken most favourably, it shows the willingness of states to use the Court to reaffirm their conviction in the legality of their position in a conflict against a stronger opponent. Seen less favourably, such cases are an unhelpful move in a propaganda war where settlement is already being pursued through other means; weak cases may be brought as a means of distracting, delaying or inconveniencing an opponent" (at 904).

154 As Matheson notes (writing in 2013), "[t]he involvement of international civil tribunals in situations of armed conflict over the past two decades stands in sharp contrast with what came before" (n. 53, at 61).

155 Sh. Rosenne, A Role for the International Court of justice in Crisis Management?, in Kreijen et al. (eds.), *State, Sovereignty, and International Governance* (2002), 195, at 217.

ic compulsory jurisdiction".[156] As regards military conflicts, international criminal justice has become the favoured project of contemporary internationalists; this seems today's equivalent to the late 19th century's fascination with inter-State arbitration, or the post-WW2 focus on disarmament. Calls to vest the world court with general compulsory jurisdiction over inter-State disputes can still be heard with some frequency,[157] but they lack the determination (or stubbornness?) of Kelsen's *Peace Through Law* and the passion of the legalists' appeal. Writing in 1996, the former ICJ President Sir Robert Jennings – by no means a cynic – offered the following cautious assessment: "International lawyers have been calling, but calling in vain, for general compulsory jurisdiction for an international court since at least 1899 at the First Hague Peace Conference. It now seems as far off as ever. Surely the time has come to look harder for the reasons why governments do not feel able to respond to the call".[158]

### *5.2 Evolution of Catholic Thinking*

The re-vitalization and re-adaptation of international adjudication over the past decades has not so far prompted a comprehensive response by the Catholic Church. And this is entirely understandable: as the debate about courts and tribunals has become granular and technical, it has moved away from the Church's core mission. (Not every ICSID award implicates world peace.) Where courts and tribunals operate as integral parts of broader sectoral regimes (as, for example, in the field of world trade law), the Church's engagement has typically been with the regime as such, not specifically its

156 O'Connell/VanderZee (n. 9), 58.

157 For recent proposals see e.g. H. Steiger, Plaidoyer pour une juridiction internationale obligatoire, in J. Makarczyk, *Theory of International Law at the Threshold of the 21st Century* (1996), 817; A.A. Cançado Trindade, The Relevance of International Adjudication: Reflections on the Need and Quest for International Compulsory Jurisdiction, in R.St.John Macdonald/D.M. Johnston, *Towards World Constitutionalism* (2005), 515. Within the United Nations, proposals tend to focus on the optional clause, which States are regularly encouraged to accept: see e.g. B. Boutros-Ghali, *An Agenda for Peace*, UN Doc. A/47/277 (1992), at para. 38; K. Annan, Statement at the Sixtieth Anniversary Celebration of the International Court of Justice, UN Doc No. SG/SM/10414 (2006). But beyond the encouragement, no real pressure is exerted; and new declarations inevitably come with significant reservations.

158 R.Y. Jennings, The Role of the International Court of Justice, British Yearbook of International Law 68 (1997), 1, at 56.

adjudicative branch.[159] As regards the potential contribution of adjudication to world peace, the picture is mixed. In their reflections on the shape of the universal political authority, John XXIII's successors have continued to engage with the existing UN Charter regime for maintaining peace and security, with its limited role for courts. At the same time, the Church has closely monitored, and facilitated, the consolidation of the contemporary system of international criminal justice; while an apostolic visit to The Hague in 1985 provided John Paul II with an opportunity to comment more systematically on the role of inter-State arbitration and adjudication in world affairs.

As regards the central features of the international order, the approach outlined in *Pacem in terris* continues to shape the Papacy's position. With the exception of John Paul I, all popes, from Paul VI to Francis, have emphasized the need to work with and through the United Nations as the "focal point"[160] of a world order of peace,[161] while at the same time calling for its reform into a true universal political authority.[162] During the late 1970s, John Paul II became involved once more in the practice of peaceful dispute settlement. The skillful handling of the Chilean-Argentinean Beagle Channel dispute drew praise, though, ironically, it was in the form of a non-binding mediation, which became necessary to 'rescue' a gridlocked arbitration process.[163]

John Paul II's interventions stand out for their detailed engagement with the legal regime governing recourse to force; they reflect the Pope's attempt to balance respect for the Charter's general ban on force with the need to protect basic principles of justice effectively. Yet, even in their detailed

159 See for example Benedect XVI's call for a "reform of economic institutions and international finance, so that the concept of the family of nations can acquire real teeth": *Caritas in veritate,* para. 67 (at http://w2.vatican.va/content/benedict-xvi/en/encyclicals/documents/hf_ben-xvi_enc_20090629_caritas-in-veritate.html).

160 See John Paul II, *Centesimus annus,* para. 21 (at http://w2.vatican.va/content/john-paul-ii/en/encyclicals/documents/hf_jp-ii_enc_01051991_centesimus-annus.html).

161 On peace as the UN's primary purpose see notably Paul VI's 1965 address to the General Assembly: "never again war, never again war! It is peace, peace, that has to guide the destiny of the nations of all mankind!" (at http://w2.vatican.va/content/paul-vi/en/speeches/1965/documents/hf_p-vi_spe_19651004_united-nations.html).

162 In his message for the celebration of the world day of peace, 2003, John Paul II reflected on the continuing relevance of *Pacem in terris* and noted that "Pope John XXIII's vision of an effective international public authority at the service of human rights, freedom and peace has not yet been entirely achieved" (para. 5) (at https://w2.vatican.va/content/john-paul-ii/en/messages/peace/documents/hf_jp-ii_mes_20021217_xxxvi-world-day-for-peace.html). See also Benedict XVI, *Caritas in veritate* (n. 158), para. 67.

163 See L.A. de la Fayette, Beagle Channel Dispute, in Max Planck Encyclopedia of Public International Law (www.mpepil.com).

interventions, the Papacy is realist enough to search for solutions for the pressing problems of war and peace within the existing systems of collective security; just as in John XXIII's *Pacem in terris,* no specific role of international courts in the process is explicitly mentioned.[164]

When looking beyond the grand designs for world peace, the picture becomes slightly more nuanced. While courts are not expected to stop wars, the Papacy has facilitated and supported attempts to establish them as instruments of international criminal justice. Building on Pius XII's early advocacy, the Church was involved in the drafting of the Rome Statute during the late 1990s, which it regarded as a contribution to a more effective protection of individual rights. In subsequent statements, John Paul II endorsed the establishment of the ICC as an "important step forward" and stated that "[t]his new institution, if built upon a sound legal foundation, could gradually contribute to ensuring on a world scale the effective protection of human rights".[165] (Attempts to prosecute John Paul's successor in connection with the Catholic Church's sexual abuse scandal seem not to have affected this position.[166]) During the Kampala review conference, which extended the ICC's jurisdiction to cover acts of aggression, the Holy See's delegation moved beyond this limited human rights perspective, and emphasized that the proposed amendment "seeks to institutionalize, in international juridical instruments, a principle which rejects war as a means for resolving disputes and seeks to replace the law of force with the force of law".[167]

Twenty-five years before Kampala, John Paul II had engaged with these bigger themes in a speech to the International Court of Justice. His address, which reflects on a century of papal involvement, contains the fullest exposition of the Church's view on the role of binding dispute resolution and

---

164 See e.g. John Paul's reflection on *Pacem in terris* (n. 161), which refers to peaceful dispute settlement only in the most general terms: "Honesty in the supply of information, equity in legal systems, openness in democratic procedures give citizens a sense of security, a readiness to settle controversies by peaceful means, and a desire for genuine and constructive dialogue, all of which constitute the true premises of a lasting peace" (at para. 8).

For a detailed assessment of John Paul II's approach see Justenhoven (n. 27), 62-90.

165 See John Paul II's messages for the celebration of the world day of peace, 2000 and 1999, at http://w2.vatican.va/content/john-paul-ii/en/messages/peace/documents/hf_jp-ii_mes_14121998_xxxii-world-day-for-peace.html and https://w2.vatican.va/content/john-paul-ii/en/messages/peace/documents/hf_jp-ii_mes_08121999_xxxiii-world-day-for-peace.html.

166 See G. Robertson, *The Case of the Pope: Vatican Accountability for Human Rights Abuse* (2010).

167 Statement during the General Debate, at http://press.vatican.va/content/salastampa/it/bollettino/pubblico/2010/06/05/0371/00849.html.

therefore may provide an appropriate conclusion to the present inquiry.[168] Unlike in Pacem in terris, and in his own addresses to the United Nations, John Paul II here recognizes a specific place for courts and tribunals within the Church's wider "collaboration with the United Nations Organization".[169] Arbitration and adjudication to him are part of the "international administration of justice", which is said to have a dual role of "peacefully resolving conflicts and as part of the evolution of a world legal system".[170] Compared to other forms of dispute settlement, arbitration and adjudication are special because they "bring an element of impartiality and objectivity to bear on dealings between States", which otherwise often remain "the province of a diplomacy determined more by self-interest than by the requirements of the common good of the international community – a common good based on what is right and just."[171] As this self-interest has had "an inhibiting influence on the work of both the International Court of Justice and the Permanent Court of Arbitration", the existing system "is no more – but it is also no less – than an initial step towards what we hope will one day be a totally effective judicial authority in a peaceful world".[172]

While few would take issue with the diagnosis, John Paul II's proposals for a reform of the status quo are indicative. Predictably, he encourages States to make greater use of arbitration and adjudication. But this call appears almost muted: it is made with the relatively modest aim of ensuring that "the judicial element can play a wider role in international relations" and forms part of a wider agenda comprising the progressive development of "a world legal system" alongside improved dispute settlement procedures.[173] As to the role of the Church, John Paul II promises "confirmation and support",[174] but it is support of a particular kind. Whereas Leo XIII had wanted to arbitrate himself, and Benedict XV intended to "spell out the ethical foundations of obligatory arbitration and urge States to establish it",[175] John Paul sees a much more indirect role for Church: "The Catholic Church is involved in this field, as can be seen, for example, by her active participation in international organizations and by the many declarations of the

168 John Paul II, Address to the International Court of Justice (1985), at https://w2.vatican.va/content/john-paul-ii/en/speeches/1985/may/documents/hf_jp-ii_spe_19850513_corte-internazionale.html.
169 John Paul II, ICJ Address (n. 167), para. 1.
170 John Paul II, ICJ Address (n. 167), para. 1.
171 John Paul II, ICJ Address (n. 167), para. 3.
172 John Paul II, ICJ Address (n. 167), paras. 3 and 4.
173 John Paul II, ICJ Address (n. 167), para. 4.
174 John Paul II, ICJ Address (n. 167), para. 5.
175 As put by Justenhoven (supra, n. 67).

Holy See in favour of them. In doing this, the Church points out the criteria which the development of an international system of law must satisfy. In legal terms, these can be expressed as the recognition of human rights: the right to life of every individual, the right to a decent existence worthy of human beings and the right to protection by the law; recognition of the right of peoples to self-determination and independence and their right to a fair share of the world's economic wealth."[176]

All this reflects both an ambitious normative agenda and a rather sober view of the prospects of international arbitration and adjudication, and on the Church's role in it: one that values the contribution of courts and tribunals to the elaboration of law, but that seeks "progress on the way to the pacification of the world"[177] through collaboration in international organizations. And one that sees the Church no longer act as an *arbitrator* (Leo XIII) or *advocate* of dispute settlement (Benedict XV), but primarily as an *auditor* of the international legal system, ensuring that it meets certain substantive standards.

## *6. Concluding Thoughts*

Fifty years after Pacem in terris, international adjudication occupies an established place in world affairs. Important areas of international relations have been effectively judicialized, in ways and degrees that neither John XXIII nor the legalist movement of the pre-WW 1 era could have predicted. Yet in rising to prominence and relevance, international adjudication has largely been de-coupled from war prevention, its original purpose. Its contributions to peace are manifold, but indirect. 200 years after Bentham's Plan for a Universal and Perpetual Peace, few would accept that, if only a court had been established, "the necessity of war no longer follows from differences of opinion".[178] International courts do not – and are no longer expected to – provide "heroic and life-saving emergency treatment"; instead they have become "providers of preventive health care and quality-of-life treatment".[179] As part of their more diverse mandates, international courts and tribunals do engage with aspects of military conflicts, but they do not today exist to prevent wars.

176 John Paul II, ICJ Address (n. 167), para. 5.
177 Cf. Kelsen (n. XX), 152.
178 See Bentham (n. 3).
179 Shany (n. 131), 80.

This development may be the result of a lack of ambition as regards the role of courts, or even be decried as a betrayal of ancient ideals.[180] But perhaps the better view is to understand the evolving roles of international courts and tribunals as part of a more profound change in the history of 20th century international relations, namely the move towards more comprehensive international organization. As has been shown, the advent of the League, and certainly that of the UN, has fundamentally affected the role of courts in 'peace through law' designs: alongside the comprehensive world organizations mandated to preserve peace and security, they no longer seemed natural dispute settlers. Adapting Stephen Neff's statement quoted at the beginning of this contribution,[181] while preferable to the "political cut and thrust" of old, dispute settlement in the "hushed calm of courtrooms" does not necessarily appear superior to collective decision-making by organs of the organized international community. From 1919 onwards, arbitration and adjudication have no longer been the most obvious, let alone only, alternatives to war: and so, they have come to occupy niches in a broader scheme that primarily sought to attain *world peace through world organization* – a "noble forward stride" of a different kind. This – rather than a betrayal of ideas – may explain the gradual move away from legalist visions over the course of the 20th century.

As the preceding discussion indicates, the shift towards more comprehensive approaches to world peace is reflected in Catholic teaching, perhaps nowhere more clearly than in John XIII's encyclical *Pacem in terris*. More clearly than earlier Catholic documents, the encyclical recognizes the central role of the United Nations as a forum, framework and instrument for the pursuit of world peace. More clearly than other documents, it identifies necessary components of a just peace, especially basic human rights. More clearly and openly, it adopts a pragmatic view of courts as useful – but no longer primary – agencies of dispute settlement. This approach is not likely to enthuse those placing their hopes in courts as guardians of world order. But in all this, *Pacem in terris* has shaped subsequent Catholic thinking and is of lasting relevance.

---

180 In this direction: Cançado Trindade (n. 56), para. 83, citing his concurring opinion in the case of Hilaire v. Trinidad and Tobago before the Inter-American Court of Human Rights: "If we are really prepared to extract the lessons of the evolution of international law in a turbulent world throughout the twentieth century, (. . .) we cannot abide by an international practice which has been subservient to State voluntarism [and] which has betrayed the spirit and purpose of the optional clause of compulsory jurisdiction".

181 See n. 1.

# The International Criminal Court: A Global Public Authority?

*Samuel T. Tessema*

## *Introduction*

Humanity has been pursuing the dream of a globe united under one authority for centuries. Some sought to realize it through conquest and war, others through diplomacy. Now we have reached a stage where global action is no longer a utopian idea but a matter of necessity and survival. The threats posed by conflicts, nuclear weapons, climate change, environmental degradation, terrorism and others, and the growing globalization of the world in all aspects of life have made it inevitable that the world community will continue to increase its global interaction exponentially. The creation of the International Criminal Court (hereinafter the ICC or the Court) is part of this global dynamic. Its aim is to tackle grave international crimes.

This chapter investigates whether the ICC is a 'global public authority'. With this query in mind, the chapter is divided into five parts. The first part explores the evolution and nature of the quest for global authority, which basically takes two forms: world government/state and global governance. The part briefly describes these two concepts. The second part shows that the ICC is one of the existing global governance institutions, which is followed by a discussion on legitimacy, as a key concept that helps to make the link between global governance and global authority. It is argued that for a global governance institution to be regarded as a public authority, it must pass the test of legitimacy, that is, normative legitimacy, which includes legal and moral legitimacy, and sociological legitimacy.

The fourth section assesses the legitimacy of the ICC using the above categories as yardsticks for assessing the acquisition and exercise of authority. The ICC only partially meets the standards set out in the Chapter, given its flaws respecting the legal, moral and sociological legitimacy of the Court. Based on these findings, the conclusion here is that the ICC is not yet a global public authority. The Court has what it takes to be one in the future, and its establishment is a development that is worth celebrating. The ICC, therefore, deserves the support necessary to become an authentic global authority. Supporting the ICC in its further development will mean defective provisions in the ICC Statute and operational procedures have to be rectified.

## 1. The Quest for Global Authority

"Nature employs the 'unsociableness of men' to motivate moral progress; thus war is a means by which nature moves states to take the step which reason could have suggested to them even without so many sad experiences—that of abandoning a lawless state of savagery and entering a federation of peoples in which every state, even the smallest, could expect to derive its security and rights not from its own power or its own legal judgment, but solely from this great federation, from a united power and the law-governed decisions of a united will".[1] Immanuel Kant

The history of humankind is a chronicle of constant strife and warfare. War remains a constant and common factor through all stages of human civilization, from the Stone Age to today's era of technology. Ironically, as humans evolve intellectually, socially, politically and technologically wars have only become more sophisticated and destructive.

The global response to such a history of war and devastation has been a sustained quest for peace. Perhaps the quest for global peace is as old as the history of conflicts. Almost every major war fought in human history revived, and continues to revive, discussions and debates on how to create a better world of harmony, unity and peace.

In this regard, the main focus has been on finding ways and means of limiting and gradually eliminating the causes and causalities of war. The establishment of a global authority that brings the world community together is believed to be a lasting solution to this seemingly interminable problem.[2] The underlying assumption is that an authoritative international entity that controls and regulates state and individual behavior will deter or at least substantially reduce conflicts and/or commission of gross violations of human rights. In recent years this vision has been invigorated by the advent of other global challenges that require collective action from the international community such as climate change, environmental degradation, terrorism, piracy, global poverty, and inequality.[3]

The ever-increasing economic globalization of the world, advancements in technology, trade, and international law have further revitalized the quest for global authority. In today's world, states, more than ever, are interde-

1 Lu, Catherine, World Government, In: Zalta, Edward (Ed.), The Stanford Encyclopedia of Philosophy, 2015, http://plato.stanford.edu/entries/world-government/ [21.10.2015].

2 Craige, Campbell, The Resurgent Idea of World Government, In: Ethics & International Affairs, 2008, Vol. 22, Issue 2, p.135.

3 Craige, The Resurgent Idea of World Government, p.135-136.

pendent and their survival and that of humanity hangs on the collective action they take and are willing to take because the state in its current form has proved time and again to be ill-equipped and ill-positioned to deal with challenges of global nature.[4]

Cognizant of these deficiencies in the state and changes in international relations, there seems to be some sort of global consensus on the need to have a global authority. However, despite the general consensus there are divergent views on the form that global authority should take. While some advocate for what they call world state or government with supreme legislative, executive, judicial and enforcement powers, others propose the creation of authoritative international and global institutions that significantly limit the powers and prerogatives traditionally attributed to the sovereign state.[5] Some also treat the two not as distinct approaches but rather as two different phases in the evolution of a global authority. In this sense, global governance institutions are believed to be transitional entities that are pivotal in paving the way for the gradual establishment of a global state or government.

### *1.1 World Government*

> "World government – the idea of all humankind united under one common political authority – arguably, has not existed so far in human history, yet proposals for a unified global political authority have existed since ancient times—in the ambition of kings, popes and emperors, and the dreams of poets and philosophers"[6]

The idea of world government was present in ancient Chinese and Indian as well as Greco-Roman thoughts. Ancient Greeks considered living in tribes and empires as a sign of barbarism.[7] Prominent among the Greeks

4 Craige, The Resurgent Idea of World Government, p. 135.

5 While medieval thinkers advocated world government under a single monarch or emperor who would possess supreme authority over all other lesser rulers, modern proponents generally do not advocate a wholesale dismantling of the sovereign states system but incremental innovations in global institutional design to move humanity toward world federalism or cosmopolitan democracy. Lu, Catherine, World Government. There are of course some strong voices that question and even oppose the relevance and viability of global authority but their importance is watered down by the ever growing phenomenon of globalization and contemporary global challenges that come with it.

6 Lu, World Government.

7 Heater, Derek, World Citizenship and Government: Cosmopolitan ideas and the History of Western Political Thought, Macmillan Press Limited, London, 1996, pp.1 & 21-26.

was Alexander the Great who envisioned a world state that includes all inhabitants of the earth where he will be a heaven-sent governor. Zeno also envisaged a world state where humanity would form one great community in which order, peace and, unity would prevail.[8]

The idea of world state is also reflected in the works of the 13th Century Italian poet and philosopher, Dante, who articulated the Christian ideal of human unity and its expression through a world governed by a universal monarch. According to Dante, having a universal monarch who rules the world is the only way to avoid wars as it is not possible to maintain peace in a divided world. Dante believed that the Roman Empire was part of God's plan for humanity.[9]

Seventeenth and eighteenth century scholars also contended that the gradual formation of an international state is inevitable.[10] In the 20th Century, the gruesome experiences of WWII and especially the devastation caused by atomic bombs in Japan, prompted scholars to call for a world government to be established as a keeper of international peace.[11] Present day scholars such as Alexander Wendt and Daniel Deudney also advocate for a world government to effectively tackle global challenges, old and new alike. Wendt argues that a formal world state, that is, a truly new sovereign political entity, will naturally evolve as peoples and nations come to realize that they cannot obtain true independence without it.[12] Deudney opines that the threat of nuclear war that may result in the destruction of life on earth

---

8 Dooley, Joseph, The World State: A Necessary Condition for World Peace, University of Ottawa, Ottawa, 1965, pp. 4-5. As Dooley rightly notes that the term 'world state' is subject to the special limitations of the world as it was known at any given period of history.

9 Heater, World Citizenship and Government, pp. 34-47.

10 Some scholars like Kant, however, cautioned that conditions were not yet ripe for that gradual transformation to occur.

11 Heater, World Citizenship and Government, pp.139-147.

12 Theorists such as Wendt who believe that a more formal world state is necessary do not necessarily disagree with the logic of global governance: it is difficult to dispute the claim that the gradual creation of supranational institutions is likely to be more feasible and peaceful than the imposition of a true world state. The problem for the governance argument, however, as Wendt puts it is "unauthorized violence by rogue Great Powers." As long as sovereign states continue to exist under a system of governance, there is nothing to prevent them from using violence to disrupt the international peace for their own purposes. Sooner or later a sovereign state will wage war, and the inability of a regime of global governance to stop it will deprive it of authority and legitimacy. International politics would then revert to the old state system. Wendt, Alexander, Why a World State is Inevitable, European Journal of International Relations, Vol. 9, Issue 4, 2003, pp. 491-542. See also Lu, World Government.

is good enough reason for states to come together and create a world government.[13] Dooley is also one of the contemporary scholars who strongly argues for a world state as a necessary condition for world peace.[14]

In Africa the concept of Ubuntu is regarded as an African philosophy for peace, harmony and unity. 'Ubuntu' is a traditional African philosophy that gives an understanding of us as human beings in relation to the rest of the world. According to Ubuntu, there exists a common link between us all as human beings. Ubuntu is a way of life that promotes harmony and humanity in the interest of building and maintaining community.[15] Though the application of the concept is commonly limited to local and at most continental level, it could be extended to all of humanity as a means of creating global unity and harmony.[16]

Ubuntu, just like most other African cultures, is a lived culture and reality as opposed to a rhetoric or idea communicated in writing. Some practical lessons and inspiration could, therefore, be drawn from it in the quest for global authority.[17]

Although proponents of a world government agree on the idea of having a common political authority at the international level that is similar to the existing structure and functions of a state, their motivation for reaching on such a conclusion are very different. Some see world government as the ultimate solution to old and new human problems such as war and the development of weapons of mass destruction, global poverty and inequality, and environmental degradation. And others advocate for world government as a proper reflection of the unity of the cosmos, under reason or God.[18]

The idea of world government is criticized by some as infeasible, unnecessary and undesirable. It is infeasible because it is deemed too utopian and too difficult to realize given the egoistic nature of human beings. Also, states are too obsessed with sovereignty and authority for a global authority to exist. The idea of World Government is deemed unnecessary because it

---

13 Deudney, Daniel, Bounding Power: Republican Security Theory from the Polis to the Global Village, Princeton University Press, New Jersey, 2006. Daniel, Bounding Power: Republican Security Theory from the Polis to the Global Village , Princeton University Press, 2006, real

14 Dooley, The World State: A Necessary Condition for World Peace, p. xvi.

15 Manda, David Suze, Ubuntu as an African Philosophy for Peace, Africa Files, 14 March 2009.

16 Manda, Ubuntu as an African Philosophy for Peace

17 Because African culture is by and large inaccessible to the rest of the world as most of it is oral rather than written and lived rather than documented, Africa is usually neglected as not having any meaningful contribution to any field of study.

18 Lu, World Government.

is not adequate to address current global challenges such as conflicts and climate change. And it is undesirable because a global authority could become oppressive, tyrannical and detached from the people.[19] Because of these concerns, some go so far as concluding that a world government is a dream that will never be realized.[20]

While it is true that current political reality is not conducive to the idea of world government, it is impossible to predict the future on this issue with certainty. World conditions could change. In this regard, one only needs to consider developments in the past two decades.

### *1.2 Global Governance*

> "Certainly, one of the most evident failures of the nation-state system in recent years has been its inability to deal successfully with problems that endanger much or most of the world's population. As the world has become more globalized—economically integrated and culturally interconnected—individual countries have become increasingly averse to dealing with international problems that are not caused by any single state and cannot be fixed even by the focused efforts of individual governments"[21].

The concept of global governance re-emerged after the end of the Cold War. It evolved and developed as a means of fostering international cooperation and collaboration in a more inclusive and consensual manner.[22] The large number of scholarly writings and studies that mushroomed after the Cold War reflect this reality. For instance, the 1995 report of the Commission on Global Governance defines global governance as "the sum of the many ways individuals and institutions, public and private, manage their common affairs. It is the continuing process through which conflict or diverse interests may be accommodated and cooperative action may be taken."[23] Similarly, Oran Young defines it as the "establishment and operation of social institutions…capable of resolving conflicts, facilitating cooperation, or

19 Lu, World Government.

20 Weiss, Thomas G, Governance, Good Governance and Global Governance: Conceptual and Actual Challenges, In: Third World Quarterly, Vol. 21, No. 5, 2010, p. 808.

21 Craige, The Resurgent Idea of World Government, p.135.

22 Barnett, Michael & Duvall, Raymond (Eds.) Power in Global Governance, Cambridge University Press, Edinburg, 2005, p. 5.

23 Our Global Neighborhood, Report of the Commission on Global Governance, 1995, http://www.gdrc.org/u-gov/global-neighbourhood/chapl.htm [26.11.2015].

more generally alleviating collective-action problems[24] in a world of interdependent actors."[25]

Supporters of global governance argue that the unique dangers created by globalization can be solved by a gradual strengthening of existing global institutions and organizations, making the imposition of a full-blown world state unnecessary. A leading scholar of globalization, Anthony McGrew, opines that global governance institutions are better placed to deal with global problems. He contends that the key is to grant more enhanced and more formal powers to such institutions and organizations, ultimately giving them greater effectiveness and influence on the international stage than nation-states.[26]

## *2. The ICC as a Global Governance Institution*

> According to Buchanan and Keohane, global governance institutions are "like governments in that they issue rules and publicly attach significant consequences to compliance or failure to comply with them – and claim the authority to do so. Nonetheless, they do not attempt to perform anything approaching a full range of governmental functions. These institutions do not seek, as governments do, to monopolize the legitimate use of violence within a permanently specified territory, and their design and major actions require the consent of states".[27]

Global governance institutions include a wide variety of multilateral entities including the World Trade Organization, International Monetary Fund and the UN Security Council. The International Criminal Court also falls into this category of global governance institutions.[28]

The history, mandate and purpose of the ICC also confirms that it is a global governance institution but destined to be more. Since the end of WWII,

24 The phrase 'collective-action problem' was coined by political scientists to refer to the dilemma that emerges when several actors have an interest in eradicating a problem that harms all of them, but when each would prefer that someone else do the dirty work of solving it. If everyone benefits more or less equally from the problem's solution, but only the actor that addresses it pays the costs, then all are likely to want to "free ride" on the other's efforts. The result is that no one tackles the problem, and everyone suffers. Craige, The Resurgent Idea of World Government, pp. 133-135.

25 Young, Oran R., International Governance: Protecting the Environment in a Stateless Society, Cornell University Press, New York, 1994, p.53.

26 Craige, The Resurgent Idea of World Government, p.137.

27 Buchanan, Allan & Keohane, Robert, The Legitimacy of Global Governance Institutions, In: Ethics & International Affairs, Vol. 20, Issue 4, 2006, p. 406

28 Buchanan & Keohane, The Legitimacy of Global Governance Institutions, p. 406.

despite the establishment of the UN to ensure world peace and security, violence and conflicts continued unabated. Acts of aggression, genocide, war crimes and crimes against humanity continued to claim the lives of millions of innocent civilians all around the world. The response of the international community to these gruesome crimes was to establish from time to time, *ad hoc* tribunals to try those top level officials responsible for the acts. But this piecemeal approach proved to be costly, short-sighted and unsustainable.[29]

It was against this backdrop that the ICC was established as the first permanent international court with jurisdiction to try individuals, including sitting heads of states, for crimes of genocide, war crimes, and crimes against humanity. The ICC is an independent international organization. It is not part of the United Nations system but maintains cooperative relationship with the UN. Its seat is at The Hague in the Netherlands. Although the Court's expenses are funded primarily by States Parties, it also receives voluntary contributions from governments, international organizations, individuals, corporations and other entities.[30]

The ICC is widely recognized as one of the many global governance institutions. In fact, it is credited for paving the way towards the creation of a global authority. Traditionally criminal matters fall within the exclusive jurisdiction of states and that is a well-recognized manifestation of state sovereignty. Therefore, the fact that states have agreed to confer criminal jurisdiction on an international institution, no matter how limited its jurisdiction might be, is indeed a step in the right direction.

But does that really make the ICC a global public authority? What is a global public authority anyway? Does the fact that the ICC is recognized as a global governance institution automatically qualify it as a global public authority? The answer to these questions lies in legitimacy, which is discussed in detail in the subsequent sections.

---

29 After the ICTY and ICTR were established, although human rights violations of similar gravity occurred in other places notably in Sierra Leone, Cambodia and East Timor, the UN Security Council did not dare to establish other *ad hoc* tribunals; rather it set up what are called mixed courts. This is particularly because at the time the UN Security Council had reached a point of what David Scheffer called 'tribunal fatigue', as the ICTY and ICTR had depleted the capabilities and resources of the UN. This fact has expedited the then ongoing process for the creation of the ICC.

30 Rome Statute of the International Criminal Court, adopted on 17 July 1998 and entered into force on 1 July 2002, https://www.icc-cpi.int/nr/rdonlyres/ea9aeff7-5752-4f84-be94-0a655eb30e16/0/rome_statute_english.pdf 29.11.2015 ; see also ICC, About the Court, https://www.icc-cpi.int/en_menus/icc/about%20the%20court/Pages/about%20the%20court.aspx [29.11.2015].

### *3. Legitimacy as the Litmus Test to the Claim of Authority*

The question of authority or power has been left out of most discussions of global governance and its introduction transforms the discourse.[31] With authority, global governance discourse moves beyond the creation and maintenance of institutional arrangements through consensual relations and voluntary choice, to the question of how global life is organized, structured and regulated.[32] When power/authority is involved global structures, processes, and institutions that shape the fates and life chances of actors around the world become the center of attention. The question of legitimacy and procedural fairness become central. Accordingly, international institutions will not only be measured based on their efficiency but also their fairness and legitimacy.[33]

The works of prominent social scientists also shows that legitimacy is a defining element in acquiring and exercising authority. In this regard, the renowned sociologist Max Weber understood authority as "the condition in which power is married to legitimacy".[34] Ruggie has a similar understanding of authority as 'fusion of power with legitimate social purpose'.[35]

When an actor sees a rule as legitimate, it means that the rule has been internalized into interests and becomes authoritative over the actor. Internalized means only occasional deviance needs to be policed. Any claim of an international institution's ascendance to global authority has to, therefore, be supported by a robust evidence of the institution's legitimacy.[36] It is inconceivable to have authority without legitimacy. Any show of power without legitimacy is coercion.

Some argue that any international institution that is engaged in any kind of governance activity should be categorized as exercising international public authority 'if it determines individuals, private associations, enterprises, states, or other public institutions' i.e. if it unilaterally shapes their legal or factual situation.[37] In certain ways global governance has also been understood to

---

31 Sometimes authority and power are used interchangeably though they do not always mean the same thing.

32 Barnett & Duvall, Power in Global Governance, pp. 7-8.

33 Barnett & Duvall, Power in Global Governance, pp. 7-8.

34 Hurd, Ian, After Anarchy: Legitimacy and Power in the United Nations Security Council, Princeton University Press, New Jersey, 2007, p.60.

35 Ruggie, John Gerard, Constructing the World Polity: Essays on International Institutionalization, Routledge, London and New York, 1998, p.64.

36 Hurd, After Anarchy, p.65.

37 Bogdandy, Armin von, Dann, Philipp & Goldman, Mathias, Developing the Publicness of Public International Law: Towards a Legal Framework for Global Governance Activities, In: Bogdandy, Armin von Dann, Philipp & Goldman,

mean public authority.[38] This, however, is a hasty assertion that may cause a political backlash as states are still reluctant, to say the least, to automatically confer authority to the swarm of existing governance institutions. A rapid transition from the national to the international would also cause confusion and even chaos. The system should be allowed to gradually evolve into an organized and structured system of authority in a democratic – all-inclusive and participatory – manner, by steadily building its legitimacy among the 'global public'. Any attempt to short-cut the process can backfire. What is instead required is to devise ways and means of expediting the process.

Success in such a transition depends on legitimacy.[39] Only global governance institutions that are legitimate can be considered to be global public authorities.[40] So now the question becomes, what is legitimacy? When do we say that global governance institutions have legitimacy and/or are legitimate? And more specifically, is the ICC a legitimate global governance institution and hence a global public authority?

### *3.1 What is Legitimacy?*

Legitimacy is perhaps one of the most commonly invoked but least defined concepts in the social sciences.[41] At the same time, a substantial body of scholarship has been devoted to define and describe the concept. For purposes of this chapter, it is not necessary or feasible to analyze the breadth of literature on legitimacy. Instead a more practical approach will be taken by first presenting the widely shared views on what legitimacy is and then explaining what it is not to avoid confusion that may be created as a result of closely related social control concepts.

According to most scholars, legitimacy has normative and sociological dimensions.[42] Simply put, normative legitimacy is having the right to rule,

---

Mathias (Eds.), The Exercise of Public Authority by International Institutions: Advancing International Institutional Law, Volume 210 of Beiträge zum ausländischen öffentlichen Recht und Völkerrecht, Springer Science & Business Media, 2010, p.5.

38 Krisch, Nico, Global Governance as Public Authority: An Introduction, Oxford University Press and New York University School of Law, 2012, http://icon.oxfordjournals.org/content/10/4/976.full.pdf [24.11.2015].

39 Buchanan & Keohane, The Legitimacy of Global Governance Institutions, p. 407.

40 Barnett & Duvall, Power in Global Governance, pp. 7-8.

41 Suchman, Mark C, Managing Legitimacy: Strategic and Institutional Approaches in The Academy of Management Review, Vol. 20, No. 3, 1995, p.573.

42 Bodansky, Daniel M., The Legitimacy of International Governance: A Coming Challenge for International Environmental Law? In The American Journal of In-

while sociological legitimacy is the belief or perception that an entity has the right to rule.[43] Sociological legitimacy is also defined as what people think is legally or morally justified or acceptable, and normative legitimacy as what really is legally or morally justified and sound.[44] Normative legitimacy is, relatively, a fact based objective assessment, and sociological legitimacy is about the perception of the public, so it is subjective.

### *3.2 What Legitimacy is not? Self-interest and Coercion*

Legitimacy co-exists with two other grand and interlinked but distinct, concepts of social control: self-interest and coercion.[45] For the purposes of this chapter it is important that the distinction is made to avoid any possible mix-up and misunderstanding. Making such distinction also helps to better understand the concept of legitimacy.

When a state or non-state actor treats rule by an institution as binding based on an instrumental and calculated assessment of the net benefits of compliance versus non-compliance, it is said to be motivated by self-interest.[46] This, of course, leads to selective compliance meaning rules are respected only if and when they promote the self-interest. Legitimacy, understood as the right to rule, is a moral notion that cannot be reduced to rational self-interest. Legitimacy implies that it has the right to rule even if it does not act in accordance with the rational self-interest of everyone who is subject to the rule.

This, in the context of the ICC means, for instance, if a government enforces an arrest warrant issued by the ICC against a rebel leader but refuses to observe a similar order against a government official or a close ally of the government, then the government can be said to be acting based on self-interest. If the government complies with orders and decisions of the ICC because it genuinely believes that it is obliged to, even when it implicates its sitting high government officials, we can perhaps deduce that the institutional rules are legitimate and hence so is the institution. This, of course, is a very rudimentary example as the reality is much more complex.

---

ternational Law, Vol. 93, 1999, p. 601. See also Hurd, After Anarchy, pp. 30-34; and Buchanan & Keohane, The Legitimacy of Global Governance Institutions, p. 405.

43 Buchanan & Keohane, The Legitimacy of Global Governance Institutions, p. 405.

44 deGuzman, Margaret, Gravity and the Legitimacy of the International Criminal Court, Fordham International Law Journal, Vol. 32, 2009, p.1438. See also Fallon, Richard H, Legitimacy and the Constitution, Harvard Law Review, Vol. 118, No. 6, 2005, pp. 1794-1801.

45 Hurd, After Anarchy, pp. 34-35.

46 Hurd, After Anarchy, pp. 37.

Coercion, on the other hand, presupposes the existence of asymmetrical power relations and a rule in such cases is obeyed for fear of punishment from a stronger power.[47] So, unlike in the case of legitimacy, where the rules are internalized and complied with willingly, coercion involves a threat or use of force to prompt compliance. It is, therefore, not the rule that results in compliance but the force behind it. As indicated above, legitimacy is not dependent on use of force but a willful internalization of rules.[48]

For the foregoing reasons, legitimacy is distinct from and hence should not be confused with observance of rules out of coercion and/or self-interest.

### *4. Putting the ICC to the Legitimacy Test*

Legitimacy in the case of global governance institutions is the "right to rule, understood to mean both the institutional agents are morally justified in making rules and attempting to secure compliance with them and that people subject to those rules have moral, content-independent reasons to follow them and/or not to interfere with others' compliance with them."[49]

The more difficult task is now assessing whether the ICC is legitimate or not. Buchanan and Keohane, mindful of the lack of standards to evaluate the legitimacy of global governance institutions, have attempted to develop a complex set of standards.[50] A combination of these standards developed by them together with others is used here in assessing the legitimacy of the ICC in three categories: legal, moral and sociological.[51]

---

47 Hurd, After Anarchy, pp. 35.

48 For a detailed discussion of why states comply with international law see O'Connell, Mary Ellen, The Power and Purpose of International Law: Insights from the Theory and Practice of Enforcement, Oxford University Press, New York, 2008. See also Koh, Harold, Why Do Nations Obey International Law?, Yale Law School Legal Scholarship Repository, 1997.

49 Buchanan & Keohane, The Legitimacy of Global Governance Institutions, p. 411.

50 See generally Buchanan & Keohane, The Legitimacy of Global Governance Institutions.

51 It should be noted that these distinctions are just functional and are rarely clear-cut. See Fallon, Richard H, Legitimacy and the Constitution, Harvard Law Review, Vol. 118, No. 6, 2005, pp. 1792-1793; and deGuzman, Gravity and Legitimacy of the ICC, p.1437.

### 4.1 Legal legitimacy

Legal legitimacy concerns the legality of norms and standards applied by an institution. It is about the correct application of laws and legal principles by the concerned institution.[52] Thus, the legal legitimacy or illegitimacy of an institution depends on legal norms; if it is legal, it is legitimate.[53]

The assessment of the legal legitimacy of an institution can be done at different levels: establishment, independence, application of substantive and procedural rules.

#### 4.1.1 Establishment

The end of the Cold War paved the way for the revival of discussions on the universality of human rights. This coupled with the breakdown of the international machinery for conflict resolution and peace enforcement following the crisis in the former Yugoslavia and Rwanda, and the 'tribunal fatigue'[54] that followed, the international community was forced to consider finding a lasting solution to this recurrent problem.[55] Accordingly, the International Law Commission was tasked to prepare a draft ICC statute, which it did, and was rigorously reviewed and revised by the Generally Assembly in 1994.[56]

In June 1998, a conference was held in Rome to draft a statute for the proposed court. More than 160 states sent their delegates who were very en-

52 deGuzman, Gravity and Legitimacy of the ICC, p. 1437

53 A court decision may be erroneous without being illegitimate. See Fallon, Legitimacy and the Constitution, p. 1794.

54 David Scheffer, who was a Senior Counsel and Advisor to the US Permanent Mission to the UN, coined the phrase, to refer to the depletion of the capabilities and resources of the UN after the establishment of the International Criminal Tribunal for the Former Yugoslavia and the the International Criminal Tribunal for Rwanda and others in the 1990s. See Bassiouni, M. Cherif, The Statute of the International Criminal Court: A Documentary History, Transitional Publishers, 1998.

55 Schiff, Benjamin N., Building the International Criminal Court, Cambridge University Press, New York, 2008, pp.37-39

56 On 4 December 1989 the General Assembly requested the ILC "to address the question of establishing an international criminal court or other international criminal trial mechanism with jurisdiction over persons alleged to have committed crimes which may be covered under such a code (draft Code of Offenses against the Peace and Security of Mankind)…" UN General Assembly, 'International Criminal Responsibility of Individuals and Entities Engaged in Illicit Trafficking in Narcotic Drugs across National Frontiers and Other Transnational Criminal Activities: Establishment of an International Criminal Court with Jurisdiction over Such Crimes' (1998). Of course, the initiative to establish a permanent court started long before the conference in the 1950s. See Schiff, Building the ICC, p. 37.

thusiastic and most of them wanted the conference to succeed. Some were also organized in groups that were playing active roles in the conference by for instance chairing working groups.[57] Even USA, though at the end vehemently opposed the Court, played an extremely important and constructive role during the negotiation process.[58] A lot of compromises were also made to appease some states and get onboard as many states as possible.[59] After the text of the Rome Statute was adopted in 1998, it was opened for ratification and to date 123 countries are parties to the Statute.[60] Civil society and international organizations also played and continue to play a significant role both before and after the adoption of the Rome Statute.

This proves that the Statute was negotiated and came into force in line with well-established norms in international law on the negotiation, adoption, ratification of and accession to treaties.[61]. All 123 states expressed their consent through internationally accepted legal procedures and hence fully submitted to the jurisdiction of the ICC.[62] The involvement and active participation of non-state actors also shows that the process of establishment

57 For instance, members of the group called the 'like-minded states' (LMS) served as chairs of most of the working groups and members of the Bureau; the 'Non-aligned movement' pushed for the inclusion of the crime of aggression in the statute; the Southern African Development Community (SADC) pressed for expanded human rights definitions; and a group of Arab states wanted to include the prohibition of nuclear weapons and a death penalty provision in the statute. For more discussion on compromises made see Kaul, Hans-Peter, The International Criminal Court: Jurisdiction, Trigger mechanism and Relationship to National Jurisdictions, In: Politi, Mauro & Nesi, Giusseppe (Eds.) The Rome Statute of the International Criminal Court: A Challenge to Impunity, Ashgate Publishing Limited, Hampshire, 2001, p. 5962.; and Schiff, Building the ICC, pp. 70-71.

58 Schiff, Building the ICC, pp. 71.

59 Some of the major compromises made were: complementarity was introduced to protect sovereignty; jurisdiction was limited to three crimes and two jurisdiction principle; Pre-trial chambers were mandated to check the independence of the Office of the Prosecutor while the Un Security Council was given the power to refer cases to the Court and to suspend its activities; although states parties are required to bring their domestic laws in line with the Statute and to cooperate with the Court, no sanctions or enforcement capacity were created to ensure either. Schiff, Building the ICC, p. 73.

60 The States Parties to the Rome Statute, International Criminal Court, https://www.icc-cpi.int/en_menus/asp/states%20parties/Pages/the%20states%20parties%20to%20the%20rome%20statute.aspx [29.11.2015]

61 See UN General Assembly, Vienna Convention on the Law of Treaties, adopted on 23 May 1969 and came into force on 27 January 1980, Part II, https://treaties.un.org/doc/Publication/UNTS/Volume%201155/volume-1155-I-18232-English.pdf [27.11.2015]

62 A well-established principle of customary international law, *pacta sunt servanda*, provides that states that ratify or accede to an international treaty are bound by it

of the Court was open, transparent and all-inclusive. In the absence of any evidence to the contrary, it can safely be concluded that the procedure followed in establishing the Court was legally acceptable or legitimate.

### *4.1.2 Independence*

Structure and source of funding and election and tenure of judges are among the vital factors commonly used to determine independence of courts, both in national and international jurisdictions.[63] And independence is vital for the legitimacy of courts. The ICC as an international court should, thus, be put to this test.

The ICC is composed of four organs: the Presidency, the Judicial Division, the Office of the Prosecutor and the Registry.[64] The Presidency is responsible for the overall administration of the Court, with the exception of the Office of the Prosecutor.[65] The Judicial Division is composed of eighteen judges organized into the Pre-Trial, Trial and Appeals divisions. The

---

and are expected to perform in good faith. See Article 26 of the Vienna Convention on the Law of Treaties, 1969.

63 See generally Seventh UN Congress on the Independence of the Prevention of Crime and the Treatment of Offenders, Basic Principles on the Independence of the Judiciary, 1985; UN General Assembly Resolution 40/32 of 29 November 1985 and Resolution 40/146 of 13 December 1985; African Commission on Human and Peoples' Rights, Principles and Guidelines on the Right to a Fair Trial and Legal Assistance in Africa, 2002, http://www.achpr.org/instruments/principles-guidelines-right-fair-trial/ [1.11.2015]; U.S. Agency for International Development (office of Democracy and Governance), Guidance for Promoting Judicial Independence and Impartiality, Washington DC, 2002; International Commission of Jurists, International Principles on the Independence and Accountability of Judges, Lawyers and Prosecutors: Practitioners Guide 1, Geneva, 2007.

64 The Court also includes a number of semi-autonomous offices such as the Office of Public Counsel for Victims and the Office of Public Counsel for Defence. These Offices fall under the Registry for administrative purposes but otherwise function as wholly independent offices. The Assembly of States Parties has also established a Trust Fund for the benefit of victims of crimes within the jurisdiction of the Court and the families of these victims. Rome Statute of the International Criminal Court, adopted on 17 July 1998 and entered into force on 1 July 2002, Part IV (articles 34-52).

65 The Presidency is composed of three judges of the Court, elected to the Presidency by their fellow judges, for a term of three years. The President of the Court is Judge Silvia Alejandra Fernández De Gurmendi (Argentina). Judge Joyce Aluoch (Kenya) is First Vice-President, and Judge Kuniko Ozaki (Japan) is Second Vice-President. See Rome Statute, article 38. See also International Criminal Court, Structure of the Court, https://www.icc-cpi.int/en_menus/icc/structure%20of%20the%20court/Pages/structure%20of%20the%20court.aspx [29.11.2015].

judges of each division sit in Chambers, which are responsible for conducting the proceedings of the Court at different stages.[66] The Office of the Prosecutor is in charge of receiving referrals and any substantiated information on crimes within the jurisdiction of the Court, for examining them and conducting investigations and prosecutions before the Court.[67] The Registry is responsible for the non-judicial aspects of the administration and servicing of the Court.[68]

The eighteen judges of the Court are nominated by states parties and elected in a secret ballot by the Assembly of States Parties.[69] In the election process, the personal character of the candidates, and their qualifications is taken into consideration.[70] Candidates are required to have prior experience in criminal law and procedure as well as competence in international humanitarian law and human rights law. In electing the judges due care is taken for a fair representation of geographical regions, legal systems, and gender.[71]

---

66 Assignment of judges to Divisions is made on the basis of the nature of the functions each Division performs and the qualifications and experience of the judge. This is done in a manner ensuring that each Division benefits from an appropriate combination of expertise in criminal law and procedure and international law. The judges of the Court are: Silvia Alejandra Fernández De Gurmendi (Argentina), Joyce Aluoch (Kenya), Kuniko Ozaki (Japan), Sanji Mmasenono Monageng (Botswana), Christine Baroness Van Den Wyngaert (Belgium), Cuno Jakob Tarfusser (Italy), Howard Morrison (United Kingdom), Olga Venecia del C. Herrera Carbuccia (Dominican Republic), Robert Fremr (Czech Republic), Chile Eboe-Osuji (Nigeria), Geoffrey A. Henderson (Trinidad and Tobago), Marc Perrin De Brichambaut (France), Piotr Hofmański (Poland), Antoine Kesia-Mbe Mindua (Democratic Republic of the Congo), Bertram Schmitt (Germany), Péter Kovács (Hungary), Chang-ho Chung (Republic of Korea) and Judge Raul Pangalangan (Philippines). ICC, Structure of the Court, https://www.icc-cpi.int/en_menus/icc/structure%20of%20the%20court/Pages/structure%20of%20the%20court.aspx [23.11.2015].

67 The Office is headed by the Prosecutor, Mrs. Fatou Bensouda (The Gambia), who was elected by the States Parties for a term of nine years. She is assisted by Deputy Prosecutor James Stewart who is in charge of the Prosecutions Division of the Office of the Prosecutor. ICC, Structure of the Court.

68 The Registry is headed by the Registrar who is the principal administrative officer of the Court. The Registrar exercises his or her functions under the authority of the President of the Court. The current Registrar, elected by the judges for a term of five years, is Mr. Herman von Hebel (The Netherlands). ICC, Structure of the Court.

69 Rome Statute, articles 36(4), & (6)(a).

70 The judges shall be chosen from among persons of high moral character, impartiality and integrity. Rome Statute, articles 36(3)(a) & (b).

71 Rome Statute, articles 36(3)(b) & (8)(a). States Parties are also required to include judges with special legal expertise such as violence against women and children.

Judges are elected for a term of nine years and are not eligible for re-election unless they were originally elected to serve three years term or they were elected to fill a vacancy.[72] Article 40 of the Rome Statute also provides for more measures that are geared towards ensuring the independence of judges. It provides that judges shall be independent in the performance of their functions and prohibits them from engaging in any activity that is likely to interfere with their judicial functions or to affect confidence in their independence. Similar provisions that are aimed at ensuring the independent functioning of the Office of the Prosecutor and the Registry are also included in the Rome Statute.[73] As indicated elsewhere the ICC is also financially independent and institutionally detached from the UN, which contributes to its actual and perceived institutional independence.

The way the Court is structured and the division of power and functions among the different organs of the Court as well as the legally acceptable procedures followed in the election of judges and in conducting their mandate are sufficient grounds for the Court to pass the standard of independence.

However, there are two major issues that dampen this conclusion on the independence of the Court. The first is related to the extensive powers given to the UN Security Council, an unpopular and highly politicized organ of the UN. Under the Rome Statute the Security Council has wide-ranging involvement in the proceedings of the ICC. The Statute allows the Council to defer the Court's proceedings at any time. Article 16 of the Rome Statute provides that no investigation or prosecution may be commenced or proceeded with for a period of twelve months if the Council requests the ICC to that effect in a resolution adopted under Chapter VII of the UN Charter. What is more is that no limits have been put on the Council on the number of deferrals that it can request, which practically means that the Council can effectively rob the Court of jurisdiction over any case that it desires.

This allows the Council to meddle with the proceedings of the Court unchecked. The situation is made worse by the fact that the Council's vague and undefined voting system and repeated abuse of veto power by its permanent members has frustrated all hopes that the Council could become a credible custodian for the application of the rule of law.[74]

---

72 Rome Statute, articles 36(9)(a),(c) & 37(2).

73 Rome Statute, articles 42-50.

74 Elaraby, Nabil, The Role of the Security Council and the Independence of the International Criminal Court: Some Reflections, In: Politi, Mauro & Nesi, Giusseppe (Eds.) The Rome Statute of the International Criminal Court: A Challenge to Impunity, Ashgate Publishing Limited, Hampshire, 2001, pp.43-44.

The second area of concern is the heavy reliance of the Prosecutor on states to undertake investigations, gather evidence, interview witnesses, or arrest suspects on the territory of states. The Prosecutor must secure the consent and cooperation of states in conducting any of these activities.[75] This lack of independence of the Office of the Prosecutor in this respect was pronounced in the case against Uhuru Kenyatta, the incumbent President of Kenya, wherein the Prosecutor was forced to drop charges against the President on grounds that the state failed to cooperate in the collection of evidence and conduct of investigation.[76] Indicting a head of state and expecting the government to fully cooperate in good faith is nothing short of daydreaming, and exposes the lack of capacity and independence of the Office of the Prosecutor in discharging its duties.

This also explains why the Prosecutor has relative success in indicting, arresting and prosecuting rebel leaders or deposed leaders as compared to sitting heads of states or high officials, because in the latter case, as it is demonstrated by the Kenyatta case, states are not willing to cooperate. This, in turn, makes the Court partial as it tends to focus on rebel leaders and ousted leaders since it is easier to get the cooperation of states in these types of cases.

Although, by and large, the way the Court is structured and constituted raises confidence in its independence, the free pass handed to the Security Council to interfere with the proceedings of the Court has affected and will continue to affect its actual as well as perceived independence. The lack of power to independently collect evidence, interview witnesses and conduct investigations by the Prosecutor equally affects the real and perceived independence of the Court.

---

75 Posner, Eric A. & Yoo, John C., Judicial Independence in International Tribunals, California Law Review, Vol. 93. No. 1, 2005, pp.68-69.

76 ICC, Statement of the Prosecutor of the International Criminal Court, Fatou Bensouda, on the withdrawal of charges against Mr. Uhuru Muingai Kenyatta, Press Release, 12.05.2014., https://www.icc-cpi.int/en_menus/icc/press%20and%20media/press%20releases/Pages/otp-statement-05-12-2014-2.aspx [26.05.2014.]; ICC withdraws charges against Kenyatta, Al Jazeera News, 05.12.2014., http://www.aljazeera.com/news/africa/2014/12/icc-case-against-kenyatta-dropped-20141251145297O3204.html [29.11.2015] ; ICC drops Uhuru Kenyatta charges for Kenya ethnic violence, BBC News, 05.12.2014., http://www.bbc.com/news/world-africa-30347019 [29.11.2015]

### *4.1.3 Applicable laws and Procedural Guarantees*

By the time the ICC was established, international law, particularly international humanitarian law, human rights law, and criminal law had evolved considerably. There were numerous international instruments and customs that guarantee a wide range of substantive and procedural rights. The lessons learned from the post-1945 tribunals such as the Nuremberg, Tokyo, Rwanda and former Yugoslavia tribunals also greatly informed the drafting of the Rome Statute.[77]

All that the drafters had to do was import those substantive and procedural norms from existing corpus of international law with necessary adaptations and inject a bit of innovation.[78] Some of the notable innovations relate to irrelevance of official capacity and referral of cases.[79] As a result, there is no issue relating to applicable laws, substantive rights and procedural guarantees that infringes legality.

In conclusion, for the Court to firmly establish its legal legitimacy, the defect that arises from the interference by the Security Council in its proceedings and lack of independence of the Prosecutor in discharging its mandate have to be cured. That can only be done by amending the Rome Statute and/or suspending article 16. Given the current international power politics, this could only be wishful thinking. And until and unless these defects are rectified, the legal legitimacy of the ICC remains open to doubt.

### *4.2 Moral Legitimacy*

Moral legitimacy connotes the moral justifiability or respect-worthiness of a judicial institution.[80] An institution could be legally legitimate and receive widespread support, but still be morally illegitimate. Moral legitimacy can be assessed based on consent.[81] Consent is a commonly used to assess moral legitimacy, though it is also considered by some as outdated because it

---

77 This is particularly evident in provisions on the mandate, structure and management of the Court; relation and cooperation with states and international institutions; funding and provisions on gender crimes and outreach. Schiff, Building the ICC, pp.42-65.
78 Schiff, Building the ICC, pp.42-65.
79 Rome Statute, articles 27 & 13.
80 Fallon, Legitimacy and the Constitution, p.1796.
81 Fallon, Legitimacy and the Constitution, p.1797.

relies on the flawed assumption that the consenting governments represent the will of the people they govern.[82]

The apparent flaw in using consent as a standard to gage moral legitimacy can be rectified by using it in combination with other standards because as it stands states are still the primary subjects of international law, and international law depends heavily on state consent. It would, therefore, not be appropriate to completely relegate consent in assessing moral legitimacy. Other standards, according to Buchanan and Keohane, that can be used to gage an institution's moral legitimacy are: minimal moral acceptability; comparative benefit; and institutional integrity.[83]

Regarding consent, all the 123 states parties consented to submit to the jurisdiction of the ICC and since international law is dependent on state consent, this segment is well covered. However, as indicated earlier consent of states does not automatically translate into consent of the citizens because there are states parties which are not democratic and so do not represent the will of the people. Even in democracies, popular opinion or support and government are not always close.

The decision of the Kenyan parliament to withdraw from the ICC and similar initiatives to do the same in South Africa, and the continuous denunciation of the ICC by African leaders and the African Union is a serious setback to the moral legitimacy of the ICC (based on consent).[84] The decision of the AU in July 2014 to confer the African Court of Justice and Human Rights with criminal jurisdiction with competence to try all crimes under the Rome Statute as well as a number of other crimes proved to be an imminent threat to the legitimacy of the Court.[85] Currently, 34 African countries are states parties to the Rome Statute constituting the

82 See deGuzman, Gravity and Legitimacy of the ICC, pp.1437-1438.

83 Buchanan & Keohane, The Legitimacy of Global Governance Institutions, pp.419-424.

84 In 2013 the Kenyan parliament voted to withdraw from the ICC after its President, Uhuru Kenyatta, and Vice-President, William Ruto, were indicted. However, the President has not endorsed the decision meaning that Kenya is still a party to the Rome Statute. In 2015 the South African ruling party, the African National Congress, called for South Africa to pull out of the ICC. Nkosi, Milton, What South Africa Leaving the International Criminal Court would mean, BBC News, 14.10.2015, http://www.bbc.com/news/world-africa-34509342 [1.11.2015].

85 International Justice Resource Center, African Union Approves Immunity for Government Officials in Amendment to African Court of Justice and Human Rights Statute, 2.7.2014. http://www.ijrcenter.org/2014/07/02/african-union-approves-immunity-for-heads-of-state-in-amendment-to-african-court-of-justice-and-human-rights-statute/ [10.11.2015].

largest bloc.[86] The lack of support and confidence from this bloc, therefore, undermines the legitimacy of the Court.

Turning to the other three standards of moral legitimacy, 'minimal moral acceptability' denotes adherence to minimum standards of justice; 'comparative benefit' is understood to mean providing benefit not otherwise obtainable; and 'institutional integrity' means exhibiting institutional integrity conforming to the goals that justify the institution's existence.[87] deGuzman succinctly summarizes how the ICC meets these standards as follows:

> "First, the Statute's provisions, particularly those affecting the accused, aim to ensure substantially more than minimal standards of justice. Second, the complementarity regime, whereby the Court cannot act if a state with jurisdiction is already doing so in good faith, ensures the Court provides a benefit that is otherwise unavailable. Finally, the gravity threshold for admissibility, along with the Statute's jurisdictional provisions, aim to ensure the Court's institutional integrity. The Statute's preamble leaves no doubt that a key component of such integrity is the adjudication of serious crimes. If the Court were routinely to exercise jurisdiction over crimes that are generally considered minor, for example, isolated instances of property theft in war, its integrity and thus its normative legitimacy would be questioned."[88]

From the forgoing, it can be concluded that though the ICC meets most of the components of the test of moral legitimacy, the withdrawal of support by some states may result in the ICC failing to measure up to the standard in the future. This concern may be dismissed by contending that those African states that denounce and threaten to withdraw do not represent the will of their people as they are undemocratic. Yet, no matter how hard this concern is downplayed, it is a fact that will slowly erode the moral legitimacy of the Court, unless it is dealt with duly and adequately. Moreover, the two countries that are threatening to withdraw, Kenya and South Africa, are two of the few African countries that are considered democratic.

---

86 ICC, States Parties to the Rome Statute, https://www.icc-cpi.int/en_menus/asp/states%20parties/Pages/the%20states%20parties%20to%20the%20rome%20statute.aspx [28.11.2015].

87 deGuzman, Gravity and Legitimacy of the ICC, p.1439.

88 deGuzman, Gravity and Legitimacy of the ICC, p. 1439. See also Rome Statute, articles 62-76.

### *4.3 Sociological Legitimacy*

Sociological legitimacy refers to the perception of relevant audiences that an institution is justified to rule and deserves support independent of any sanction or reward associated with such support.[89] In addition to factors that make up legal and moral legitimacy, fairness or procedural correctness serve as sources of perceived legitimacy.[90] As to whose perception is considered, states and affected communities are commonly identified as relevant stakeholders.[91]

In this regard, the selection of cases by the Prosecutor and the Security Council's ability to refer cases to the Court have met serious opposition. The lack of guidelines and transparency by the Office of the Prosecutor in the selection of cases, coupled with the fact that all the cases before the ICC are from Africa, have prompted African states to label it as a biased and neo-imperialist institution that is unfairly targeting Africans.[92] Mr. Jean Ping, the former Chairperson of the African Union Commission (AUC), has accused the ICC of hypocrisy, charging that "there are two systems of measurement…the ICC seems to exist solely for judging Africans".[93] In 2013, the then Chairperson of the African Union, Prime Minister Hailemariam Desalegn of Ethiopia, accused the ICC of 'hunting Africans' on the basis of race.[94]

Currently, all the nine cases before the ICC are from Africa.[95] And this is regardless of the existence of credible claims of equally grave, if not

89 Fallon, Legitimacy and the Constitution, p.1795.

90 Hurd, After Anarchy, pp.67-73.

91 deGuzman, Gravity and Legitimacy of the ICC, pp.1445-1449.

92 Thus far the ICC has indicted 36 individuals. Those in the public eye have been Laurant Gbagno, former President of Ivory Coast, Maummar Gaddafi, President Uhuru Kenyatta, Deputy William Ruto and President Omar al-Bashir of Sudan. The Sudanese leader was the subject of media headlines in South Africa recently. There was an order on behalf of ICC that South Africa must arrest him. Pheko, Motsoko, Africa: The ICC is Now an Instrument of Imperialism, In: allAfrica, 25.6.2015. http://allafrica.com/stories/201507011622.html [26.11.2015].

93 Arieff, Alexis et al, International Criminal Court Cases in Africa: Status and Policy Issues, 2011, p. 26 https://www.fas.org/sgp/crs/row/RL34665.pdf [24.11.2015].

94 Laing, Aislinn, International Criminal Court is 'Hunting' Africans, The Telegraph, 27.5.2013. http://www.telegraph.co.uk/news/worldnews/africaandindianocean/10082819/International-Criminal-Court-is-hunting-Africans.html 29.11.2015. See also ICC targets Africans on race basis: African Union Chair, [27.5.2015]. http://www.nation.co.ke/News/politics/ICC-targets-Africans-on-race-basis-African-Union-chair/-/1064/1864200/-/14tyb02z/-/index.html [28.11.2015].

95 The nine situations currently under investigation are from the Democratic Republic of the Congo, Uganda, Central African Republic, Sudan (Darfur), Kenya, Libya,

worse, human rights violations in countries such as Afghanistan, Colombia, Iraq and Palestine.[96] The former Prosecutor, Luis Moreno Ocampo, validated apprehensions expressed by some African leaders when he publicly announced in 2006 that he had received many complaints on the situation in Iraq but he had no competence to prosecute the crime of aggression[97], although there were, arguably, alleged crimes that fall within the jurisdiction of the Court.

ICC prosecutions in Sudan, prior to the indictment order against President Bashir, drew criticism for targeting mid-level officials rather than those with alleged higher-order responsibility for abuses in Darfur. Some have criticized the ICC prosecutions in Uganda, the Democratic Republic of Congo (DRC), Central African Republic (CAR), Libya and Cote d'Ivoire for focusing on alleged abuses committed by rebel fighters or deposed leaders to the exclusion of those reportedly committed by government troops.[98] In Uganda, some observers suggest that the ICC is locally associated with the administration of President Museveni, as only Lord Resistance Army (LRA) commanders have been the focus since the prosecutor's investigation in northern Uganda began despite reported abuses by Government troops.[99] The decision to pursue DRC opposition leader Jean-Pierre Bemba Gombo provoked accusations that the prosecutor was swayed by political bias, as Bemba was seen as a leading opposition figure in the DRC before he went into exile and was arrested.[100]

The other most persistent criticism of the ICC's actions in Africa has been that by prosecuting active participants in ongoing or settled conflicts, the ICC risks prolonging violence or endangering fragile peace processes. By removing the bargaining chip of amnesty from the negotiating table, critics allege, the ICC may remove incentives for peace settlements while encouraging perpetrators to remain in power in order to shield themselves

---

Cote d'Ivoire, Mali, and Central African Republic II. See International Criminal Court, https://www.icc-cpi.int/en_menus/icc/Pages/default.aspx

96 All these four situations are under preliminary examination, but are unlikely to be referred to the Court because of the powers and interests involved in the conflicts that led to alleged violations of the provisions of the Rome Statute. See International Criminal Court, https://www.icc-cpi.int/en_menus/icc/Pages/default.aspx

97 Jalloh, Charles Chernor, Regionalizing International Criminal Law? International Criminal Law Review, Vol. 9, 2009, pp.492-493.

98 See Waddel, Nicholas & Clark, Phil, (Eds.) Courting Conflict? Justice, Peace and the ICC in Africa, London, 2008.

99 Clark, Phil, law, Politics, and Pragmatism: The ICC and Case Selection in Uganda and the Democratic Republic of Congo, In: Waddel, Nicholas & Clark, Phil, (Eds.) Courting Conflict? Justice, Peace and the ICC in Africa, London, 2008, pp. 37-46.

100 Phil, Politics and Pragmatism, pp.37-46.

from prosecution. Some observe that in such cases, "it is difficult to tell victims of these conflicts that the prosecution of a small number of people should take precedence over a peace deal that may end the appalling conditions they endure and the daily risks they face".[101]

Concerns that the aims of 'justice' and 'peace' may conflict have been particularly prominent in Uganda and Sudan. In Uganda some argue that ICC arrest warrants against LRA commanders have acted as an impediment to achieving a final peace agreement. Ugandan critics reportedly include ethnic Acholi elders, a community most affected by the conflict in Northern Uganda, who support the use of traditional reconciliation mechanisms instead of international prosecution.[102] In Sudan, President Bashir's prosecution raised serious concerns that the ICC actions could endanger peace processes in Darfur and the then southern Sudan.[103]

Another challenge to the sociological legitimacy of the Court emanates from the ability of the Security Council to refer a situation of alleged commission of international crimes within the jurisdiction of the ICC to the Prosecutor. This makes it a very influential organ in the functioning of the ICC, regardless of its political nature. Five members of the UN Security Council are permanent members with veto powers. Out of these five permanent members, three, USA, Russia and China, are not signatories to the Rome Statute. The problem arises when an organ with five permanent members, out of which three are not parties to the Rome Statute, is empowered to refer cases to the Prosecutor. The Security Council used its referral powers in the case of Sudan and Libya, both not parties to the Rome Statute. Allowing the USA, Russia and China to refer cases against non-state parties, while they themselves are not parties, raises question of procedural fairness. What is more is that since they have veto power they can easily thwart any attempt to indict their citizens or close allies. This demonstrates a categorical deficiency in procedural fairness as well as in the equal treatment of states and people.

101 Grono, Nick & O'Brien, Adam, Justice in Conflict? The ICC and Peace Process, In: Waddel, Nicholas & Clark, Phil, (Eds.) Courting Conflict? Justice, Peace and the ICC in Africa, London, 2008.

102 Wierda, Marieke & Otim, Michael, Justice at Juba: International Obligations and Local Demands in Northern Uganda, In: Waddel, Nicholas & Clark, Phil, (Eds.) Courting Conflict? Justice, Peace and the ICC in Africa, London, 2008, pp. 21-28; Arieff, Alexis et al, ICC Cases in Africa, p.27.

103 de Waal, Alex, Darfur, the Court and Khartoum: The Politics of State Non-Cooperation, In: Waddel, Nicholas & Clark, Phil, (Eds.) Courting Conflict? Justice, Peace and the ICC in Africa, London, 2008, pp. 29-36.

Adding insult to injury, the USA has not only refused to ratify the Rome Statute, but has greatly undermined the moral and practical force of the instrument, by passing a law which "prohibits the US from participating in peace keeping missions in countries that have ratified the Rome Statute and makes most countries that are state parties to the treaty ineligible for military aid unless they guarantee that they will not hand over US citizens to the ICC, and gives the President the authority to use force to liberate US military personnel in the ICC's custody".[104] As a further means of ensuring the immunity of its citizens from prosecution before the ICC, the US has continued signing bilateral agreements with several nations including African states using Article 98 of the Rome Statute.[105] Consequently, this has reinforced the perception that the ICC is just another form of neo-imperialist institution designed to control economically and politically weak states by wealthier states with larger militaries. The colonial past of the continent coupled with the persistent bashing of the ICC by state media in many African countries is making the general public wary of the Court.

USA has also gone to the extent of threatening countries like Belgium whose national courts invoked universal jurisdiction to indict the then US Defense Secretary, Donald Rumsfeld, and Israeli Prime Minister Ariel Sharon. The indictments were dropped and even the national law that allowed Belgian courts to exercise universal jurisdiction scrapped as USA threatened to advocate for the relocation of the NATO headquarters from Brussels.[106]

These concerns are not only causing some states that are parties to the Statute to reconsider their decisions, but it is also preventing others from joining the ICC. As President Paul Kagame of Rwanda once said, "Rwanda cannot be party to the ICC for one simple reason.., with ICC all the injustices of the past including colonialism, imperialism, keep coming back in different forms. They control you. As long as you are poor, weak there is always some rope to hang you. ICC is made for Africans and poor countries..... Two thirds of the countries that have signed for this ICC are these poor countries. When they were signing (the treaty) they didn't know what they were signing. They don't know they were signing for a rope to hang themselves"[107].

---

104 Delaet, Debra L. The Global Struggle for Human Rights: Universal Principles in World Politics, Stamford, 2006, p.175; see also US Congress, American Service Members Protection Act of 30 July 2003, Sec 2004 – 2008.

105 Delaet, The Global Struggle for Human Rights, pp. 175-176.

106 Jalloh, Regionalizing International Criminal Law? p. 494.

107 David, Kezio-Musoke, Kagame tells why he is against ICC charging Bashir, Daily Nation, 3.8.2008. http://www.nation.co.ke/news/africa/-/1066/446426/-/3huvkb/-/

Irrespective of the genuineness or otherwise of the aforementioned claims, the sociological legitimacy of the ICC is thinning out slowly in Africa, a continent where the largest number of states parties come from. What needs to be done, before things deteriorate further, is to effectively address the identified legal and procedural deficits, which are serving as springboards to lash out the ICC and to justify withdrawal. This is the proper way of laying the foundations for the legitimacy of the Court and its gradual ascendance to a global public authority. A defensive and dismissive approach will only make the situation worse, and thwart the long time coming dream of creating an international authority, in the true sense of the term.

The ICC's claim of global authority is also undermined by a couple of other factors. The first is related to the complementary nature of the Court. Complementarity means that state sovereignty and authority is still given primacy over international jurisdiction.[108] Under such circumstances it is hard to talk of the ICC as a global authority.

The other is related to the Court's lack of universal jurisdiction. The Court may only exercise jurisdiction if: the accused is a national of a State Party or a State otherwise accepting the jurisdiction of the Court; the crime took place on the territory of a State Party or a State otherwise accepting the jurisdiction of the Court; or the United Nations Security Council has referred the situation to the Prosecutor, irrespective of the nationality of the accused or the location of the crime. This raises questions on the ICC's true global nature or universality of jurisdiction.

Another challenge related to this is the absence of what is called the 'global public'. The 'global public' as a result of the weaknesses of the international system, has not yet evolved and hence the exercise of global public authority in the absence of a 'global public' would be mockery of the concept.

index.html 28.1.2015.

108 The principle of complementarity provides that certain cases will be inadmissible even though the Court has jurisdiction. In general, a case will be inadmissible if it has been or is being investigated or prosecuted by a State with jurisdiction. However, a case may be admissible if the investigating or prosecuting State is unwilling or unable to genuinely to carry out the investigation or prosecution. For example, a case would be admissible if national proceedings were undertaken for the purpose of shielding the person from criminal responsibility. In addition, a case will be inadmissible if it is not of sufficient gravity to justify further action by the Court.

## 5. Conclusion

It is argued in this chapter that a true global authority has to have normative as well as sociological legitimacy, if it is here to stay. It has to embody, reflect and apply the values of democracy, rule of law and governance. These values have to be manifest from the establishment to the way it operates and dispenses justice. The ICC, as one of the existing global governance institutions, should also be put, and continue to be put, to this rigorous test before it is fully recognized as a worthy global authority. This is the only way we can ensure that the system is all inclusive and democratic, and hence can be relied upon to carry the long awaited dream of humanity for unity. We cannot afford to hurriedly give such title and responsibility to an institution, no matter how long overdue it might be, only to find that it failed half-way.

Based on this understanding and with this purpose in mind, the legitimacy test, as outlined in this chapter, is decisive for the ICC to be called a global public authority. We can, of course, agree that the ICC is an international authority, in the loose sense of the term, to mean an institution that is authorized or mandated through a treaty to exercise jurisdiction over certain matters. However, this does not suffice for an institution to be bestowed with the task of realizing a long awaited dream of uniting the international community through and by its authority. This is the reason why a more rigorous requirement is proposed in this chapter.

From the analysis and findings here, we can safely conclude that the ICC partially meets the standards of legitimacy, which are key to acquiring and the exercise of authority, but it is not yet at the place where we can call the ICC a global public authority. The existing gaps cannot be underestimated, and, as explained in detail, have clouded its legitimacy and hence its authority.

It would not be possible for the ICC to become a global public authority when it is ridden with multitude of problems. As suggested in this chapter all the defects have to be rectified. In particular, the power of the Security Council to request deferment of ongoing investigations and its power to refer situations to The Prosecutor should be suspended. Or at least the Security Council should be allowed to exercise such powers only when all its members, including the permanent members, become States Parties to the Rome Statute.

It would be inconceivable for the ICC to become a legitimate global court when some states that are not parties to the ICC are allowed to refer cases against others, and these same states are capable of legally protecting their citizens or allies against indictment and prosecution by the Court through their veto power.

The Courts ascendance to global authority is also seriously hindered by the fact that big and powerful countries such as China, India, USA and Russia that together have more than half of the world's population are not parties to the Rome Statute. A Court that does not have jurisdiction over more than half of the world's population cannot be, by any measure, considered global. Add to this the population living in more than 65 countries that are not parties to the Rome Statute, the situation looks bleak.

The Office of the Prosecutor has to also develop clear guidelines for the selection of cases and conduct its examination in line with those guidelines in a transparent way. It is only then that it can have smooth relations with states, which is pivotal for the legitimacy of the Court.

The concerns raised by African leaders and their regional organization, the AU, should also be looked into and addressed properly so that they would not have any legitimate ground to lament. Though their allegations are exaggerated and at times unsubstantiated, there are legitimate concerns that require serious consideration. ICC's relation with Africa is very crucial for its existence not only because Africa has the largest number of states parties but also because Africa is also the 'biggest client' and will for at least sometime be its 'repeat customers'. As the former judge of the Court, Philip Kirsch, rightly observed 'without Africa the ICC would not exist as it does today; and because of the relationship between the Court and African states, cooperation with the AU is particularly important to the Court"[109].

In conclusion, it should be noted that the ICC has what it takes to be a global public authority, but it will get there only when the gaps identified are duly and adequately addressed. The quest for a global public authority is long overdue and the ICC has paved the way towards it in many ways, and there is a long journey ahead, a bumpy and arduous one. All in all, the ICC's establishment is a heartening development for the quest for global public authority.

109 Jalloh, Regionalizing International Criminal Law? pp. 466-467.

# Authors

*Nigel Biggar* is Regius Professor of Moral and Pastoral Theology, and Director of the McDonald Centre for Theology, Ethics, and Public Life, at the University of Oxford; and the author of In Defence of War (2013) and Between Kin and Cosmopolis: An Ethic of the Nation (2014).

*Andreas Hasenclever* is Professor of International Relations and Peace Studies at the Eberhard Karls University of Tübingen, Germany. His research focuses on the analysis of international institutions and the role of religion in armed conflicts.

*Heinz-Gerhard Justenhoven* is director of the ithf since 1995. Since 2010 he is adjunct professor at the Faculty of Theology at University of Freiburg. He has published on Catholic peace teaching and contemporary issues of political ethics.

*Matthias Lutz-Bachmann*, since 1994 Professor of Philosophy at Goethe University, Frankfurt. Main research areas are the History of Medieval and Early Modern Philosophy, Philosophy of Kant, Ethics, Political Philosophy and Philosophy of Religion.

*Karsten Nowrot*, LL.M. (Indiana) is Professor of Public Law, European Law and International Economic Law as well as Head of the Department of Law at the School of Socio-Economics of the Faculty of Business, Economics and Social Sciences at Hamburg University, Germany.

*Mary Ellen O'Connell* holds the Robert and Marion Short Chair in Law and is Research Professor of International Dispute Resolution—Kroc Institute for Peace Studies at the University of Notre Dame.

*Stefan Oeter* is Professor of Public, European and International Law and director of the Institut für internationale Angelegenheiten at the University of Hamburg since 1999. His main interests lie on issues about humanitarian intervention, civil protection against military forces and combating terrorism.

*Dietmar von der Pfordten* is Professor of Philosophy of Law and Social Philosophy at the Georg-August-University Göttingen and there the director of the Section for Philosophy of Law and Social Philosophy. He was visiting professor at the universities of Cagliari and Groningen.

*Michael Reder* is Professor of Practical Philosophy at the Munich School of Philosophy. He is member of the Institute for Social and Development Studies (IGP) and Head for the project "Global Solidarity".

*Annette Schramm* is a research associate at the Collaborative Research Centre 923 "Threatened Order - Societies under Stress" working in a project on protest against Land Grabbing. Her main research interests are land conflicts, non-state violent conflicts, as well as conflict resolution and mediation.

*Christian Tams* is Professor of International Law at the University of Glasgow and an Academic Member of Matrix Chambers, London. During 2015–16, he is a Senior Fellow at the Centre for Global Cooperation Research at the University of Duisburg-Essen.

*Samuel T. Tessema* is currently a J.S.D. candidate and a Teaching Assistance in International Law at the University of Notre Dame Law School. He is also a consultant to the African Commission's Working Group on Indigenous Populations/Communities.

*Johan Verstraeten* is Professor at the Catholic University of Leuven and coordinator of the Research Unit Theological and Comparative Ethics. His research focuses on peace ethics, catholic social thought and the link between leadership and spirituality.

# Previous Publications

## Theologie und Frieden

Band 23

Gerhard Beestermöller,
Hans-Richard Reuter (Hrsg.)
**Politik der Versöhnung**
Eine philosophisch-theologische Begleitung zu Expeditionen in ein wenig vermessenes Land
2002. 264 Seiten, gebunden,
€ 29,-
ISBN 3-17-017348-0

Band 24

Gerhard Beestermöller (Hrsg.)
**Die humanitäre Intervention – Imperativ der Menschenrechtsidee?**
Rechtsethische Reflexionen am Beispiel des Kosovo-Krieges
2003. 176 Seiten, gebunden,
vergriffen

Band 25

Heinz-Gerhard Justenhoven
Rolf Schumacher (Hrsg.)
**„Gerechter Friede" – Weltgemeinschaft in der Verantwortung**
Zur Debatte um die Friedensschrift der deutschen Bischöfe
2003. 256 Seiten, gebunden,
vergriffen

Band 26

Norbert Brieskorn
Markus Riedenauer (Hrsg.)
**Suche nach Frieden:**
Politische Ethik in der Frühen Neuzeit III
2003. 448 Seiten, gebunden,
ISBN 3-17-018154-8

Band 27

Heinz-Gerhard Justenhoven
Joachim Stüben (Hrsg.)
**Kann Krieg erlaubt sein?**
Eine Quellensammlung zur politischen Ethik der Spanischen Spätscholastik
2006. 548 Seiten, gebunden,
€ 40,-
ISBN 978-3-17-018324-7

Band 28

Timo J. Weissenberg
**Die Friedenslehre des Augustinus**
Theologische Grundlagen und ethische Entfaltung
2005. 564 Seiten, gebunden,
€ 53,-
ISBN 3-17-018744-9

Band 29

Guido Brune
**Menschenrechte und Menschenrechtsethos**
Zur Debatte um eine Ergänzung der Menschenrechte durch Menschenpflichten
2006. 192 Seiten, gebunden,
€ 29,-
ISBN 3-17-019036-9

Band 30

Heinz-Gerhard Justenhoven
**Internationale Schiedsgerichtsbarkeit**
Ethische Norm und Rechtswirklichkeit
2006. 302 Seiten gebunden,
€ 29,80
ISBN 3-17-019529-8

Band 31

Markus Kremer
Hans-Richard Reuter (Hrsg.)
**Macht und Moral**
Politisches Denken im 17. und 18. Jahrhundert
2007. 365 Seiten gebunden,
€ 39,-
ISBN 3-17-019695-7

Band 32

Markus Riedenauer
**Pluralität und Rationalität**
Die Herausforderung der Vernunft durch religiöse und kulturelle Vielfalt nach Nikolaus Cusanus
2007. 562 Seiten gebunden,
€ 49,-
ISBN 3-17-019797-8

Band 33

Tania Wettach-Zeitz
**Ethnopolitische Konflikte und interreligiöser Dialog**
Die Effektivität interreligiöser Konfliktmediationsprojekte am Beispiel der World Conference on Religion and Peace Initiative in Bosnien-Herzegowina
2008. 284 Seiten, gebunden,
€ 34,-
ISBN 3-17-019969-9

Band 34

Volker Stümke
**Das Friedensverständnis Martin Luthers**
Grundlagen und Anwendungsbereiche seiner politischen Ethik
2007. 533 Seiten, gebunden,
vergriffen
ISBN 3170199706

Band 35

Markus Kremer
**Den Frieden verantworten**
Politische Ethik bei Francisco Suárez (1548-1617)
2007. 293 Seiten, gebunden,
€ 38,-
ISBN 3-17-020165-1

Band 36

Dieter Baumann
**Militärethik**
Theologische, menschenrechtliche und militärwissenschaftliche Perspektiven
2007. 620 Seiten, gebunden,
€ 48,-
ISBN 3-17-020157-6

Band 37

Thomas R. Elßner
**Josua und seine Kriege in jüdischer und christlicher Rezeptionsgeschichte**
2008. 336 Seiten, gebunden,
€ 39,-
ISBN 3-17-020520-8

Band 38

Stephanie van de Loo
**Versöhnungsarbeit**
Kriterien – theologischer Rahmen – Praxisperspektiven
2009. 418 Seiten, gebunden,
€ 39,-
ISBN 3-17-020717-2

Band 39

Sebastian Friese
**Politik der gesellschaftlichen Versöhnung**
Eine theologisch-ethische Untersuchung am Beispiel der Gacaca-Gerichte in Ruanda
2010. 204 Seiten, gebunden,
€ 39,80
ISBN 3-17-0213159

Band 40

Heinz-Günther Stobbe
**Religion, Gewalt und Krieg**
Eine Einführung
2010. 418 Seiten, gebunden,
€ 39,90
ISBN 3-170213722

Band 41

Marco Hofheinz
**Johannes Calvins theologische Friedensethik**
2012. 258 Seiten, gebunden,
€ 39,90
ISBN 978-3-17-020967-1

Band 42

Volker Stümke
Matthias Gillner (Hrsg.)
**Friedensethik im 20. Jahrhundert**
2011. 279 Seiten, gebunden,
€ 44,80
ISBN 3-17-021837-6

Band 43

Andrea Keller
**Cicero und der gerechte Krieg**
2012. 249 Seiten, gebunden,
€ 39,90
ISBN 3-17-022340-0

Band 44

Jörg Lüer
**Die katholische Kirche und die „Zeichen der Zeit“**
Die Deutsche Kommission Justitia et Pax nach 1989
2013. 340 Seiten, gebunden,
€ 39,90
ISBN 3-17-023029-3

## Beiträge zur Friedensethik

Band 39

Thomas Bruha
Dominik Steiger
**Das Folterverbot im Völkerrecht**
2006. 57 Seiten. Kart.
€ 14,-
ISBN 3-17-019438-0

Band 40

Gerhard Beestermöller
Heinz-Gerhard Justenhoven (Hrsg.)
**Der Streit um die iranische Atompolitik**
Völkerrechtliche, politische und friedensethische Reflexionen
2006. 148 Seiten. Kart., € 16,-
ISBN 3-17-019548-4

Band 41

Klaus Ebeling
**Militär und Ethik**
Moral- und militärkritische Reflexionen zum Selbstverständnis der Bundeswehr
2006. 90 Seiten. Kart., vergriffen
ISBN 3-17-019733-9

Band 42

Hans-Georg Ehrhart
Heinz-Gerhard Justenhoven (Hrsg.)
**Intervention im Kongo**
Eine kritische Analyse der Befriedungspolitik von UN und EU
2008. 217 Seiten. Kart.
€ 24,-
ISBN 3-17-020781-3

Band 43

Dirk Ansorge (Hrsg.)
**Der Nahostkonflikt**
Politische, religiöse und theologische Dimensionen
Stuttgart 2010,332 Seiten. Kart.
€ 29,80
ISBN 3-17-021500-9

Band 44

Jochen Bohm
Thomas Bohrmann
Gottfried Küenzlen (Hrsg.)
**Die Bundeswehr heute: Berufsethische Perspektiven für eine Armee im Einsatz**
Stuttgart 2011. 90 Seiten.
€ 19,80
ISBN 978-3-17-021654-9

Band 45

Heinz-Gerhard Justenhoven
Ebrahim Afsah (Hrsg.)
**Das internationale Engagement in Afghanistan in der Sackgasse?**
Eine politisch-ethische Auseinandersetzung
Baden-Baden 2011. 182 Seiten.
€ 29,-
ISBN 978-3-8329-6689-8

## Studien zur Friedensethik

Band 46

Gerhard Beestermöller (Hrsg.)
**Friedensethik im Frühmittelalter**
Münster 2014, 327 Seiten,
gebunden, € 56,-
ISBN 978-3-402-11690-6

Band 47

Bernhard Koch (Hrsg.)
**Den Gegner schützen?**
Zu einer aktuellen Kontroverse in der Ethik des bewaffneten Konflikts
Baden-Baden 2014, 293 Seiten,
gebunden, € 64,-
ISBN 978-3-8487-0784-3

Band 48

Gerhard Beestermöller (Hrsg.)
**Libyen: Missbrauch der Responsibility to Protect?**
Baden-Baden 2014, 139 Seiten,
gebunden, € 26,-
ISBN 978-3-8487-0763-8

Band 49

Matthias Gillner
Volker Stümke (Hrsg.)
**Kollateralopfer**
Die Tötung von Unschuldigen als rechtliches und moralisches Problem
Münster 2014, 258 Seiten,
gebunden, € 46,-
ISBN 978-3-402-11693-7

Band 50

Heinz-Gerhard Justenhoven
Mary Ellen O'Connell (Hrsg.)
**Peace through Law: Reflections on Pacem in Terris from philosophy, law, theology and political science**
Baden-Baden 2016

Band 51

Veronika Bock
Johannes J. Frühbauer
Arnd Küppers
Cornelius Sturm (Hrsg.)
**Christliche Friedensethik vor den Herausforderungen des 21. Jahrhunderts**
Münster 2015, 266 Seiten,
gebunden, € 46,-
ISBN 978-3-402-11695-1

Band 52

Stefan Brüne
Hans-Georg Ehrhart
Heinz-Gerhard Justenhoven (Hrsg.)
**Frankreich, Deutschland und die EU in Mali**
Chancen, Risiken, Herausforderungen
Baden-Baden 2015, 251 Seiten,
gebunden, € 46,-
ISBN 978-3-8487-1895-5

Band 53

Myroslava Rapp
**The Public Role of the Church in Contemporary Ukrainian Society**
The Contribution of the Ukrainian Greek-Catholic Church to Peace and Reconciliation
Baden-Baden 2015, 500 Seiten,
gebunden, € 89,-
ISBN 978-3-8487-2704-9

Band 54

Alexander Merkl
**"Si vis pacem, para virtutes"**
Ein tugendethischer Beitrag zu einem Ethos der Friedfertigkeit
Münster 2015, 480 Seiten,
gebunden, € 89,-
ISBN 978-3-402-11698-2